Nurse's Clinical Guide

NEONATAL CARE

D0791809

Nurse's Clinical Guide

NEONATAL CARE

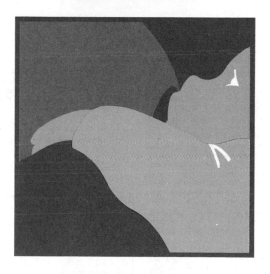

CAROLE ANN KENNER, RN,C, DNS
Assistant Professor
College of Nursing and Health
University of Cincinnati

Springhouse Corporation
Springhouse, Pennsylvania

STAFF

Executive Director, Editorial
Stanley Loeb

Director of Trade and Textbooks
Minnie B. Rose, RN, BSN, MEd

Art Director
John Hubbard

Drug Information Editor
George J. Blake, RPh, MS

Associate Acquisitions Editor
Betsy Steinmetz

Copy Editors
Mary Hohenhaus Hardy, Elizabeth Kiselev

Editorial Assistant
Mary Madden

Designers
Stephanie Peters (associate art director),
Elaine Ezrow (book designer),
Julie Carleton Barlow

Art Production
Robert Perry (manager), Anna Brindisi,
Nancy Frazier, Donald Knauss,
Anet Oakes, Ann Raphun, Thomas Robbins,
Robert Wieder

Typographers
David Kosten (director), Diane Paluba
(manager), Elizabeth Bergman,
Joy Rossi Biletz, Phyllis Marron, Robin
Rantz, Valerie L. Rosenberger

Manufacturing
Deborah Meiris (manager), T.A. Landis,
Jennifer Suter

Production Coordinator
Caroline Lemoine

Adapted from *Maternal, Neonatal, and Women's Health Nursing* by Susan M. Cohen, Carole Ann Kenner, and Andrea O. Hollingsworth. © 1991 by Springhouse Corporation. Authorization to photocopy items for internal or personal use, or the internal or personal use of specific clients, is granted by Springhouse Corporation for users registered with the Copyright Clearance Center (CCC) Transactional Reporting Service, provided that the base fee of $.75 per page is paid directly to CCC, 27 Congress St., Salem, MA 01970. For those organizations that have been granted a photocopy license by CCC, a separate system of payment has been arranged. The fee code for users of the Transactional Reporting Service is: 0874343844/92 $00.00 + $.75.

Library of Congress Cataloging-in-Publication Data

Kenner, Carole.
  Nurse's clinical guide to neonatal care / Carole Ann Kenner.
     p.   cm.
  Includes bibliographical references and index.
  1. Infants (Newborn) – Diseases – Nursing – handbooks, manuals, etc. I. Title.
  [DNLM: 1. Maternal-Child Nursing – handbooks.
WY 39 K36n]
RJ253.K46   1992
610.73′62 – dc20
DNLM/DLC   91-5082
ISBN 0-87434-384-4   CIP

TABLE OF CONTENTS

ADVISORY BOARD

CONTRIBUTORS

Ann E. Brueggemeyer, RN, MBA, MSN, Manager, Education Services, Middletown Regional Hospital, Middletown, Ohio

Darlene Nebel Cantu, RN,C, MSN, Nurse Educator, School of Professional Nursing, Baptist Memorial Hospital System, San Antonio, Tex.

Brook Gumm, RN, MSN, Clinical Nurse Specialist, Discharge Planning and Apnea Team, Children's Hospital Medical Center, Cincinnati

Laurie Porter Gunderson, RN, PhD, Assistant Professor, College of Nursing and Health, University of Cincinnati

Carole Ann Kenner, RN,C, DNS, Assistant Professor, Parent-Child Nursing, College of Nursing and Health, University of Cincinnati

Judy Wright Lott, ARNP, MSN, Assistant Professor, College of Nursing, University of Florida, Gainesville

Mary E. Lynch, RN, MS, Assistant Clinical Professor, Department of Family Health Care Nursing, University of California, San Francisco

Gail Blair Storr, RN, MN, MEd, Assistant Professor, Faculty of Nursing, University of New Brunswick (Canada), Fredericton

Laura Rodriguez Vaello, RN,C, MSN, NNP, Neonatal Nurse Practitioner-Clinical Nurse Specialist, Baptist Medical Center, San Antonio, Tex.

Neonatal care has changed dramatically in the past decade. The advent of single-room labor, delivery, recovery, and postpartum (LDRP) care and combined mother-neonate units has necessitated specialized training for the nurse. To cope with these conditions, a nurse must think critically, assess accurately, and intervene efficiently. A giant shadow behind all these events is early discharge of the neonate and mother. Neonatal stay under 48 hours is not unusual, thus requiring the nurse to use quick reference materials to supplement current nursing knowledge.

Nurse's Clinical Guide to Neonatal Care provides concise information in an easy-to-use format that is small enough to be carried in a pocket or stored in a nearby locker. The guide is organized into seven chapters. The first chapter surveys the biological and behavioral changes the neonate experiences during the critical 24 hours following birth, emphasizing the importance of successful adaptation to the extrauterine environment. It begins by discussing the biological characteristics of adaptation, detailing the physiologic adjustments occurring in all body systems. It highlights such important changes as the conversion from fetal to neonatal circulation and onset of independent breathing. It details thermoregulation in the neonate and illustrates neonatal circulation and lung fluid removal within moments of birth.

Chapter 1 also discusses the behavioral aspects of neonatal adaptation. It investigates the neonate's interaction with the environment through sensory and behavioral capacities, elaborating on visual and hearing abilities, tactile perception, taste, and smell. The chapter concludes with a description of the periods of neonatal reactivity — a series of distinctive behavioral and physiologic characteristics — and a discussion of neonatal sleep and awake states.

Chapter 2 describes the assessment techniques that yield important baseline information about the neonate's physiologic status and adaptation to the extrauterine environment. First, it presents general assessment guidelines, delineating the proper timing and sequence of the various types of assessment. It points out key health history factors to consider and explains how periods of neonatal reactivity may affect physical findings.

Next, Chapter 2 explains how to conduct a brief physical assessment to gather data about the neonate's general appearance, obtain vital signs, and take anthropometric measurements. Then it explores gestational-age assessment. After explaining how a neonate's gestational age helps predict perinatal problems, the chapter identifies the physical and neurologic features that help reveal gestational age. It shows how to correlate gestational age with birth weight, body length, and head circumference.

The chapter then presents the essentials of a complete physical assessment. It highlights assessment of neonatal reflexes and presents a comprehensive chart detailing normal and abnormal head-to-toe assessment findings and listing possible causes of abnormal findings. The chapter concludes by discussing behavioral assessment as a means of exploring the neonate's behavioral state and responses.

Chapter 3 outlines the nurse's role in ensuring successful neonatal adaptation, helping the family adjust to the neonate, and promoting optimal parent-infant interaction. Using a nursing process framework, it presents pertinent assessment information and nursing diagnoses for the normal neonate.

Chapter 3 then discusses nursing interventions that maintain a stable physiologic status and foster parent-infant bonding. It focuses on measures that ensure neonatal oxygenation, hydration, nutrition, hygiene, safety, and thermoregulation, highlighting interventions that combat cold stress. The chapter presents step-by-step procedures illustrating how to provide routine neonatal care, including bathing, nasal and oral suctioning, administering medications, obtaining a urine specimen, and caring for circumcision and umbilical cord sites.

Chapter 4 assists the nurse in promoting optimal infant nutrition. After delineating nutrient and fluid requirements for neonates and infants, it discusses the circumstances that impose special nutritional needs and limitations on neonates and infants, and then it reviews nutritional assessment.

Next, Chapter 4 compares and contrasts breastfeeding and formula-feeding, and then it explores the factors that influence parents' choice of infant feeding method. It begins by describing the health benefits of breast-feeding, then reviews the physiology of lactation and the composition of breast milk and examines infant sucking dynamics during breast-feeding. It illustrates the lactating breast and offers step-by-step procedures showing how to assess a neonate's sucking reflex and how to train a neonate to suck properly. Then the chapter provides basic information about formula feeding, describing commercial formulas and equipment, providing formula intake requirements, and detailing nutritional options for the non-breast-feeding infant.

Chapter 4 then presents nursing care for breast-feeding and formula-feeding clients and their infants. It explains how to assess a breast-feeding client's knowledge of feeding techniques and describes how to assess the client's breasts for consistency and nipple condition. For the client using infant formula, the chapter prepares the nurse to assess client knowledge of formula-feeding techniques and infant formula intake requirements. It follows with a discussion of nursing interventions, focusing on general infant-feeding guidelines and client teaching. This section includes detailed client-teaching aids on such topics as breast-feeding positions, initiating breast-feeding, and expressing milk. It touches on drug use during lactation and breast-feeding in special situations, and it offers a breast-feeding schedule for the working mother. Addressing the client using infant formula, the chapter describes interventions that help ensure proper formula preparation and effective burping technique, and it explains how the nurse can promote physical contact between the client and her infant during formula-feeding.

Chapter 5 prepares the nurse to care for the high-risk neonate. First, it surveys some important concepts in neonatal intensive care, describing the regionalization of perinatal care and comparing the three levels of perinatal care provided in perinatal care centers. It examines associated ethical and legal issues, including withholding life-support for the critically ill neonate. Then the chapter focuses on the perinatal problems that lead to high-risk status, ranging from respiratory problems, metabolic disorders, and infection to congenital anomalies and effects of maternal substance abuse. It describes the pathophysiology and etiology of these problems, then highlights the causes and consequences of birth-weight and gestational-age variations, and it discusses child abuse and failure to thrive in the high-risk neonate.

Next, Chapter 5 presents nursing care for the high-risk neonate and explains how to assess for each perinatal problem described earlier. After listing pertinent nursing diagnoses for the high-risk neonate, the chapter addresses nursing interventions. Highlighting emergency measures, the chapter features illustrated procedures of neonatal resuscitation and suctioning of an endotracheal tube. It also presents a chart showing indications and nursing considerations for resuscitation drugs. Then Chapter 5 elaborates on general nursing interventions for high-risk neonates, including measures that support oxygenation, thermoregulation, and nutrition. It explains how to prevent or control infection, provide preoperative or postoperative care, and carry out special procedures. The chapter concludes with a discussion of specific medical and nursing management of selected perinatal problems.

Chapter 6 guides the nurse in providing practical and psychosocial support for the family with a high-risk neonate. To establish a theoretical framework for understanding a family's reactions to the birth of a high-risk neonate, the chapter begins by discussing theories of grief and common coping mechanisms.

The chapter then applies these concepts to nursing care. It explains how to assess the parents' socioeconomic and cultural backgrounds, experience with health care facilities, and grieving behavior and coping mechanisms. It describes how to evaluate the family's support systems and examines cultural influences on the expression of grief. After offering pertinent nursing diagnoses, Chapter 6 identifies nursing interventions that help the family deal with their crisis and attain the skills to care for the neonate after discharge. The chapter examines the family's teaching needs and explains how the nurse can bolster the family's internal and external support systems and enhance their bonding with the neonate. Chapter 6 features an examination of nursing measures to support the siblings and grandparents of a high-risk neonate, and it outlines interventions to help families cope with neonatal or fetal death.

Chapter 7 addresses discharge planning and home health care services—the tools that extend neonatal care to the home. After delineating the factors that have increased the demand for home health care over the past decade, the chapter discusses the nurse's role in discharge planning and reviews discharge planning systems and resources. It instructs the nurse in assessing the discharge planning needs of the neonate and family, including ways to determine whether the family's circumstances make home health care feasible, and presents a sample discharge planning questionnaire. Next, Chapter 7 explains how to implement the discharge care plan by preparing the parents for the neonate's discharge and helping them select and arrange payment for health care services.

Chapter 7 then explores home health care in depth, describing available services, equipment, and supplies and reviewing case management of home care. It identifies the types of home health care a neonate may need – routine and basic care for normal, healthy neonates, and specialized care for others.

Next, the chapter presents nursing care for the neonate receiving health care at home. It describes the essentials of assessment during the first home visit and on subsequent visits. It focuses on how to evaluate parental knowledge, caregiving skills, and support needs; how to assess whether health care can be delivered safely and adequately in the home; and how to gauge parent-infant interaction. For planning and implementation, Chapter 7 discusses the importance of nursing flexibility and innovation, then addresses such interventions as ensuring parental caregiving knowledge and skills, promoting parent-infant interaction, and helping siblings adjust. Other highlights of Chapter 7 include discussions of nutritional assessment and home nutrition therapy and a chart showing how to assess the neonate requiring special equipment. The chapter includes parent teaching aids on dealing with an infant who has acquired immunodeficiency syndrome and on use of such equipment as a home apnea monitor and nasal cannula for oxygen administration.

The book concludes with four appendices. The first covers the NANDA taxonomy of nursing diagnoses as of summer 1990. The diagnoses are grouped into nine human response patterns – exchanging, communicating, relating, valuing, choosing, moving, perceiving, knowing, and feeling. The second appendix provides a table that converts customary weight units to metric units and vice versa. The third appendix shows Fahrenheit and Celsius conversions from 93.2° F (34.0° C) to 109.4° F (43.0° C). The fourth appendix lists support organizations for the families of special-needs neonates. The final appendix is an extensive glossary.

Nurse's Clinical Guide to Neonatal Care follows the nursing process and demonstrates through specific diagnoses how this process is applied to the neonate and family. It emphasizes family-centered care and considers the role that culture may play in a client's needs or wishes. Further, it spotlights research findings that are applicable in clinical practice and groups useful information in the three domains of learning – cognitive, psychomotor, and affective. Finally, its client teaching pages support the nurse by speaking directly to the client and to the family. In short, this guide will be of major and practical use to any nurse who is preparing for or delivering level I or level II neonatal care.

Neonatal Adaptation

Immediately after delivery, the neonate must assume the life-support functions performed by the placenta in utero. Birth begins a critical 24-hour phase, called the *transitional period,* that encompasses the neonate's adaptation from intrauterine to extrauterine life.

To survive outside the womb, the neonate must successfully navigate the transitional period. Statistics reflect the difficulty of this task: Mortality is higher during this period than at any other time; two-thirds of all neonatal deaths occur in the first 4 weeks after birth (Avery, 1987).

The transitional period imposes changes in all body systems and exposes the neonate to a wide range of external stimuli. Conditions that prevent successful adaptation to extrauterine life pose a serious threat. By becoming familiar with the normal events of transition, the nurse may recognize signs of poor adaptation and intervene promptly when they occur.

BIOLOGICAL CHARACTERISTICS OF ADAPTATION

Crucial physiologic adjustments take place in all body systems after birth. The cardiovascular and pulmonary systems undergo immediate drastic changes as soon as the umbilical cord is clamped and respiration begins. Although cardiovascular and pulmonary changes occur simultaneously, they are discussed separately to facilitate understanding.

CARDIOVASCULAR SYSTEM

To ensure the neonate's survival, fetal circulation must convert to neonatal circulation during the transitional period. Fetal circulation involves four unique anatomic features that shunt most blood away from the liver and lungs. The *placenta* serves as an exchange organ through which the fetus absorbs oxygen, nutrients, and other substances and excretes wastes (such as carbon dioxide). The *ductus venosus* links the inferior vena cava with the umbilical vein, permitting most placental blood to bypass the liver. The *foramen ovale* and *ductus arteriosus* direct most blood away from the pulmonary circuit. Although a small portion of pulmonary arterial blood enters the pulmonary circuit to perfuse the lungs, the ductus arteriosus shunts most to the aorta to supply oxygen and nutrients to the trunk and lower extremities.

Conversion from fetal to neonatal circulation

Beginning at birth, fetal shunts undergo changes that establish neonatal circulation. (For an illustration of blood flow in the neonate, see *Tracing circulation.*) As the umbilical cord is clamped and the neonate draws the first breath, systemic vascular resistance increases and blood flow through the ductus arteriosus declines. Most of the right ventricular output flows through the lungs, boosting pulmonary venous return to the left atrium. In response to increased blood volume in the lungs and heart, left atrial pressure rises. Combined with increased systemic resistance, this pressure rise results in functional closure of the foramen ovale. (*Functional closure* refers to cessation of blood flow, resulting from pressure changes, that renders a structure nonfunctional.) Within several months, the foramen ovale undergoes *anatomic closure* (structural obliteration from constriction or tissue growth).

Onset of respiratory effort and the effects of increased partial pressure of arterial oxygen (PaO_2) constrict the ductus arteriosus, which functionally closes 15 to 24 hours after birth. By age 3 to 4 weeks, this shunt undergoes anatomic closure.

Clamping of the umbilical cord halts blood flow through the ductus venosus, functionally closing this structure. The ductus venosus closes anatomically by the first or second week. After birth, the umbilical vein and arteries no longer transport blood and are obliterated.

Because anatomic closure lags behind functional closure, fetal shunts may open intermittently before closing completely. Intermittent shunt opening most commonly stems from conditions causing increased vena caval and right atrial pressure (such as crying); clinically insignificant functional murmurs may result. Also, because

TRACING CIRCULATION

With birth comes functional closure of the fetal shunts (ductus venosus, foramen ovale, and ductus arteriosus) that direct blood flow away from the lungs and liver and separate the systemic and pulmonary circulations. As the shunts close, blood flows from the pulmonary arteries to the lungs and through the portal system to the liver. In the large illustration, the darker areas represent regions of high arterial oxygen saturation; the lighter areas, regions of low saturation. The boxed illustrations show the shunts as they previously existed.

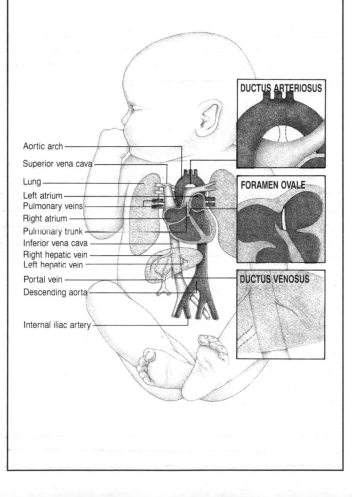

Aortic arch
Superior vena cava
Lung
Left atrium
Pulmonary veins
Right atrium
Pulmonary trunk
Inferior vena cava
Right hepatic vein
Left hepatic vein
Portal vein
Descending aorta
Internal iliac artery

DUCTUS ARTERIOSUS

FORAMEN OVALE

DUCTUS VENOSUS

shunts allow unoxygenated blood to pass from the right to left side of the heart, bypassing the pulmonary circuit, they may cause transient cyanosis. Both cyanosis and murmurs in the neonate should be carefully monitored and evaluated so that any underlying abnormalities can be detected. (See Chapter 2, Neonatal Assessment, for more information about assessing the neonate's cardiovascular system.)

Blood volume

The blood volume of the full-term neonate ranges from 80 to 90 ml/kg of body weight, depending on the amount of blood transferred from the placenta after delivery. Delayed umbilical cord clamping increases blood volume by up to 100 ml (1 dl), possibly increasing heart rate, respiratory rate, and systolic blood pressure. Changes caused by increased blood volume may persist for about 48 hours, possibly leading to crackles and cyanosis.

RESPIRATORY SYSTEM

Throughout gestation, biochemical and anatomic respiratory features develop progressively, preparing the fetus for the abrupt respiratory changes brought on by birth. Between weeks 25 and 30 of gestation, Type II pneumocytes (alveolar cells) begin limited secretion of surfactant. A phospholipid, surfactant decreases the surface tension of pulmonary fluids and prevents alveolar collapse at the end of expiration. Reduction of surface tension facilitates gas exchange, decreases inflation pressures needed to open the airways, improves lung compliance, and decreases labor of breathing.

Onset of neonatal respiration

The fetal lungs contain fluid secreted by the lungs, amniotic cavity, and trachea. The fluid volume, which correlates with the neonate's functional residual capacity (FRC), typically reaches 30 to 25 ml/kg of body weight (West, 1985). For the neonate to assume the tasks of ventilation and oxygenation, air must rapidly replace lung fluid. In the healthy neonate, replacement occurs with the first few breaths.

Lung fluid removal. As the neonate's chest squeezes through the birth canal, compression forces out roughly one-third of the lung fluid through the nose and mouth. The pulmonary circulation and

STIMULI FOR RESPIRATION

In response to various stimuli, the neonate draws the first breath within about 20 seconds of delivery. Asphyxia is the most important stimulus for neonatal respiration. However, as the flowchart below shows, other biochemical stimuli also come into play, as do various mechanical, thermal, and sensory factors.

INITIAL STIMULUS	RECEPTOR STIMULATION	RESPONSE
Sensory Bright lights, touch, pain	Visual, auditory, and proprioceptive chemoreceptors	• Stimulation of medullary respiratory center • Efferent nerve impulses (via spinal cord) • Diaphragmatic contraction
Biochemical Asphyxia	Aortic and carotid chemoreceptors	
Thermal Heat loss	Thermal receptors	
Mechanical Thoracic squeeze, elastic recoil	Stretch receptors	• Glossopharyngeal breathing

lymphatic system absorb the remaining two-thirds after respiration begins.

After the neonate's chest clears the birth canal, elastic recoil pulls 7 to 42 ml of air into the lungs to replace the fluid that was forced out. Consequently, the neonate may cough before the first inspiration. Glossopharyngeal or frog breathing, which involves involuntary muscle contraction, pulls another 5 to 10 ml of air into the lungs. Each breath increases the neonate's FRC.

The time needed to clear the lungs varies from 6 to 24 hours after vaginal delivery of a healthy, full-term neonate (West, 1985). Inadequate lung fluid removal may cause transient tachypnea, a common problem in neonates.

Breathing stimuli. Normally, the neonate breathes within 20 seconds of delivery, stimulated by the medullary respiratory center. (For an overview of the factors leading to respiration, see *Stimuli for respiration.*) Asphyxia — the combination of hypoxemia, hypercapnia, and acidosis — provides the strongest stimulus for the first breath. Before the first breath, the neonate has an arterial oxygen saturation (SaO_2) of only 10% to 20%, reflecting hypoxemia; a partial pressure of arterial carbon dioxide ($PaCO_2$) of approximately 58 mm Hg, reflecting hypercapnia; and an arterial pH of approximately 7.28, reflecting acidosis.

Because the final stage of delivery interrupts gas exchange, even the healthy neonate has some degree of asphyxia at birth. Asphyxia stimulates chemoreceptors in the carotid bodies and aorta. As this stimulation increases, efferent impulses travel to the diaphragm, contracting it. The negative intrathoracic pressure that results draws air into the lungs, increasing intrathoracic volume.

Other stimuli that help trigger breathing include cord occlusion, thermal changes (from rapid heat loss caused by increased energy expenditure), tactile stimulation, and other environmental changes (such as bright lights and noise).

The onset of respiration and lung expansion indirectly decreases pulmonary vascular resistance because of the direct effect of oxygen and carbon dioxide on vessels. As oxygen saturation increases and the $PaCO_2$ value declines, the decrease in pulmonary vascular resistance leads to increased pulmonary blood flow. This further improves oxygen saturation.

Neonatal respiratory function

The respiratory rate varies over the first day, stabilizing by about 24 hours after birth. Maintained by the effects of biochemical and environmental stimulation, the neonate's respiratory function requires:
• a patent airway
• a functioning respiratory center
• intact nerves from the brain to chest muscles
• adequate calories to supply energy for labor of breathing.

HEMATOPOIETIC SYSTEM

Like other body systems, the hematopoietic system is not fully developed at birth. The hematologic features that ensured adequate tissue oxygenation in utero must be replaced by more mature elements after birth.

Red blood cells

Erythropoiesis—production of erythrocytes, or red blood cells (RBCs)—is stimulated by the renal hormone erythropoietin. In the fetus, low oxygen saturation causes erythropoietin release to rise;

to ensure adequate tissue oxygenation, RBC production increases. At birth, the increased oxygen saturation that follows the onset of respiration inhibits erythropoietin release, reducing RBC production.

Fetal RBCs have a life span of about 90 days, compared to 120 days for normal RBCs. As fetal RBCs deteriorate, the neonate's RBC count decreases, sometimes resulting in physiologic anemia before stabilization. By age 2 to 3 months, however, the RBC count rises to within acceptable neonatal limits. (For normal neonatal laboratory values, see Chapter 2, Neonatal Assessment.)

Hemoglobin

Blood's oxygen-carrying component, hemoglobin is produced by developing RBCs. After birth, the hemoglobin value decreases simultaneously with the RBC count. Fetal RBCs produce hemoglobin F (fetal hemoglobin), which has a higher affinity for oxygen than hemoglobin A (produced by adult RBCs). This compensatory mechanism helps ensure adequate oxygenation in utero. As RBCs are replaced, hemoglobin A replaces hemoglobin F.

White blood cells

White blood cells (WBCs, leukocytes) serve as the neonate's major defense against infection. WBCs exist in five types: neutrophils, eosinophils, basophils, lymphocytes, and monocytes. Neutrophils account for 40% to 80% of total WBCs at birth; lymphocytes account for roughly 30%. However, by age 1 month, lymphocytes outnumber neutrophils.

Neutrophils and monocytes are phagocytes — cells that engulf and ingest foreign substances. They form part of the mononuclear phagocytic system, which defends the body against infection and disposes of cell breakdown products. Despite the presence of these phagocytic properties, however, the neonate's immature inflammatory tissue response may not localize an infection.

Thrombocytes

Thrombocytes (platelets) are crucial to blood coagulation. The neonate usually has an adequate platelet count and function. (Brown, 1988).

HEPATIC SYSTEM

The neonate's hepatic system—responsible for bilirubin clearance, blood coagulation, carbohydrate metabolism, and iron storage—is immature. Nonetheless, under normal circumstances, it functions adequately.

Bilirubin clearance

A yellow bile pigment, bilirubin is a by-product of heme after RBC breakdown. As RBCs age, they become fragile and eventually are cleared from the circulation by the mononuclear phagocytic system. The iron and protein portions are removed and recycled for further use. After leaving the mononuclear phagocytic system, bilirubin binds to plasma albumin. In this water-insoluble state, it is called indirect (unconjugated) bilirubin.

Indirect bilirubin must be conjugated—converted to direct bilirubin—for excretion. Conjugation occurs in the liver as bilirubin combines with glucuronic acid with the assistance of the enzyme glucuronyl transferase; a water-soluble bilirubin form results. Urobilinogen and stercobilinogen, the bilirubin compounds resulting from breakdown, can be excreted in the urine and stool.

Jaundice (icterus). If unconjugated bilirubin accumulates faster than the liver can clear it, the neonate may develop the yellow pallor known as jaundice. Slow or ineffective bilirubin clearance results in some degree of jaundice in approximately half of full-term neonates and 90% of preterm neonates. Fortunately, most full-term neonates avoid toxic bilirubin accumulation because they have adequate serum albumin binding sites and sufficient liver production of glucuronyl transferase. Factors that may increase the risk of unconjugated hyperbilirubinemia (an elevated serum unconjugated bilirubin level) include asphyxia, cold stress (ineffective heat maintenance), hypoglycemia, and maternal salicylate ingestion (Avery, 1987).

Ineffective excretion of conjugated bilirubin may cause conjugated hyperbilirubinemia (an elevated serum conjugated bilirubin level). Always abnormal in the neonate, this condition warrants evaluation.

Jaundice types. Four types of jaundice occur in the neonate—physiologic jaundice, pathologic jaundice, breast milk jaundice (BMJ), and breast-feeding–associated jaundice (BFAJ).

Physiologic jaundice arises 48 to 72 hours after birth. The serum bilirubin level peaks at 4 to 12 mg/dl by the third to fifth day after birth. On average, the bilirubin level increases by less than 5 mg/dl/day. Physiologic jaundice normally disappears by the end of the seventh day (Wilkerson, 1988). Five conditions that may cause physiologic jaundice are decreased hepatic circulation, increased bilirubin load, reduced hepatic bilirubin uptake from the plasma, decreased bilirubin conjugation, and decreased bilirubin excretion.

In contrast, pathologic jaundice occurs within the first 24 hours after birth; the serum bilirubin level rises above 13 mg/dl. Pathologic jaundice may stem from such conditions as blood group or blood type incompatibilities; hepatic, biliary, or metabolic abnormalities; or infection. (See Chapter 5, High-Risk Neonates, for further information on pathologic jaundice.)

BMJ was first identified in the 1960s. Although various causes have been suggested, current theory focuses on increased breast milk levels of the enzyme beta-glucuronidase. Researchers believe this enzyme causes increased intestinal bilirubin absorption in the neonate, thus blocking bilirubin's excretion. BMJ appears as physiologic jaundice subsides (after the seventh day). The serum bilirubin level peaks at 15 to 25 mg/dl between days 10 and 15. BMJ may persist for several weeks or, rarely, several months. A serum bilirubin level that decreases 24 to 48 hours after discontinuation of breast-feeding confirms the diagnosis.

Controversy exists over whether BMJ warrants treatment. Some physicians and breast-feeding advocates consider treatment unnecessary. Conservative treatment involves temporarily stopping breast-feeding until the bilirubin level declines; this usually takes 24 to 48 hours. The mother should maintain lactation by expressing milk by hand or pump.

BFAJ correlates with the neonate's breast-feeding patterns. The underlying cause of BFAJ is poor caloric intake that leads to decreased hepatic transport and removal of bilirubin from the body. Typically, the neonate who develops BFAJ has not been able to stimulate an early and adequate supply of breast milk. BFAJ usually appears 48 to 72 hours after birth. The serum bilirubin level peaks at 15 to 19 mg/dl by 72 hours. The average serum bilirubin level increases by less than 5 mg/dl/day. Treatment of BMAJ involves measures that ensure an adequate breast milk supply. Wilkerson (1988) recommends breast-feeding the neonate every 2 hours to stimulate the mother's milk production and the neonate's intestinal motility. The mother who quickly identifies signs of hunger in her infant should initiate feeding instead of waiting for the infant to cry vigorously. If the bilirubin level approaches 18 to 20 mg/dl, phototherapy (discussed in Chapter 5, High-Risk Neonates) may be necessary.

Bilirubin encephalopathy (kernicterus). Unconjugated serum bilirubin levels of approximately 20 mg/dl or higher may lead to bilirubin encephalopathy, a life-threatening condition characterized by bilirubin deposition in the basal ganglia of the brain. To assess the risk for bilirubin encephalopathy, the neonate's condition and gestational and chronological ages must be considered in conjunction with the bilirubin level. The condition may be treated with phototherapy or exchange transfusions (discussed in Chapter 5, High-Risk Neonates).

Blood coagulation

For the first few days after birth, the gastrointestinal (GI) tract lacks the bacterial action to synthesize adequate vitamin K. Vitamin K catalyzes synthesis of prothrombin by the liver, thereby activating four coagulation factors (II, VII, IX, and X). Consequently, the neonate is at special risk for hemorrhage (hemorrhagic disease of the neonate). All neonates now receive a prophylactic injection of vitamin K soon after delivery to help prevent hemorrhage (Putnam, 1984).

Carbohydrate metabolism

The major energy source during the first 4 to 6 hours after birth, glucose is stored in the liver as glycogen. The increased metabolic demands of labor, delivery, and the first few hours after birth cause rapid glycogen depletion (approximately 90% of liver glycogen is used within the first 3 hours). Skeletal muscle glycogen stores also decline rapidly (Streeter, 1986). If the neonate does not receive exogenous glucose, glycogenolysis (breakdown of glycogen into a usable glucose form) occurs. Until the neonate takes in sufficient glucose, glycogenolysis causes release of sufficient glucose into the bloodstream to maintain a serum glucose level of approximately 60 mg/dl. However, such stresses as hypothermia, hypoxia, and delayed feeding may rapidly exhaust glycogen stores, leading to hypoglycemia (Korones, 1986). (For more information on hypoglycemia, see Chapter 5, High-Risk Neonates.)

Iron storage

By term, the liver contains enough iron to produce RBCs until about age 5 months (provided the mother ingested adequate iron during pregnancy). Removed from destroyed RBCs, iron is stored in the liver, then recycled into new RBCs. The neonate must ingest sufficient dietary iron to maintain adequate RBC production.

RENAL SYSTEM

A relatively immature renal system makes the neonate susceptible to dehydration, acidosis, and electrolyte imbalance if vomiting and diarrhea occur (Gomella, 1988). The neonate's short, narrow renal tubules inhibit urine concentration and acidification and increase the fraction of excreted amino acids, phosphates, and bicarbonate. Also, the neonate's kidneys are relatively inefficient at secreting hydrogen ions in the tubule to promote acid-base balance.

Glomerular filtration rate

In utero, glomerular perfusion pressure is relatively low and arteriolar resistance high. These conditions contribute to a low fetal glomerular filtration rate (GFR), defined as the volume of glomerular filtrate formed over a specific period. A low GFR limits the capacity of the kidneys to excrete excess solutes and regulate body water composition.

In the last trimester of pregnancy, the fetal kidneys undergo tremendous growth and maturation. At 34 weeks of gestation, the GFR — and consequently renal function — improve markedly (Avery, 1987). Thus, neonatal GFR varies with gestational age; the full-term neonate has a higher GFR than the preterm neonate. The GFR reaches 30% of adult values within the first 2 days of extrauterine life, but it does not attain full adult values until about age 2.

Fluid balance

During the neonate's transition after birth, changes occur in extracellular, intracellular, and total body water volume. At birth, water makes up approximately 70% of the body composition, compared to approximately 58% by adulthood. Extracellular fluid accounts for about 40% of the neonate's total body water. As cell mass increases, this percentage drops; by adulthood, extracellular fluid accounts for 20% of total body water.

The neonate usually voids within 24 hours of birth. The first urine may be dark red and cloudy from urate and mucus (the slight reddish stain has no clinical significance). The neonate's urine usually is odorless; specific gravity ranges from 1.005 to 1.015.

As the neonate's fluid intake increases, urine output increases and urine becomes clear or light straw in color. The breast-fed neonate may require 10 to 12 diaper changes daily. The bottle-fed neonate typically requires about 6 diaper changes daily.

Loss of fluid through urine, feces, insensible (imperceptible) losses, intake restrictions related to small gastric capacity, and increased metabolic rate contributes to a reduction of 5% to 15% of the birth weight over the first 5 days of extrauterine life. However, in the period before the mother's milk supply is established, increased extracellular fluid volume protects the breast-fed neonate from dehydration. The neonate should regain the birth weight within 10 days (Avery, 1987). Typically, the infant doubles the birth weight by age 5 to 6 months and triples it by the first birthday.

GI SYSTEM

At birth, the neonate must assume the digestive functions previously performed by the placenta—including metabolism of sufficient amounts of water, proteins, carbohydrates, fats, vitamins, and minerals for adequate growth and development.

Gastric capacity

Despite a relatively immature GI system, the healthy neonate can ingest, absorb, and digest nutrients. Gastric capacity is between 40 and 60 ml on the first day after birth; it increases with subsequent feedings. Because of this limited capacity, nutrient needs must be met through frequent small-volume feedings. Gastric emptying time—typically 2 to 4 hours—varies with the volume of the feeding and the neonate's age. Peristalsis is rapid.

Many neonates regurgitate a small amount of ingested matter (1 to 2 ml) after feedings because of an immature cardiac sphincter (a muscular ring constricting the esophagus). Persistent, forceful, or large-volume regurgitation is abnormal and warrants investigation.

GI enzymes

Compared to the adult's intestine, the neonate's is longer relative to body size and has more secretory glands and a larger absorptive surface. The neonate's ability to digest nutrients depends on enzyme action and gastric acidity. The stomach lining consists of chief cells (which secrete pepsinogen and promote protein digestion) and parietal cells (which secrete hydrochloric acid to maintain gastric acidity). Salivary glands secrete only minimal amounts of saliva until age 2 to 3 months, when drooling becomes apparent. Milk digestion begins in the stomach and continues in the small intestine. Secretions from the pancreas, liver, and duodenum aid digestion.

Enzyme deficiencies limit the neonate's absorption of complex carbohydrates and fats. Deficiency of amylase, an enzyme produced in the salivary glands and pancreas, persists until age 3 to 6 months, restricting the conversion of starch to maltose. Deficiency of lipase, which the pancreas secretes in minimal amounts, impedes fat digestion (Avery, 1987). Lipase production increases in the first few weeks after birth.

Vitamin K synthesis

Synthesis of vitamin K through bacterial action is another important GI function. Although initially sterile, the GI tract establishes normal colonic bacteria within the first week after birth, allowing adequate vitamin K synthesis.

Initiation of feedings

In most cases, feedings should begin as soon as the neonate is physiologically stable and exhibits adequate coordination of the sucking and swallowing reflexes. An extended delay before feedings may deplete the neonate's limited glycogen reserves — already taxed by the increased energy demands of the transitional period. This may result in hypoglycemia (reflected by a serum glucose level below 35 mg/dl), which poses a threat to the glucose-dependent brain.

Feedings should be offered by breast or bottle. In some health care facilities, the neonate receives sterile water as the first feeding to verify the sucking and swallowing reflexes without risking aspiration of formula into the airway.

Neonatal stools

Initially, the neonate's intestines contain meconium, a thick, dark-green, odorless fecal substance consisting of amniotic fluid, bile, epithelial cells, and hair (from in utero shedding of lanugo – the fine, soft hair covering the fetus's shoulders and back). Typically, the neonate passes the first meconium stool within 24 hours of birth.

After enteric feedings begin, fecal color, odor, and consistency change. Transitional stools usually appear on the second or third day after feedings begin. These greenish brown stools have a higher water content than meconium.

The type of feeding determines the characteristics of subsequent stools. The formula-fed neonate passes pasty, pale-yellow stools with a strong odor. Stools from the breast-fed neonate are golden-yellow, sweet smelling, and more liquid.

The gastric distention that results from food ingestion causes relaxation and contraction of colonic muscles, commonly leading to a bowel movement during or after a feeding. Typically, the breast-fed neonate has more frequent bowel movements than the formula-fed neonate because breast milk digests more rapidly than formula.

IMMUNE SYSTEM

The immune system is deficient at birth. With delivery comes exposure to substances (for example, bacteria) not normally present in utero. Such exposure activates components of the immune response. The first year is the period of greatest vulnerability to such serious infections as *Haemophilus influenzae*. Bacterial infections (including those caused by group B streptococci and staphylococci) occur in about 2% of neonates; viral infections – such as varicella and cytomegalovirus (CMV) – in about 8% (Berkowitz, 1984).

Immune response

The various elements of the immune system recognize, remember, respond to, and eliminate foreign substances called antigens. Primarily proteins, antigens may invade the body's protective barriers (such as the skin and mucous membranes) or arise from malignant cell transformation.

When local barriers and inflammation fail to fight off antigenic invasion, the immune system initiates a humoral or cell-mediated response. The response is carried out by the mononuclear phagocytic system, which includes cells in the thymus, lymphoid tissue, liver, spleen, and bone marrow. Cells involved in the immune response include lymphocytes (specifically, T cells and B cells), granulocytes, monocytes, RBCs, and platelets.

Humoral immunity. This response is mediated by humoral antibodies. Also called immunoglobulins, these proteins are synthesized in response to a specific antigen. B cells, coated with immunoglobulins, recognize invaders and produce antibodies, which are molecules that react specifically with a matching site on a corresponding antigen. This antigen-antibody reaction activates the complement system, a series of chemical reactions that removes the antigen from the body. Humoral immunity is most important against bacterial and viral reinfections.

Immunoglobulins have one or more molecules, each of which consists of four polypeptide chains. Properties of these chains determine the immunoglobulin's classification.

Immunoglobulin G (IgG). The most abundant immunoglobulin, IgG (gamma globulin) is synthesized in response to bacteria, viruses, and fungal organisms. Maternal IgG, transferred to the fetus via the placenta, confers passive acquired immunity (a short-lived immunity in which no antibodies are produced). Fetal IgG appears by the twelfth week of gestation, with levels increasing significantly during the last trimester.

IgG is active against gram-positive cocci (pneumococci and streptococci), meningococci, *H. influenzae*, some viruses, and diphtheria and tetanus toxins (if the mother has been exposed to these agents). The neonate also has protection against most childhood diseases — including diphtheria, measles, and smallpox — provided the mother has antibodies to these diseases. Because IgG does not act against gram-negative rods (such as *Escherichia coli* and *Enterobacter*), the neonate is more susceptible to infection by these agents.

Passive immunity may interfere with infant immunization by preventing a challenge to the infant's immune system, which ordinarily would cause the immune system to make antibodies to the disease for which the immunization was given. Thus, when the IgG level drops, the infant may contract the disease. For example, an infant may contract pertussis despite receiving the first DPT (diphtheria, pertussis, tetanus) injection.

By about age 3 months, maternally acquired IgG is depleted. By then, however, the body usually produces enough IgG to replace the lost antibodies.

Immunoglobulin M (IgM). The first immunoglobulin produced by antigenic challenge, IgM is the major antibody in blood type incompatibilities and gram-negative bacterial infections. Maternal IgM does not cross the placenta. By the twentieth week of gestation, however, the fetus produces IgM in response to antigenic exposure. IgM provides active immunity (a long-lasting or permanent immunity resulting from antigenic stimulation through inoculation or natural immunity). High IgM levels in the neonate may signal perinatal infection.

Immunoglobulin A (IgA). The major antibody in the mucosal linings of the intestines and bronchi, IgA appears in all body secretions. It does not cross the placenta and normally is absent in the neonate. Combining with a mucosal protein, IgA is secreted onto mucosal surfaces as a secretory antibody (secretory IgA). Present in breast milk, this substance confers some passive immunity on the breast-fed infant. Secretory IgA also limits bacterial growth in the GI tract.

Cell-mediated immunity. This immune response is most apparent in localized inflammations triggered by fungi, viruses, tissue transplants, and tumors. Various types of T cells carry out cell-mediated immunity. Recognizing a foreign antigen, T cells mobilize tissue macrophages in the presence of migration inhibitory factor. This substance triggers chemical reactions that convert local macrophages into phagocytes and prevent macrophages from leaving the invasion site until they have destroyed the antigen. The breast-fed infant may acquire passive immunity to such diseases as polio, mumps, influenza, and chicken pox through the cell-mediated response.

Congenital infections

Usually, congenital infections — those acquired in utero — result from exposure to such viruses as CMV, rubella, hepatitis B, herpes simplex, herpes zoster, varicella, and Epstein-Barr. However, they also may stem from such nonviral agents as toxoplasmosis, syphilis, tuberculosis, trypanosomiasis, and malaria. Collectively, these viral and nonviral agents are called TORCH—an acronym for toxoplasmosis, others, rubella, CMV, and herpes.

Fetal infection by a TORCH agent follows a systemic maternal infection with placental involvement and fetal spread. TORCH infections can cause a wide range of sequelae, from spontaneous abortion and fetal death to overt or asymptomatic infection at birth. In the early prenatal period, infection by certain TORCH agents (such as rubella and toxoplasmosis) causes disruption of embryogenesis, resulting in severe congenital anomalies (Avery, 1987). (For further information on TORCH infections, see Chapter 5, High-Risk Neonates.)

Congenital bacterial infections may arise from bacterial organisms that travel to the fetus through the placenta. Organisms causing such infections include *Listeria monocytogenes, E. coli, Klebsiella,* and *Streptococcus pneumoniae.* The fetus also may become infected by organisms that reach the amniotic cavity via the mother's cervix. Other routes of infection include the fetal skin and mucous membranes, intervillous placental spaces, umbilical cord to the fetal circulation, and respiratory airways (via aspiration). Infectious agents that may take these routes include group B streptococci, *E. coli, L. monocytogenes,* and herpes simplex. An infected neonate may be acutely ill at birth with septicemia, pneumonia, or both (Berkowitz, 1984).

NEUROLOGIC SYSTEM

Although not fully developed, the neonate's neurologic system can perform the complex functions required to regulate neonatal adaptation—stimulate initial respirations, maintain acid-base balance, and regulate body temperature. The neonate's neurologic function is controlled primarily by the brain stem and spinal cord. The autonomic nervous system and brain stem coordinate respiratory and cardiac functions. All cranial nerves are present at birth; however, the nerves are not yet fully sheathed with myelin, a substance essential for smooth nerve impulse transmission.

The neonate has a functioning cerebral cortex, although the degree to which it is used remains unknown. At birth, the brain measures about one-fourth the size of the adult brain. The brain grows and matures in a cephalocaudal (head-to-toe) direction.

The brain needs a constant supply of glucose for energy and a relatively high oxygen level to maintain adequate cellular metabolism (Volpe and Hill, 1987). For this reason, the neonate's oxygenation status and serum glucose levels must be assessed and monitored carefully to detect impaired gas exchange or signs of hypoglycemia.

Nerve tract development

Sensory, cerebellar, and extrapyramidal nerve pathways are the first to develop. This accounts for the neonate's strong sense of hearing, taste, and smell. The cerebellum governs gross voluntary movement and helps maintain equilibrium. The extrapyramidal tract controls reflexive gross motor movement and postural adjustment by regulating reciprocal flexion and extension of muscle groups, thus maintaining smooth, coordinated movement.

Neonatal reflexes

The neonate's reflexes — categorized as feeding, protective, postural, and social — include such primitive reflexes as sucking and rooting (which causes the neonate to turn toward and search for the nipple). Crucial to survival, these reflexes serve as the basis for neonatal neurologic examination. Persistence of the neonatal reflexes beyond the age at which they normally disappear may indicate a neurologic abnormality.

ENDOCRINE AND METABOLIC SYSTEMS

At birth, the endocrine system is anatomically mature but functionally immature. Complex interactions between the neurologic and endocrine systems help coordinate adaptation to extrauterine life. Such interactions take place along three major feedback pathways:
- the parasympathetic-adrenal medulla pathway
- the hypothalamic-anterior pituitary pathway
- the hypothalamic-posterior pituitary pathway (Volpe and Hill, 1987).

Hormonal role in transition

Many extrauterine adaptations are regulated by hormones secreted by the endocrine glands, including growth hormone, thyroid-stimulating hormone, adrenocorticotropic hormone, cortisol, and catecholamines. However, the posterior pituitary gland secretes only a limited amount of antidiuretic hormone (ADH), a substance that limits urine production. Insufficient ADH contributes to the neonate's increased risk of dehydration.

Metabolic changes at birth

Interruption of placental circulation at birth halts the supply of oxygen, nutrients, electrolytes, and other vital substances to the neonate. Withdrawal of maternally supplied glucose and calcium necessitates significant and immediate metabolic changes to ensure successful neonatal adaptation. During the first few hours after birth, serum glucose and calcium levels change rapidly.

Glucose. At birth, the neonate's serum glucose level usually measures 60% to 70% of the maternal serum glucose level. Over the next 2 hours, this level falls, stabilizing between 35 and 40 mg/dl. By 6 hours after birth, however, it usually rises to about 60 mg/dl, unless the neonate experiences cold stress, delayed feeding, metabolic abnormalities, or sepsis.

Calcium. The serum calcium level decreases at birth but usually stabilizes between 24 and 48 hours after birth. A level below 7 mg/dl reflects hypocalcemia. Most commonly, hypocalcemia arises within the first 2 days or at 6 to 10 days after birth. Hypocalcemia may result from hypoxemia, interrupted maternal calcium transfer (early-onset hypocalcemia), or infant formula with an improper calcium-to-phosphorus ratio (later-onset hypocalcemia). In most cases, the full-term neonate given sufficient amounts of the proper formula or breast milk achieves the normal calcium-to-phosphorus ratio of 2:1 (Philip, 1987).

Thermoregulation

Body temperature maintenance — essential for successful extrauterine adaptation — is regulated by complex interactions between environmental temperature and body heat loss and production. The understanding and appropriate management of thermoregulation were among the earliest advances in neonatology.

The neonate has limited thermoregulatory capacity, achieved by body heating and cooling mechanisms. When the neonate no longer can maintain body temperature, cooling or overheating results; exhaustion of thermoregulatory mechanisms brings death. (For a depiction of the progressive effects of hypothermia, see *Dangers of hypothermia,* page 20.)

As the neonate makes the transition to extrauterine life, the core temperature decreases by an amount that varies with the environ-

DANGERS OF HYPOTHERMIA

Hypothermia prevention ranks among the most important goals of neonatal nursing care. As shown, untreated hypothermia can have grave consequences—culminating in death.

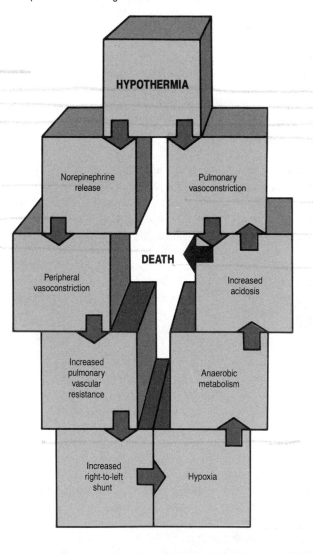

mental temperature and the neonate's condition. Initially, the full-term neonate's core temperature falls by approximately 0.54° F (0.3° C) per minute. Thus, under normal delivery conditions, it may drop 5.4° F (3° C) before the neonate leaves the delivery room.

Maintaining normal body temperature in the neonate can contribute significantly to successful adaptation. Neonatal morbidity and mortality can be favorably influenced by the nurse who takes steps to prevent cold stress.

Neutral thermal environment (NTE). Encompassing a narrow range of environmental temperatures, NTE requires the least amount of energy to maintain a stable core temperature. For an unclothed, full-term neonate on the first day after birth, NTE ranges from 89.6° to 93.2° F (32° to 34° C). Within this temperature range, oxygen consumption and carbon dioxide production are lowest and core temperature is normal. To maintain body temperature within the NTE, the neonate makes vasomotor adjustments—vasoconstriction to conserve heat and vasodilation to release heat. Environmental temperatures below or above the NTE increase oxygen consumption and boost the metabolic rate—the amount of energy expended over a given unit of time (Gomella, 1988).

The following characteristics place the neonate at a physiologic disadvantage for thermoregulation, increasing the risk of hypothermia:

• a large body surface relative to mass
• limited subcutaneous fat deposition to provide insulation
• vasomotor instability
• limited metabolic capacity.

Mechanisms of heat loss. Heat loss, which begins at delivery, can occur through four mechanisms—evaporation, conduction, radiation, and convection.

Evaporation. Evaporative heat loss occurs when fluids (insensible water, visible perspiration, and pulmonary fluids) turn to vapor in dry air. The drier the environment, the greater the evaporative heat loss. The pronounced evaporative heat loss occurring with delivery can be minimized by immediately drying the neonate and discarding the wet towels.

Conduction. This form of heat loss takes place when the skin directly contacts a cooler object – for example, a cold bed or scale. Therefore, any metal surface on which the neonate will be placed should be padded.

Radiation. A cooler solid surface not in direct contact with the neonate can cause heat loss through radiation. Common sources of radiant heat loss include incubator walls and windows. Occurring even with warm air temperatures, radiant heat loss may be minimized through the use of a thermoplastic heat shield (such as Plexiglas).

Convection. Heat loss from the body surface to cooler surrounding air occurs through convection. It increases in drafty environments. Thus, a delivery room cooled for the comfort of personnel may cause significant convective heat loss in the neonate.

Defenses against hypothermia. In a cold environment or in other stressful circumstances, the neonate defends against heat loss through vasomotor control, thermal insulation, muscle activity, and non-shivering thermogenesis.

Vasomotor control. Peripheral nervous stimulation activates vaso-motor control and metabolic processes to regulate thermal control. The neonate conserves heat through peripheral vasoconstriction and dissipates heat through peripheral vasodilation.

Thermal insulation. Provided by subcutaneous (white) fat, thermal insulation guards against rapid heat loss. The amount of subcutaneous fat determines the degree of thermal insulation. (Subcutaneous fat commonly accounts for 11% to 17% of the full-term neonate's weight.)

Muscle activity. Muscle activity increases heat production. Initially, the neonate reacts to a cold environment with increased movements (often perceived as irritability). For instance, the neonate may assume a tightly flexed posture that reduces heat loss by limiting body surface area.

Whether the neonate can produce heat by shivering remains unknown. Experts now believe the neonate may have some shivering ability. Nonetheless, even if shivering does occur in response to severe cold stress, it does not serve as a major heat source (Avery, 1987).

Nonshivering thermogenesis. Defined as the production of heat through lipolysis of brown fat, nonshivering thermogenesis is the neonate's most efficient heat production mechanism because it increases the metabolic rate minimally. A type of adipose tissue, brown fat accounts for up to 1.5% of a full-term neonate's total weight. Named for its brown color — a result of its rich vascular supply, dense cellular content, and numerous nerve endings — brown fat is deposited around the neck, head, heart, great vessels, kidneys, and adrenal glands; between the scapula; behind the sternum; and in the axillae.

The brain, liver, and skeletal muscles take part in nonshivering thermogenesis. In response to heat loss, sympathetic nerves stimulate the release of norepinephrine, the major mediator of nonshivering thermogenesis. Norepinephrine stimulates oxidation of brown fat, causing increased heat production. Heat produced by brown fat oxidation is distributed throughout the body by the blood, which absorbs heat as it flows through fatty tissue.

INTEGUMENTARY SYSTEM

The healthy neonate is moist and warm to the touch. Lanugo — fine, downy hair — may appear over the shoulders and back.

As with adults, the neonate's skin serves as the first line of defense against infection. The outermost skin layer, the stratum corneum, is fused with the vernix caseosa. A greasy white substance produced by sebaceous glands, the vernix caseosa coats the fetal skin and protects it from the amniotic fluid. (Because of its protective properties, the vernix caseosa should not be scrubbed off.) With maturation, the stratum corneum becomes an effective protective barrier (Guyton, 1985).

The full-term neonate's skin may appear erythematous (beefy red) for several hours after birth but soon takes on a normal color. In many neonates, vasomotor instability, capillary stasis, and high hemoglobin levels lead to acrocyanosis, characterized by bluish discoloration of the hands and feet. Skin color and circulation usually improve with warming of the hands and feet. (Acrocyanosis, a common condition, should not be confused with central cyanosis, which reflects impaired gas exchange. In central cyanosis, the neonate's skin and mucous membranes turn blue.)

MUSCULOSKELETAL SYSTEM

Ossification (bone development) is incomplete at birth but proceeds rapidly afterward. The neonate's skeleton consists mainly of bone.

Six thin, unjoined bones form the neonate's skull; these bones accommodate subsequent brain and head development. Separating the skull bones are sutures—fibrous joints in which the apposed bones are joined by a thin layer of fibrous connective tissue. Fontanels, soft-tissue areas covered with tough membranes, separate the sutures. Typically, vaginal delivery causes overriding sutures, a spontaneously resolving condition in which the sutures appear to be pushed together.

The muscles are anatomically complete at term birth. With age, muscle mass, strength, and size increase. Increasing muscle strength is crucial to the development of postural control and mobility (Lawrence, 1984).

REPRODUCTIVE SYSTEM

The reproductive system is anatomically and functionally immature at birth. However, the female's ovaries contain all potential ova, which decrease in number from birth to maturity by roughly 90%. In approximately 90% of males, the testes have descended into the scrotum by birth, although no sperm appear until puberty.

High maternal estrogen levels may cause transient side effects in the neonate. For example, breast hypertrophy with or without witch's milk (a thin, watery secretion similar to colostrum) may appear in both the male and female neonate. The female may have pseudomenstruation, a mucoid or blood-tinged vaginal discharge caused by the sudden drop in hormone levels after birth (Gomella, 1988). Clinically insignificant, breast hypertrophy and pseudomenstruation resolve spontaneously as the influence of maternal hormones subsides.

Normally, the male neonate has adhesions of the prepuce (penile foreskin) that prevent separation of the prepuce and glans. During fetal development, prepuce tissue is continuous with the epidermal glans covering.

BEHAVIORAL CHARACTERISTICS OF ADAPTATION

Research on neonatal development in the past 10 to 20 years has shown that the neonate has remarkable sensory, cognitive, and social abilities.

NEONATE-ENVIRONMENT INTERACTIONS

The full-term neonate not only perceives the environment but attempts to control it through behavior. Able to see, hear, and differentiate among tastes and smells, the neonate responds to touch and movement, defends against stimulation, and gives signals that, when interpreted by a responsive caregiver, can satisfy the neonate's needs. For example, a neonate uncomfortable in a wet diaper cries; the mother responds by changing the diaper.

NEONATAL SENSORY CAPACITIES

Using the sensory capacities — vision, hearing, touch, taste, and smell — the neonate perceives, interacts with, modifies, and learns from the environment. Combined with the neonate's attractive physical features, these sensory capacities play a major role in parent-infant bonding (sometimes called attachment).

Vision

Although the neonate can see, visual acuity is limited to a distance of approximately 9″ to 12″. The neonate has a preference for geometric shapes, such as squares, rectangles, or circles roughly 3″ in diameter. Black and white images hold the neonate's gaze longer than color images (Ludington-Hoe, 1983).

The neonate can conjugate the eyes (move them in unison) at or just after birth. However, immature neuromuscular control limits visual accommodation (the ability to adjust for distance) for the first 4 weeks after birth. Incomplete muscle control of ocular movements sometimes causes transient strabismus (deviation of the eyes, or "crossed" eyes). Also, the epicanthal fold covering the inner canthus of the eye may narrow the visible width of the sclera beside the iris, giving a neonate the appearance of having crossed eyes (pseudostrabismus).

The neonate apparently finds the human face intriguing and typically fixes the eyes and gazes intently at a face in proximity, as during feeding or cuddling. Such behavior strongly reinforces parent-infant bonding.

Visual acuity improves quickly; by age 6 months, adult-level visual acuity is achieved. In the neonate exposed to various pleasing objects in a range of colors, shapes, and contrasts, visual acuity may improve even more rapidly. Placing crib gyms, mobiles, and pictures within view may help stimulate visual development. Because the neonate prefers more color, greater contrast, and more interesting patterns than the light pastels of the traditional nursery, a change in nursery decor and infant clothing may be warranted.

Sensitive to light, the neonate grimaces or frowns and turns the head away from a bright light directed toward the eyes and opens the eyes more readily in a dimly lit room. Thus, by dimming the lights, parents may improve eye contact with the neonate, facilitating bonding.

The neonate responds to movement in the environment, fixing on and following bright or shiny objects soon after birth. For instance, the neonate fixes on and follows a parent's eyes; while gazing at a parent's face, the neonate may appear to imitate that parent's facial expressions, thereby rewarding the parent's response. The ability to fix on and gaze at objects improves rapidly.

Hearing

The neonate can hear at birth. In fact, hearing begins even earlier: The fetus can hear extrauterine sounds (for instance, voices or music) as well as noises originating in maternal body systems, including variable low-pitched sounds in the maternal cardiovascular and GI systems (Kramer and Pierpont, 1976).

Hearing is well established after aeration of the eustachian tube and drainage of blood, vernix caseosa, amniotic fluid, and mucus from the outer ear. Shortly after birth, the neonate turns toward sounds and startles in response to loud noises, such as a ringing telephone, dropped chart, or slammed door. Able to differentiate sounds on the basis of frequency, intensity, and pattern, the neonate responds more readily to sounds below 4,000 Hz. (Human speech usually is between 500 and 900 Hz.)

The neonate responds variously to different vocal pitches. Most women have higher-pitched voices than men and instinctively raise their pitch when talking to an infant. A high-pitched voice attracts the attention of the neonate, who turns toward the sound with increased alertness. In contrast, the lower-pitched male voice seems to have a soothing effect. Mothers commonly make use of this effect by talking in a much lower pitch when trying to calm or console the neonate (Redshaw, Rivers, and Rosenblatt, 1985).

Touch

The neonate has well-developed tactile perception, which serves as a stimulus for the first breath. The most sensitive body areas include the face (especially around the mouth), hands, and soles.

Until recently, experts believed that incomplete nerve myelination prevented the neonate from experiencing pain, except perhaps to a limited degree. Current knowledge, however, refutes this assumption. Anand and Hickey (1987) concluded that the pain pathways and cortical and subcortical centers crucial to pain perception are well developed and that the neurochemical systems associated with pain transmission are intact and functional as term approaches. Physiologic changes associated with pain in the neonate include increased blood pressure and pulse during and after a painful procedure. During such a procedure, the neonate's $PaCO_2$ level fluctuates widely and palmar sweating increases. In neonates undergoing painful procedures, researchers also have documented marked hormonal changes — including increased plasma renin levels soon after venipuncture and elevated plasma cortisol levels during and after circumcision without anesthesia. Also, painful stimuli have elicited simple motor responses (flexion and adduction of extremities); distinct facial expressions (pain, sadness, surprise); and characteristic crying. Some preliminary studies suggest that neonates have pain memory as well as pain perception.

Pleasant cutaneous stimulation, on the other hand, induces muscle relaxation — another key factor in parent-infant bonding. As the mother becomes acquainted with the neonate by lightly touching the face, extremities, and trunk, the neonate's muscle tone and movement decrease and crying stops or declines, reinforcing the mother's attachment (Redshaw, Rivers, and Rosenblatt, 1985).

Handling of the neonate provides sensory stimulation from motion as well as from touch. Such stimulation elicits alertness and orienting responses. These responses, in turn, influence neonatal development and parent-neonate interaction. However, the neonate may tire if handled too much.

Taste

The neonate differentiates among tastes by the first or second day after birth. In response to a tasteless solution (such as sterile water), the neonate's facial expression remains unchanged. A sweet solution, on the other hand, elicits satisfied sucking; a sour solution induces a grimace and cessation of sucking; and a bitter solution provokes an angry facial expression, cessation of sucking, and in many cases, turning away of the head. Breast-feeding mothers also find that neonates prefer bottled breast milk to commercial formula during periods when they cannot nurse (Als, 1982).

Smell

Although little research has been conducted on neonatal olfaction, the neonate is known to react to strong or noxious odors by averting the head from the odor. Sensitivity to olfactory stimuli increases over the first 4 days after birth.

CHARACTERISTIC PATTERNS OF SLEEP AND ACTIVITY

During the transitional period, the neonate experiences a series of changes encompassing state of consciousness, behavioral response to stimuli, and physiologic parameters. Various neonatal sleep and awake states also have been identified.

PERIODS OF NEONATAL REACTIVITY

The neonate's initial hours are characterized by a predictable, identifiable series of behavioral and physiologic characteristics (Arnold, Putman, Barnard, Desmond, and Rudolph, 1965). Desmond and Associates (1966) described this series collectively as the periods of neonatal reactivity.

All neonates experience the same sequence of periods. However, when each period begins and how long it lasts varies from one neonate to another. Maternal medication, anesthesia, labor duration, and any stress affecting the neonate may influence the duration of a given period.

First period of reactivity

Beginning just after birth, this period lasts roughly 60 minutes. In this phase of intense activity and awareness of external stimuli, the neonate is alert and attentive to the environment and may exhibit vigorous activity, crying, and rapid respiratory and heart rates. The neonate has a strong desire to suckle during this period, so breast-feeding may be initiated. Gradually, the neonate becomes less alert and active and falls asleep.

Neonatal adaptations during this initial period are regulated mainly by the sympathetic nervous system. Irregular respirations, tachypnea, and nasal flaring unrelated to respiratory distress may occur. Other visible features of this period include spontaneous startles, the Moro reflex (in which the neonate extends and moves the limbs away from the body when the head is dropped backward suddenly), grimacing, sucking motions, sudden cries that stop abruptly, fine tremors of the jaw or extremities, blinking, and jerking eye movements.

The first period of reactivity provides a good opportunity for early parent-neonate interaction. Studying the attachment of mothers and neonates, Klaus and Kennell (1976) concluded that this is the optimal time for promoting mother-infant bonding. They referred to this phase as a sensitive period, necessary to some degree for successful mother-infant bonding. Although the importance of this period to bonding has since been questioned, the work of Klaus and Kennell led to changes in routine obstetric and neonatal nursery care to prevent unnecessary separation of parents and neonate.

The nurse can enhance bonding by allowing the mother and neonate to remain together during this period (provided the neonate is healthy). After drying the neonate and performing initial care, the nurse should allow the parents to see and hold their child. Instillation of prophylactic eye medication should be delayed until after this period so that the neonate's heightened visual awareness can enhance parent-infant bonding.

Temperature must be monitored and maintained carefully during this period to prevent cold stress. For example, the nurse should carefully dry the neonate or use warmed blankets or overhead warming lights to supply heat and prevent heat loss. Although temperature maintenance should never be forfeited to allow parent-neonate contact, the nurse should keep in mind that skin-to-skin contact between parent and neonate usually maintains the neonate's temperature adequately.

Sleep stage

The neonate typically falls asleep about 2 to 3 hours after birth and remains asleep from a few minutes to 2 to 4 hours. Some authorities classify sleep as a distinct, self-contained period of reactivity. Others consider it a transitional phase bridging the first and second periods.

While asleep, the neonate's respiratory rate increases while the heart rate ranges from 120 to 140 beats/minute. Skin color improves, although some acrocyanosis persists. Because the neonate has little response to external stimuli during the sleep period, attempts at breast-feeding will elicit no response. However, the mother may wish to hold and cuddle her child.

Second period of reactivity

Beginning when the neonate awakens, this period is characterized by an exaggerated response to internal and external stimuli. The heart rate is labile, and episodes of bradycardia and tachycardia occur. The neonate's skin usually appears pink-tinged or ruddy (although skin color naturally varies with racial background). Thick oral secretions frequently cause gagging and emesis. The respiratory rate, ranging from about 30 to 60 breaths/minute, is irregular and may include brief apneic pauses and periodic tachypnea. The neonate usually expels meconium from the GI tract during this period.

The second period may last from 4 to 6 hours. As it ends, the neonate becomes more stable and the respiratory and cardiac rates normalize. A dynamic equilibrium emerges, with the neonate alternating between alert activity and sleep and establishing a pattern of sleeping, crying, activity, and feeding. Although the environment influences the neonate's diurnal and circadian rhythms, temperament also strongly affects behavior.

Nursing measures appropriate for this period include monitoring vital signs, maintaining temperature, and ensuring a patent airway. The nurse also should encourage the parents to get acquainted with their infant at this time. The neonate may exhibit vigorous sucking motions and may appear hungry. (For a discussion of assessment during the two periods of reactivity, see Chapter 2, Neonatal Assessment.)

SLEEP AND AWAKE STATES OF THE NEONATE

Brazelton (1979) classified the neonate's state of consciousness into six states—two sleep states and four awake states. The sleep and awake states encompass the behavioral states used in the Brazelton Neonatal Behavioral Assessment Scale (BNBAS). Developed by Brazelton to measure a neonate's capabilities, the BNBAS assesses neonatal behavioral responses and elicited responses as well as behavioral states. (For details on the BNBAS, see Chapter 2, Neonatal Assessment.)

The neonate's ability to regulate the state of consciousness reflects central nervous system integrity. The state of consciousness may be affected by medication, hunger, diurnal cycles, stress (such as from noise, pain, and bright lights), and any other physical discomfort. Normally, the neonate in a sleep state responds to stimuli with increased activity, whereas a neonate in the crying state responds with decreased activity.

According to Brazelton, when confronted with external interferences (such as a heel prick or another painful stimulus), the neonate attempts to control the state of consciousness in one of four ways:
• by trying to withdraw physically
• by trying to push away the stimulus with the hands or feet
• by trying to withdraw emotionally (for example, turning away from the stimulus or falling asleep)
• by crying or fussing in an effort to interrupt the stimulus.

State of consciousness serves as a key focus of nursing assessment and as the basis for care of both neonate and parents. The nurse must be sufficiently familiar with neonatal sleep and awake states to recognize the neonate's state and any changes in it. By using this information, the nurse may more skillfully assess the neonate, plan neonatal care, and help promote parent-neonate interaction. (See Chapter 2, Neonatal Assessment, for details on assessing specific sleep and awake states.)

Deep sleep

In this sleep state, the neonate's eyes are closed and no rapid eye movements (REMs) appear. Except for occasional startle reflexes, no spontaneous activity occurs. Respirations are even and regular. The neonate in deep sleep usually cannot be aroused by external stimuli and will not breast-feed. Attempts by the mother to feed the neonate will cause frustration.

Light sleep

During this period, the neonate's eyes are closed and REMs occur. Variable breathing patterns, random movements, and sucking motions typify light sleep. External stimuli may arouse the neonate in this state.

Drowsy state

In this transitional state, the neonate attempts to become fully alert. The eyes may be open or closed and the eyelids may flutter frequently. Muscle movements are smooth, with intermittent spontaneous activity and startles. Tactile or auditory stimuli may evoke a response, but the response may be sluggish until the neonate approaches the next state.

Alert state

In this state, the eyes are open, bright, and shining and the neonate focuses on the source of stimulation. Aware of and responsive to the environment, the neonate makes purposeful movements and shows good eye-hand coordination. The neonate attempts to attain and maintain this state.

The alert state is considered the optimal state of arousal, ideal for parent-neonate contact or breast-feeding initiation. Although only minimally active, the neonate remains alert and responsive to visual and auditory stimulation for prolonged periods. Additional stimulation may cause a change of state (although the response to external stimulation is delayed).

Active state

The neonate's movements increase in this state, and external stimuli cause eye and body movements. The level of this activity increases as the next state approaches.

Crying state

In this state, the neonate responds to both internal and external stimuli. Usually beginning with slight whimpering and minimal activity, the neonate in the crying state typically progresses to increased motor activity, with thrusting movements of the extremities and spontaneous startles. The chance for successful feeding or interaction may improve if the parents or nurse can calm the neonate through such motions as rocking.

BIBLIOGRAPHY

Avery, G.B. (1987). *Neonatology: Pathophysiology and management of the newborn* (3rd ed.). Philadelphia: Lippincott.

Brown, B.A. (1988). *Hematology: Principles and procedures.* Philadelphia: Lea & Febiger.

Cloherty, J.P., and Stark, A.R. (1985). *Manual of neonatal care (The Boston manual)* (2nd ed.). Boston: Little, Brown.

Gomella, T.L. (1988). *Neonatology: Procedures, "on-call" problems, diseases, drugs.* Norwalk, CT: Appleton & Lange.

Guyton, A. (1985). *Textbook of Medical Physiology* (7th ed.). Philadelphia: Saunders.

Klaus, M.H., and Kennell, J.H. (1976). *Maternal infant bonding.* St. Louis: Mosby.

Korones, S.B. (1986). *High-risk newborn infants: The basis for intensive nursing care* (3rd ed.). St. Louis: Mosby.

March of Dimes. (1985). *Report on child health.* White Plains, NY.

Philip, A.G. (1987). *Neonatology: A practical guide.* Philadelphia: Saunders.

Redshaw, M.E., Rivers, R.P.A., and Rosenblatt, D.B. (1985). *Born too early: Special care for your preterm baby.* New York: Oxford University Press.

Streeter, N.S. (1986). *High-risk neonatal care.* Rockville, MD: Aspen.

West, J.B. (1985). *Respiratory physiology – the essentials* (3rd ed.). Baltimore: Williams & Wilkins.

Neonatal physical and behavioral assessment

Berkowitz, I.D. (1984). Infections in the newborn. In M. Ziai, T. Clarke, and T. Merritt (Eds.), *Assessment of the newborn: A guide for the practitioner* (pp. 59-80). Boston: Little, Brown.

Brazelton, T.B. (1973). Neonatal behavior assessment scale. *Clinics in Developmental Medicine,* No. 50. Philadelphia: Lippincott.

Brazelton, T.B. (1979). Behavioral competence of the newborn infant. *Seminars in Perinatology,* 3(1), 35-44.

Eisenberg, R. (1965). Auditory behaviors in the human neonate: Methodological problems. *Journal of Research,* 5, 159-177.

Ingelfinger, J.R. (1985). Renal conditions in the newborn period. In J.P. Cloherty and A.R. Stark (Eds.), *Manual of neonatal care* (2nd ed.; pp. 377-394). Boston: Little, Brown.

Lawrence, R. (1984). Physical examination. In M. Ziai, T. Clarke and T. Merritt (Eds.), *Assessment of the newborn: A guide for the practitioner* (pp. 86-111). Boston: Little, Brown.

Ludington-Hoe, S.M. (1983). What can newborns really see? *AJN,* (9), 1286-1289.

Putnam, T.C. (1984). Gastrointestinal bleeding. In M. Ziai, T. Clarke, and T. Merritt (Eds.), *Assessment of the newborn: A guide for the practitioner* (pp. 207-209). Boston: Little, Brown.

Volpe, J.J., and Hill, A. (1987). Neurologic disorders. In G.B. Avery (Ed.), *Neonatology, pathophysiology, and management of the newborn* (pp. 1073-1132). Philadelphia: Lippincott.

Nursing management during transition

Als, H. (1982). Toward a synactive theory of development. Promise for the assessment and support of infant individuality. *Infant Mental Health Journal, 3*(4), 229-243.

Anand, K. and Hickey, P.R. (1987). Pain and its effects in the human neonate and fetus. *New England Journal of Medicine,* 317(21), 1321-1329.

Arnold, H.W., Putman, N.J., Barnard, B.L., Desmond, M.M., and Rudolph, A.J. (1965). Transition to extrauterine life. *AJN,* 65(10), 77-80.

Desmond, M.M., and Associates. (1966). The transitional care nursery. *Pediatric Clinics of North America,* 13(3), 651-668.

Maisels, I. (1987). Neonatal jaundice. In G.B. Avery (Ed.), *Neonatology: Pathophysiology and management of the newborn* (3rd ed.; pp. 86-111). Philadelphia: Lippincott.

Wilkerson, N. (1988). A comprehensive look at hyperbilirubinemia. *MCN,* 13(5), 360-364.

Nursing research

Greer, P.S. (1988). Head coverings for neonates under radiant heat warmers. *JOGNN,* 17(4), 265-271.

Kramer, L.I., and Pierpont, M.E. (1976). Rocking waterbeds and auditory stimuli to enhance growth of preterm infants. *Journal of Pediatrics,* 88(2), 297-299.

Neonatal Assessment

The neonate undergoes many physiologic changes during the neonatal period—the first 28 days after birth. To make a successful transition to the extrauterine environment, the neonate must adapt to these changes as smoothly as possible. The nurse plays a critical role in the neonate's transition by conducting a thorough, systematic assessment that provides baseline information about the neonate's physiologic status and the adequacy of neonatal adaptation.

Besides knowing how to conduct such an assessment, the nurse also must understand the significance of assessment findings. For example, by identifying gestational age, the nurse can determine whether the neonate has a gestational-age variation necessitating special care. Early detection of a potential or actual problem reduces the risk of complications; in some cases, it may mean the difference between life and death.

GENERAL ASSESSMENT GUIDELINES

The nurse must adapt the assessment to the neonate's tolerance, delaying any maneuvers that could compromise the neonate and combining overlapping portions of the various assessments to help conserve the neonate's energy. For instance, gestational-age assessment includes certain characteristics also evaluated during the physical and behavioral assessments; the nurse should examine these characteristics only once. Also, the nurse should allow a neonate who falls asleep during the assessment to sleep undisturbed to recuperate from the stress of birth, then resume the assessment when the neonate awakens.

ASSESSMENT SEQUENCE

Neonatal assessment proceeds from an immediate determination of the Apgar score to a complete physical assessment.

The immediate assessment – determination of the Apgar score – takes place in the delivery area. Within the next few hours, the nurse should conduct a complete physical assessment to determine how well the neonate is adapting to the extrauterine environment and to check for obvious problems and major anomalies. This assessment includes evaluation of general appearance, vital sign measurement, and anthropometric measurements.

The nurse then estimates the neonate's gestational age and, if necessary, conducts a formal gestational-age assessment, using a special assessment tool, to determine gestational age precisely. Based on education and experience, the nurse may assist with a behavioral assessment.

HEALTH HISTORY

Determination of preterm or postterm status usually is established by the time of delivery. However, the nurse may want to review the maternal history for factors that increase the risk of a gestational-age variation so that the health care team can anticipate potential perinatal problems more accurately. For instance, the risk of preterm delivery increases with:

• various intrapartal factors, such as multiple gestation (more than one fetus), fetal infection, preeclampsia, premature rupture of the membranes, abruptio placentae, hydramnios (excessive amniotic fluid), placenta previa, and poor prenatal care

• chronic maternal disease, such as cardiovascular disease, renal disease, or diabetes mellitus

• maternal history of abdominal surgery, trauma, uterine anomalies, cervical incompetency, infection, or previous preterm delivery

• maternal age under 19.

With a postterm neonate, the intrapartal history may include weight loss, decreased abdominal circumference, and reduced uterine size – signs of an altered fetal growth pattern (fetal dysmaturity).

The prenatal and intrapartal history also may suggest a birth-weight variation. Such variations include small for gestational age (SGA), defined as a birth weight that falls below the tenth percentile for gestational age on the Colorado intrauterine growth chart, and large for gestational age (LGA), defined as a birth weight that exceeds the ninetieth percentile for gestational age on the growth chart.

Like a gestational-age variation, a birth-weight variation increases the risk of perinatal problems. Women identified as high risk by history or clinical assessment deliver about two-thirds of SGA neonates (Cassady and Strange, 1987). Risk factors for delivery of an SGA neonate include low socioeconomic status, an age under 19 or over 34, multiparity, short stature, low prepregnancy weight, and previous delivery of an SGA neonate.

Typically, the diagnosis of LGA is established during the antepartal period, when fundal height appears disproportionate to gestational weeks. Also, because diabetes mellitus is a leading cause of accelerated intrauterine growth, an elevated maternal serum glucose level may result in an LGA fetus.

PERIODS OF NEONATAL REACTIVITY

During the first hours after birth, the neonate experiences gradual, predictable changes in physiologic characteristics and behavioral responses, reflecting the periods of neonatal reactivity. The two reactivity periods are separated by a sleep stage (considered a discrete period of reactivity by some authorities).

With each period of reactivity, vital signs, state of alertness, and responsiveness to external stimuli change. The nurse must be able to recognize the characteristics of each period and use them when interpreting assessment findings. (For key features associated with each reactivity period, see *Assessment findings during periods of reactivity,* page 38.) Although a specific assessment for the period of reactivity is not necessary, the nurse should stay alert for deviations from normal findings because such deviations may signify a disorder. (For more information on the periods of reactivity, see Chapter 1, Neonatal Adaptation.)

INITIAL PHYSICAL ASSESSMENT

The neonate's cardiopulmonary rates and rhythms may be irregular and high during the periods of reactivity. This is especially true

ASSESSMENT FINDINGS DURING PERIODS OF REACTIVITY

The nurse should consider the period of reactivity when assessing the neonate—especially when using the Brazelton neonatal behavioral assessment scale to evaluate behavior. This chart shows the normal assessment findings associated with each reactivity period.

PARAMETER	FIRST PERIOD	SECOND PERIOD
Skin color	Fluctuates from pale pink to cyanotic (blue)	Fluctuates from pale pink to cyanotic, with periods of mottling
Alertness level	Awake and alert, progressing to sleep	Hyperactive, with exaggerated responses
Cry	Rigorous, diminishing as sleep begins	Periodic
Respiratory rate	Up to 80 breaths/minute when crying	40 to 60 breaths/minute, with periods of more rapid respirations
Respiratory effort	Irregular and labored, with nasal flaring, expiratory grunts, and retractions	Usually unlabored
Heart rate	Up to 180 beats/minute when crying	120 to 160 beats/minute, with periods of more rapid beating
Heart rhythm	Fluctuating, progressing to regular	Fluctuating as the neonate falls asleep, progressing to regular
Bowel sounds	Absent	Present
Stool	May not be passed	Meconium stool passed
Voiding	Rare	Usually begins
Mucus production	Minimal, diminishing gradually	Present, may be excessive
Sucking reflex	Strong, diminishing as sleep begins	Strong

during the first few minutes after birth. Even nasal flaring and grunting may be noted immediately following birth. The neonate may or may not be crying. The nurse must report these irregularities if they continue, even though they represent only the normal transition to postnatal life for some neonates. For other neonate's, however, they may be the earliest signs of respiratory difficulties or cardiac problems.

GENERAL APPEARANCE

By assessing general appearance, the nurse quickly gauges the neonate's maturity level (a reflection of gestational age) and may detect obvious problems. Features to assess in the general survey include posture, head size, lanugo, vernix caseosa, cry, and state of alertness. (For details on normal and abnormal findings when evaluating general appearance, see "Complete physical assessment" later in this chapter.)

VITAL SIGNS AND BLOOD PRESSURE

After assessing general appearance, the nurse measures vital signs (temperature, respiratory rate, and pulse) and blood pressure – not strictly a vital sign but usually included. (For details on how to take neonatal vital signs, see *Psychomotor skills: Taking vital signs,* pages 40 and 41.)

ANTHROPOMETRIC MEASUREMENTS

To take anthropometric measurements (weight, head-to-heel length, head and chest circumference, and crown-to-rump length), the nurse weighs and measures the neonate (as described in *Psychomotor skills: Obtaining anthropometric measurements,* page 42 to 44).

GESTATIONAL-AGE ASSESSMENT

Gestational-age assessment determines the neonate's physical and neuromuscular maturity, helping health care providers anticipate perinatal problems associated with preterm or postterm status. Correlation of gestational age with birth weight may suggest perinatal problems related to SGA or LGA status. (For information on specific perinatal problems associated with gestational-age and birth-weight variations, see Chapter 5, High-Risk Neonates.)

The average full-term gestation lasts about 38 weeks from fertilization, or 40 weeks from the first day of the last menstrual period. Traditionally, gestational age has been calculated from the latter. However, irregular menstrual cycles and fetal growth variations can lead to erroneous calculation.

TAKING VITAL SIGNS

The nurse should measure the neonate's vital signs every 15 minutes for the first hour after birth. If they remain stable during this time, measure them at least every hour for the next 6 hours, then at least once every 8 hours until discharge.

1 Measuring temperature. Place the thermometer in the axilla and hold it along the outer aspect of the neonate's chest, between the axillary line and the arm. Keep the thermometer in place for at least 3 minutes (axillary temperature takes this long to register).

If the measured axillary temperature is outside the normal range—97.5° to 99° F (36.4° to 37.2° C)—check it again 15 to 30 minutes later. If the temperature still is abnormal, report this finding. A subnormal temperature may indicate infection; an elevated temperature, dehydration. (To ensure consistency of subsequent measurements, document the route used to take the temperature.)

2 Measuring respiratory rate. Count respirations for at least 1 minute. Depending on the neonate's period of reactivity, the respiratory rate should range from 40 to 80 breaths/minute. An abnormally rapid rate (tachypnea) may signal a perinatal problem. A lapse of 15 seconds or more after a complete respiratory cycle (one expiration and inspiration) indicates apnea.

Assess the neonate's breathing pattern for regularity. An irregular pattern may indicate respiratory dysfunction. Also check for signs of labored breathing, such as uneven chest expansion, nasal flaring, visible chest retractions, expiratory grunts, and inspiratory stridor (a high-pitched sound audible without a stethoscope). In some cases, labored breathing indicates blockage of nasal passages (the neonate is an obligate nose breather).

To evaluate breath sounds, auscultate the anterior and posterior lung fields, placing the stethoscope over each lung lobe for at least 5 seconds (for a total time of 1 minute). Normally, breath sounds are clear and equal bilaterally. However, immediately after birth, a few crackles (rales) may be audible because of retained fetal lung fluid. Document any abnormal breath sounds.

Observe the movement of the chest as it rises and falls; it should be symmetrical. Also determine the ratio between the anterior and posterior diameters of the chest. A ratio exceeding 1 suggests lung hyperinflation or respiratory distress.

3 Assessing pulse. Place the stethoscope over the apical impulse on the fourth to fifth intercostal space at the left midclavicular line over the cardiac apex. Listen for 1 minute to count

TAKING VITAL SIGNS   *(continued)*

the pulse and detect any abnormalities in the quality or rhythm of the heartbeat.

If heart rhythm is irregular, assess whether the irregularity is regular (follows an identifiable pattern) or irregular (lacks an identifiable pattern). This helps identify the type of abnormality present; for example, atrial fibrillation is an irregular rhythm with an irregular pattern.

Also auscultate for variations from the normal sounds ("lub-dub") of systole and diastole. Determine if the first and second heart sounds are separate and distinct or split into two sounds. Also assess for extra heart sounds and for sounds that seem to stretch into the next sound. Such abnormal sounds may signify a heart murmur, such as from a patent ductus arteriosus (in which blood rushes through the abnormal opening).

4 **Taking blood pressure.** When using a Doppler probe (an electronic blood pressure monitor), place the cuff directly over the brachial or popliteal artery to ensure an accurate reading; the machine automatically inflates the cuff. For the most accurate reading, keep the cuffed arm or leg extended during cuff inflation. Also observe the color of the extremity; duskiness signifies reduced blood flow.

When measuring blood pressure by the cuff-and-stethoscope method, make sure to choose the correct cuff size. Cuff width should be half the circumference of the neonate's arm. A cuff that is too large or too small may cause a misleading reading.

Place the cuff one to two fingerbreadths above the antecubital or popliteal area. With the stethoscope held directly over the chosen artery, hold the cuffed extremity firmly to keep it extended, then inflate the cuff.

To determine if blood pressure is within the neonate's normal range, compare the readings to baseline values; report any significant deviation.

GESTATIONAL-AGE AND BIRTH-WEIGHT CLASSIFICATIONS

Previously, health care professionals used birth weight alone to classify neonates. However, in the past few decades, as experts recognized the importance of gestational age, new classifications have been developed and mortality and morbidity rates identified

(Text continues on page 45.)

OBTAINING ANTHROPOMETRIC MEASUREMENTS

Anthropometric measurements include weight, head-to-heel length, head and chest circumference, and crown-to-rump length. If abnormal, these measurements may indicate a significant problem or anomaly. The nurse should follow the illustrated procedure for taking anthropometric measurements.

1 Measuring weight. Take this measurement before—not after—a feeding, preferably with the neonate undressed. If the neonate must be weighed with clothing or equipment (such as an I.V. armboard), make sure to note this information.

Before the weighing, place one or two pieces of disposable scale paper over the scale to prevent cold stress. When taking the measurement, keep one hand directly above the neonate. However, avoid touching the neonate, which could affect the accuracy of the measurement. Birth weight averages 2,500 to 4,000 g (5 lb, 6 oz to 8 lb, 13 oz).

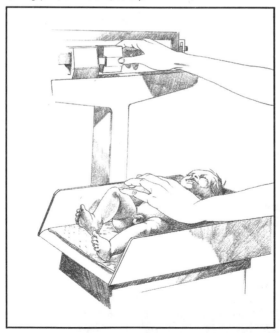

OBTAINING ANTHROPOMETRIC MEASUREMENTS
(continued)

2 Measuring head-to-heel length. Position the neonate supine with legs extended and measure from head to heel. To make this measurement easier, use a length board. Length averages 45 to 53 cm (18″ to 21″).

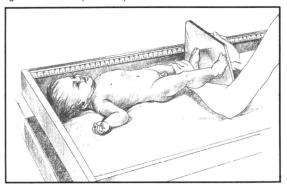

3 Measuring chest circumference. Place a tape measure around the neonate's chest at the nipples. Take the measurement after the neonate inspires, before expiration begins. Chest circumference usually measures about 2 cm less than head circumference, averaging 30 to 33 cm (12″ to 13″).

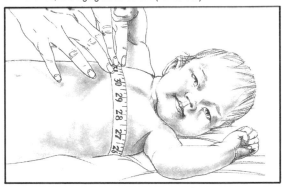

(continued)

OBTAINING ANTHROPOMETRIC MEASUREMENTS
(continued)

4 **Measuring head circumference.** Place a tape measure securely around the fullest part of the caput, from the middle of the forehead to the midline of the back of the skull. Record the result. Keep in mind that if delivery caused molding or swelling of the head, the measured head circumference may be misleading.

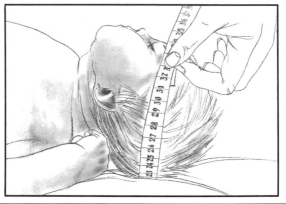

5 **Measuring crown-to-rump length.** With the neonate lying on one side, measure from the crown of the head to the buttocks. This measurement should approximate head circumference.

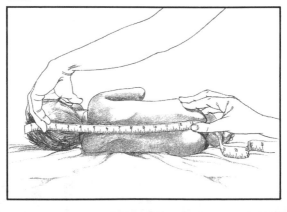

for each classification. (For more information, see *Classifying by gestational age and birth weight,* pages 46 and 47.)

GESTATIONAL-AGE ASSESSMENT TOOLS

Gestational age should be assessed for any neonate who weighs less than 2,500 g (5½ lb) or who has a suspected alteration in the intrauterine growth pattern. Gestational-age assessment tools rely on external physical features and neurologic maturity—not birth weight—as indices of growth and maturation. Developing in an orderly manner during gestation, external physical features usually are not affected by labor and delivery and thus can be assessed immediately. Evaluation of neurologic maturity, however, may have to be postponed for 24 hours or so—especially if the neonate suffered fetal central nervous system depression, which may skew assessment findings.

The most common gestational-age assessment tools are the Dubowitz tool (1970) and the Ballard tool (revised in 1988). The Dubowitz tool includes 11 external and 10 neurologic signs. The examiner evaluates and scores each external sign, then totals the scores. After following the same procedure for neurologic signs, the examiner adds the two totals and plots the sum on a graph to identify the neonate's gestational age. (With early client discharge now routine, the Dubowitz tool has become somewhat impractical because the neurologic part of the examination must be delayed.)

The Ballard tool, an abbreviated version of the Dubowitz tool, consists of 7 physical maturity and 6 neuromuscular maturity criteria. This tool is refined periodically in response to research. The 1988 revision incorporates criteria for gestational-age assessment of neonates at 20 to 44 weeks' gestation.

ASSESSMENT PHYSICAL FEATURES

Certain physical features vary with gestational age and thus reflect neonatal maturity. (These features are called external signs on the Dubowitz tool and physical maturity criteria on the Ballard tool.)

Skin texture, color, and opacity

The preterm neonate has thin, translucent, ruddy skin with easily seen veins and venules (especially over the abdomen). As term approaches, the skin thickens and becomes pinker; also, the number of large vessels visible over the abdomen decreases. The postterm

CLASSIFYING BY GESTATIONAL AGE AND BIRTH WEIGHT

Organ system maturity depends largely on gestational age. Thus, the greater a neonate's gestational age, the more fully developed the organ systems. At the First World Health Assembly in 1948, the World Health Organization (WHO) defined an "immature" neonate as one weighing 5½ lb (2,500 g) or less; or, if the weight was not specified, one whose gestation lasted less than 37 weeks. In 1950, the WHO Expert Group on Prematurity defined the premature (preterm) neonate as one weighing 2,500 g or less.

However, health care professionals recognized that some neonates weighing less than 2,500 g were term or postterm but small for gestational age. Consequently, in 1961, the WHO Expert Committee on Maternal and Child Health redefined the premature neonate as one born before 37 weeks from the first day of the mother's last menstrual period. The committee defined low birth weight (LBW) as 2,500 g or less and subdivided neonates in this category into term and preterm LBW neonates.

In the 1980s, an additional classification — very low birth weight (VLBW) — was added to describe the neonate weighing 500 g to 1,499 g. Most VLBW neonates have a gestational age of 23 to 30 weeks. VLBW neonates have had a tremendous impact on medical research and have sparked important advances in neonatal care — even though they account for only a tiny percentage of neonates. (According to Usher [1987], only 0.87% of live births occur before 31 weeks; VLBW neonates make up just 0.85% of these births.)

Currently, neonates are classified according to the Colorado intrauterine growth chart. Developed by Battaglia and Lubchenco (1967), this chart correlates gestational age with birth weight. After weighing the neonate and determining gestational age, the examiner plots these two parameters on the graph. The neonate whose weight falls between the tenth and ninetieth percentiles for gestational age on this chart is classified as appropriate for gestational age. One whose birth weight falls outside this range is considered to be small or large for gestational age, with an increased risk for certain perinatal problems. Thanks largely to

neonate typically has thick, parchmentlike skin with peeling and cracking; few if any blood vessels appear over the abdomen.

Lanugo

Soft, downy hair, lanugo appears at approximately 20 weeks' gestation. From 21 to 33 weeks, it covers the entire body. It begins to vanish from the face at 34 weeks and by 38 weeks may appear only on the shoulders. Lanugo rarely appears after 42 weeks' gestation.

improved knowledge and technology, however, such a neonate has an
improved chance for survival.

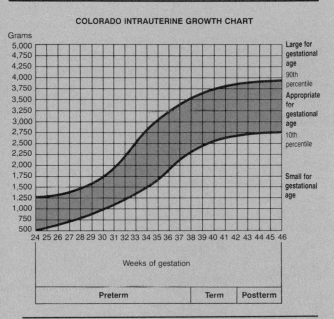

COLORADO INTRAUTERINE GROWTH CHART

Battaglia, F.C., and Lubchenco, L.O. (1967). A practical classification of newborn infants by weight and gestational age. *Journal of Pediatrics*, 71, 159-163. Graph used with permission from C.V. Mosby Company.

Plantar (sole) creases

Plantar creases should be assessed immediately after birth because
the drying effect of environmental exposure causes additional creases
to form. The preterm neonate of 34 to 35 weeks' gestation has one
or two anterior creases; at 36 to 38 weeks' gestation, creases cover
the anterior two-thirds of the sole. In the term neonate, creases
appear over both the sole and heel. In the postterm neonate, deeper
creases line the entire sole.

Breast size

The examiner assesses breast tissue through observation and palpation. To measure breast tissue, palpate the nipple gently between the second and third fingers. Do not use the thumb and index finger because surrounding skin may be measured inadvertently this way.

Breast tissue and areola size increase with gestation. The areola appears slightly elevated at 34 weeks' gestation. By week 36, a breast bud of 1 to 2 mm is visible; the bud may grow to 12 mm by week 42. Increased breast tissue may indicate subcutaneous fat accumulation from accelerated intrauterine growth (such as occurs in the LGA neonate). In contrast, the SGA or postterm neonate may have decreased breast tissue from inadequate fetal growth or lost fetal weight.

Ear form and firmness

In the preterm neonate of less than 28 weeks' gestation, decreased cartilage distribution prevents the ear from recoiling after it is folded forward against the side of the head and released. The ear appears flat and shapeless until 28 weeks' gestation when incurving of the pinna (the external part of the ear) begins. At 36 weeks' gestation, the upper two-thirds of the pinna are incurved and the pinna recoils instantly. In the term neonate, the pinna has well-defined incurving. The ear of the postterm neonate is firm and set apart slightly from the head.

Genitalia

In the male neonate, the genitalia should be assessed for testicular descent, scrotal size, and number of rugae (skin folds). In the preterm neonate of less than 28 weeks' gestation, the testes remain within the abdominal cavity and the scrotum appears high and close to the body. At 28 to 36 weeks' gestation, the testes can be palpated in the inguinal canal and a few rugae appear. At 36 to 40 weeks' gestation, the testes are palpable in the upper scrotum and rugae appear on the anterior portion. After 40 weeks' gestation, the testes can be palpated in the scrotum and rugae cover the scrotal sac. The postterm neonate has deep rugae and a pendulous scrotum.

The female preterm neonate of 30 to 36 weeks' gestation has a prominent clitoris extending from the labia minora and majora; the labia majora are small and widely separated. (This appearance occasionally complicates sex determination and may upset parents.)

At 36 to 40 weeks' gestation, the labia majora are larger, almost covering the clitoris. Labia majora that cover the labia minora and clitoris suggest more than 40 weeks' gestation.

ASSESSMENT OF NEUROLOGIC MATURITY

Assessment of neurologic features (called neurologic signs on the Dubowitz tool and neuromuscular maturity criteria on the Ballard tool) determines the degree of neuromuscular tone — an index of neurologic maturity. Unlike other neurologic characteristics, which develop in a cephalocaudal (head-to-tail) direction, neuromuscular tone begins in the lower extremities and progresses upward.

The Dubowitz neurologic examination initially includes evaluation of posture and of arm and leg recoil. The remaining neurologic criteria are assessed 24 hours after birth to eliminate the effects of maternal analgesia, increased handling from additional assessments, and the normal physiologic fluctuations (such as vital sign changes) of the first few hours.

Correlating gestational age with birth weight

After determining the neonate's gestational age with an assessment tool, the examiner plots the age on the Colorado intrauterine growth chart to correlate it with birth weight. This reveals whether the neonate is SGA, LGA, or appropriate for gestational age — information that helps caregivers anticipate perinatal problems.

Correlating gestational age with length and head circumference

The examiner also plots gestational age against length and head circumference on an appropriate growth chart to determine whether these measurements fall within the normal range — the tenth to nine-tieth percentile for the corresponding gestational age.

COMPLETE PHYSICAL ASSESSMENT

When conducting the complete physical assessment, the nurse may use a systematic, head-to-toe approach tailored to the neonate's size and age, or may assess heart and lung sounds first because these assessments require a quiet neonate. Ensure thermoregulation by placing the neonate under a radiant heat warmer and examining only

ASSESSING REFLEXES

To evaluate neurologic status during the complete physical assessment, the nurse should test neonatal reflexes. The chart below describes testing methods and normal responses. A weak, absent, or asymmetrical response is considered abnormal. Some reflexes (such as the pupillary, blink, and gag reflexes) persist throughout life; others (including the doll's eye, sucking, grasp, Babinski, Moro, fencing, and Galant reflexes) normally disappear a few weeks or months after birth.

REFLEX	TESTING METHOD	NORMAL RESPONSE
Babinski	Stroke one side of the neonate's foot upward from the heel and across the ball of the foot.	Neonate hyperextends the toes, dorsiflexes the great toe, and fans the toes outward.
Blink (corneal)	Momentarily shine a bright light directly into the neonate's eyes.	Neonate blinks.
Crawl	Place the neonate prone on a flat surface.	Neonate attempts to crawl forward using the arms and legs.
Crossed extension	Position the neonate supine; extend one leg and stimulate the sole with a light pin prick or finger flick.	Neonate swiftly flexes and extends the opposite leg as though trying to push the stimulus away from the other foot.
Doll's eye	With the neonate supine, slowly turn the neonate's head to the left or right.	Neonate's eyes remain stationary.
Fencing (tonic neck)	With a swift motion, turn the neonate's head to either side.	Neonate extends the extremities on the side to which the head is turned and flexes the extremities on the opposite side.
Galant	Using a fingernail, gently stroke one side of the neonate's spinal column from the head to the buttocks.	Neonate's trunk curves toward the stimulated side.
Grasp	Palmar reflex: Place a finger in the neonate's palm.	Neonate grasps the finger.
	Plantar reflex: Place a finger against the base of the neonate's toe.	Neonate's toes curl downward and grasp the finger.
Moro	Suddenly but gently drop the neonate's head backward (relative to the trunk).	Neonate extends and abducts all extremities bilaterally and symmetrically; forms a "C" shape with the thumb and forefinger; and adducts, then flexes, the extremities.
Pupillary (light)	Darken the room and shine a penlight directly into the neonate's eye for several seconds.	Pupils constrict equally bilaterally.

ASSESSING REFLEXES (continued)

REFLEX	TESTING METHOD	NORMAL RESPONSE
Rooting	Touch a finger to the neonate's cheek or the corner of mouth. (The mother's nipple also should trigger this reflex.)	Neonate turns the head toward the stimulus, opens the mouth, and searches for the stimulus.
Startle	Make a loud noise near the neonate.	Neonate cries and abducts and flexes all extremities.
Stepping (automatic walking)	Hold the neonate in an upright position and touch one foot lightly to a flat surface (such as the bed).	Neonate makes walking motions with both feet.
Sucking	Place a finger in the neonate's mouth. (The mother's nipple also should trigger this reflex.)	Neonate sucks on the finger (or nipple) forcefully and rhythmically; sucking is coordinated with swallowing.

one area at a time. For assessments requiring advanced skills, seek appropriate assistance.

Check vital signs before the examination begins; if they are unstable or if the neonate has a temperature below 96° F (35.5° C), do not proceed with the examination. Instead, swaddle the neonate, rewrapping securely. Because the period of reactivity affects assessment findings, record the neonate's behavioral state and age (in hours or days after birth) at the time of the examination.

For details on normal and abnormal assessment findings and their significance, see *Assessing reflexes* and *Head-to-toe physical assessment findings,* pages 52 to 72.

BEHAVIORAL ASSESSMENT

The behavioral assessment allows the nurse to evaluate the neonate's behavioral capacities and interaction with the environment.

Various tools are available for behavioral assessment. For best results, the assessment should be conducted in a quiet, softly lit setting. Findings must be interpreted in light of the period of reactivity and the neonate's gestational age.

If possible, the parents should observe the assessment so they can learn about their child's behavioral capacities.

(Text continues on page 72.)

HEAD-TO-TOE PHYSICAL ASSESSMENT FINDINGS

Comprehensive physical assessment of the neonate proceeds from head to toe. For each body area, the chart shows normal findings and common variations, and abnormal findings and their possible causes.

PARAMETER	NORMAL FINDINGS AND COMMON VARIATIONS	ABNORMAL FINDINGS	POSSIBLE CAUSES
General appearance and behavior			
Body shape and posture	Well-rounded torso with sufficient subcutaneous tissue and no obvious anomalies	Thin extremities, muscle wasting, loose skin, little or no subcutaneous tissue, obvious anomalies	Malnourishment, fetal stress, congenital defect (such as cleft lip or palate, omphalocele, gastroschisis, meningomyelocele)
	Flexed extremities, bowed legs	Fetal position (fists clenched, arms adducted and flexed, hips abducted, knees flexed)	Prematurity
		Frog position (flexed hips and thighs, extended arms)	Prematurity
		Opisthotonos (acute arching of back, with head bent back on neck, heels bent back on legs, and rigid arm and hand flexion)	Brain damage, birth asphyxia, neurologic abnormality
Muscle tone	Pronounced	Reduced or flaccid	Birth asphyxia, prematurity
	Spontaneous symmetrical movement (possibly slightly tremulous), bilaterally equal flexion and extension	No movement or asymmetrical, irregular, tremulous movement	Birth asphyxia, neurologic dysfunction, prematurity, drug-induced birth injury
Alertness level	Usually easy to console when upset	Decreased alertness, hard to arouse and console	Prematurity, stress, sepsis, neurologic disorder
Cry	Strong	Weak, high-pitched, or absent	Brain damage, neonatal drug addiction, increased intracranial pressure (ICP)
		Raspy	Upper airway problem
		Expiratory grunt during crying	Respiratory distress

HEAD-TO-TOE PHYSICAL ASSESSMENT FINDINGS *(continued)*

PARAMETER	NORMAL FINDINGS AND COMMON VARIATIONS	ABNORMAL FINDINGS AND POSSIBLE CAUSES	
Neuromuscular maturity			
Scarf sign	Elbow reaches midline when extended across chest	Elbow extends beyond midline	Prematurity
		Elbow does not reach midline	Postmaturity
Arm recoil	Brisk	Sluggish	Prematurity
Ankle dorsi-flexion	0-degree angle	Angle greater than 0 degrees	Prematurity
Popliteal angle	90 degrees or less	Greater than 90 degrees	Prematurity
Heel-to-ear maneuver	Heel reaches only to shoulders	Heel approaches or reaches ear	Prematurity
Skin			
Texture	Moist and warm	Gelatinous with visible veins	Prematurity
		Dry, peeling, cracking	Postmaturity
		Edematous, shiny, taut	Kidney dysfunction, cardiac or renal failure
Color	Varies with ethnic background; may deepen with crying and activity • Asian: pink or rosy red to yellow tinge • Black or Native American: pale pink with yellow or red tinge • Caucasian: pale pink to ruddy • Hispanic: pink with yellow tinge Cyanotic discoloration of hands and feet during first 24 hours after birth caused by transition to relatively cool extrauterine environment	Cyanotic discoloration of hands and feet lasting longer than first 24 hours	Poor peripheral circulation, possibly with cardiac compromise
		Dusky or cyanotic discoloration over entire body	Poor circulation, respiratory compromise
		Plethora (florid complexion), accompanied by elevated hematocrit or hemoglobin level	Polycythemia or blood hyperviscosity
		Pallor	Cardiopulmonary compromise or failure

(continued)

HEAD-TO-TOE PHYSICAL ASSESSMENT FINDINGS *(continued)*

PARAMETER	NORMAL FINDINGS AND COMMON VARIATIONS	ABNORMAL FINDINGS AND POSSIBLE CAUSES	
Color *(continued)*	Reddish tinge just after birth caused by adjustment of central oxygen levels to extrauterine environment	Mottling	Prematurity or cardiopulmonary disorder (if associated with cold stress, color changes, bradycardia, or apnea)
	Yellow discoloration (jaundice) arising in first 48 to 72 hours after birth and normally disappearing by the seventh day (physiologic jaundice)	Jaundice on first day after birth (pathologic jaundice)	Isoimmune hemolytic disease (such as Rh or ABO incompatibility), polycythemia, enzyme deficiency, excessive bruising or bleeding, Hirschsprung's disease, pyloric stenosis (or other intestinal obstruction that increases blood supply or shunts blood to liver), maternal diabetes, small-for-gestational-age (SGA) status
Vernix caseosa	Present over entire body	Absent	Severe prematurity
		Minimal or absent	Postmaturity
Lanugo (soft, downy hair)	Sparse or present only on shoulders	Abundant over entire body	Prematurity
		Absent	Postmaturity
Turgor	Adequate (indicated by brisk return of skin to original position after examiner pinches it between fingers)	Poor (indicated by tenting or sluggish return to original position)	Dehydration
Skin variations	Ecchymosis of presenting part Harlequin (clown) sign (pink or reddish skin on one side of body, with color division at midline; caused by vasomotor instability)	Café-au-lait spots (small, light tan macules)	Possible early sign of neurofibromatosis, especially if appearing in group of seven or more

HEAD-TO-TOE PHYSICAL ASSESSMENT FINDINGS *(continued)*

PARAMETER	NORMAL FINDINGS AND COMMON VARIATIONS	ABNORMAL FINDINGS AND POSSIBLE CAUSES	
Skin variations *(continued)*	Mongolian spots (blue-black macules over buttocks, possibly extending to sacral region; most common in dark-skinned neonates)	Meconium staining	Fetal distress
		Petechiae	Hematopoietic disorder
	Milia (minute white epidermal cysts caused by sebaceous gland obstruction; commonly seen on face)	Cutaneous papilloma (small brownish or flesh-colored outgrowth of skin; also called skin tag)	Possible congenital anomaly
	Miliaria (rash consisting of minute vesicles and papules, resulting from sweat duct blockage; occurs mainly on forehead and in skin folds, also called prickly heat)		
	Erythema toxicum neonatorum (pink, papular rash covering thorax, back, abdomen, and groin; commonly appears within 24 to 48 hours after birth)		
	Nevus flammeus (permanent birthmark; flat, capillary hemangioma ranging from pale red to deep red-purple; also called port wine stain)		
	Telangiectatic nevi (flat, deep pink, localized areas of capillary dilation; typically appear on upper eyelids, across nasal bridge and occipital bone, or along neck; also called stork bite)		

(continued)

HEAD-TO-TOE PHYSICAL ASSESSMENT FINDINGS *(continued)*

PARAMETER	NORMAL FINDINGS AND COMMON VARIATIONS	ABNORMAL FINDINGS AND POSSIBLE CAUSES	
Respiratory system			
Respiratory effort and rhythm	Easy, unlabored effort; abdominal breathing; possible irregular rhythm and apneic episodes lasting less than 15 seconds	Dyspnea; substernal, supracostal, intercostal, or supraclavicular retractions; nasal flaring; stridor; grunting	Respiratory distress
Chest excursion	Symmetrical	Asymmetrical	Diaphragmatic hernia, pneumothorax, phrenic nerve damage
Anteroposterior (AP) diameter	1:1 ratio (almost round)	Ratio > 1:1 (barrel chest)	Poorly developed rib cage and chest musculature, possible prematurity
Breath sounds	Clear; equal bilaterally, anteriorly, and posteriorly; crackles during first few hours after birth (unless accompanied by color changes or cyanosis)	Unequal	Pneumothorax or diaphragmatic hernia
		Crackles after first day, rhonchi, expiratory grunts, wheezing	Pulmonary congestion or edema, respiratory distress, pneumonia
Chest percussion	No increase in tympany over lung fields	Increased tympany over lung fields	Lung hyperinflation
Cardiovascular system			
Heart rate and rhythm	120 to 160 beats/minute (higher during active or crying periods); regular	Less than 100 beats/minute (bradycardia) or more than 160 beats/minute (tachycardia)	Prematurity, respiratory compromise, increased cardiac workload, sepsis, congenital heart defect
		Persistent arrhythmias	Congenital heart anomaly
Heart sounds	No audible murmur (however, slight murmur heard over base or left sternal border until foramen ovale closes)	Heart sounds on right side of chest	Possible dextrocardia
		Persistent murmur (usually heard at left sternal border or above apical impulse)	Persistent fetal circulation, congenital heart anomaly

HEAD-TO-TOE PHYSICAL ASSESSMENT FINDINGS *(continued)*

PARAMETER	NORMAL FINDINGS AND COMMON VARIATIONS	ABNORMAL FINDINGS AND POSSIBLE CAUSES	
Apical impulse	Located at fourth or fifth intercostal space at midclavicular line; point of maximum impulse located at fourth intercostal space just right of midclavicular line (may shift to the right in first few hours after birth)	Displaced	Cardiac defect or cardiomegaly
Thrill	Absent (except for first few hours after birth)	Present beyond first few hours after birth	Increased cardiac activity

Head and neck

Head size	Slightly large in proportion to body (average head circumference of term neonate is 32 to 35 cm)	Abnormally small	Microcephaly, caused by congenital syndrome or decreased brain development (such as from intrauterine growth retardation)
		Extremely small	Anencephaly (absent cerebral tissue or absent or minimal skull)
		Abnormally large	Macrocephaly, possibly caused by hydrocephalus (abnormal accumulation of cerebrospinal fluid within cranial vault) resulting from congenital anomaly (such as meningomyelocele, tumor, trauma, or infection)
Fontanels	Anterior fontanel open until age 12 to 18 months; diamond shaped; measures 2 x 3 x 5 cm; located at juncture of coronal, frontal, and sagittal sutures	Premature closure of anterior fontanel	Poor brain development

(continued)

HEAD-TO-TOE PHYSICAL ASSESSMENT FINDINGS *(continued)*

PARAMETER	NORMAL FINDINGS AND COMMON VARIATIONS	ABNORMAL FINDINGS AND POSSIBLE CAUSES	
Fontanels *(continued)*	Posterior fontanel open until age 2 to 3 months (may be closed at birth); triangular shaped; measures 1 x 1 x 1 cm; located at juncture of sagittal and lambdoidal sutures	Bulging fontanel (usually anterior fontanel)	Increased ICP
		Sunken fontanel	Dehydration
Head and scalp variations	Molding (cranial distortion lasting 5 to 7 days, caused by pressure on cranium during vaginal delivery)	Herniation of brain tissue through skull defect	Encephalocele (congenital or traumatic defect)
		Bradycephalus, premature closure of coronal suture line, increased AP diameter and lateral growth	Anomalies, such as congenital or traumatic defects
		Premature closure of skull sutures (craniosynostosis)	Genetic disorder
		Overriding sutures, caused by excessive pressure on cranium during vaginal delivery	Prematurity
		Localized pitting edema of scalp possibly extending over sutures	Caput succedaneum, caused by pressure on fetal occiput (as during extended labor)
		Forceps marks; edematous or reddened area	Forceps delivery
		Localized scalp swelling	Cephalhematoma (collection of blood between skull and periosteum that does not cross suture lines; commonly caused by forceps trauma; may last up to 8 weeks)
	No masses or soft areas over skull	Masses or soft areas (such as craniotabes)	Possible anomaly of internal organs

HEAD-TO-TOE PHYSICAL ASSESSMENT FINDINGS *(continued)*

PARAMETER	NORMAL FINDINGS AND COMMON VARIATIONS	ABNORMAL FINDINGS AND POSSIBLE CAUSES	
Head and scalp variations *(continued)*		over parietal bones (may be insignificant if no other abnormality exists)	
	No bruits in temporal area over anterior or posterior fontanel	Bruits in vascular areas of head	Cerebral arteriovenous malformation
Head lag	No greater than 10 degrees	Greater than 10 degrees	Hypotonia or prematurity
Hair distribution and texture	Distributed over top of head; single identifiable strands of hair	Fine or fuzzy hair	Prematurity
Eyes and eyelids	Symmetrical; aligned with ears, face, nose midline	Wide-eyed, apprehensive look	Postmaturity, SGA status, intrauterine growth retardation
	Eyes spaced approximately 2.5 cm apart	Abnormally wide distance (greater than 2.5 cm) between eyes (hypertelorism)	Fetal hydantoin syndrome (from maternal hydantoin use during pregnancy)
		Abnormally small distance (less than 2.5 cm) between eyes (hypotelorism)	Trisomy 13
	Clear sclera	Yellow sclera	Jaundice (however, slight yellow tinge may reflect only ethnic influence)
		Blue sclera	Osteogenesis imperfecta (fatal genetic syndrome characterized by fragile bones and shortened limbs)
		Scleral hemorrhage	Birth trauma
	Clear conjunctiva	Pink conjunctiva	Conjunctivitis (possibly resulting from silver nitrate or erythromycin instillation)
		Conjunctival hemorrhages	Birth trauma

(continued)

HEAD-TO-TOE PHYSICAL ASSESSMENT FINDINGS *(continued)*

PARAMETER	NORMAL FINDINGS AND COMMON VARIATIONS	ABNORMAL FINDINGS AND POSSIBLE CAUSES	
Eyes and eyelids *(continued)*	Even, bilateral iris color	Gold flecks in iris (Brushfield's spots)	Down's syndrome (trisomy 21), if accompanied by other anomalies
		Coloboma (cleft usually affecting iris, ciliary body, or choroid; extends inferiorly)	Possible congenital malformation of internal organs
	Bilaterally equal pupil reaction to light	Absent or bilaterally unequal pupil reaction to light	Brain damage or increased ICP
	Clear cornea	Hazy, milky cornea	Prematurity; congenital cataract (possibly from congenital rubella)
	Transparent, intact retina	Pigmented retinal areas; tortuous or poorly demarcated retinal vessels	Retinal damage or hemorrhage
	Patent, palpable lacrimal duct	Blocked or absent lacrimal duct	Congenital obstruction
	Positive blink reflex (eyes blink in response to bright light)	Absent blink reflex	Facial nerve paralysis or optic nerve damage
	Positive red reflex (luminous bilateral red appearance of retina)	Absent red reflex	Congenital cataract
	Positive doll's eye reflex (eyes remain stationary when head is moved to left or right)	Absent doll's eye reflex	Trochlear, oculomotor, or abducens nerve damage
	No eye slant or slant reflecting ethnic background	Pronounced upward eye slant	Down's syndrome
		Downward eye slant	Treacher Collins' syndrome (congenital syndrome characterized by small mandible, beaked nose, and lower lid and external ear malformations)

HEAD-TO-TOE PHYSICAL ASSESSMENT FINDINGS *(continued)*

PARAMETER	NORMAL FINDINGS AND COMMON VARIATIONS	ABNORMAL FINDINGS AND POSSIBLE CAUSES	
Eyes and eyelids *(continued)*		"Sunset" eyes (upper lid retraction causing sclera to show above iris)	Hydrocephalus
		Edematous eyelids	Birth trauma or irritation from silver nitrate or erythromycin instillation
		Ptosis (drooping) of eyelids	Oculomotor nerve damage
		Epicanthal folds	Down's syndrome; cri du chat (cat's cry) syndrome
Nose	Located at midline	Located off midline	Congenital malformation or syndrome (such as Apert's syndrome, characterized by premature closure of sutures)
	Appropriate size for face	Beaked	Treacher Collins's syndrome
		Enlarged or bulbous	Trisomy 13
	Patent nares	Nonpatent nares	Nasal obstruction; choanal atresia
		Missing nares	Congenital syndrome or malformation (such as cleft lip)
	Grimace or cry in response to strong odors passed under nose	No response to strong odors passed under nose	Olfactory nerve damage
		Flattened nasal bridge	Congenital syndrome, such as arthrogryposis (characterized by persistent contractures)
	Positive sneeze reflex (indicated by sneezing when both nares are occluded for 1 to 2 seconds)	No response	Possible nonpatent nares

(continued)

HEAD-TO-TOE PHYSICAL ASSESSMENT FINDINGS *(continued)*

PARAMETER	NORMAL FINDINGS AND COMMON VARIATIONS	ABNORMAL FINDINGS AND POSSIBLE CAUSES	
Ears	Symmetrical in size, shape, and placement; top of ear parallel to an imaginary line drawn through the outer and inner canthi of the eye	Low-set, slanted	Congenital syndrome (such as Down's syndrome)
		Pinpoint holes or sinus tracts along preauricular surface	Possible congenital renal anomaly
	Well-curved pinna; rigid cartilage; instant recoil after folding	Flattened or folded pinna; slow recoil	Prematurity
	Positive startle reflex (indicated by startling or crying in response to loud noise)	Absent or minimal startle reflex	Deafness or auditory nerve impairment
	Umbo (cone) of light visible on otoscopic examination; pearl gray, movable tympanic membrane with no bulges (membrane may be covered with vernix caseosa)	Umbo dull or absent; dull, immobile, or red tympanic membrane	Infection
		Blue tympanic membrane	Hemorrhage
		Bulging tympanic membrane	Otitis media (middle ear infection)
Mouth	Symmetrical; appropriate size for face; located at midline	Droops or slants unilaterally when neonate cries or moves mouth	Palsy or damage to seventh cranial or facial nerve, possibly resulting from birth trauma (such as from forceps delivery)
		Birdlike, with shortened vermilion border (exposed red portion of lips) and shortened philtrum (groove from upper lip to nose)	Fetal alcohol syndrome
		Extremely wide (macrostomia)	Metabolic disorder (such as hypothyroidism)
		Unusually small (microstomia)	Down's syndrome

HEAD-TO-TOE PHYSICAL ASSESSMENT FINDINGS *(continued)*

PARAMETER	NORMAL FINDINGS AND COMMON VARIATIONS	ABNORMAL FINDINGS AND POSSIBLE CAUSES	
Mouth *(continued)*	Lips pink, moist, and formed completely	One or more clefts in upper lip, possibly extending to nasal floor	Cleft lip (congenital anomaly in which maxillary and median nasal processes fail to fuse)
Mucous membranes	Moist and pink	Dry, dusky, or cyanotic	Dehydration, poor oxygenation
	Moderate salivation	Excessive salivation	Tracheoesophageal fistula, esophageal atresia
Palate	Intact with no arching or fissures	Markedly arched	Turner's syndrome
	Epstein's pearls (small, hard, white patches that resolve gradually)	Midline fissure	Cleft palate (congenital anomaly in which two sides of palate fail to fuse; may occur in conjunction with cleft lip)
Tongue	Appropriate size for face	Abnormally large (macroglossia)	Hypothyroidism
		Abnormally small (microglossia)	Congenital syndrome (such as Möbius's syndrome)
	Located at midline	Located off midline	Cranial nerve damage
	Juts forward when touched	Fails to jut forward when touched	Short frenulum
Uvula	Located at midline; rises with crying	Fails to rise with crying	Neurologic dysfunction
Chin	Slightly receding; appropriate size for face	Extremely receding; underdeveloped (micrognathia)	Congenital syndrome (such as Pierre Robin's syndrome)
Oral reflexes	Sucking, swallowing, rooting, and gag reflexes present; sucking and swallowing reflexes well coordinated	Absent gag reflex	Neurologic dysfunction
		Absent sucking or rooting reflex	Prematurity or neurologic dysfunction
Neck	Symmetrical	Asymmetrical	Unusual fetal position
	Short, no webbing (excessive skin)	Short and webbed	Down's syndrome

(continued)

HEAD-TO-TOE PHYSICAL ASSESSMENT FINDINGS *(continued)*

PARAMETER	NORMAL FINDINGS AND COMMON VARIATIONS	ABNORMAL FINDINGS AND POSSIBLE CAUSES	
Neck *(continued)*	Full range of motion (head can turn to each side equally)	Partial range of motion or tilting of head to one side (torticollis)	Birth injury; muscle spasm resulting in contraction of sternocleidomastoid muscles
	Weak, asymmetrical tonic neck reflex	Strong, asymmetrical tonic neck reflex	Prematurity
		Symmetrical tonic neck reflex	Neurologic dysfunction
	Thyroid located at midline; appropriate in size	Enlarged thyroid	Goiter
		Palpable lymph nodes	Congenital infection
		Palpable neck masses	Cystic hygroma
	Regular, bilaterally equal, strong carotid pulses	Weak or irregular carotid pulses	Cardiac defect or circulatory problem
		Enlarged sternocleidomastoid muscle	Torticollis; birth or fetal injury resulting in sternocleidomastoid hematoma
Thorax			
Clavicles	Even; symmetrical; nontender; without masses or lumps	Uneven; asymmetrical; masses or lumps present	Clavicular fracture; shoulder dystocia (as from birth injury); brachial plexus damage or palsy
Chest circumference	30 to 33 cm (12″ to 13″)	Less than 30 cm	Prematurity or SGA status
		Barrel chest (circumference greater than 33 cm)	Respiratory compromise; large-for-gestational-age (LGA) status
Chest excursion	Bilaterally equal	Bilaterally unequal	Phrenic nerve damage
Ribs	Symmetrical, flexible, without masses or crepitus	Asymmetrical	Birth injury or congenital syndrome
		Masses or crepitus present	Fracture or subcutaneous air pocket caused by air leakage resulting from pulmonary dysfunction

HEAD-TO-TOE PHYSICAL ASSESSMENT FINDINGS *(continued)*

PARAMETER	NORMAL FINDINGS AND COMMON VARIATIONS	ABNORMAL FINDINGS AND POSSIBLE CAUSES	
Breasts	1 cm of palpable breast tissue	Less than 1 cm (possibly only 5 mm) of palpable breast tissue	Prematurity
	Raised areolas	Flat areolas	Prematurity
	Horizontally aligned, well-spaced nipples; no extra nipples	Misaligned or supernumerary (more than two) nipples	Possible internal organ anomaly
	Breast hypertrophy, possibly with white nipple discharge (witch's milk) from maternal hormonal influence; appears within the first 2 to 3 days after birth, and usually diminishes during the first or second week	Purulent nipple discharge	Mastitis
Xiphoid process	Intact	Absent or depressed	Fracture (may result from resuscitation)
Abdomen			
Shape	Symmetrical; rounded	Asymmetrical	Abdominal mass
		Scaphoid	Diaphragmatic hernia
		Distended	Intestinal obstruction, renal disorder, ascites, edema resulting from congenital renal or cardiac defect, prematurity, fetal hydrops
		Distended left upper quadrant	Pyloric stenosis, duodenal or jejunal obstruction
Abdominal muscles	Strong	Weak	Prune-belly syndrome, possible renal problems (such as hypoplastic kidneys)
		Visible abdominal wall defect over bladder	Bladder exstrophy

(continued)

HEAD-TO-TOE PHYSICAL ASSESSMENT FINDINGS *(continued)*

PARAMETER	NORMAL FINDINGS AND COMMON VARIATIONS	ABNORMAL FINDINGS AND POSSIBLE CAUSES	
Abdominal muscles *(continued)*	No visible peristaltic waves	Visible peristaltic waves moving in left-to-right direction	Intestinal obstruction (rarely manifests immediately after birth)
Umbilical cord remnant	Bluish white, three vessels (two arteries and one vein) present	Two vessels (one artery and one vein) present	Possible internal congenital anomalies (especially renal anomalies)
		Thick	LGA status
		Small	SGA status or malnourishment
		Red, with discharge	Infection
		Meconium stained	Fetal distress
		Mass (hernia) present, with protrusion of abdominal viscera	Omphalocele
		Hernia	Gastroschisis (congenital fissure of the abdominal wall, not located at umbilical cord insertion site, accompanied by intestinal protrusion)
Abdominal palpation	Abdomen soft, without tenderness or masses	Abdomen tense, rigid, and tender	Intestinal deformity or obstruction
		Masses present	Renal or urinary tract deformity
	Minor separation of rectus abdominis muscles	Wide separation of rectus abdominis muscles (diastasis recti abdominis)	Prematurity
Abdominal auscultation	Two to four bowel sounds per minute	Absent bowel sounds	Intestinal obstruction
		More than five bowel sounds per minute (except immediately after feeding)	Intestinal obstruction or hypermotility
	No audible bruit	Bruit over abdominal aorta	Arteriovenous malformation
		Bruit over kidneys	Renal artery stenosis

HEAD-TO-TOE PHYSICAL ASSESSMENT FINDINGS *(continued)*

PARAMETER	NORMAL FINDINGS AND COMMON VARIATIONS	ABNORMAL FINDINGS AND POSSIBLE CAUSES	
Abdominal percussion	Tympany over all areas except liver, spleen, and bladder (where dullness is heard)	Increased tympany	Increased fluid or air
		Increased areas of dullness (if liver or spleen is enlarged, dullness extends below costal margins; if bladder is enlarged, dullness extends toward umbilicus)	Mass or enlarged organ at increased area of dullness
	Tympany over gastric bubble, just below left costal margin toward midline	No tympany over gastric bubble	Esophageal atresia or gastric defect
Kidneys	Located in lumbar area; right kidney lower than left; 4 to 5 cm long	Enlarged	Polycystic kidney disease
		Both kidneys absent	Potter's syndrome
Liver	Firm	Hard	Liver damage or cardiopulmonary disorder
	Sharp edge of liver palpable just above right costal margin during inspiration	Sharp edge of liver palpable more than 1 cm below right costal margin during inspiration	Enlarged liver (from respiratory distress or congestive heart failure)
Spleen	Palpable 1 cm below left costal margin	Absent or not palpable	Congenital heart defect
		Enlarged	Erythroblastosis fetalis (ABO incompatibility)
Bladder	No visible distention (except just before voiding)	Distended (may be visible above pubic bone)	Urinary tract obstruction or full bladder
Groin	Smooth, no palpable masses	Masses present	Inguinal hernia
Back			
Spinal column	Straight	Curved	Vertebral misalignment (if caused by fetal position, condition usually resolves gradually)

(continued)

HEAD-TO-TOE PHYSICAL ASSESSMENT FINDINGS *(continued)*

PARAMETER	NORMAL FINDINGS AND COMMON VARIATIONS	ABNORMAL FINDINGS AND POSSIBLE CAUSES	
Spinal column *(continued)*	No visible deviations or defects	Visible defect, such as mass, dimple, or bulge (possibly with tuft of hair)	Spina bifida
		Hernial sac (may be open or covered with portion of spinal cord, meninges, and cerebrospinal fluid)	Meningomyelocele
		Sinus tracts or pinpoint holes	Pilonidal cysts
	No vertebral enlargement or tenderness	Vertebral bulge, mass, cyst, enlargement, or tenderness	Vertebral fracture, spina bifida, occult meningomyelocele, pilonidal cyst
Buttocks	Symmetrical midline crease	Asymmetrical midline crease	Congenital hip dysplasia
Anus and genitalia			
Anus	Patent, located at midline	Nonpatent or dimpled	Imperforate anus
		Shifted anteriorly or posteriorly	Anal defect
	Anal wink present (indicated by anal sphincter constriction in response to light stroking of anal area)	Anal wink absent	Neurologic deficit
Perineum	Smooth	Dimpled or with extra opening	Urinary or genital malformation; urinary fistula
Female genitalia	Distinguishable as female Enlarged clitoris (from maternal hormonal influence)	Ambiguous genitalia; some structures resembling male genitalia (such as a greatly enlarged clitoris)	Trisomy 18; adrenocortical insufficiency
	Labia majora extend beyond labia minora	Labia majora smaller than labia minora	Prematurity
	Well-formed labia minora	Labia minora larger than labia majora	Prematurity

HEAD-TO-TOE PHYSICAL ASSESSMENT FINDINGS *(continued)*

PARAMETER	NORMAL FINDINGS AND COMMON VARIATIONS	ABNORMAL FINDINGS AND POSSIBLE CAUSES	
Female genitalia *(continued)*	Urethral meatus located anterior to vaginal orifice	Displaced urethral meatus	Urinary malformation
	Patent vagina, possibly with discharge or slight bleeding (pseudomenstruation)	Vagina opening completely covered by thickened hymen, possibly with slight bleeding (pseudomenstruation)	Vaginal malformation
Male genitalia	Penis straight; appropriate size for body (2.8 to 4.3 cm long)	Penis curved	Chordee (fibrous constriction of penis)
		Penis enlarged	Renal disorder
	Urinary meatus located at midline, at tip of glans	Urinary meatus displaced to ventral surface	Hypospadias
		Urinary meatus displaced to dorsal surface	Epispadias
	Urine stream flowing straight from penis	Crooked urine stream or urine leakage from patent urachus (abnormal fetal opening between bladder and umbilicus)	Urinary fistula; phimosis
	Full testes; numerous rugae	Smooth or few rugae	Prematurity
	Darkly pigmented testes	Bluish testes or scrotum	Testicular torsion
		Enlarged or edematous scrotum	Hydrocele or breech delivery
		Dimpled testes	Testicular torsion
	Testes descended on at least one side	Testes not palpable or found high in inguinal canal	Prematurity
Voiding onset	Within first 24 hours	Later than 24 hours	Renal or urinary obstruction or malformation

(continued)

HEAD-TO-TOE PHYSICAL ASSESSMENT FINDINGS (continued)

PARAMETER	NORMAL FINDINGS AND COMMON VARIATIONS	ABNORMAL FINDINGS AND POSSIBLE CAUSES	
Arms			
General appearance	Of appropriate length relative to body; bilaterally equal; straight	Shortened or asymmetrical	Maternal diabetes or drug use, congenital syndrome
	Humerus, radius, and ulna symmetrical; no masses present	Humerus, radius, or ulna asymmetrical or absent	Possible syndrome, such as thrombocytopenia-absent radius syndrome
		Mass present on humerus, radius, or ulna	Fracture (as from birth injury)
Range of motion	Full	Limited	Birth injury or trauma
		Limited flexion	Prematurity
		Limited shoulder motion or flexion	Dystocia, brachial plexus damage or palsy
		Limited clavicular motion	Clavicular injury, osteogenesis imperfecta (genetic disorder resulting in fragile bones)
		Limited elbow, wrist, or hand motion	Possible birth injury
Hands and wrists	Hand straight	Hand turned outward	Possible congenital absence of radius
	No simian crease in palm	Simian crease in palm	Down's syndrome
	10 equally spaced fingers; no webbing	More than 10 fingers (polydactyly)	Possible congenital syndrome (such as trisomy 13)
		Webbed fingers, digital tags (syndactyly), unequal finger spacing	Congenital syndrome (such as Apert's syndrome)
	Nails extending beyond nail beds to tips of fingers	Spoon-shaped nails that do not reach beyond nail beds	Congenital syndrome (such as fetal alcohol syndrome)
		Absent nails	Possible congenital absence of radius
		Meconium-stained nails	Fetal distress

HEAD-TO-TOE PHYSICAL ASSESSMENT FINDINGS *(continued)*

PARAMETER	NORMAL FINDINGS AND COMMON VARIATIONS	ABNORMAL FINDINGS AND POSSIBLE CAUSES	
Hands and wrists *(continued)*	Nail beds regain pink color equally bilaterally and briskly (within 3 seconds) during capillary refill test	Nail beds remain dusky or regain pink color unequally bilaterally or slowly (longer than 3 seconds)	Poor peripheral perfusion or oxygenation
	Carpal and metacarpal bones of bilaterally equal length; no masses	Carpal and metacarpal bones absent or bilaterally unequal; masses present	Fracture or absence of bone, possibly associated with congenital syndrome
	Strong palmar grasp	Weak palmar grasp	Prematurity
Pulses	Brachial and radial pulses strong and bilaterally equal; equal to femoral pulses	Brachial or radial pulse weak, absent, or bilaterally unequal	Poor peripheral perfusion, possible cardiac defect
Legs			
General appearance	Of apportionate length relative to body; bilaterally equal; straight	Disproportionate length relative to body, short or bilaterally unequal, crooked, internally rotated or bowed	Congenital hip dysplasia
	Fibula, tibia, trochanter, and femur bilaterally symmetrical	Fibula, tibia, trochanter, or femur absent or bilaterally asymmetrical	Fracture or absence of bone (may be associated with congenital syndrome)
		Limited hip motion; audible click heard with Ortolani's or Barlow's maneuver	Congenital hip dysplasia
Femoral pulses	Strong and bilaterally regular	Weak or bilaterally absent	Coarctation of the aorta
		Bounding	Patent ductus arteriosus
Feet	Straight	Turned out (valgus deformity)	Absent fibula, fetal positioning (apparent clubfoot), true clubfoot
		Turned in (varus deformity)	Absent tibia, fetal positioning (apparent clubfoot), true clubfoot

(continued)

HEAD-TO-TOE PHYSICAL ASSESSMENT FINDINGS *(continued)*

PARAMETER	NORMAL FINDINGS AND COMMON VARIATIONS	ABNORMAL FINDINGS AND POSSIBLE CAUSES	
Feet *(continued)*		Pedal edema	Pressure caused by fetal positioning, poor peripheral perfusion, or congenital syndrome (such as Turner's syndrome)
	Plantar creases covering sole	Few plantar creases; may cover only anterior third of sole	Prematurity
	Tarsal and metatarsal bones present and bilaterally equal	Tarsal and metatarsal bones absent or bilaterally unequal	Fracture or absence of bone (may be associated with congenital syndrome)
	10 equally spaced toes; no webbing	More than 10 toes; unequal toe spacing, webbing present	Possible congenital syndrome (such as trisomy 13)
Reflexes	Symmetrical plantar and patellar reflexes (knee jerk)	Absent, weak, or asymmetrical plantar reflex	Neurologic deficit, prematurity
		Absent, weak, or asymmetrical patellar reflex	Neurologic deficit, prematurity

BRAZELTON NEONATAL BEHAVIORAL ASSESSMENT SCALE

Developed by pediatrician T. Berry Brazelton in 1973, the Brazelton neonatal behavioral assessment scale (BNBAS) is the most commonly used behavioral evaluation tool. To score the BNBAS reliably, the examiner must take an intensive 2-day course. The nurse without such preparation may want to use the BNBAS as a guideline for assessing neonatal behavior in a more general way, without scoring the neonate.

Areas evaluated by the BNBAS include the neonate's behavioral state (level of wakefulness) and behavioral responses, including elicited responses.

Behavioral state

Begin the BNBAS assessment by observing the neonate's behavioral state (degree of alertness). The neonate experiences six behavioral states.

• Deep sleep is a quiet period during which the neonate makes few or no spontaneous movements; any movements that occur are brief and jerky. No rapid eye movements (REMs) are detected. Respirations are even and regular. The neonate can be aroused from this state only for a few moments.

• In light sleep, the neonate can be aroused and brought to wakefulness easily; REMs can be detected. The arms or legs may move occasionally, and movements are smoother than during deep sleep. The breathing pattern varies as the neonate drifts from light sleep to drowsiness.

• The drowsy state is characterized by an attempt to become fully alert. Movements become more frequent and regular and the eyes open periodically. Although the neonate responds to auditory and tactile stimuli, the response may be sluggish until the next state approaches.

• In the alert state, the neonate seems to be transfixed by external stimuli and has limited motor activity.

• The active state is characterized by regular eye and body movements in response to external stimuli.

• In the crying state, the neonate responds to both internal and external stimuli, cries vigorously and without interruption, and makes thrusting movements.

The neonate should move successively through these states, although the time spent in each may vary widely from one neonate to the next. The sleep-awake pattern also varies, depending on gestational age and other factors. The typical neonate sleeps 10 to 20 hours daily, with deep sleep accounting for only about 4 hours of total sleep. A neonate affected by maternal drug use may have an extremely labile sleep-awake pattern (Blackburn, 1987).

Behavioral responses

Neonatal behavioral responses fall into six categories: habituation, orientation, motor maturity, variations, self-quieting ability, and social behaviors.

Habituation. A protective mechanism, habituation refers to the process of becoming accustomed (habituating) to environmental stimuli, such as noise and light. For example, if one neonate in the nursery starts to cry, a neonate in light sleep will startle initially. If a second neonate then cries, the neonate who was in light sleep may move about. As the other neonates continue crying, the neonate in light sleep gradually becomes less stimulated, reflecting habituation. Normally, habituation occurs after three consecutive presentations of a stimulus (in this example, the continued crying of both neonates is the third presentation).

A neonate's ability to become habituated to a stimulus varies with the behavioral state. Habituation should be tested only during deep sleep, light sleep, or the drowsy state. If habituation does not occur after three presentations of a stimulus, the neonate may be hyperresponsive to external stimuli. A slowed or diminished response from the outset of the first presentation (except during deep sleep) suggests lethargy or hyporesponsiveness. These variations commonly reflect neurologic immaturity or impaired neurologic function.

Orientation. This term refers to the neonate's responsiveness to visual and auditory stimuli. For best results, orientation should be tested while the neonate is in the alert or active state.

Normally, the neonate orients to (follows) a visual or auditory stimulus by moving both the head and eyes. No response or lack of head movement is abnormal. Also observe for nystagmus (rapid, darting eye movements) and for gaze aversion after direct eye contact — both normal responses.

A neonate is more responsive to a human face — either real or represented in a picture — than an inanimate object. (This especially is apparent when the neonate is held in the en face — face-to-face — position). If the parents are observing the behavioral assessment, show them how closely their child attends to visual stimuli by holding a brightly colored object, such as a ball, in front of the neonate. As the ball moves from side to side, the neonate's eyes will follow it and the head will turn from side to side.

In response to an auditory stimulus, such as a human voice or noise from a rattle, the neonate typically stops an activity to attend to the sound. If the sound comes from outside the visual field, the neonate will turn toward it. (If the neonate fails to respond, repeat the sound at a different pitch – many neonates alert better to higher pitches.) A sudden or loud stimulus usually causes crying.

Motor maturity. Best assessed with the neonate in the alert state, motor maturity refers to posture, muscle tone, muscle coordination and movements, and reflexes. Evaluate smoothness and equality of arm and leg movements. In the term neonate, asymmetrical or absent movement of an extremity calls for further investigation, as do muscle flaccidity or hypotonia, extreme tremors, and excessive jerking movements.

Keep in mind that the first 24 hours after birth represent a period of progressive changes; thus, motor responses may vary greatly. Neurologic stability typically is established by the third day. However, with early discharge, few neurologic assessments can be delayed until this time. If any abnormalities are detected, the examination must be repeated later.

Variations. This term refers to the frequency of changes in activity level, state, and skin color. Document these changes throughout the behavioral assessment.

Self-quieting ability. To test this, observe how soon and how effectively the neonate self-quiets when crying. Attempts to self-quiet include such behaviors as moving the hands toward the mouth, sucking on the fist, changing position, and attending to auditory or visual stimuli.

If the neonate does not attempt to self-quiet, the nurse or a parent should attempt to console the neonate by singing, talking, rocking, walking, cuddling, or facing the neonate directly. The degree to which this attempt succeeds reflects the neonate's consolability. If the attempt fails to elicit self-quieting, the neonate may be hyperactive or hypersensitive to the environment. Consolability is documented in terms of whether and to what degree the neonate self-quiets after introduction of a visual or an auditory stimulus.

Social behaviors. Neonatal social behaviors include smiling, cuddling, and exhibiting distinct cues. Such cues — signals that indicate the neonate's needs — include crying to be fed and stopping sucking when hunger has been sated. These behaviors should be tested with the neonate in the alert or active state.

Social behaviors are especially important to the parents, who commonly gauge their ability to provide care by their child's response to their actions. During this part of the behavioral assessment, the nurse can demonstrate to the parents that the neonate is an active partner in the relationship, giving as well as responding to cues from the parents.

Als's synactive theory of development

Extending Brazelton's work, Heidelise Als developed a theoretical model for assessing neonatal behavior based on developmental potential. Als's theory holds that the neonate both shapes and is shaped by the environment, of which the parents form a part. According to Als, whose work spans the past decade, the neonate's physiologic status depends on the environmental stimuli received and processed. Further, neonatal behavior consists of functional subsystems (autonomic-visceral, motoric [motor], and state-attentional), each with distinctive behavioral stress responses.

BIBLIOGRAPHY

American Academy of Pediatrics and American College of Obstetricians and Gynecologists. (1988). *Guidelines for Perinatal Care* (2nd ed.). Washington DC: Staff.

Behavioral assessment

Als, H. (1982). Toward a synactive theory of development: Promise for the assessment and support of infant individuality. *Infant Mental Health Journal,* 3(4), 229-243.

Brazelton, T. (1984). *Neonatal behavioral assessment scale* (2nd ed.). Philadelphia: Lippincott.

Gestational-age assessment

Ballard, J.L., Novak, K.K., and Driver, M. (1979). A simplified score for assessment of fetal maturation of newly born infants. *Journal of Pediatrics,* 95(5, Pt.1), 769-774.

Ballard, J. (1988). *Maturational assessment of gestational age.* Cincinnati: University of Cincinnati.

Battaglia, F.C., and Lubchenco, L.O. (1967). A practical classification of newborn infants by weight and gestational age. *Journal of Pediatrics,* 71, 159-163.

Cassady, G., and Strange, M. (1987). The small-for-gestational-age (SGA) infant. In G.B. Avery (Ed.), *Neonatology: Pathophysiology and management of the newborn* (3rd ed.; pp. 299-378). Philadelphia: Lippincott.

Dubowitz, L., and Dubowitz, V. (1977). *Gestational age of the newborn.* Reading, MA: Addison-Wesley.

Dubowitz, L.M.S., Dubowitz, V., and Goldberg, C. (1970). Clinical assessment of gestational age in the newborn infant. *Journal of Pediatrics,* 77(1), 1-10.

Usher, R. (1987). Extreme prematurity. In G.B. Avery (Ed.), *Neonatology: Pathophysiology and management of the newborn* (3rd ed.). Philadelphia: Lippincott.

Physical assessment

Blackburn, S. (1987). Sleep and awake states of the newborn. In K. Barnard (Ed.), *NCAST learning resource manual* (pp. 25-28). Seattle: University of Washington.

Bliss-Holtz, J. (1989). Comparison of rectal, axillary, and inguinal temperatures in full-term newborn infants. *Nursing Research,* 38(2), 85-87.

Smith, D.W. (1988). Minor anomalies. In K.L. Jones (Ed.), *Smith's recognizable patterns of human malformation: Genetic, embryologic and clinical aspects* (4th ed.; pp. 662-681). Philadelphia: Saunders.

Nursing research

Beal, J.A. (1986). The Brazelton neonatal behavioral assessment scale: A tool to enhance parental attachment. *Journal of Pediatric Nursing,* 1(3), 170-177.

Care of the Normal Neonate

The neonate undergoes various physiologic changes during the neo-natal period – the first 28 days after birth. To make a successful transition from dependent fetus, the neonate must adapt to these changes effectively, especially during the first 24 hours (known as the transitional period).

The nurse plays a crucial role during the neonatal period by promoting a stable physiologic status. For instance, the nurse maintains oxygenation, hydration, nutrition, elimination, hygiene, and thermoregulation; prevents and detects complications; and ensures environmental safety.

Neonatal nursing care also calls for a family-centered approach that helps ease the neonate's transition to the home and promotes positive parent-infant interaction. The nurse must assess parent-teaching needs regarding neonatal care and identify risk factors for poor parent-infant bonding. Parent teaching can be enhanced if the nurse serves as a caregiver role model and provides positive reinforcement during the parents' supervised attempts at caring for their child.

While providing care, the nurse must remain aware of cultural differences that may affect the parents' neonatal care decisions – for example, cultural attitudes toward circumcision. Considering these differences when planning, promoting, and implementing holistic neonatal and family care is essential.

ASSESSMENT

During the first few days after the neonate's birth, the nurse should conduct a comprehensive assessment (as described in Chapter 2,

Neonatal Assessment). Throughout the neonate's hospitalization, however, the nurse should conduct ongoing assessment to ensure optimal neonatal adaptation and to detect changes in the neonate's status.

The nurse evaluates the neonate continually for obvious or subtle changes from baseline clinical findings (including heart and respiratory rate and rhythm, skin color, cry, response to stimuli, alertness level, and irritability level) or laboratory values. The nurse also assesses for indications of neonatal distress. These include:

- abdominal distention
- apprehensive facial expression
- bile-stained emesis
- cyanosis (other than acrocyanosis or periorbital cyanosis)
- excessive mucus production or meconium in the nasal passages
- frequent apneic episodes
- hypotonia during active and alert periods
- jaundice
- labored respirations accompanied by skin or mucous membrane color changes
- lethargy during periods of expected activity
- meconium-stained skin
- persistent, pronounced increase or decrease in heart and respiratory rates from baseline vital signs
- temperature instability.

Such distress could lead to serious complications. (For information on the comprehensive neonatal assessment and a thorough discussion of other characteristics to assess, see Chapter 2, Neonatal Assessment.)

NURSING DIAGNOSIS

After gathering assessment data, the nurse reviews it carefully to identify pertinent nursing diagnoses for the neonate. (For a partial list of applicable diagnoses, see *Nursing diagnoses: Normal neonate,* page 80.)

NURSING DIAGNOSES

NORMAL NEONATE

For the normal neonate, the nurse may find the following examples of nursing diagnoses appropriate.

- Altered family processes related to the neonatal feeding schedule
- Altered nutrition: less than body requirements, related to decreased oral intake and increased caloric expenditure
- Altered parenting related to the addition of a new family member
- Altered patterns of urinary elimination related to inability to maintain fluid balance
- Altered patterns of urinary elimination related to renal immaturity
- Altered tissue perfusion: peripheral, related to transition to the extrauterine environment
- Anxiety (parental) related to lack of confidence in parenting ability
- Constipation related to GI immaturity
- Diarrhea related to GI immaturity
- Fluid volume excess related to renal immaturity
- Hypothermia related to cold stress
- Ineffective airway clearance related to the presence of mucus
- Ineffective breathing pattern related to respiratory dysfunction
- Ineffective breathing pattern related to transition to the extrauterine environment
- Potential altered body temperature related to radiant, conductive, convective, or evaporative heat loss or gain
- Potential altered parenting related to lack of knowledge about neonatal care
- Potential altered parenting related to transition to the role of parent
- Potential fluid volume deficit related to insensible fluid losses
- Potential fluid volume deficit related to poor oral intake
- Potential for infection related to immunologic immaturity
- Potential for infection related to the circumcision site
- Potential for infection related to transition to the extrauterine environment
- Potential for infection related to umbilical cord healing
- Potential for injury related to environmental influences during transition to the extrauterine environment
- Potential for injury related to slippage while bathing
- Potential for trauma related to decreased vitamin K levels

PLANNING AND IMPLEMENTATION

After assessing the neonate and formulating nursing diagnoses, the nurse develops and implements a plan of care. For the normal neonate, the plan centers on promoting optimal neonatal adaptation and parent-neonate interaction and includes such routine therapeutic interventions as umbilical cord care and vitamin K administration. Nursing goals include:

- ensuring oxygenation
- maintaining thermoregulation
- maintaining optimal hydration and nutrition
- promoting adequate urinary and bowel elimination
- providing hygienic care
- preventing and detecting complications
- ensuring environmental safety
- providing care for the family
- performing routine therapeutic interventions.

The American Academy of Pediatrics (1988) recommends that the neonate be kept in a transitional care or observation area in the nursery during the transition period to allow close observation. Then the neonate may be moved to the mother's room to avoid separating mother and neonate. This area should have oxygen and suction outlets, resuscitation equipment, and multiple electrical outlets with safety grounds.

ENSURING OXYGENATION

At birth, the neonate must begin breathing through the nose and drawing air into the lungs. Closure of the fetal shunts (ductus arteriosus, ductus venosus, and foramen ovale) after birth changes the circulatory direction and facilitates peripheral circulation and alveolar gas exchange. (See Chapter 1, Neonatal Adaptation, for more information on fetal shunt closure and neonatal respiration.) To ensure successful respiratory adaptation, maintaining adequate oxygenation is crucial.

A few hours after birth, the gastrointestinal (GI) tract begins secreting gastric juices; this leads to increased saliva and mucus production. Mucus production peaks in the first 2 to 3 days after birth. For the neonate with a nursing diagnosis of *ineffective airway clearance related to the presence of mucus,* suctioning with a bulb syringe or sterile catheter may be necessary to prevent aspiration of mucus. A bulb syringe may be kept at the bedside; clean it with warm, soapy water after each use to reduce the risk of bacterial growth. (For details on how to suction with a bulb syringe, see *Psychomotor skills: Performing routine care,* pages 83 to 93.)

A suction catheter should be used only if absolutely necessary because suctioning carries a risk of apnea, reflex bradycardia, cardiopulmonary arrest, and laryngospasm. For this procedure, the neonate is placed in a side-lying or prone position. Lubricate the end of the catheter with sterile water, then insert the catheter into the oral cavity without applying pressure. When the catheter reaches the pharynx, apply pressure for 5 seconds, then withdraw. After suctioning the pharynx, suction each naris (nostril). Before each new suctioning attempt, the catheter tip must be lubricated and the catheter rinsed with sterile water.

While suctioning, observe for skin and mucous membrane color changes. If the neonate is attached to a cardiopulmonary monitor, check for changes in the heart and respiratory rates. If the neonate becomes cyanotic (indicated by a bluish color), withdraw the catheter and stop suctioning. The amount and appearance of any secretions and the neonate's tolerance for the procedure should be documented.

An irregular respiratory pattern, including periodic breathing and slight chest retractions, is common in the first few hours after birth while the neonate adapts to the new environment. However, stay alert for changes in the respiratory pattern that persist for several hours or become increasingly severe; these may indicate respiratory distress. If skin or mucous membrane color changes from pink to dusky or cyanotic, check for grunting, nasal flaring, crackles, rhonchi, and other abnormal signs. The neonate with these signs may have a nursing diagnosis of ***ineffective breathing pattern related to transition to the extrauterine environment***. Immediately report any significant deviations from normal cardiopulmonary parameters, and assess vital signs continually to help prevent complications.

MAINTAINING THERMOREGULATION
The term neonate has protective mechanisms to promote heat conservation—layers of adipose tissue and areas of brown fat, most prominent over the scapula and flank. Brown fat supplies fatty acids

(Text continues on page 93.)

PERFORMING ROUTINE CARE

During routine neonatal care, the nurse may perform such procedures as cleaning the neonate's scalp and face, suctioning with a bulb syringe, instilling eye medications, administering I.M injections, performing heel sticks, and obtaining urine specimens. The instructions below provide guidelines for these procedures.

Cleaning the scalp and face

The nurse who bathes a neonate should expose only one area at a time, washing and drying thoroughly before exposing the next area. Follow these steps to ensure safety when cleaning the scalp and face.

1 Hold the neonate in the football position, which supports the back and head and frees one hand for bathing.

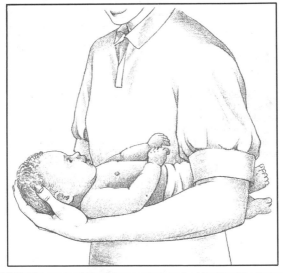

2 If shampooing is necessary, extend the neonate's head slightly while keeping the neonate supine, and tilt the head backward over a small basin. This position allows water to run from the front to the back of the head, preventing soapy water

(continued)

PERFORMING ROUTINE CARE (continued)

from getting into the eyes. Gently lather the scalp in a circular motion by hand or with a small cloth or soft brush containing mild, nonmedicated shampoo.

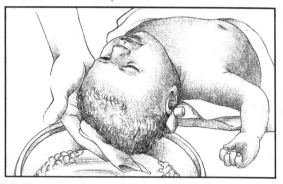

3 To rinse, fill a small cup with tepid water and pour the water over the scalp. Dry the hair quickly and thoroughly with a soft towel to minimize heat loss.

4 To wash the eyes, wrap a small washcloth around one hand so that no ends dangle. (This reduces the risk of dragging a wet cloth across the neonate, which could cause chilling from the dripping water or cross-contamination from contact with a soiled surface.) Moisten the washcloth with water, then gently stroke from the inner aspect of the lacrimal duct to the outer portion of the eyelid.

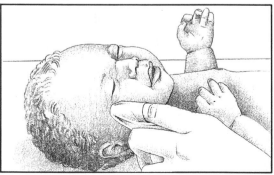

PERFORMING ROUTINE CARE *(continued)*

5 Wash the ears by wrapping a cloth around one finger and gently cleaning the external part of the ear (including the posterior portion). Never use a cotton-tipped applicator to clean the ears because this may damage the delicate internal ear structures and lead to infection.

6 To clean the nose, insert the twisted end of a washcloth into the naris (nostril). Remove any crusted matter or nasal secretions at the surface of the nostril. To help detect excessive nasal drainage (which may indicate infection), document any nasal drainage and secretions.

7 Next, wash each side of the face with mild soap.

Suctioning with a bulb syringe

If the neonate has excess mucus in the respiratory tract, the nurse may need to aspirate the mouth and nasal passages using a bulb syringe. To perform this procedure, which demands skill and sensitivity to touch, follow these steps.

1 Depress the bulb to remove air. Then insert the tip of the syringe into the neonate's mouth until it reaches the pharyngeal area.

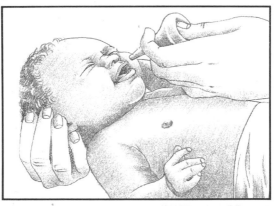

(continued)

PERFORMING ROUTINE CARE *(continued)*

2 Suction one side of the mouth by releasing the bulb end of the syringe. This action pulls the mucus into the tip of the syringe.

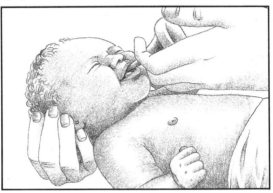

3 Suction the other side of the mouth the same way. Be sure to avoid touching the midline of the throat because this could activate the gag reflex.

4 Finally, suction the nasal passages, one nostril at a time, using the same approach.

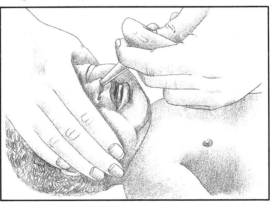

PERFORMING ROUTINE CARE *(continued)*

Administering eye medications

Eye prophylaxis is an essential part of neonatal nursing care. Most states require the administration of 1% silver nitrate ophthalmic solution, 1% tetracycline ointment, or 0.5% erythromycin ointment to prevent ophthalmia neonatorum, a severe eye infection.

To administer the medication, wash the hands thoroughly. Position the neonate securely so that the head remains still. While holding the eyelid open, instill the medication into the conjunctival sac. Repeat with the other eye.

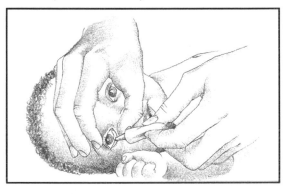

Giving an I.M. injection

When caring for the normal neonate, the nurse may have to administer prophylactic vitamin K or other medications by I.M. injection. In most cases, a 25-gauge (25G), ⅝″ needle should be used to allow medication to reach the muscle without causing excessive pain or trauma. A 22G needle is warranted only for thick medications, such as some penicillins.

Before administering any medication, confirm the route, dose, time, and medication, and cross-check the neonate's identification with the medication order and identification bracelet. Also check the neonate's history for reactions to previous medications; although rare, medication or allergic reactions do occur in

(continued)

PERFORMING ROUTINE CARE (continued)

neonates. Check the medication record for the previously used injection site. To minimize bruising and increase medication absorption, rotate the injection site from one leg to the other.

To administer the injection, follow these steps.

1 Put on clean gloves to guard against contamination from potentially infected blood. Then examine and palpate the neonate's leg above the knee and below the groin fold to determine how much muscle tissue is present. To find a safe injection site away from the bone and nerves, palpate along the femur. Place two fingers below the groin fold and two fingers above the knee. The thigh surface between these areas contains much muscle tissue and no major blood vessels or nerves, making it a good choice for injection.

The injection may be given along the top of the thigh or in the vastus lateralis, along the side of the thigh above the femur (the shaded area in the illustration). Do not give the injection in the buttocks; because the muscle mass here is not well developed, the needle or medication can enter a major vessel or nerve more easily.

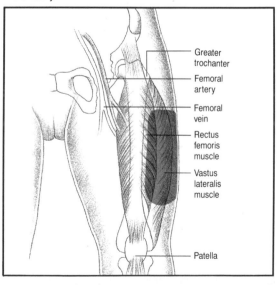

- Greater trochanter
- Femoral artery
- Femoral vein
- Rectus femoris muscle
- Vastus lateralis muscle
- Patella

PERFORMING ROUTINE CARE *(continued)*

2 To keep the neonate still and reduce tissue trauma, gently restrain the leg. If possible, ask an assistant to help with this; as one person holds the leg, the other can give the injection.

If a pinchable amount of muscle or a large, solid muscle mass is palpated (as in a term neonate), stretch the skin and hold it taut. This reduces the risk of medication entering the subcutaneous tissue. If the muscle is small and soft to a gentle pinch with little palpable mass, gently pinch about 1 cm of skin during needle insertion to allow the injection to reach the muscle mass.

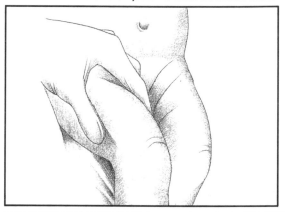

3 Without releasing the leg, aim the needle at a 90-degree angle toward the thigh. Then, using a quick, darting wrist motion, insert the needle almost down to the hub.

Next, release the skin that has been pinched or stretched. Gently aspirate the plunger to check for a flash of blood. Blood indicates that the needle has pricked a blood vessel; if the medication enters the vessel, an adverse reaction may result. If blood appears, withdraw the needle immediately. Then discard the needle and start the procedure over, using new medication and a new syringe and needle.

If no blood appears, inject the medication steadily by applying gentle pressure on the plunger. When the barrel is empty, withdraw the needle quickly by pulling it straight out (this makes the

(continued)

PERFORMING ROUTINE CARE *(continued)*

injection less painful). Do not recap the needle – this may lead to an accidental needle stick. Instead, keep it out of the neonate's reach until it can be discarded.

4 Massage the site with alcohol and soothe the neonate. Besides having a quieting effect, massage increases circulation and enhances medication absorption. In most cases, the site does not need to be covered by an adhesive bandage because any bleeding that occurs is minimal and stops rapidly. Also, removing the bandage might tear the skin, causing more pain than a small injection site.

Performing a heel stick

In some facilities, the nurse who cares for normal neonates is required to perform a heel stick to obtain blood for measurement of glucose level and hematocrit. The blood also is used to test for phenylketonuria, galactosemia, and hypothyroidism.

1 Before beginning, wash the hands and put on gloves. Next, clean the neonate's heel with alcohol and dry with a sterile 2″ x 2″ gauze pad.

PERFORMING ROUTINE CARE *(continued)*

2 Choose a capillary site for venipuncture (as shown in the shaded area) to avoid the plantar artery.

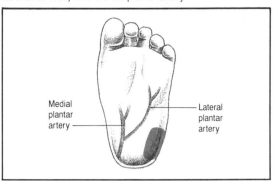

Medial plantar artery

Lateral plantar artery

3 Using the appropriate blade, quickly puncture the heel deeply enough to trigger a free flow of blood. Discard the first drop by wiping it away with another sterile gauze pad.

4 Collect blood into the appropriate capillary tubes. Clean the heel of any blood and cover with a bandage.

Obtaining a urine specimen from a urine collection bag

The nurse may collect a urine specimen from a neonate for routine urinalysis, cultures, specific gravity measurement, or other studies. Follow these steps when using a urine collection bag to obtain the specimen.

1 Remove the diaper and place the neonate in the supine position. With a male neonate, clean the urinary meatus, if soiled, with water and a towelette. Then clean the meatus with povidone-iodine swabs, using one swab for each stroke.

With a female neonate, clean the labia from front to back to avoid contamination from the anal area. Next, clean the urinary meatus with water and a towelette, then with povidone-iodine swabs, again using a front-to-back motion.

(continued)

PERFORMING ROUTINE CARE   *(continued)*

2 In an uncircumcised male, retract the foreskin until resistance is met, then clean the glans with povidone-iodine swabs. Release the foreskin, returning it to its natural position. In the circumcised male, clean the glans penis in the same manner.

3 To place the urine collection bag over the urinary meatus, remove the tabs from either side of the bag and uncover the adhesive sides. With a female neonate, apply the bag one side at a time to the labia majora and extend the tab to the femoral (groin) fold.

FEMALE NEONATE

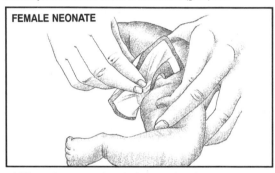

With a male neonate, place the bag over the urinary meatus in the same manner, enclosing the penis and scrotum in the bag if possible.

MALE NEONATE

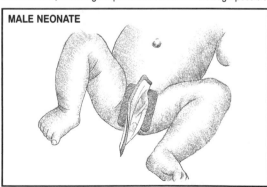

PERFORMING ROUTINE CARE *(continued)*

With any neonate, make sure the bag does not cover the anus, because this may contaminate the specimen. After the bag has been positioned, press the tabs in place to ensure a secure fit. If the adhesive does not hold, apply a small amount of benzoin tincture to the skin under the tab to help keep the bag in place. However, use benzoin tincture only if absolutely necessary; the strong adhesion it provides may deter removal of the bag and can cause irritation.

4 Place a clean diaper over the bag and secure it. The diaper holds the bag in place and collects any stool or overflow from the bag.

5 When 1 to 2 ml of urine has been obtained, gently remove the bag and observe for skin irritation. Aspirate the specimen with a syringe, then place the specimen in a sterile plastic tube or culture bottle and send it to the laboratory immediately.

6 Document that a specimen was obtained and sent to the laboratory.

for heat production (thermogenesis), a process that begins when the neonate starts to lose heat. To maintain a stable core (rectal) temperature, the body breaks down fats, burns calories, consumes oxygen, and increases the metabolic rate.

The preterm neonate, in contrast, has insufficient adipose tissue and brown fat insulation and may suffer cold stress from heat loss. The posture of the preterm neonate also contributes to heat loss. Unlike the term neonate—who assumes a fetal position to reduce the exposed surface area and thus minimize convective heat loss—the preterm neonate lies flaccid with arms and legs extended, exposing a greater surface area.

Cold stress may occur in any neonate who is exposed to a cold environment without adequate protection or whose caloric expenditure exceeds caloric consumption. When oxygen and nutritional reserves are depleted, the neonate loses protein and muscle tissue as well as weight. Anabolic metabolism ensues, leading to metabolic acidosis.

To stabilize the neonate's body temperature and thus minimize oxygen, caloric, and fat expenditure, maintain a neutral thermal environment. This narrow temperature range maintains a stable core temperature with minimal caloric and oxygen consumption, allowing calories and oxygen to be used for growth and adaptation rather than thermoregulation. (For further information on the mechanisms of heat loss and gain, see Chapter 1, Neonatal Adaptation. For specific nursing measures that help prevent heat loss, see *Preventing heat loss.*)

Throughout the neonate's nursery stay, enforce measures to conserve body heat — especially for the neonate with a nursing diagnosis of *potential altered body temperature related to radiant, conductive, convective, or evaporative heat loss.* For example, always keep the neonate dry; a warm, wet neonate loses heat to the surrounding environment through evaporation and convection. Keep the neonate's head covered at all times. The head accounts for 25% of the neonate's total body surface; substantial heat can be lost to surrounding cool surfaces and air through radiation, conduction, and convection unless the head is covered with a blanket, hat, or stockinette. (For more information on neonatal head coverings, see Chapter 1, Neonatal Adaptation.)

Even if the neonate is placed under a radiant warmer and dried to reduce heat loss, wide temperature fluctuations are common in the first few hours after birth. If the neonate has been in an open warmer for 2 to 3 hours and the core temperature measures 96.8° F (36° C), wrap the neonate in a blanket and place in an open, clear basinette. Monitor skin temperature, which should measure 32° to 32.9° F (0° to 0.5° C) below the core temperature (Carlo and Chatburn, 1988).

Using an incubator or radiant warmer

If the core temperature drops below an acceptable level, keep the neonate in a thermally controlled environment. Depending on health care facility policy, this may necessitate use of an incubator or a radiant warmer. (An incubator is a fully enclosed, single-walled or double-walled bed containing a heating source and a humidification chamber. A radiant warmer is an open bed with an overhead radiant heat source.) Because the neonate requires close observation during the transitional period, keep the incubator or radiant warmer in clear view at all times.

PREVENTING HEAT LOSS

Preventing heat loss is an important part of neonatal nursing care. Heat loss can occur through four mechanisms—conduction, convection, evaporation, and radiation. The chart below describes some nursing measures that help prevent heat loss by each mechanism.

CONDUCTIVE HEAT LOSS

- Preheat the radiant warmer bed and linen.
- Warm the stethoscope before use.
- Wrap the neonate in a warm blanket or allow the mother to hold the neonate to provide the warming effect of skin contact.
- Pad the scale with paper or a preweighed, warmed sheet to weigh the neonate.
- Check the temperature of any surface before placing the neonate on it.

CONVECTIVE HEAT LOSS

- Place the neonate's bed out of direct line with an open window, a fan, or an air-conditioning vent.
- Cover the neonate with a blanket when moving the neonate to another area.
- Raise the sides of the radiant warmer bed to prevent exposing the neonate to air currents.
- Avoid using fans in the delivery room or nursery.

EVAPORATIVE HEAT LOSS

- Dry the neonate immediately after delivery.
- When the neonate is not in a warming bed, keep the neonate dry and swaddled in warmed blankets.
- Remove wet blankets.
- Delay the bath until the neonate's temperature is stable.
- When bathing the neonate, expose only one body part at a time; wash each part thoroughly, then dry it immediately.
- When assessing the neonate, uncover only the specific area to be assessed.
- Place a cap on the neonate's head in the delivery room.

RADIANT HEAT LOSS

- Use a radiant heat warmer for initial post-delivery stabilization.
- Place the neonate in a double-walled incubator.
- Keep the neonate away from areas with cold surfaces (such as a cold formula bottle or a window in winter).

With an incubator, temperature can be controlled externally or servo-controlled by taping a flat probe to the neonate's skin and setting the thermostat to maintain a skin temperature of 96° to 97.7° F (35.5° to 36.5° C). Do not tape the probe to areas of brown fat, such as the scapula and flank; these areas generate more heat, causing a falsely elevated skin temperature reading. With a radiant warmer, control the temperature by positioning the skin probe, then setting the thermostat of the bed to maintain a stable skin temperature.

Observing and intervening for cold stress

Signs of cold stress include an accelerated respiratory rate, labored respirations, and an increased metabolic rate accompanied by hypoglycemia (indicating greater use of glucose stores). In the neonate with a nursing diagnosis of *hypothermia related to cold stress,* check for signs of hypoglycemia, such as a serum glucose level below 30 mg/dl before the third day after birth or below 40 mg/dl on or after the third day.

Other signs of hypoglycemia include tremors, seizures, irritability and lethargy (from breakdown of fats and proteins to maintain body heat), and apnea or bradycardia (from changes in arterial oxygen saturation and a shift to anaerobic metabolism). Neurologic immaturity may prevent homeostasis in the hypoglycemic neonate, leading to unstable vital signs.

If the neonate suffers cold stress, rewarm gradually to avoid hyperthermia and its complications; closely observe the neonate and check vital signs every 15 to 30 minutes. Hyperthermia may cause skin reddening, irritability, and an initial increase — then gradual drop — in the heart and respiratory rates, leading to apnea and bradycardia. To prevent complications, report any status changes immediately.

MAINTAINING OPTIMAL HYDRATION AND NUTRITION

Hydration and nutrition are vital to immune system development and maintenance. The American Academy of Pediatrics (1988) recommends that the initial feeding never be delayed more than 6 hours after birth. If the mother plans to breast-feed, the neonate can be put to the breast in the delivery room.

Assessing the adequacy of fluid intake

To maintain adequate output and hydration and help avert a nursing diagnosis of *potential fluid volume deficit related to poor oral intake,* assess fluid intake frequently and compare it to urine output. The term neonate requires a fluid intake of 140 to 160 ml/kg/day to maintain hydration (Streeter, 1986). This requirement increases with illness, preterm birth, and excessive evaporative or radiant fluid loss. Urine output should measure 1 to 2 ml/kg/hour. In the first 24 hours after birth, the neonate may void only once or twice, although output from these first voidings exceeds output from later voidings.

The bottle-fed neonate who requires a diaper change every 2 to 3 hours is receiving adequate fluids. (Diapers should be moderately saturated.) The breast-fed neonate usually voids less frequently but at least six times a day. With any neonate, scanty or infrequent voiding (less than five times a day) suggests impaired fluid intake or a urinary problem. Document this finding and notify the physician.

Assessing for insensible fluid loss

The neonate experiences insensible fluid loss, such as radiant and evaporative fluid loss resulting from the transition to the relatively cool extrauterine environment. For the neonate with a nursing diagnosis of *potential fluid volume deficit related to insensible fluid loss*, assess for and guard against such loss, including that caused by environmental sources. For example, phototherapy (used to treat jaundice) increases GI motility, causing diarrhea and fluid loss in the stool. Also, phototherapy increases radiant fluid loss by warming the neonate. (For specific interventions to maintain thermoregulation, see the previous section on "Maintaining thermoregulation.")

Giving the first feeding

For the first feeding, the bottle-fed neonate usually is given sterile water because it is less irritating than formula or glucose water if it is aspirated. (Some facilities suggest an initial sterile water feeding for the breast-fed neonate as well to determine if the neonate is prone to aspiration or other complications.) If the neonate takes the sterile-water feeding without problems, glucose water or formula then may be given. In some facilities, the neonate is given a few milliliters of sterile water followed by 15 to 30 ml of glucose water to prevent hypoglycemia.

During the first feeding, assess the neonate's sucking ability and observe how well the neonate coordinates the sucking, swallowing, and gag reflexes. Immediately after the feeding, check for salivation, mucus production, aspiration, and regurgitation. The neonate produces more saliva and mucus in the first few hours after birth than at later times. Consequently, regurgitation — especially of a combination of mucus and feeding matter — is common. To promote digestion, place the neonate in a right side-lying position, which allows food to move more easily through the stomach and into the GI tract for absorption. This intervention helps prevent a nursing diagnosis of *altered nutrition (less than body requirements) related to decreased oral intake and increased caloric expenditure*.

Continue to check for signs of excessive salivation or mucus production, which may indicate a blind esophageal pouch (esophageal atresia) or a fistula between the esophagus and trachea (tracheoesophageal fistula). A neonate who aspirates or regurgitates copious amounts of mucus or the entire feeding also may have esophageal atresia or a tracheoesophageal fistula.

Regurgitation after a feeding also may indicate an immature cardiac sphincter that allows reflux of feeding matter through the weak muscle. This condition may cause esophageal irritation from acidic gastric juices, possibly leading to aspiration. Projectile vomiting or bile-colored emesis indicates GI blockage. If the vomiting is accompanied by abdominal distention, suspect an intestinal obstruction — a condition that requires immediate intervention.

A neonate with excessive mucus production may require nasopharyngeal suctioning. Be sure to use caution when performing this procedure because it may trigger the gag reflex, causing aspiration.

To prevent aspiration and facilitate digestion, place the neonate in semi-Fowler's position after feeding. The neonate who becomes cyanotic or extremely fatigued during a feeding may have a cardiac or respiratory problem. A respiratory rate above 60 to 80 breaths/minute increases the risk of aspiration.

If aspiration or regurgitation occurs, stop the feeding immediately and allow the neonate to rest before attempting further feeding. Document the incident thoroughly, and report it for further assessment.

Supporting the parents' choice of feeding method

Optimal enteral nutrition may be achieved by breast-feeding, bottle-feeding, or both. Support the parents' choice of feeding method. Their choice may be based on such factors as economic and financial considerations, the mother's occupational status, and sociocultural influences as well as neonatal health implications. (For more information on feeding methods, see Chapter 4, Infant Nutrition.)

PROMOTING ADEQUATE URINARY AND BOWEL ELIMINATION

Urinary and bowel elimination must be adequate to maintain hydration and nutrition. Elimination patterns are established in the first few days after birth.

Urinary elimination patterns

Although the kidneys begin functioning in utero (fetal urine is the major component of amniotic fluid), the neonate's kidneys do not concentrate urine as effectively as an adult's. The neonate also has an immature glomerular filtration system (restricting elimination of water and solutes) and limited tubular reabsorption (impairing the ability of bicarbonate ions and buffers to maintain the glomerular filtration system at a homeostatic pH).

Monitoring for voiding onset

Despite the limitations described above, voiding should begin by 48 hours after birth. (Some neonates even void on the delivery table.) Over 90% of term neonates void within 24 hours of birth; all but 1% within 48 hours (Kim and Mandell, 1988). Failure to void within 48 hours may indicate a renal disorder, inadequate fluid intake, increased water loss, or fluid retention (edema). The neonate with any of these problems may have a nursing diagnosis of *altered patterns of urinary elimination related to renal immaturity*.

Assessing urine characteristics

Initially, urine should be cloudy and amber (from urinary protein, blood, and mucus); specific gravity should measure 1.005 to 1.015. In the female neonate, blood in the urine represents pseudomenstruation; in the circumcised male neonate, blood originates from the surgical site.

After the first 24 hours or so, urine should appear clear and amber. A specific gravity below 1.005 may indicate excessive fluid loss unless the neonate has been edematous and is eliminating excess fluids. A specific gravity above 1.025 may indicate fluid retention unless the neonate has been dehydrated (in which case it represents an attempt to restore fluid balance).

A deviation from the usual urinary pattern — too few or too many saturated diapers, a high specific gravity, or dilute urine — may warrant a nursing diagnosis of *altered patterns of urinary elimination related to inability to maintain fluid balance.* If the neonate is losing excessive fluids, check skin turgor and assess the fontanels and eye area. With dehydration, skin turgor is decreased and the anterior fontanel and eye orbits appear sunken. Edema, indicated by shiny, taut skin, may suggest fluid retention caused by a cardiac or renal disorder. All of these signs warrant further evaluation to help prevent complications.

Bowel elimination patterns

The first stool (usually passed in the delivery room or within 48 hours after birth) consists of meconium, a thick, dark green, sticky, odorless material made up of amniotic fluid and shed GI mucosal cells. Failure to pass meconium within 48 hours may indicate anal or bowel malformation or Hirschprung's disease (aganglionic megacolon), a congenital disorder characterized by incomplete bowel innervation.

Once feeding patterns have been established, stools change in color and consistency, the GI tract starts to secrete digestive enzymes, and intestinal bacteria (especially *Escherichia coli*) start to colonize. Transitional stools — thinner, lighter green, and seedier than meconium — then appear. After 2 or 3 days, stools change again, taking on distinctive characteristics that vary with the feeding method. (For details on characteristics of the neonate's stools, see Chapter 1, Neonatal Adaptation.)

Feeding method affects stool consistency and output. The stool of a breast-fed neonate is looser and paler yellow than that of a formula-fed neonate. Also, the breast-fed neonate typically passes 2 to 10 stools daily; the formula-fed neonate usually passes one stool daily or every other day.

Assess for deviations in stool pattern or consistency. A neonate with such a deviation may have a nursing diagnosis of *diarrhea related to GI immaturity* or *constipation related to GI immaturity*. If the neonate has diarrhea, a condition that increases fluid loss, assess for signs of dehydration (described above). If the neonate fails to pass stool or passes a hard, ribbon-like stool, suspect an intestinal obstruction. Also assess for abdominal distention, and palpate the abdomen for fecal masses. Observe the neonate during and just after feeding; an abdominal obstruction may cause vomiting and irritability at these times. Report any problem with stools, feedings, and related changes in the neonate's status so that prompt diagnosis and treatment can begin.

PROVIDING HYGIENIC CARE

Maintaining hygiene is an important aspect of neonatal care. The epidermal layer of the skin protects against traumatic injury, helps minimize heat loss, and serves as a barrier against bacterial infection by maintaining the pH of the skin at 4.9.

Bathing the neonate

Because scented, medicated, and harsh soaps can alter the pH of the skin, use only mild soap (or the soap specified by the health care facility) when bathing the neonate. To prevent cross-contamination and bacterial growth, a soap dispenser should be assigned for each neonate. Avoid scrubbing the skin because this may cause abrasions through which microorganisms can enter.

To guard against heat loss during bathing, bathe the neonate only after temperature and vital signs have stabilized — especially if the core temperature is below normal. In the first hour or so after birth, use a soft sterile cotton pad soaked with warm water to remove dried blood, meconium, and debris arising from delivery; then dry the skin thoroughly. Removing these contaminants reduces the risk of infection by the hepatitis B, herpes simplex, and human immunodeficiency viruses (American Academy of Pediatrics, 1988). Also, gently wash off the vernix caseosa, the grayish white substance that covers the skin of the term neonate.

Proceed from head to toe, washing the cleanest areas first to reduce the risk of infection from any contaminated areas and help avoid a nursing diagnosis of *potential for infection related to transition to the extrauterine environment.* Do not immerse the neonate in a tub; this could cause chilling or infection of the umbilical cord or an unhealed circumcision. During bathing, inspect the neonate's body for such variations as skin tags, unusual hair distribution, palmar creases, and other minor abnormalities. These variations may indicate more serious abnormalities. (For more information, see Chapter 2, Neonatal Assessment.)

Assess the neonate's response to each portion of the bath. For example, a change in appearance or skin color may indicate stress, fatigue, or chilling. (If any of these changes occurs, stop the bath immediately and dry the neonate.) Observe for drainage (exudate), discoloration, swelling, and redness around the eyes, which may signal infection or chemical irritation.

Washing the neonate's hair and scalp may decrease the risk of seborrheic dermatitis (cradle cap) — a potential cause of skin breakdown and infection. However, cradle cap also may occur in a neonate whose hair is washed frequently. The exact cause of this condition remains unknown.

Wash the neonate's face only after feedings, if milk or formula remains on the skin. If necessary, wash the chin and mouth more often. (For an illustrated procedure of techniques used to clean the scalp and face, see *Psychomotor skills: Performing routine care*, pages 83 to 93.)

After drying the neonate's head and face, wash the rest of the body one part at a time, covering each part immediately after drying it to avoid evaporative heat loss. In the female neonate, clean the perineal region from front to back, proceeding from the cleanest area to the most soiled. In the male neonate, gently clean the penis to remove smegma. Use plain warm water or soapy water followed by a plain warm water rinse. Gently pat the penis dry to avoid causing abrasions. Some health care facilities recommend applying a thin layer of petrolatum gauze or a bactericidal ointment over the circumcision site.

In the uncircumcised male, gently retract the foreskin until encountering resistance, then expose the glans penis. If the foreskin cannot be retracted, do not force it; simply wash the penis as is. Make sure to return a retracted foreskin to its natural position — the neonate's skin is so tight that the foreskin rarely retracts on its own; the glans may become inflamed and swollen if the foreskin is left retracted. Next, lift the scrotal sac — a potential infection source because of accumulated stool — and wash the underlying surface.

Wash the anal region from front to back to avoid cross-contamination from stool and dry the area thoroughly. Also clean the buttocks and genitalia at each diaper change to prevent infection and skin irritation.

Excessive bathing — more frequently than every other day — may dry the skin, increasing the infection risk. Although relatively aggressive washing may be needed to remove the vernix caseosa and dried blood found in natural creases (such as the neck, axillae, and groin), always use care to keep the skin intact.

Ensuring safety during bathing

All neonates have a nursing diagnosis of *potential for injury related to slippage while bathing.* Make sure to maintain a secure grip while bathing the neonate. Using the forearm, support the neonate's back and head; wash with the other hand. Then dry each body part thoroughly. Immediately place the neonate in a bath blanket, making sure the neonate is thoroughly dry. Then redress and swaddle in a dry blanket.

PREVENTING AND DETECTING COMPLICATIONS

To prevent and detect neonatal complications, assess continually, staying alert for subtle changes in the neonate's condition. Document and report any changes immediately. Also monitor laboratory values and report any deviations. (For more information, see *Normal laboratory values,* page 104; for a more detailed discussion of complications occurring in neonates, see Chapter 5, High-Risk Neonates.)

Respiratory dysfunction

The most common neonatal complication, respiratory dysfunction may be mild (such as transient tachypnea) or severe (such as respiratory distress syndrome). In a neonate with a nursing diagnosis of *ineffective breathing pattern related to respiratory dysfunction,* stay alert for respiratory distress by assessing for changes in the respiratory rate and effort and checking for accompanying skin color changes, such as duskiness or cyanosis. If cyanosis is present, supplemental oxygen may be necessary. Be sure to allow the neonate to rest between nursing procedures to minimize oxygen consumption.

Hypocalcemia

The neonate who experienced birth asphyxia, is premature, or was born of an insulin-dependent diabetic mother is at risk for hypo-

NORMAL LABORATORY VALUES

The physician may order various laboratory tests to check for such neonatal complications as infection, hematologic problems, and metabolic disorders (such as hypoglycemia). The chart below shows normal laboratory values for commonly ordered tests. However, because values differ among laboratories, the nurse must check the values for the laboratory used.

TEST	NORMAL VALUES
Hematocrit	51% to 56%
Hemoglobin	16.5 g/dl (cord blood)
Platelets	150,000 to 400,000/mm³
Serum electrolytes Bicarbonate	18 to 23 mEq/liter
Calcium	7 to 10 mg/dl
Carbon dioxide	15 to 25 mEq/liter
Chloride	90 to 114 mEq/liter
Potassium	4 to 6 mEq/liter
Sodium	135 to 148 mEq/liter
Serum glucose	40 to 80 mg/dl
Total protein	4 to 7 g/dl
White blood cell total	18,000/mm³
White blood cell differential Band neutrophils	1,600/mm³ (9%)
Segmented neutrophils	9,400/mm³ (52%)
Eosinophils	400/mm³ (2.2%)
Basophils	100/mm³ (0.6%)
Lymphocytes	5,500/mm³ (31%)
Monocytes	1,050/mm³ (5.8%)

calcemia (a serum calcium level below 7 mg/dl). Hypocalcemia also may occur if enteral feedings must be delayed (such as in the neurologically impaired neonate). Signs of hypocalcemia include twitching of extremities, cyanosis, apneic episodes, seizures, and listlessness. To detect hypocalcemia early and help prevent complications, monitor the serum calcium level. Expect to give enteral or parenteral calcium supplements to a hypocalcemic neonate.

Physiologic jaundice

Physiologic jaundice (yellow skin discoloration accompanied by an increased serum bilirubin level) is a common neonatal complication resulting from hepatic immaturity. It develops in the full-term neonate 48 to 72 hours after birth. Suspect physiologic jaundice if the neonate's skin appears abnormally yellow. To verify the disorder, apply pressure to the tip of the neonate's nose. With jaundice, a yellow tinge appears instead of the normal blanching as circulation is impeded. (This test is accurate in dark-skinned as well as light-skinned neonates.)

If the neonate has jaundice, pathologic jaundice must be ruled out. Unlike physiologic jaundice, pathologic jaundice develops within 24 hours.

Infection

Infection, another common complication, stems from immunologic immaturity. Thorough hand washing significantly reduces the risk of neonatal infection and may help avoid a nursing diagnosis of *potential for infection related to immunologic immaturity*. Before and after performing any nursing procedure, wash the hands. Also emphasize to parents the importance of frequent hand washing and proper hand-washing technique.

Because the neonate does not have localized immune reactions, infection causes only subtle, nonspecific signs. Such signs may include a high, low, or unstable body temperature; a weak or high-pitched cry; pallor; cyanosis; feeding problems or fatigue after feedings; diminished peripheral perfusion causing reduced skin temperature; sudden onset of apneic or bradycardic episodes; and jaundice.

If the neonate has signs that suggest infection, immediately document and report them. Obtain vital signs every 1 to 2 hours, observe closely for behavioral changes, and expect the physician to order a complete diagnostic workup for sepsis. Depending on health care facility policy and updated recommendations from the Centers for Disease Control, isolation procedures may be necessary.

Neonatal ophthalmia, an eye infection caused by *Neisseria gonorrhoea* or *Chlamydia trachomatis,* can be prevented if 1% silver nitrate solution, 1% tetracycline ointment, or 0.5% erythromycin ointment is applied to the eyes shortly after delivery. (Tetracycline and erythromycin are less irritating than silver nitrate.) Previously, the medication was administered in the delivery room. However, in many facilities, the procedure now is delayed until the neonate arrives in the nursery. This allows clear vision during the first period of reactivity, facilitating parent-infant bonding. (For details on administering eye medication, see *Psychomotor skills: Performing routine care,* pages 83 to 93.)

ENSURING ENVIRONMENTAL SAFETY

Environmental safety is an important concern of neonatal nursing, particularly for the neonate with a nursing diagnosis of *potential for injury related to environmental influences during transition to the extrauterine environment.*

When the neonate is ready for discharge, confirm that an infant car seat (not a carrier seat, which cannot be locked into place) is available for the trip home. Most states require such seats for children under age 4.

PROVIDING CARE FOR THE FAMILY

Nursing care must involve the entire family—not just the neonate. By facilitating bonding and offering parent teaching, the nurse can help prepare the family for the neonate's discharge.

Promoting parent-infant bonding

Bonding—the reciprocal relationship between parents and infant—may begin even before delivery. For instance, many parents imagine how their child will look and act or may think of the child as male or female. This helps the parents adjust after the neonate's arrival.

How easily a couple makes the transition to parenthood depends on many variables, including their ages, length of time they have been together, previous experience with children, available social support, teaching needs, coping patterns, perception of the neonate, and knowledge of neonatal behavior. Various relationships – between the parents, among the parents and any existing children, and among siblings – also play a role in the assumption of the parenting role.

The parents' perceptions of their parenting abilities also affect bonding. Many new parents have doubts about their ability to care for a dependent person, leading to a nursing diagnosis of *potential altered parenting related to transition to the role of parent.* Call attention to the neonate's positive responses to the parents' initial caregiving attempts. Such responses include recognizing each parent's voice; smiling when a parent smiles; quieting in response to a parent's consoling efforts; and taking feedings well from parents.

Bonding between parents and infant increases after delivery and continues to grow in the coming days through skin contact. The parents usually examine their child for physical features that link their child with the rest of the family. Putting the neonate to the breast and breast-feeding successfully reinforce the mother's confidence in her ability to nourish her child.

Reassure the parents that bonding will occur and that the neonate will be ready to interact with them when the sleep phase (which follows the first period of reactivity) ends and the second period of reactivity begins.

Ask the parents to describe the child they imagined during the pregnancy – for example, a son or daughter, a light-haired or dark-haired child. If their child does not conform to this image, they may need to mourn the loss of the imagined child before they can bond with the real one.

Providing parent teaching

Ongoing parent teaching is an essential part of discharge planning. Such teaching includes bathing, providing cord and diaper rash care, changing diapers, observing stool and voiding patterns, ensuring environmental safety, and integrating the neonate into the family. (For details, see *Parent teaching: Caring for your infant,* pages 108 to 111. For information on discharge planning, see Chapter 7, Discharge Planning and Care at Home.)

The nurse also should serve as a caregiver role model for the parents and reinforce their caregiving behaviors. Steele (1987) found that active parental involvement in neonatal care before discharge led to a strong parent-infant bond. Encourage the parents to ask

(Text continues on page 111.)

PARENT TEACHING

CARING FOR YOUR INFANT

Basic infant care techniques include bathing, diaper changing, umbilical cord care, and environmental safety measures. These help ensure your infant's well-being, and they give you an opportunity to learn about your infant and to bond through close contact. The guidelines and techniques described below will help you provide the best possible care.

BATHING YOUR INFANT

• Use only nonmedicated, unscented soap. A harsh soap may alter the skin's pH and impair the skin's ability to provide a barrier against infection. Also, be sure to use a mild shampoo, such as a baby shampoo or an unscented product, to reduce the risk of chemical irritation of your infant's eyes from the soap.
• Before bathing your infant, test bath water temperature; it should be warm to the touch.
• Use a firm grasp to hold your infant. Never let go, because the infant might slide down in the tub or fall out.
• Do not immerse your infant in a tub until the umbilical cord and circumcision site (if present) have healed because these are potential infection sites. Wash the umbilical cord and circumcision site with water and pat dry gently. Avoid excessive rubbing.
• The use of powder after a bath is unnecessary and possibly unsafe. Powder particles that disperse into the air may enter the infant's lungs. If these particles are inhaled, they could cause irritation and infection.
• Baby oil is not recommended. The extra lubrication is unnecessary and may block pores. Also, it makes the infant harder to hold.

PROVIDING UMBILICAL CORD CARE

• The umbilical cord dries gradually during the first week, then falls off. To clean the cord, gently rub its surface with alcohol swabs or cotton balls saturated with rubbing alcohol. As an alternate mathod, use an antibiotic ointment, if prescribed. Lift the cord away from the abdomen, then coat the stump or base with alcohol. (This is the area most likely to become infected.)
• Call the physician if you see pus or drainage at the base of the cord or if the cord remains moist. Pus or drainage may indicate infection. The physician may recommend a 1% silver nitrate solution to dry a moist cord.
• To keep the cord as dry and bacteria-free as possible, fold the diaper down below the cord and avoid giving your infant tub baths. Typically, the umbilical cord dries and falls off within the first 2 weeks after birth.

CARING FOR YOUR INFANT *(continued)*

CHANGING DIAPERS

• Clean and dry the perineal area, observing for diaper rash (for a girl, always clean the perineal area from front to back; for a boy, always be sure to clean and dry under and around the scrotum). Then place a cloth or disposable diaper on the infant. For a snug fit, wrap the diaper from back to front, then check for gaps at the waist and abdominal areas and around the thighs. (If the diaper is not secure, stool or urine will leak, soiling the infant and bed and possibly causing chilling.) However, make sure the diaper is loose enough to allow the legs to move freely.
• For a boy wearing cloth diapers, fold the diaper so that a double thickness covers the penis. If the infant has been circumcised, allow enough room in front so that the cloth does not irritate the circumcision site.
• When diapering a girl, keep in mind that urine will fall to the front of the diaper when the infant lies on her stomach and to the back when she is on her back.
• If your infant develops a diaper rash after wearing disposable diapers, consider switching to cloth diapers, which allow air to reach the skin surface and promote healing. However, do not place a disposable diaper over a cloth diaper because this will seal in moisture and may promote bacterial growth.
• If your infant is wearing cloth diapers, use a mild detergent when laundering and rinse these items thoroughly to ensure soap removal.

CARING FOR YOUR INFANT'S CIRCUMCISION SITE

• The circumcision site may appear yellow in light-skinned infants and lighter than the surrounding skin in dark-skinned infants. This signifies healing and is not a cause for concern. Observe the circumcision site regularly for pus or bloody discharge, which may indicate delayed healing or infection. If these signs appear, call the physician.
• The rim of the device used for circumcision may remain in place after discharge. Do not be alarmed if you find the rim in your infant's bed; typically, it falls off 3 or 4 days after circumcision. If the rim does not come loose 1 week after the circumcision, call the physician. A retained rim may lead to infection.
• For the first 1 to 2 hours after circumcision, keep the neonate in a side-lying position with the diaper off.

(continued)

CARING FOR YOUR INFANT *(continued)*

MONITORING STOOL PATTERNS

• Report any changes in your infant's stool pattern or appearance — especially if they are accompanied by fever or behavioral changes, such as irritability or fussiness.
• If your infant cries excessively with a bowel movement or produces small, hard fecal pellets, constipation may be the cause. This problem usually can be corrected by giving additional water between feedings or by introducing fruit juice (if the physician approves).
• In some cases, constipation results from iron supplements or from iron-containing infant formula. If this happens, the physician may recommend that you switch to another formula.
• Diarrhea may result from a particular infant formula, introduction of new foods, or — in the breast-fed infant — changes in the mother's diet. If your infant normally passes stool only once a day but begins to pass loose, watery stools more than 5 times in a 24-hour period, notify the physician. Diarrhea may lead to excess fluid loss.
• In a breast-fed infant, loose, watery stools or a water ring appearing in the diaper around more solid fecal matter may indicate infection. If this sign appears, call the physician. Loose, seedy, dark-green stools with a foul odor suggest an intestinal infection.

MONITORING VOIDING PATTERNS

• The infant's urine should appear amber and clear. Although usually odorless, it occasionally may take on an ammonia-like odor, which is normal.
• Five diaper changes a day indicate adequate urine output. (The diapers should be at least moderately saturated.)

ENSURING ENVIRONMENTAL SAFETY

• Maintain adequate lighting, temperature, and humidity in the infant's room. Keep room temperature at 80° F for the first week, then 75° F. Keep the humidity level at 35% to 70% to maintain moist mucous (nasal) membranes (which serve as an important infection barrier).
• If your infant has nasal secretions that must be removed, remove them with a bulb syringe. Depress the bulb to remove air,

---

CARING FOR YOUR INFANT *(continued)*

ENSURING ENVIRONMENTAL SAFETY *(continued)*

then insert the syringe in the infant's nostrils and release the bulb to withdraw the secretions. This technique adequately removes most nasal secretions without injuring the inside of the nostrils.
• Never prop a formula bottle against the infant because this may lead to inhalation of formula or otitis media (middle ear infection). Bottle propping also eliminates an opportunity for the closeness and touch between you and your infant that is necessary for bonding.
• Never look away or leave the neonate unattended during bathing or weighing. Before leaving the neonate, make sure crib side rails are up and locked in place.

PROVIDING VISUAL AND AUDITORY STIMULATION

• Keep in mind that your infant can see bright objects and will follow a brightly colored ball or a human face. To provide visual stimulation, hang a mobile over the infant's bed. A mobile that turns is better than a stationary mobile because it offers greater variation.
• To provide auditory stimulation or quiet the infant, place a radio (on low volume) or a music box in the infant's room.
• Because infants can become used to noise, you do not have to reduce the noise level in your home when the infant sleeps. Some infants even sleep better with quiet music in the room.

---

questions about their child or the required care. Also urge them to interact with their child to enhance bonding. For parents with a nursing diagnosis of ***anxiety related to lack of confidence in parenting ability,*** explain how to detect early signs of potential problems, such as cold stress, infection, and dehydration to help prevent life-threatening complications. The parents may be eager for their child to establish regular sleep-awake and eating patterns. However, inform them that a neonate typically sleeps 10 to 20 hours a day at first. Also emphasize that sleep patterns vary and that a deviation from the typical pattern does not necessarily indicate an abnormality.

Point out that the mother will have an increased need for support after discharge and would benefit by having relatives or friends available to help her. This is especially important for the single mother who may have to serve as the sole caregiver.

PERFORMING ROUTINE THERAPEUTIC INTERVENTIONS

Routine nursing care of the normal neonate includes umbilical cord care, vitamin K administration, circumcision care, and collection of urine specimens.

Providing umbilical cord care

Immediately after birth, the umbilical cord is moist, making it an excellent breeding ground for bacteria. To avoid a nursing diagnosis of *potential for infection related to umbilical cord healing,* aim to promote drying of the cord and prevent infection. Depending on health care facility policy, one of several methods may be used to clean the cord. The American Academy of Pediatrics (1988) does not recommend a particular method.

Administering vitamin K

The neonate has a vitamin K deficiency, which results partly from lack of intestinal bacterial flora necessary to synthesize vitamin K. Because only small amounts of bacterial flora cross the placenta, this deficiency continues until enteral feedings are established and milk or formula is digested. Without sufficient vitamin K, the liver cannot synthesize coagulation factors II, VII, IX, and X (Streeter, 1986). This deficiency predisposes the neonate to hemorrhage and may lead to a nursing diagnosis of *potential for trauma related to inability to process vitamin K.* Thus, the American Academy of Pediatrics (1988) recommends a prophylactic I.M. injection of 0.5 to 1 mg of vitamin K_1 (phytonadione) during the first hour after birth. (For an illustrated procedure of I.M. injection in the neonate, see *Psychomotor skills: Performing routine care*, pages 83 to 93.)

Caring for a circumcision site

Circumcision has become controversial. The main advantage of circumcision is hygienic. The circumcised penis is easier to keep clean and free of smegma, a sebaceous secretion that accumulates under the foreskin. Because the neonate's tight skin makes foreskin retraction difficult, bacterial growth is less common with a circumcised penis. Wiswell, Enzenauer, Holton, Cornish, and Hankins (1987) found an increase in urinary tract infections in male neonates as the circumcision rate declined.

The major disadvantage of circumcision is the pain and discomfort it causes. After circumcision, the neonate cries and has a disturbed sleep-awake pattern. To reduce pain, the neonate may receive a topical anesthetic (Stang, Gunnar, Snellman, Condon, and Kestenbaum, 1988).

Various factors may influence the parents' decision whether to circumcise their child, including religious beliefs, the perception that circumcision is a sign of manhood, and the fear that an uncircumcised male will be stigmatized.

Apply petrolatum gauze over the penis to prevent bleeding and encrustation and to serve as a protective layer against abrasion from the diaper. To reduce the risk of contamination from fecal matter or urine – and thereby avoid a nursing diagnosis of *potential for infection related to the circumcision site* – change the petrolatum gauze at each diaper change. The gauze is necessary for only 2 to 3 days after the procedure. The neonate should not be under a radiant warmer once the petrolatum gauze is in place because burning may occur.

Collecting urine specimens

When caring for the normal neonate, urine specimens sometimes must be collected for urine cultures, for routine urinalysis, or to determine urine specific gravity, pH (by dipstick testing), protein, ketones, glucose, bilirubin, or blood.

To obtain urine for a specific gravity measurement or dipstick test, withdraw the specimen from a collection bag (via the covered port at the bottom of the bag) or from a disposable diaper. Both urine collection methods yield accurate results. For an illustrated procedure of urine specimen collection from a collection bag, see *Psychomotor skills: Performing routine care,* pages 83 to 93.

EVALUATION

During this step of the nursing process, the nurse evaluates the effectiveness of the care plan by ongoing evaluation of subjective and objective criteria. Evaluation findings should be stated in terms

of actions performed or outcomes achieved for each goal. The following examples illustrate appropriate evaluation statements for the normal neonate.
- The neonate did not appear cyanotic or dusky.
- The neonate maintained a stable body temperature of 96° to 97.7° F (35.5° to 36.5° C).
- The neonate voided clear amber urine six times in 24 hours.
- The neonate passed a meconium stool 24 hours after birth.
- The parents exhibited appropriate bonding behavior with their infant.

DOCUMENTATION

All steps of the nursing process should be documented as thoroughly and objectively as possible. Thorough documentation not only allows the nurse to evaluate the effectiveness of the care plan, but it also makes the data available to other members of the health care team, helping to ensure consistency of care.

Documentation for the normal neonate should include:
- vital signs, including temperature, heart rate and rhythm, and respiratory rate and rhythm
- strength and symmetry of peripheral pulses
- capillary refill time
- general appearance
- size and shape of fontanels
- umbilical cord description
- circumcision site description (as appropriate)
- stool and urine passage, including times, amounts, and characteristics
- any abnormal physical or behavioral findings
- parent teaching provided.

BIBLIOGRAPHY

American Academy of Pediatrics. (1988). Guidelines for perinatal care (2nd ed.). Washington, DC: American Academy of Pediatrics and American College of Obstetricians and Gynecologists.

Carlo, W.A., and Chatburn, R.L. (1988). *Neonatal respiratory care* (2nd ed.). Chicago: Year Book Medical Pubs.

Kim, M., and Mandell, J. (1988). Renal function in the fetus and neonate. In L.R. King (Ed.), *Urologic surgery in neonates and young infants* (pp. 59-76). Philadelphia: Saunders.

Stang, H., Gunnar, M.R., Snellman, L., Condon, L.M., and Kestenbaum, R. (1988). Local anesthesia for neonatal circumcision. *JAMA,* 259(10), 1507-1511.

Streeter, N.S. (1986). *High-risk neonatal care.* Rockville, MD: Aspen.

Nursing research

Steele, K.H. (1987). Caring for parents of critically ill neonates during hospitalization: Strategies for health-care professionals. *MCN,* 16(1), 13-27.

Wiswell, T.E., Enzenauer, R.W., Holton, M.E., Cornish, J.D., and Hankins, C.T. (1987). Declining frequency of circumcision: Implications for changes in the absolute incidence and male to female sex ratio of urinary tract infections in early infancy. *Pediatrics,* 79(3), 338-342.

4

Infant Nutrition

The rapid physical and developmental growth of the first year necessitates optimal nutrition. Besides playing a crucial part in infant health, nutrition also provides an opportunity for positive feeding experiences and important interactions between infant and caregiver. Parents may view positive feeding experiences and a satisfied infant as a measure of their parenting ability; for the infant, repeated pleasurable feeding experiences help develop trust in the caregiver.

Teaching about infant nutrition is a major role of the nurse who works with young families. By understanding the nutritional needs of the first year, the nurse can provide the client with accurate and practical rationales for feeding recommendations.

INFANT NUTRITIONAL NEEDS

The neonate's immature organ systems and the unparalleled growth of the first year impose special requirements for nutrients and fluids. These factors also limit the types and amounts of foods a neonate can ingest and digest. Recommendations for the introduction of solid foods are based on these limitations.

NUTRIENT AND FLUID REQUIREMENTS
As with all diets, the neonate's must contain sufficient amounts of carbohydrates, proteins, fats, vitamins, minerals, and fluids.

Energy
Three basic nutrients — carbohydrates, proteins, and fats — supply the body's caloric needs. Carbohydrates should serve as the body's main source of calories. Proteins promote cellular growth and maintenance, aid metabolism, and contribute to many protective sub-

stances. Fats provide a concentrated energy storage form, transport essential nutrients (such as fatty acids needed for neurologic growth and development), and insulate vital organs. Carbohydrates, which contain 4 calories per gram, should provide 35% to 55% of the neonate's total calories; fats, which contain 9 calories per gram, 30% to 55%; and proteins, which contain 4 calories per gram, the remaining calories.

Vitamins and minerals

Vitamins regulate metabolic processes and promote growth and maintenance of body tissues. Fat-soluble vitamins (A, D, E, and K) in excess of needs can be stored in the body to some extent and normally are not excreted; therefore, reserves may accumulate. Water-soluble vitamins (C, B_1, B_2, B_6, B_{12}, niacin, folic acid, pantothenic acid, and biotin) are stored only in small amounts. Consequently, if these vitamins are not ingested regularly, deficiencies may develop relatively quickly.

All major minerals and most trace minerals are essential for a wide range of body functions, including regulation of enzyme metabolism, acid-base balance, and nerve and muscle integrity. Calcium and iron are particularly important for growth — calcium for the rapid bone mineralization of the first year and iron for hemoglobin synthesis.

Fluids

The neonate's difficulty concentrating urine plus a high extracellular water content result in a much greater need for fluids (150 ml/kg/day) compared to the adult (20 to 30 ml/kg/day). By age 1, the daily fluid requirement is roughly 700 ml.

SPECIAL CONSIDERATIONS

The neonate has limited gastric capacity. Also, fat absorption does not reach adult levels until ages 6 to 9 months. For the first 3 months, limited synthesis of the starch-splitting salivary enzyme ptyalin and absence of pancreatic amylase restrict digestion of complex starches found in solid foods.

Because of the neonate's low glomerular filtration rate (GFR) and difficulty concentrating urine, high renal solute loads may cause fluid imbalance. (Renal solute load is a collective term for solutes that must be excreted by the kidneys.) The major solutes are sodium, potassium, and urea (an end product of protein metabolism). Some commercial infant formulas have a higher renal solute load than breast milk. Coupled with the neonate's low GFR, the solutes can cause too much fluid to be excreted, increasing the neonate's fluid needs even more.

Although the basic components of the neurologic system are present at birth, myelinization (development of the myelin sheath that protects nerve fibers) is incomplete. Only breast milk, infant formula, and whole milk contain enough linoleic acid to facilitate myelinization; for this reason, milk that contains less than 2% milk fat is not recommended before age 1.

Sleeping through the night — a significant developmental milestone — usually occurs earlier in the formula-fed infant than in the breast-fed infant. Parents may feel compelled to introduce solid foods early, believing this will lengthen the infant's sleep and help this milestone occur sooner (Wright, 1987). However, before age 3 months, the infant is ill-equipped to ingest solids. The extrusion reflex, in which the tongue pushes out food placed on it, does not diminish until approximately age 4 months. Also, an infant under age 3 months lacks the tongue motion needed to pass solids from the front to the back of the mouth. These limitations indicate unreadiness for solid foods.

NUTRITIONAL ASSESSMENT

Weight, length, and head circumference are the major nutritional assessment indices in the infant. In North America, growth charts with standardized measurements for these indices are used to compare an infant to others of the same age. Repeat measurements at various ages show whether the infant is growing at the expected rate. However, current charts are based on formula-fed infants and may be unreliable for exclusively breast-fed infants, who grow rapidly during the first 3 months and more slowly from ages 3 to 6 months (Wood, Isaacs, Jensen, and Hilton, 1988).

The neonate typically loses an average of 10% of the birth weight in the first few days. This may alarm parents, who commonly view weight as a reflection of their infant's health status. However, the formula-fed neonate usually returns to birth weight by day 10 and the breast-fed neonate by 3 weeks (Lauwers and Woessner, 1989). Birth weight typically doubles by ages 5 to 6 months and triples by age 1 year. Body length increases by about 50% by age 1; head circumference expands along with the rapidly growing brain.

INFANT FEEDING METHODS

Choice of an infant feeding method involves more than a simple comparison of the biophysical properties of breast milk and formula. (See *Nutritional and immunologic properties of breast milk and infant formulas,* pages 120 to 124.) Cultural, psychosocial, and other factors also come into play. Although various health groups have endorsed breast-feeding, many women still choose to use infant formula or to breast-feed only briefly. Consequently, the nurse must be familiar with the basic techniques of both breast-feeding and formula-feeding. Also, the nurse must recognize any personal biases toward a particular feeding method and make sure they do not influence the interaction with the family.

Because many clients make infant feeding decisions during pregnancy, the nurse should be prepared to offer guidance at that time to ensure an informed decision. Working with the client after delivery, the nurse helps her gain skills and confidence in the method she has chosen.

BREAST-FEEDING

Breast-feeding is an evolving, interdependent, and reciprocal relationship between mother and infant. Although the reflexes involved are natural, many of the techniques of breast-feeding must be learned by both mother and infant. The nurse who strives to work successfully with the breast-feeding client must have a comprehensive understanding of the physiology of lactation and a genuine commitment to facilitating practices that promote breast-feeding.

Breast-feeding has preventive health potential in both developing and industrialized countries. It has been endorsed officially by the World Health Organization (WHO), the International Pediatrics Association, the American Academy of Pediatrics, and the Canadian Pediatric Society.

Nearly all researchers agree that breast-feeding has health benefits, although they do not concur on the extent of such benefits (Cunningham, 1988; Jason, Nieburg, and Marks, 1984; Kovar, Ser

(Text continues on page 125.)

NUTRITIONAL AND IMMUNOLOGIC PROPERTIES OF BREAST MILK AND INFANT FORMULAS

Health experts recommend breast-feeding over formula-feeding. The chart below compares the nutritional and immunologic properties of breast milk and infant formulas and provides an overview of the health implications of these feeding methods.

COMPONENT AND FUNCTION	BREAST MILK CONTENT	COMMON FORMULA CONTENT	HEALTH IMPLICATIONS AND SPECIAL CONSIDERATIONS
Protein Promotes cellular growth and maintenance	Casein-whey protein ratio of 40:60[A]	Casein-whey protein ratio of 82:18[B] (Some milk-based formulas provide casein-whey ratio closer to that of breast milk.)	Whey proteins are acidified in the stomach; resulting curds are soft and readily digested with minimal energy expenditure. Casein forms tougher, less digestible curd that require more energy expenditure.
Methionine-cysteine (amino acids) Promote somatic (body tissue) growth	Methionine-cysteine ratio close to 1:1	Methionine-cysteine ratio seven times higher than that of breast milk[C]	More abundant methionine in formulas is poorly tolerated by some infants.[D]
Taurine (an amino acid) Allows early brain and retinal development	Present	Present since 1984[E]	Taurine is an essential amino acid for the neonate; therefore, it must be included in the diet.
Fat Serves as most concentrated calorie source	Breast milk fat content varies throughout the day. Concentration is lowest during the first morning feeding, highest at midmorning, then gradually declines.[F] Fat concentration also increases toward the end of feeding (hindmilk). Breast milk also contains lipase, an enzyme that breaks down triglycerides to fatty acids	Vegetable oils are major fat constituent.	Fat is absorbed to virtually the same degree in breast milk and infant formulas.[G] However, lipase in breast milk provides initial energy supply.

[A]Canadian Pediatric Society, 1978; Neville, 1983; Ogra and Greene, 1982. [B]Canadian Pediatric Society, 1978; Casey and Hambridge, 1983. [C]Lawrence, 1985. [D]Ogra andGreene, 1982. [E]Minchin, 1985. [F]Casey and Hanbridge, 1983. [G]American Academy of Pediatrics, 1978.

NUTRITIONAL AND IMMUNOLOGIC PROPERTIES OF BREAST MILK AND INFANT FORMULAS *(continued)*

COMPONENT AND FUNCTION	BREAST MILK CONTENT	COMMON FORMULA CONTENT	HEALTH IMPLICATIONS AND SPECIAL CONSIDERATIONS
Fat *(continued)*	and glycerol and supplies initial energy before milk reaches the intestine.		
Cholesterol May be needed for synthesis of nerve tissue and bile acids.[H]	Present	Absent	Cholesterol ingestion during infancy may promote synthesis of enzymes linked to cholesterol metabolism, resulting in lower serum cholesterol levels later in life.[I]
Carbohydrate Serves as main calorie source	Lactose is primary carbohydrate in breast milk; small quantities of galactose and fructose also are present.	Lactose is primary carbohydrate in many formulas.	Lactose enhances calcium absorption and metabolizes readily to galactose and fructose, which supply energy for the infant's rapidly growing brain. Lactose promotes lactobacilli growth and increases intestinal acidity. The combination of lactobacilli and an acidic environment helps prevent diarrhea.[J]
Iron Promotes cellular oxygen transport and storage and carbon dioxide removal; increases resistance to infection	Present in small amounts; high levels of lactose and vitamin C in breast milk facilitate iron absorption.[C]	Present in higher amounts than in breast milk but more poorly absorbed because of lower lactose and vitamin C levels in formulas[C]	Iron in breast milk meets the requirements of an exclusively breast-fed term infant until birth weight triples.[I]
Zinc Promotes cellular growth and repair	Present; zinc-binding ligand (molecule that forms coordinate covalent bonds with metallic ions) in breast milk enhances zinc absorption.[D]	Present in roughly same amount as in breast milk	Zinc is essential for growth and skin integrity and must be included in the neonate's diet.[H]

[C]Lawrence, 1985. [D]Ogra and Greene, 1982. [H]Lewis, 1986. [I]Canadian Pediatric Society, 1978. [J]Hayward, 1983.

(continued)

NUTRITIONAL AND IMMUNOLOGIC PROPERTIES OF BREAST MILK AND INFANT FORMULAS *(continued)*

COMPONENT AND FUNCTION	BREAST MILK CONTENT	COMMON FORMULA CONTENT	HEALTH IMPLICATIONS AND SPECIAL CONSIDERATIONS
Calcium, phosphorus, potassium, and **sodium** Calcium promotes bone formation and blood clotting. Phosphorus is involved in bone and tooth formation and other biochemical processes. Potassium and sodium promote fluid and electrolyte balance. Calcium, phosphorus, potassium, and sodium also are renal solutes.	Present	Present in higher amounts than in breast milk	The lower renal solute load of breast milk poses less danger to the infant's immature renal system.[G]
Vitamins Important in various metabolic processes. For example, vitamin D promotes calcium and phosphorus metabolism, vitamin K is crucial to synthesis of coagulation factors, and vitamin E protects retinal and pulmonary cell membranes.	All vitamins, both fat-soluble and water-soluble, present at levels reflecting mother's nutritional status and vitamin intake. Although vitamin D is considered fat-soluble, it has been found in water-soluble as well as fatty portion of breast milk.[K] Vitamin K is present in small amounts. High quantities of vitamin E are present in both colostrum and mature breast milk.	All vitamins present in breast milk in equal or higher amounts.	Vitamin D supplements may be recommended for breast-fed infants to prevent deficiency (rickets), although some authorities question need for this.[L] Vitamin K prophylaxis is recommended at birth for both breast-fed and formula-fed infants to prevent hemorrhagic disease of the newborn.[M]

[G]American Academy of Pediatrics, 1978. [K]Lauwers and Woessner, 1983. [L]Fomon, 1987. [M]Shapiro, Jacobson, Armon, Manco-Johnson, Hulac, Lane, and Hathaway, 1986.

NUTRITIONAL AND IMMUNOLOGIC PROPERTIES OF BREAST MILK AND INFANT FORMULAS *(continued)*

COMPONENT AND FUNCTION	BREAST MILK CONTENT	COMMON FORMULA CONTENT	HEALTH IMPLICATIONS AND SPECIAL CONSIDERATIONS
Fluoride Protects against dental caries	Present in small amounts, which do not increase significantly if mother takes supplements.	Present in controlled amounts	Fluoride supplements at birth are controversial. However, supplements are recommended by age 6 months.[N] Need for supplements may depend on fluoride content of local water. Current fluoride recommendation: 0.25 mg/day if local water supply contains less than 0.3 parts per million.
Thyroid hormone Promotes carbohydrate, protein, and fat metabolism and helps regulate metabolic rate	Present in significant amounts	Present in negligible amounts	Value of breast milk thyroid hormone in protecting against congenital hypothyroidism is unknown.[O]
Immunoglobulins (particularly IgA and IgG) Offer protection against antigens (such as viruses and bacteria) and decrease risk of food allergy. Secretory IgA bathes body surfaces and prevents pathogens from entering the body.[P] IgG increases phagocytosis.[Q]	All immunoglobulins are present in both colostrum and breast milk. Secretory IgA accounts for most IgA during first year of breast-feeding.[R] Breast milk has higher IgA levels than formulas; it also contains antibodies to food proteins and thus may decrease risk of food allergy.[S]	Present in negligible amounts	IgA does not readily cross the placenta and therefore is deficient at birth. IgA levels increase slowly in the infant's first few months.
Lysozymes Protect against micrococci and *Escherichia coli*	Present in amounts up to 3,000 times higher than in cow's milk[C]	Present in minimal amounts	Breast milk lysozymes provide protection up to 6 months after birth as the infant loses transplacentally acquired passive immunity.[R]

[C]Lawrence, 1985. [N]American Academy of Pediatrics, 1986. [O]Hartman and Kent, 1988. [O]Ogra and Greene, 1982. [P]Marieb, 1989. [Q]Seeley, Stephens, and Tate, 1989. [R]Goldman, Garza, Nichols, and Goldblum, 1982. [S]Hanson, Adlerberth, Carlsson, Castrignano, Hahn-Zoric, Dahlgren, Jalil, Nilsson, and Robertson, 1988.

(continued)

NUTRITIONAL AND IMMUNOLOGIC PROPERTIES OF BREAST MILK AND INFANT FORMULAS (continued)

COMPONENT AND FUNCTION	BREAST MILK CONTENT	COMMON FORMULA CONTENT	HEALTH IMPLICATIONS AND SPECIAL CONSIDERATIONS
Lactoferrin (bacteriostatic and iron-binding protein) Exerts antimicrobial effect by preventing bacteria from obtaining iron necessary for survival	Abundant	Absent	In combination with IgA, lactoferrin in breast milk destroys pathogenic strains of *E. coli* and *Candida albicans*.[T]
Bifidum factor (a nitrogen-containing carbohydrate) Creates unfavorable environment for enteropathic bacteria	Present	Absent	Bifidum factor fosters favorable GI bacterial flora—predominantly *Lactobacillus bifidum*—thus helping to protect against several pathogenic organisms.[G]
Antistaphylococcal factor Resists staphylococci, especially *Staphylococcus aureus*	Present	Absent	Antistaphylococcal factor may promote infant health.
Leukocytes Destroy pathogens by phagocytosis	Present	Absent	Leukocytes may promote infant health.
Interferon Protects against viral infections	Present	Present in negligible amounts	Interferon may promote infant health.
Respiratory syncytial virus (RSV) antibodies Protect against RSV	Present	Present in negligible amounts	RSV antibodies may promote infant health.
Prostaglandins Affect cellular function in all organ systems	Present	Present in negligible amounts	Prostaglandins may promote infant health.
Lactoperoxidase Kills streptococci	Present	Absent	Lactoperoxidase may promote infant health.

[G]American Academy of Pediatrics, 1978. [T]Rumball, 1988.

dula, Marks, and Fraser, 1984; Kramer, 1988; Leventhal, Shapiro, Aten, Berg, and Egerter, 1986). Several studies show that breast milk has distinct advantages over formulas; in contrast, no studies have reached the opposite conclusion (Baer, 1981).

In North America, an increasing percentage of women are breast-feeding their neonates. Approximately 60% of American women breast-fed in 1985, compared to 25% in 1971 (Fomon, 1987). The trend is similar in Canada, where 79% of women breast-fed in 1984, compared to roughly 25% in the 1970s (Myres, 1988). Internationally, a marketing code for breast milk substitutes established by WHO in 1979 helped promote breast-feeding in developing countries.

The U.S. Surgeon General has established as a goal for 1990 that 75% of American women breast-feed at the time of discharge after delivery and that 35% continue to breast-feed by the infant's sixth month (U.S. Department of Health and Human Services, 1984). Canada developed a national program to promote breast-feeding in 1978 (Myres, Watson, and Harrison, 1981).

Physiology of lactation

Lactation operates on a supply-meets-demand basis: The more milk the infant removes, the more milk the breast produces. Hormones control milk production and ejection to make milk available to the infant, as described below.

Milk production. Milk is produced in the breast alveoli — tiny sacs made up of epithelial cells. The female breast has a rich blood supply from which the alveoli extract nutrients to produce milk. The alveoli are situated in lobules — clusters leading to ductules that merge into lactiferous ducts. These larger ducts widen further into ampullae, or lactiferous sinuses, located behind the nipple and areola.

Lactogenesis — initiation of milk production — begins during the third trimester of pregnancy under the influence of human placental lactogen, a hormone secreted by the placenta. The lactating breast functions in synchrony with maternal hormones; along with effective infant attachment on the breast, these hormones mediate milk flow through the alveoli and ductules.

After delivery of the placenta and the resultant decrease in circulating estrogen and progesterone, the anterior pituitary gland releases prolactin, one of many hormones that stimulate mammary gland growth and development. In response, alveolar secretory cells begin extracting nutrients from the blood and converting them to milk. Initial prolactin production also hinges on tactile stimulation of the nipple-areola junction by infant sucking or milk expression (Neville, 1983).

Prolactin is secreted intermittently throughout the day, with secretion rising markedly during sleep (Neville, 1983) and night feedings (Glasier, McNeilly, and Howie, 1984). Thus, frequent feeding over the entire 24-hour period enhances prolactin secretion and significantly increases milk production (Klaus, 1987). Prolactin secretion also creates a calm, relaxed feeling in the mother, which may enhance mother-infant bonding.

Milk ejection. The hormone oxytocin makes breast milk available to the infant through the let-down reflex. In this reflex, nipple stimulation or an emotional response to the infant causes the hypothalamus to trigger release of oxytocin by the posterior pituitary gland. Myoepithelial cells surrounding the alveoli then contract and eject milk into the ductules and sinuses, making milk available through nipple openings. A conditioned reflex, let-down occurs after 2 to 3 minutes of sucking during the first days of breast-feeding; several let-downs occur over the course of a feeding.

Some women have no symptoms of let-down. Others experience it as a tingling sensation, a momentary pain in the nipple, or a warm rush from the chest wall toward the nipple. In the early postpartal period, other let-down symptoms may include uterine cramps (afterpains), caused by the action of oxytocin on the involuting uterus, and a slight increase in lochia (the vaginal discharge emitted after delivery). Also, the breasts may leak. However, let-down may occur even in the absence of milk leakage. In some women, the sphincters controlling milk expulsion from the lactiferous sinuses to the nipple function so effectively that only active sucking on the breast leads to milk release.

Restricting sucking time — a practice based on the erroneous notion that prolonged sucking causes nipple soreness — can disrupt optimal function of the let-down reflex by preventing the infant from completely emptying the milk ducts. This, in turn, leads to milk buildup and signals the body to stop producing milk. The breasts become engorged and harden; the nipples may become flat, hindering proper infant attachment. The body responds to engorgement by halting milk production. In the early days of breast-feeding, restricted sucking time may establish a negative feedback system that can lead to insufficient milk production. Also, it may force the infant to feed more often to satisfy hunger.

Breast milk composition and digestion

The composition of breast milk undergoes various changes. Initial feedings provide colostrum, a thin, serous fluid. Unlike mature breast milk, which has a bluish cast, colostrum is yellow (Casey and Hambridge, 1983). However, its color may vary considerably from one woman to the next.

Colostrum contains high concentrations of protein, fat-soluble vitamins, minerals, and immunoglobulins, which function as antibodies. (For more on the immunologic properties of breast milk, see Chapter 1, Neonatal Adaptation.) Colostrum's laxative effect promotes early passage of meconium. Also, the low colostrum volumes produced do not tax the neonate's limited gastric capacity or cause fluid overload.

The breasts may contain colostrum for up to 96 hours after delivery. The maturation rate from colostrum to breast milk varies (Humenick, 1987). With increased breast-feeding frequency and duration in the first 48 hours, colostrum matures to milk more rapidly (Humenick, 1987). This discovery helped disprove the theory that breast-feeding frequency should be limited until mature milk comes in. (However, in some cultures, infants never receive colostrum, as described in *Cultural considerations: Cultural aspects of infant feeding,* page 128.)

Breast milk composition also changes over the course of a feeding. The foremilk — thin, watery milk secreted when a feeding begins — is low in calories but contains abundant water-soluble vitamins. It accounts for about 60% of the total volume of a feeding. Next, whole milk is released. The hindmilk, available 10 to 15 minutes after the initial let-down, has the highest concentration of calories for satisfying hunger between feedings.

The rate of milk transfer to the infant varies among mother-infant couples (Woolridge, 1989). Consequently, limiting feeding times or insisting that the woman use both breasts at each feeding may prevent the infant from obtaining the maximum benefit of variable breast milk content.

> ### CULTURAL CONSIDERATIONS
>
> # CULTURAL ASPECTS OF INFANT FEEDING
>
> When caring for a client whose background is different from yours, keep the following cultural considerations in mind.
>
> > Infant feeding practices vary with geography and culture. In Finland, where no infant formula is manufactured, breast-feeding is the norm (Carr, 1989). Some developing countries (for example, Colombia, Brazil, Thailand, and New Guinea) have reversed the recent decline in breast feeding through vigorous breast-feeding promotion.
> >
> > Filipinos, Mexican Americans, Vietnamese, and some Nigerians do not give colostrum to neonates; mothers in these groups begin breast-feeding only after milk ejection begins. Some Korean women delay breast-feeding until 3 days after delivery; others begin breast-feeding immediately and breastfeed whenever the infant cries (Choi, 1986).
> >
> > In Kenya, mothers feed premature neonates only by breast and begin breast-feeding them much earlier than in North America. Kenyans never use gavage tubes and feed neonates from small cups until they are ready to suck (Armstrong, 1987).

The whey proteins that predominate in breast milk lead to formation of soft, easily digested curds. The infant typically digests breast milk within 2 to 3 hours after a feeding and thus may become hungry more often than the formula-fed infant, who typically feeds every 4 hours. In the first few weeks after birth, the breast-fed neonate may feed eight to twelve times every 24 hours.

Infant sucking

The dynamics of sucking on a breast and sucking on an artificial nipple differ dramatically. No frictional movement occurs during breast-feeding (Woolridge, 1986); therefore, it should be painless, provided the infant is properly attached (Royal College of Midwives, 1988). Misinformation about the dynamics of sucking has led to such practices as limiting feeding times. Incorrect infant sucking technique — not prolonged feeding — causes nipple soreness. Some infants must be taught to suck correctly.

Using images generated by real-time ultrasound studies, investigators have observed the dynamics of breast sucking. Smith, Erenberg, and Nowak (1988) found that the human nipple is a highly elastic structure that elongates to nearly twice its resting length during active feeding. Little change occurs in the nipple's lateral dimension, confirming the theory that the cheeks serve as a passive seal. The researchers also observed that nipple compression between the infant's tongue and palate reduces the tongue's height by half and causes milk ejection.

This sucking pattern was confirmed by Weber, Woolridge, and Baum (1986), who found that the breast-fed infant uses a rolling or peristaltic tongue action in contrast to the squeezing or pistonlike tongue action of the bottle-fed infant. The researchers also noted that the tongue's resting position between bursts of sucking differs in breast-fed and bottle-fed infants.

Intake requirements

A breast-fed infant typically needs to be fed every 2 to 3 hours. During the first 3 to 4 weeks, before the feeding pattern is established fully, parents may wonder if the neonate is receiving adequate nourishment. Signs of adequate intake include 10 to 12 wet diapers in 24 hours, steady weight gain, and contentedness after feeding.

Duration

Despite an increase in breast-feeding rates of women at the time of discharge after delivery, 65% of American women who breast-feed stop before 4 months (Fomon, 1987); 23% of Canadian women stop before 3 months (Tanaka, Yeung, and Anderson, 1987). By anticipating the reasons why a client may choose to stop breast-feeding, the nurse can identify strategies that may help reduce barriers to continued breast-feeding.

Lactation insufficiency (lack of milk) is the most common reason for stopping breast-feeding in the early weeks (Newman, 1986). The incidence of primary lactation insufficiency is unknown. However, lactation insufficiency most commonly stems from mismanagement of lactation (Neifert and Seacat, 1987); this in turn may result from such institutional practices as routine supplementation with bottled glucose and water, omission of night breast-feeding until mature milk comes in, and arbitrary feeding schedules. These practices may strain the adaptability of the mother-infant couple and interrupt the interactions necessary for successful breast-feeding (Winikoff, Laukaran, Myers, and Stone, 1986). Also, indiscriminate use of bottles to supplement breast-feeding in the neonate's first days may cause nipple confusion, making the neonate refuse the breast the next time it is offered. When such problems occur, ready availability of an alternative infant food source may cause the mother to switch to formula rather than try to correct the problems.

Like the client's decision to breast-feed initially, her decision to stop involves many factors, including her age, family or social attitudes toward breast-feeding, and her socioeconomic status or educational level. For example, an adolescent mother may stop breast-feeding when she realizes how much time and energy it requires; a new mother who is the first woman in her family to breast-feed may feel pressured to stop if problems arise.

Maternal ambivalence toward breast-feeding also may play a role (Jones, West, and Newcombe, 1986). However, with proper antepartal teaching, a client may learn to adjust her expectations about breast-feeding and thus avoid becoming so discouraged that she stops when problems occur. For instance, she can learn to anticipate ambivalence and doubt about her ability to breast-feed and to expect such physical discomforts as leaking breasts and frequent feedings.

Hewat and Ellis (1986) compared women who breast-fed for prolonged periods with those who discontinued breast-feeding early. They concluded that those who continued:

• fed their neonates more frequently in the early days of breast-feeding

• showed less anxiety about initial neonatal weight loss and interpreted neonatal behavior in a positive light

• demonstrated a greater ability to relax

• showed more flexibility in their daily routines

• more readily incorporated siblings into the feeding experience

• received more support from their partner.

The nurse can help prevent a poor breast-feeding outcome by teaching the client about the physiology of lactation, providing anticipatory guidance about the normal course of breast-feeding, and making sure the client knows how to obtain information and support after discharge. Although the availability of follow-up support varies, some community health nurses make routine home visits after a neonate's birth. Also, the assistance of a lactation nurse has significantly prolonged breast-feeding during the first 4 weeks and among women of lower socioeconomic status (Jones and West, 1985). Professional and lay breast-feeding support may be available from a lactation consultant or a local LaLeche League group.

FORMULA-FEEDING

Because of the current emphasis on breast-feeding, the client who chooses formula-feeding may feel uncertain about her choice and react defensively if she feels it is being questioned. By recognizing the many factors that go into infant feeding decisions, the nurse can convey respect and offer support to the client who has made an informed decision to formula-feed. Also, by working with the client in the antepartal period, the nurse can help ensure that she receives relevant information in a way that would allow her to revise her choice (Gabriel, Gabriel, and Lawrence, 1986).

Although choice of specific formula and preparation method are important aspects of formula-feeding, the feeding process goes beyond simply giving the infant a bottle. As with breast-feeding, formula-feeding involves a developing relationship between mother and infant. The nurse who remains aware of this added dimension can provide the family with appropriate anticipatory guidance during the early learning period of infant feeding.

COMMERCIAL FORMULAS AND EQUIPMENT

Commercial infant formulas fall into three categories — milk-based, soy-based, and casein hydrolysate-based. (For a comparison of these formula types, see *Nutritional options for the formula-fed infant,* page 132.) The American Academy of Pediatrics recommends commercially prepared formulas over other formulas for infants up to age 1 year. Commercial formulas provide all necessary vitamins, so infants receiving them do not require vitamin supplements. However, use of noncommercial formulas necessitates vitamin supplementation.

Product convenience, personal preference, and economic status influence the client's choice of formula equipment. Commercially available equipment includes glass bottles, boilable plastic bottles, disposable plastic bags (which the preparer places in a hollow plastic holder), and artificial nipples. Because sucking action on the NUK nipple (which is flat and broad) most closely resembles sucking action on the human nipple, some authorities recommend this nipple for breast-fed infants who receive an occasional supplemental bottle.

Infant sucking

Sucking on a regular latex nipple is largely a squeezing action. The bottle-fed infant tends to swallow with every suck at the beginning

NUTRITIONAL OPTIONS FOR THE FORMULA-FED INFANT

Commercial formulas are recommended for non-breast-feeding infants. The table below compares three major types of commercial formulas.

OPTION	RECOMMENDATIONS FOR USE	FORM AND ENERGY CONTENT
Milk-based commercial formula (Enfalac, Similac, SMA, Milumil)	• Infants with no family history of food allergy who receive little or no breast milk	Liquid concentrate, powdered concentrate, ready-to-serve Energy content: 68 kcal/dl
Soy-based commercial formula (Isomil, Nursoy, ProSobee)	• Infants with galactosemia or primary lactase deficiency • Infants recovering from secondary lactose intolerance • Infants with a family history of food allergy but no clinical manifestations • Infants in strict vegetarian families that wish to avoid animal protein formulas	Liquid concentrate, powdered concentrate, ready-to-serve Energy content: 68 kcal/dl
Casein hydrolysate-based commercial formula (Nutramigen, Pregestimil, Alimentum)	• Infants with clinical manifestations of food allergy	Liquid or powdered concentrate Energy content: 68 kcal/dl

Adapted with permission of the Minister of Supply and Services Canada, 1991, from Health and Welfare Canada publication *Feeding babies: A counselling guide on practical solutions to common infant feeding questions*, 1986.

of a feeding. If milk flow is restricted (for instance, from vacuum buildup that makes the nipple collapse), the suck-swallow ratio may rise to 2:1 or even higher, until sucking stops completely.

Intake requirements

The amount and frequency of formula-feedings vary with infant size, maturity, and activity level. Daily formula intake averages 180 ml/kg.

Like parents of the breast-fed infant, parents of the formula-fed infant may believe all crying signals hunger. The nurse can help them interpret infant behavior more accurately by reviewing guidelines on feeding frequency. (For formula intake requirements and feeding frequency for infants up to age 1 year, see *Formula guidelines*.)

FORMULA GUIDELINES

The table below shows recommended formula volume and feeding frequency for infants up to age 1 year who are receiving commercial formula exclusively.

AGE	FORMULA VOLUME PER FEEDING	FEEDINGS PER DAY
1 month	126 ml (4.1 oz)	6
2 months	142 ml (4.6 oz)	5
3 months	161 ml (5.2 oz)	5
4 months	168 ml (5.4 oz)	5
5 months	191 ml (6.2 oz)	4
6 months	170 ml (6.8 oz)	5
7 to 9 months	131 ml (4.2 oz)	5
10 months	136 ml (4.4 oz)	5
11 months	125 ml (4.0 oz)	5
12 months	141 ml (4.5 oz)	4

Adapted from data analysis performed by Ross Laboratories, 1985. Used with permission.

Digestion

The casein proteins predominating in formula result in tougher, less digestible curds than the whey in breast milk. Consequently, infant formula takes more time and energy to digest than breast milk. (However, homogenization and heat treatment of commercially prepared formulas have improved curd digestibility somewhat.)

ASSESSMENT

The nurse should begin client assessment by collecting general data and then make specific assessments related to the feeding method.

THE BREAST-FEEDING CLIENT AND NEONATE

Ideally, assessment should begin in the early antepartal period as the nurse determines how much the client knows about infant nutrition and breast-feeding techniques. Also, the nurse should evaluate nipple graspability and protractility by determining whether the nipples are slightly everted, flat, or inverted. The slightly everted nipple, the most common type, becomes more graspable when stimulated. A flat nipple is hard to distinguish from the areola and changes shape only slightly when stimulated. Inverted nipples fall into three categories. A pseudoinverted nipple appears inverted but becomes erect with stimulation. A semi-inverted nipple initially appears graspable but retracts with stimulation. A truly inverted nipple is inverted both at rest and when stimulated.

For the client in the postpartal period, after breast-feeding has begun, the nurse should assess:

• consistency of the breasts (softness, mobility, engorgement, and warmth)

• condition of the nipples (tenderness, abrasions, and discoloration)

• sensations experienced during breast-feeding (such as tingling).

For the breast-feeding neonate, the nurse should assess the sucking reflex before the first feeding because improper sucking will prevent adequate feeding. Clues that the neonate is sucking properly include puffing out of the cheeks and absence of biting.

Also assess for signs of lactose intolerance, including abdominal cramps and distention and severe diarrhea. The major carbohydrate in milk, lactose normally is broken down by the enzyme lactase. Lactose intolerance occurs from the absence of lactase in the border of the intestinal villi. Most common among non-Caucasian neonates, lactose intolerance may warrant the use of a soy-based formula, which provides corn syrup solids and sucrose as the primary carbohydrates.

The nurse also should assess for proper client and infant positioning. The client may assume a sitting or reclining position, bringing the infant to her. A pillow can be placed under the arms to prevent shoulder elevation, which could cause muscle tension. The client should hold the infant facing her and level with the breast so that the infant's neck need not twist or flex.

The nurse should assess the client and infant during a feeding to determine if the infant is correctly attached on the breast, as indicated by a wide open mouth with lips curved backward.

Assessment of the client and infant after discharge can promote breast-feeding success. Many life-style adjustments must be made when a neonate joins the family. These adjustments may cause role

NUTRITIONAL AID FOR MOTHERS AND INFANTS

In the United States, a government program called the Women, Infants, and Children Nutrition Program (WIC) provides supplemental foods, access to health care, and nutrition education during critical stages of growth and development. Those eligible include pregnant and postpartal women, infants up to age 1 year, and children up to age 5 whom a health care professional has classified as being at nutritional risk. Although federally funded, WIC is administered by states; consequently, eligibility requirements may vary. Further information can be obtained from the Department of Agriculture or from state health departments.

In Canada, access to health care is universal. However, no universal social assistance program exists specifically for mothers and infants. Instead, each Canadian province has its own program. In special cases, government subsidies are available for infant feeding equipment and formulas. Otherwise, a woman receiving social assistance is expected to meet her and her child's nutritional needs with the monthly allowance she receives. Provincial community health nurses employed by the government can provide specific information about health care for Canadian mothers with infants.

strain and conflict. Postdischarge nursing assessment may reveal breast-feeding problems caused by such role strain and conflict.

THE CLIENT USING INFANT FORMULA

For the client in the antepartal period, the nurse should assess for:
- knowledge of proper feeding techniques
- understanding of types of formula
- previous experience with infant formula.

Also, the nurse should find out what equipment and facilities the client will use to prepare formula and determine if the client will need financial aid to meet the infant's nutritional needs. (For information on sources of financial aid for mothers of young children, see *Nutritional aid for mothers and infants.*)

For the client in the postpartal period, the nurse should assess bottle and infant positioning during feeding and the client's ability to adjust feeding technique in response to infant cues. The nurse also should inspect the client's breasts for signs of engorgement, such as tenderness, swelling, warmth, hardness, shininess, and redness.

Infant factors to assess for include:

• excessive drooling, coughing, gagging, or respiratory distress during feeding (which may indicate tracheal or esophageal fistula, as discussed in Chapter 5, High-Risk Neonates)
• amount of formula the infant takes
• regurgitation after feeding
• mucus in regurgitated matter
• how readily the infant burps
• signs of lactose intolerance (discussed under "The breast-feeding client and neonate")
• presence of circumoral cyanosis (bluish skin around the mouth) during feeding. This may reflect insufficient oxygen to meet the infant's increased metabolic needs.

NURSING DIAGNOSIS

After gathering all assessment data, the nurse must review it carefully to identify pertinent nursing diagnoses for the client or neonate. (For a partial list of applicable diagnoses, see *Nursing diagnoses: Infant nutrition.*)

PLANNING AND IMPLEMENTATION

After assessing the client and formulating nursing diagnoses, the nurse develops and implements a plan of care. For example, if the client has a nursing diagnosis of *knowledge deficit related to breast-feeding,* the nurse should plan what and how to teach her about breast-feeding. Although the plan will depend on the client's abilities, it may include written materials, discussion of proper feeding methods and infant positioning, and client demonstration of breast-feeding.

CARE FOR THE BREAST-FEEDING CLIENT

The nurse's role in working with the breast-feeding client includes teaching of proper feeding techniques and intervention to correct any related problems. The nurse also helps the client deal with physiologic or psychosocial problems related to breast-feeding.

NURSING DIAGNOSES

INFANT NUTRITION

The following are potential nursing diagnoses for problems and etiologies that a nurse may encounter when caring for a client as she begins to nourish her neonate. Specific nursing interventions for many of these diagnoses are provided in the "Planning and implementation" section of this chapter.

- Altered family processes related to breast-feeding
- Altered family processes related to infant feeding
- Altered nutrition: potential for more than body requirements, related to breast-feeding
- Altered parenting related to infant prematurity and the mother's wish to breast-feed
- Altered role performance related to the new task of breast-feeding
- Altered sexuality patterns related to requirements of the breast-feeding infant
- Anxiety related to change in infant feeding pattern secondary to a growth spurt
- Anxiety related to the ability to breast-feed multiple infants
- Anxiety related to the ability to properly feed the infant
- Body image disturbance related to physiologic changes secondary to breast-feeding
- Ineffective breast-feeding related to improper positioning at the breast
- Knowledge deficit related to breast-feeding
- Knowledge deficit related to formula-feeding
- Pain related to breast engorgement
- Potential fluid volume deficit related to breast-feeding
- Potential for infection related to improper expression and storage of breast milk
- Potential for injury related to improper nipple care
- Sleep pattern disturbance, related to the infant's nutritional needs

Client teaching

Ideally, teaching about breast-feeding should begin in the antepartal period and continue postpartum until breast-feeding is well established.

Antepartum. In the antepartal period, teaching should focus on practical knowledge that will help the client establish and maintain lactation after delivery. Some general topics that could be incorporated into antepartal teaching include:

• physiologic, emotional, and social factors that influence lactation

• the role of the neonate and the client's partner in breast-feeding outcome

• common breast-feeding problems and possible solutions

• the possibility of continuing to breast-feed after the client returns to work

• the role of support groups or professional services and how to gain access to them.

Antepartal teaching also can help prepare the client to deal with incorrect advice about breast-feeding. Such advice — which may come from friends, relatives, or even health care professionals — typically is based on emotion rather than scientific principles that promote a positive breast-feeding outcome. When initiating breast-feeding, the client is especially vulnerable to such outside interference. To make her less vulnerable, the nurse can establish credibility as a knowledgeable professional during the pregnancy. Then, the nurse may use role-playing techniques, asking the client to predict who might offer advice and having her play the role of each of those persons. Practicing this technique in the antepartal period prepares the client to react rationally to incorrect advice once she begins breast-feeding.

Postpartum. The nurse should encourage the client to take advantage of the neonate's early responsiveness by breast-feeding as soon as possible. For the healthy full-term neonate, no contraindications exist to feeding immediately after delivery. In the first 30 minutes or so after birth, the neonate is highly responsive and eager to suck. Many neonates breast-feed shortly after delivery; all at least make licking or nuzzling motions, helping to stimulate the mother's prolactin production. Also, during this time the client's breasts may be soft and easily manipulated, facilitating proper attachment. Immediate breast-feeding also offers the chance for intimate contact that can enhance mother-infant bonding and have a positive psychological effect on the parents.

Valid reasons for delaying breast-feeding immediately after delivery include such obvious contraindications as life-threatening illness of the mother or neonate. In less obvious cases, the nurse must exercise good judgment. For example, immediate breast-feeding may be inappropriate if the neonate has anomalies that warrant evaluation, if the mother is heavily sedated or fatigued, or if the neonate has a 5-minute Apgar score of 6 or less.

General breast-feeding guidelines

Although lactation is a natural process, breast-feeding skills must be learned and practiced. The nurse can promote breast-feeding success through timely intervention to correct any problems. (See *Client teaching: Breast-feeding your infant,* pages 140 to 142.)

Helping the client initiate breast-feeding. In many cases, the nurse must help the client initiate feeding. However, the client who believes breast-feeding should be entirely natural may feel like a failure for needing help. Especially for a client with a nursing diagnosis of **knowledge deficit related to breast-feeding,** the nurse should point out that some infants must learn to breast-feed. Others may need to be wakened for every feeding.

Providing comfort measures and promoting hygiene. Before a feeding begins, the nurse should meet the client's comfort needs — for example, by having her void or by administering an analgesic, if prescribed. Also, the nurse should encourage her always to wash her hands just before breast-feeding.

Ensuring proper positioning. The nurse should emphasize the importance of correct positioning. The client may breast-feed in three different positions — cradle position, side-lying position, or football hold. Whichever position the client uses, her back and arms should be firmly supported; pillows may be placed under the arm on the breast-feeding side to keep the infant close to the breast.

Help the client into the chosen position and instruct her to hold the infant so that the infant looks down on her breast, then tilt the breast so that the nipple points toward the roof of the infant's mouth. This position typically places the infant's lower lip and jaw well below the nipple.

In the client's eagerness to ensure that breast-feeding goes well, she may lean in toward the infant, believing this facilitates attachment. However, to avoid discomfort, the client should bring the infant toward her instead.

(Text continues on page 143.)

BREAST-FEEDING YOUR INFANT

Before you begin breast-feeding, review the guidelines below to gain confidence and help both you and your infant get the most from the experience.

Starting to breast-feed

The first time you breast-feed your infant can be exciting, especially if the infant sucks and feeds properly at once. If your infant does not, however, breast-feeding still can succeed.

During the first days, you and your infant are getting to know each other. Here are some tips that may help.

• No hard and fast rules exist for the first feeding. Do not follow rigid guidelines for feeding times or frequency because these can impede milk production.

• Do not offer the infant a bottle when establishing breast-feeding. Sucking on a nipple differs from sucking on a bottle; nipple confusion may make the infant refuse the breast the next time you offer it.

• Keep the infant in the room with you and breast-feed every 2 to 3 hours or on demand—whichever comes first.

• Feed the infant through the night to help increase milk production.

• Let the infant decide when to stop breast-feeding rather than breaking suction yourself and pulling the infant off your breast. Also, let the infant finish feeding on one breast before offering the other. Keep in mind that reducing breast-feeding time will not prevent sore nipples and may cause milk drainage problems.

• Give yourself and your infant time to develop a mutually satisfying breast-feeding pattern.

• Keep in mind that a breast-fed infant usually needs to be fed more often than a formula-fed infant, so avoid comparing your infant's feeding pattern to that of a formula-fed infant.

Breast-feeding positions

You may use the cradle position, side-lying position, or football hold to breast-feed your infant. By alternating positions, you rotate the infant's position on the nipple to avoid constant friction on the same area.

Cradle position. To use this position—the most common one—sit in a comfortable chair and rest the infant's head in the bend of your arm. You may want to place pillows under your elbow to minimize tension and fatigue. Tuck the infant's lower arm alongside your body so it stays out of the way. The infant's mouth should remain even with your nipple and the stomach should face and touch your stomach.

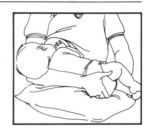

Side-lying position. You may find this position useful for night feedings or if you are recovering from a cesarean delivery. Lie on your side with your stomach facing the infant's stomach and the infant's head near your breast. Lift your breast; as the infant's mouth opens, pull the infant toward your nipple.

Football hold. This may be the most comfortable position if you have large breasts, if the infant is very small or premature, or if you have had a cesarean delivery and find other positions uncomfortable. Sit in a chair with a pillow under your arm on the nursing side. Place your hand under the infant's head and bring it close to your breast; place the fingers of your other hand above and below the nipple. As the infant's mouth opens wide, pull the head close to your breast.

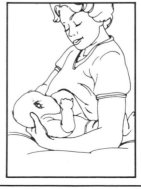

(continued)

BREAST-FEEDING YOUR INFANT *(continued)*

Removing the infant from the breast

When removing the infant from the breast to feed from the other breast or to end the feeding, you can use a special technique to minimize pulling or tension on the nipple. Place your little finger in the corner of the infant's mouth, as shown here, and release suction before pulling the infant away.

Burping your infant

You may burp your infant in any of the three positions described below. Be sure to place a cloth diaper or pad under the infant's mouth to protect your clothing from any expelled matter.

Upright position. Position the infant upright, with the head resting on your shoulder. Supporting the infant with one hand, pat or rub the infant's back with your other hand.

Across your lap. Place the infant face down across your lap. While holding the infant's head with one hand, rub or pat the infant's back with the other.

Upright on your lap. With the infant upright on your lap, hold the head from the front with one hand while patting or rubbing the back with the other hand. To help bring up air, gently rock the infant back and forth.

For a client with a nursing diagnosis of *ineffective breast-feeding related to improper positioning of the infant at the breast,* the nurse should check for common positioning mistakes, such as placing the infant so low that the neck must hyperextend to grasp the nipple or so high that the neck must flex to grasp it.

Ensuring correct infant attachment. To ensure that the infant is correctly attached on the breast and getting enough nipple tissue to suck properly, instruct the client to cup the breast with her thumb well away from the nipple and fingers. After tickling the infant's lip with the nipple to stimulate rooting, the client should wait for the infant to open the mouth wide (with the tongue pointing downward), then center the nipple in the mouth and pull the infant toward her breast. Sometimes a slight delay before bringing the infant to the breast makes the infant open the mouth wider.

Assess the infant's jaw action to confirm proper attachment. The jaws should move rhythmically (possibly accompanied by slight ear movement). Gumming jaw motions and a clicking sound signal improper attachment. The let-down reflex also confirms proper attachment. If the client lacks the experience to recognize let-down internally from the drawing sensation in the ducts, teach her to place her finger lightly across the top of her breast; with proper attachment, she will feel the drawing sensation externally with her finger.

Establishing a breast-feeding pattern. Advise the client that the infant may need to feed for at least 15 minutes on each breast at each feeding. The client should let the infant complete a feeding on one breast before offering the other (Woolridge, 1989). As milk volume adjusts to the infant's needs, the client may change this pattern several times, offering only one breast at a feeding, then offering both breasts again.

The nurse also should tell the client to expect to breast-feed every 2 to 3 hours during the day and every 4 to 5 hours at night (or sooner, if the infant awakens). On average, the neonate should feed at least once every 3 to 4 hours.

Unless feeding time is extremely long (which may indicate inadequate attachment and let-down), the client should let the infant determine the length of a feeding by continuing to breast-feed until the infant begins to release the nipple.

Encouraging night feedings. Because more prolactin is released during night feedings than day feedings, the client should breast-feed at night to take advantage of the nocturnal boost in milk production. This boost proves especially important in the early post-partal period when milk production begins. Early postpartal night feedings also give the mother added experience in handling her breasts and attaching the infant while the breasts are still relatively soft and easily manipulated. Also, increased breast-feeding frequency helps widen and stretch the lactiferous ducts, promoting breast drainage and emptying.

Helping the client cope with growth spurts. Occurring at ages 10 to 14 days, 6 weeks, 3 to 4 months, and 6 months, growth spurts seem much more noticeable in the breast-fed than the formula-fed infant. During a growth spurt, a previously satisfied infant will want to feed much more frequently. The infant's behavior — chewing on fists, crying, and settling down only for short periods — may make the client fear that her milk supply is inadequate and that the infant is malnourished. If a growth spurt coincides with the client's return to work, this may raise particular concern about milk supply.

To minimize these fears in the client with a nursing diagnosis of *anxiety related to change in infant feeding pattern secondary to a growth spurt,* point out that the breasts may take up to 48 hours to produce enough milk to meet the increased demands of a growth spurt. The required time may vary somewhat, however, depending on how efficiently the infant feeds and how the client's body responds. (For more information on helping the client deal with fears about her milk supply, see *Client teaching: Coping with fears about your milk supply.*)

Providing nipple and breast care. Usually, the breasts require no care other than daily cleaning with clear water. However, the nipples may become sore, especially during the first days of breast-feeding, necessitating special care.

Nipple soreness. Although proper infant attachment and sucking help prevent nipple soreness, some soreness is common in the first few days or weeks of breast-feeding until the nipples become more elastic. For the client with a nursing diagnosis of *potential for injury*

COPING WITH FEARS ABOUT YOUR MILK SUPPLY

While breast-feeding, you may worry that you are not producing enough milk. At times, you may even fear that your milk supply has stopped. Anxiety about adequacy of milk supply is most common during the first few days of breast-feeding and during your infant's growth spurts, which occur at ages 10 to 14 days, 6 weeks, 3 to 4 months, and 6 months. To prepare for growth spurts, mark them on your calendar so that you can build up your milk supply in advance. Also keep in mind the following points about breast milk.

- Milk supply grows in response to demand: The more milk your infant removes, the more you will produce.
- Expect to breast-feed every 2 to 3 hours while building up your milk supply.
- Use the number of wet diapers to gauge your infant's milk intake. An infant who wets 10 to 12 diapers daily is getting adequate intake.
- Do not skip feedings because that tells your body it does not need to make milk.
- Breast-feed long enough for your infant to receive the rich, more filling hindmilk—about 15 minutes on each breast in the early days.
- Rest as often as possible to increase your milk production. Especially try to rest when your infant is sleeping.
- Accept all offers of help in caring for the infant and doing household chores.
- Offer both breasts at a feeding even if your infant has lately been feeding only at one breast.
- Review your fluid and nutrient intake to ensure that your own needs are met. Remember to drink fluids each time your infant breast-feeds.
- Remember that the need to increase your milk supply during a growth spurt is only temporary.
- Motivate yourself by keeping in mind how much your infant benefits from breast-feeding.

related to improper nipple care, teach about proper infant attachment.

These measures can help relieve sore nipples:
- Apply ice compresses just before feeding (this numbs the nipples and makes them firmer and more graspable).

• Lubricate the nipples with a few drops of expressed milk before the feeding. This helps prevent tenderness as effectively as lanolin-based creams (Adcock, Burleigh and Scott-Heads, 1988). Also, such creams have come under question because of possible contamination with pesticides resulting from sheep dipping (Food and Drug Administration, 1988).

• Let the nipples air dry thoroughly after feeding to promote healing and comfort.

• Avoid applying soaps directly to the nipples when washing the breasts.

The value of antepartal nipple preparation in reducing nipple tenderness is controversial. Some breast-feeding experts do not recommend it (Lauwers and Woessner, 1989). Others have found the practice helpful (Storr, 1988).

Breast engorgement. Breast engorgement may involve excessive fullness of the breast veins or alveoli. Vascular engorgement occurs in all lactating women as blood flow to the breasts increases to prepare for breast-feeding. However, vascular engorgement commonly is confused with alveolar (milk) engorgement, which refers to alveolar overdistention with milk. Initially, vascular and alveolar engorgement may coincide.

If breast milk is insufficiently removed (as through restricted sucking time, incorrect infant attachment, or improper sucking technique), milk volume will exceed alveolar storage capacity, causing extreme discomfort. For a client with a nursing diagnosis of *pain related to breast engorgement,* encourage frequent feeding throughout the day and night in the initial days to alleviate engorgement. One study demonstrated that prophylactic breast massage after each feeding in the first 4 days after delivery also helped prevent breast engorgement (Storr, 1988).

Determine the cause of breast engorgement by assessing the client's breast-feeding technique and frequency. Suggest any necessary changes. Because milk engorgement can create serious drainage problems unless treated, teach the client what causes milk engorgement and remind her not to limit feeding time at the first breast offered in the mistaken belief that this will relieve engorgement. If the infant does not feed at the second breast, advise the client to express milk from the second breast, then offer this breast at the next feeding.

To help soften the breasts and facilitate attachment, the client with engorged breasts should express some milk gently before a feeding. Also, the client may massage her breasts after a warm shower or bath (applying mineral oil or a similar lubricant to the hands may make breast massage easier and reduce any discomfort it causes). Cold compresses applied to the breasts between feedings also may reduce discomfort, although no evidence shows that this relieves engorgement (Royal College of Midwives, 1988).

Milk expression. Milk expression by hand or pump may be indicated for a client who needs relief from breast engorgement or who is separated from the infant by infant illness or prematurity or by employment outside the home. Also, milk expression by pump helps improve graspability of flat or retracted nipples.

Hopkinson, Schanler, and Garza (1988) found that women who express their milk can improve milk volume in the early postpartal period by minimizing the interval between delivery and the start of milk expression. They also linked optimal milk production with five or more milk expressions and total pumping time exceeding 100 minutes daily.

Warn the client who has a nursing diagnosis of ***potential for infection related to improper expression and storage of breast milk*** that expressed milk probably is not sterile. Urge her to minimize bacterial contamination through frequent hand washing, aseptic handling of equipment, and aseptic transfer of her milk to storage containers (McCoy, Kadowski, Wilks, Engstrom, and Meier, 1988).

Breast pumps are available as hand-operated, battery-operated, and electric models. (For more information about expressing milk by hand and pump, see *Client teaching: Expressing your milk,* pages 148 and 149. For more information on breast pumps, see *Client teaching: Types of breast pumps,* page 150.)

Advising the client about supplemental bottles. Some health care facilities continue the outmoded, unscientific practice of giving supplemental bottled fluids to breast-feeding neonates. Besides causing nipple confusion, supplemental bottles given in the early weeks of breast-feeding may interfere with the fragile dynamics of milk supply and demand. The nurse should advise the client to avoid

(Text continues on page 151.)

EXPRESSING YOUR MILK

You may express milk when your breasts are engorged, when weaning your infant, or when you want to provide breast milk during periods of separation from your infant. Refer to the guidelines below for milk expression by hand or pump.

Expressing milk by hand

You may want to practice expressing milk by hand at a time when you feel relaxed. The illustrated steps below show the proper expression sequence. Keep in mind that you must squeeze milk from the back of the milk reservoirs forward. To push milk out of nipple openings, start the squeezing motion well behind the areola and move forward. For the final squeeze, keep your fingers behind the areola's outer edge — not on the areola or nipple.

1 Form a "U" with your fingers, as shown here, by placing your thumb above the areola and the other fingers below it.

2 While pushing your fingers away from the nipple, squeeze your thumb and fingers together.

3 Now change direction by squeezing toward the nipple.

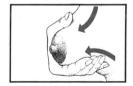

4 Rotate the thumb and fingers a quarter turn around the breast, then return to step 1 and continue until you have rotated 360 degrees around the breast.

CLIENT TEACHING —————————

EXPRESSING YOUR MILK   *(continued)*

Pumping and storing breast milk

Breast pumps generate a suck-release action via an adapter (flange) that you place over the areola. The adapter presses on milk reservoirs, pushing out milk. Available in pharmacies and maternity shops, breast pumps come in several varieties (see the illustrations). Here are some guidelines to follow when using a breast pump and storing milk.

You can begin pumping breast milk as soon after delivery as you feel well enough. (If your infant was born prematurely, you may begin pumping within 24 hours after delivery.)

First, wash your hands and gather all equipment (make sure the equipment has been thoroughly cleaned). You may want to apply warm, wet washcloths to your breasts or take a warm shower to help release the milk.

Before you begin pumping, stimulate the nipple and areola by rolling the nipple between your thumb and forefinger for a minute or two. This helps trigger the release of milk-producing hormones.

Pump each breast for at least 10 minutes every 3 to 4 hours during the day; at night, pump only if you are awake. Try to pump for a total of at least 100 minutes every 24 hours.

To obtain the most milk, switch breasts several times while pumping. For example, pump for 5 to 8 minutes on each breast, then for 3 to 5 minutes on each breast, and finally for 2 to 3 minutes on each breast.

Transfer milk from the collection bottle to a sterile container (preferably plastic) and refrigerate it immediately. Breast milk can be kept refrigerated for 24 to 48 hours before use.

For longer storage periods (up to 6 months), breast milk must be frozen. Let frozen breast milk thaw in the refrigerator or at room temperature, or set the container in warm water. However, be careful not to overheat it. Once thawed, it must be used within 24 hours. Also, it must not be refrozen.

If you must transport your milk to the hospital, store it in the refrigerator until transport time to prevent bacterial growth. (Some health care facilities may request that you freeze your milk before transporting it. Others freeze it after it arrives.)

TYPES OF BREAST PUMPS

Battery-operated pump. This pump has a battery-operated motor and can be used with one hand. Easy to clean, it is a good choice if you work outside the home or need a breast pump only for short-term use.

Electric pump. Usually used in hospitals, this pump is efficient and gentle and requires only one hand for operation. It is available as a small, 2-lb model or as a larger model about the size of a small sewing machine (the latter can be rented from a pharmacy or medical supply company).

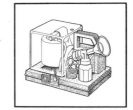

Cylinder pump. This pump has two plastic cylinders, one inside the other, that create gentle suction as you move the cylinder back and forth. Because you must use two hands to operate it, you may find it tiring. Easily cleaned and portable, this pump proves relatively efficient for short-term or intermittent use.

Rubber bulb or bicycle horn pump. To operate this pump, squeeze the rubber bulb, then release it slowly. This pump usually is not recommended because it is inefficient and tends to cause nipple and areola trauma. Also, sterility cannot be maintained because milk commonly becomes trapped inside the bulb.

giving supplemental bottles until her milk supply is well established (which typically takes 4 to 6 weeks).

Although some mothers have successfully combined breast-feeding and formula-feeding (Morse and Harrison, 1988), a client who feels she must use formula supplements should be advised to give bottles at a separate time from breast-feeding. This will disrupt the milk supply less than giving a bottle just after breast-feeding. (Parents with a family history of food allergies may wish to avoid any use of formula until the infant's gastrointestinal mucosa has matured and is less susceptible to allergic reactions.)

Ensuring adequate maternal fluid and food intake. Advise the breast-feeding client to maintain a fluid intake sufficient to keep her urine clear and amber. For a client with a nursing diagnosis of *potential fluid volume deficit related to breast-feeding,* provide fluids at each feeding. Also advise the client to restrict intake of caffeine-containing fluids because caffeine accumulates in the body and transfers to the infant in breast milk, possibly making the infant fussy in the evening.

Although many obstetricians still advise lactating women to consume 500 extra calories daily, the Royal College of Midwives (1988) now recommends that hunger — rather than a rigid caloric requirement — should guide food intake during breast-feeding.

When counseling the client with a nursing diagnosis of *altered nutrition: potential for more than body requirements, related to breast-feeding,* help her establish a well-balanced diet and assure her that she can consume any food in moderation. However, if the infant develops symptoms of food allergy, she may have to restrict some foods. The client with a family history of food allergy may need to modify her diet (ideally, modification should begin during pregnancy).

Advising the client about drug use. Almost any drug the client consumes potentially transfers to the infant through breast milk. However, the client need not necessarily stop breast-feeding during drug therapy. Instead, she should seek her physician's advice. Usually, the breast-feeding woman can safely use therapeutic doses of such drugs as analgesics, antibiotics, stool softeners, and bulk-forming laxatives. On the other hand, potent diuretics, antineoplastic drugs, stimulant laxatives, and radioactive drugs nearly always warrant temporary discontinuation of breast-feeding. Use of oral contraceptives during breast-feeding is controversial.

Promoting family support. The breast-feeding client needs practical and emotional support from those close to her. The client's partner can play an especially key role. Hewat and Ellis (1986) found that mothers of neonates view three types of support from the father as important: physical support (such as helping with housework or other children), verbal reinforcement (such as ensuring the mother that breast-feeding is progressing well), and psychological support or sensitivity to the mother's feelings.

Childbirth education groups can serve as a source of support for new parents dealing with role adjustment. For a family with a nursing diagnosis of *altered family processes related to breast-feeding,* urge the partner to provide physical support by helping the client rest when she is establishing her milk supply. Also, encourage the partner to prevent visitors from overwhelming the client in the early breast-feeding days. Further, incorporate the partner in client teaching about such topics as infant positioning and attachment and determining if the infant is getting adequate nourishment.

Grandparents also may be expected to provide support. However, many of today's grandparents formula-fed their infants and thus know little about breast-feeding. Promote grandparent involvement in breast-feeding by developing teaching materials designed specifically for them.

Encouraging cuddling and eye contact. Breast-feeding brings the infant into close contact with the mother, allowing interaction that facilitates attachment. The nurse can encourage such interaction — for example, by suggesting that the client stroke the infant during feeding (especially if the client breast-feeds while lying down, which frees both hands). If the client breast-feeds while sitting, she can make eye contact with the infant.

Breast-feeding in special situations
Few circumstances completely rule out breast-feeding. The nurse with limited exposure to special breast-feeding situations should develop contacts with such groups as the International Lactation Consultant Association (ILCA) or the LaLeche League for information or client referral.

The premature infant. Many premature infants can be breast-fed. Providing breast milk may be the only role the mother of a premature infant is permitted or able to perform; doing so may help her feel she is mothering her infant (Driscoll and Sheehan, 1985). For a client with a nursing diagnosis of *altered parenting related to infant prematurity and the mother's wish to breast-feed,* provide accurate information and ongoing support.

In North America, feeding schedules for premature infants typically are based on infant weight, gestational age, and ability to bottle-feed without signs of distress. However, none of these parameters is a research-based index of readiness to breast-feed (McCoy, Kadowski, Wilks, Engstrom, and Meier, 1988). Some data suggest that the premature infant can coordinate sucking and swallowing earlier for breast-feeding than for bottle-feeding (Meier and Pugh, 1985) and that breast-feeding creates less physiologic stress than bottle-feeding (Meier, 1988). However, most premature infants breast-feed for shorter durations than full-term neonates (Neifert and Seacat, 1988).

Besides coping with the stress of premature delivery, the client who wishes to breast-feed her premature infant but who cannot do so directly must establish and maintain a milk supply by expressing milk.

Multiple infants. Many mothers have successfully breast-fed twins and even triplets and quadruplets (Keith, McInnes, and Keith, 1982). For a client with a nursing diagnosis of *anxiety related to the ability to breast-feed multiple infants,* help instill confidence by relating these findings. However, also promote realistic expectations about the additional time needed to initiate and maintain a milk supply for multiple infants. If the client chooses to breast-feed the infants simultaneously, she may need help in positioning them. Refer her to a Parents of Twins group for support and information if the community has one.

The client with premature multiple infants may have to delay breast-feeding until the infants can tolerate it (Storr, 1989). However, if the infants were born close to term and are permitted to breast-feed, the client should keep them together while breast-feeding to accustom her to breast-feeding multiple infants (Lauwers and Woessner, 1989).

If the client wishes to breast-feed exclusively, this pattern should be initiated in the health care facility. If she plans to supplement breast-feeding with formula, however, advise her that this practice will decrease breast milk production and may create nipple confusion in the infants.

Working outside the home. The client who plans to continue breast-feeding after returning to work will need guidance and support. Although breast-feeding in this circumstance calls for extra commitment and effort, both mother and infant may reap rewards. For instance, knowing that her breast milk is meeting the infant's nutritional and immunologic needs may help ease any misgivings she has about returning to work.

The client may breast-feed at home and pump milk at work, schedule work around feeding times, or wean the infant from work-time feedings. Weaning should be done gradually to avoid adverse effects in both infant and mother. The client who wants to wean may decrease milk production by pumping only minimally, for comfort; as the demand for milk drops, so does milk production. Instruct the client to give the infant a bottle for the feeding that will be eliminated and warn her that her body will probably need several days to adjust to the elimination of each feeding.

Help the working mother devise a breast-feeding schedule that meets her individual needs, especially if she has a nursing diagnosis of *altered role performance related to the new task of breast-feeding*.

The client's work wardrobe should include clothes that can be easily unbuttoned or pulled aside to express milk to feed to the infant later. Breasts may leak in the first few weeks after she returns to work as they readjust to the new schedule. To help prevent or minimize breast leakage, the client can press against the breasts when she feels the tingling that signals let-down. Instruct her to place breast pads in her bra so that milk will not stain clothing and to change the pads frequently to avoid skin irritation from milk. She may prefer to wear patterned fabrics, which disguise milk stains better than solid colors. Taking a sweater and a spare blouse to work will avoid embarrassment caused by milk stains.

Warn the client that anxiety and fatigue caused by her return to work may reduce her milk production for a week or so. Maintaining an adequate fluid intake at work may minimize this problem.

CARE FOR THE CLIENT USING INFANT FORMULA

For the client who plans to formula-feed her infant, teaching on such topics as formula preparation can begin in the antepartal period. As with breast-feeding, initial formula-feeding experiences can prove crucial for both mother and infant. A positive first feeding experience can enhance maternal confidence and set the right tone for subsequent feedings. The nurse who observes early feedings has a unique opportunity to assess client-infant interaction and, if necessary, provide timely intervention.

Client teaching

The nurse should consider both short-term and long-term goals to anticipate guidance needed by the client who chooses formula-feeding. In the antepartal period, develop varied client teaching methods (perhaps using such items as films and books) to present current recommendations about formula-feeding. Discuss with the client specific feeding situations that might arise and plan a strategy for handling them. For example, ask the client what she would do if a friend or relative told her the infant was not eating enough or if the infant did not sleep through the night as early as a friend's did. Usually, antepartal discussion of growth spurts, of alternatives to early introduction of solid foods, and of support systems is more effective than discussion during the postpartal period, when the client may be fatigued from sleep deprivation and anxiety accompanying new parenthood.

Ensuring proper formula preparation

To teach the client about formula preparation, find out what preparation facilities and equipment will be available as well as which formula the client will use. Where water and refrigeration are readily available, rigorous sterilization practices largely have been replaced with an emphasis on cleanliness of the equipment and preparer. However, a client who lacks easy access to refrigeration and running water may have to modify preparation procedures.

Preparation methods. Four basic methods may be used to prepare infant formula.

Aseptic method. In this method, the preparer sterilizes formula equipment (including the mixing pitcher, measuring spoons, tongs, bottles, nipples, and nipple caps) by boiling it for 10 minutes. After reconstituting the formula according to manufacturer's instructions, the preparer pours the specified amount into each bottle, applies nipples and caps, and stores the bottles in the refrigerator until needed.

Terminal method. The preparer thoroughly washes the equipment and prepares the formula under clean (not sterile) conditions. After pouring reconstituted formula into bottles (with nipples and caps applied loosely), the preparer places the bottles in a pot with a tightly covered lid and boils them for 25 minutes. Once the bottles have cooled slightly, the preparer screws the caps down tightly and refrigerates them. Formula prepared by this method may take up to 2 hours to cool sufficiently to give to the infant.

One-bottle method. Using clean equipment, the preparer reconstitutes enough formula for one feeding, then pours it in a bottle. Prepared formula should be used within 30 minutes; the can containing the remaining unreconstituted formula must be refrigerated.

Clean method. With this method, an entire day's formula is prepared at one time and placed in clean bottles. The preparer reconstitutes the formula, applies clean nipples and caps, and refrigerates the bottles immediately.

General principles. Some common principles are basic to all formula preparation methods. The preparer must use good hand-washing technique – a point to reinforce frequently. Also, before opening the can, the preparer should wash the can opener and the top of the formula can with soap and water.

Prepared formula should be used within 24 hours (or 30 minutes with the one-bottle method). Opened formula cans should be covered with plastic or foil and refrigerated. Equipment used in formula preparation may be cleaned in an automatic dishwasher (providing the temperature reaches 140° F) or in warm, soapy water. However, latex nipples cleaned in a dishwasher may need to be replaced frequently because repeated exposure to heat weakens them. Instruct the client to place latex nipples in a covered basket in the dishwasher to prevent their displacement to the heating element, where they could melt. Also instruct the client to inspect nipples regularly to ensure that no milk particles block the opening, forming a bacterial breeding ground.

Giving the first feeding

No research-based guidelines support delaying formula-feeding. Nonetheless, in many health care facilities, the first feeding is given when the neonate is about 4 hours old. In other facilities, it is given when physiologic and behavioral cues suggest the neonate is ready to feed. Such cues include active bowel sounds, lack of abdominal distention, and sucking and rooting responses to stimulation of the lips. Neonates fed according to these cues are less likely to gag during the first feeding because their sucking and rooting responses are active. In some health care facilities, a nurse — rather than the mother — gives the first bottle (usually sterile water). However, this practice is based on tradition rather than research.

Helping the client with early feedings

Contrary to popular belief, the client using infant formula may require help with early feedings, especially if she has a nursing diagnosis of *knowledge deficit related to formula-feeding*.

Provide comfort measures (such as encouraging voiding and administering an analgesic, if prescribed) and have the client wash her hands before preparing the formula and feeding the infant. Then, help the client to a comfortable position with good back support and instruct her to hold the infant close to her in a semi-reclining position, with the bottle tilted so that the nipple always is filled with formula. This position minimizes air swallowing and permits air to rise to the top of the infant's stomach.

Some neonates will take an artificial nipple into the mouth readily; others must be coaxed. Instruct the client to stroke the infant's lips gently with the nipple; usually, this causes the mouth to open wide enough for nipple insertion. The first-time mother may be reluctant to place more than the tip of the nipple in the infant's mouth; urge her to insert the nipple further to trigger the sucking reflex.

Instruct the client to check nipple openings by holding the bottle upside down and noting whether formula drips freely from the nipple. (Formula that runs in a continuous stream is flowing too quickly.) The client can assume that nipple openings are the correct size if feedings take roughly 15 to 20 minutes — long enough to meet the infant's nutritional needs without causing fatigue. Warn the client to discard any formula left in the bottle at the end of a feeding because of the risk of bacterial contamination.

Most health care facilities use glass bottles with standard latex nipples; when the infant sucks, air bubbles may appear in these bottles, indicating that the infant is obtaining milk. However, point out that at home, the client may use a feeding system with a collapsible bag in which she cannot see air bubbles move. Instead, she should watch for the bag to collapse gradually — as a sign that the infant is obtaining formula.

Ensuring good burping technique. The infant should be burped after every ounce of formula and again at the end of the feeding. Burping can be done in three positions — upright, across the lap, or upright on the lap. Because a neonate's cardiac sphincter does not function fully, the infant may expel milk along with air; a towel or cloth diaper placed in front of the infant will protect the client's clothing.

Helping the client establish a feeding pattern. Like the breast-fed infant, the formula-fed infant should be fed on a flexible demand schedule, not a rigid regimen. The formula-fed infant may awaken for feedings as often as every 2 hours or as infrequently as every 5 hours; many feed satisfactorily on a 3- or 4-hour schedule. If the client worries that the infant is not getting enough nourishment, explain that the initial feeding pattern does not necessarily indicate the pattern that will emerge later.

Promoting physical contact. Although formula-feeding allows less intimate contact than breast-feeding, it still provides an opportunity to cuddle the infant. Encourage the client to make eye contact and to vocalize with the infant during feeding.

Encouraging family support. A commonly cited benefit of formula-feeding is that it allows other family members to help with feedings. This help can be particularly valuable if the mother is fatigued. However, encourage family members to do such chores as preparing formula and cleaning formula equipment rather than insisting on giving the infant the bottle — an activity the mother may find relaxing. Siblings may or may not want to assist with feedings; parents should let them decide for themselves, especially in the early feeding days.

For the client with a nursing diagnosis of *altered family processes related to infant feeding,* discuss how to spend adequate time with the infant while obtaining help for more tiring chores.

EVALUATION

Evaluation findings should be stated in terms of actions performed or outcomes achieved for each goal. The following examples illustrate appropriate evaluation statements for the breast-feeding client:
• The client demonstrated appropriate techniques for attaching the infant to the breast.
• The client showed no signs of breast problems, such as sore nipples or excessive engorgement.
• The client expressed an understanding of breast-feeding dynamics.
• The client expressed confidence in her ability to seek help for breast-feeding problems.

The following examples illustrate appropriate evaluation statements for the client who uses infant formula:
• The client expressed an understanding of formula preparation and feeding techniques.
• The client maintained close contact with the neonate during feeding.
• The client expressed confidence in her ability to seek support for feeding problems.

Objective infant criteria include hydration status and weight-gain pattern.

DOCUMENTATION

When assisting a client with breast-feeding, include the following points in the documentation:
• maternal vital signs
• maternal fluid intake and output
• maternal position and comfort level during feeding
• maternal understanding of breast-feeding technique

• maternal understanding of proper infant positioning and ability to achieve proper positioning
• maternal attitude toward breast-feeding
• maternal understanding of dietary needs and breast care
• condition of the nipples and breasts
• infant sucking ability.

When assisting a client with formula-feeding, include the following points in the documentation:
• maternal vital signs
• maternal comfort level when feeding the infant
• maternal understanding of formula preparation
• maternal understanding of normal infant feeding patterns, including amount of formula taken and feeding frequency
• infant sucking ability.

BIBLIOGRAPHY

Health and Welfare, Canada. (1986). Feeding babies: A counselling guide on practical solutions to common infant feeding questions. Minister of Supply and Services, Canada.

Morse, J., and Harrison, M. (1988). Patterns of mixed feeding. *Midwifery,* 4(1), 19-23.

Myres, A. (1988). Tradition and technology in infant feeding — achieving the best of both worlds. *Canadian Journal of Public Health,* 79(2), 78-80.

Seeley, R., Stephens, T., and Tate, P. (1989). *Anatomy and physiology.* Redwood City, CA: Benjamin-Cummings.

Shapiro, A., Jacobson, L., Armon, M., Manco-Johnson, M., Hulac, P., Lane, P., and Hathaway, W. (1986). Vitamin K deficiency in the newborn infant: Prevalence and perinatal risk factors. *Journal of Pediatrics,* 109(4), 675-680.

Tanaka, P., Yeung, D., and Anderson, G. H. (1987). Infant feeding practices: 1984-85 versus 1977-78. *Canadian Medical Association Journal,* 136(9), 940-944.

Winikoff, B., Laukaran, V., Myers, S., and Stone, R. (1986). Dynamics of feeding: Mothers, professionals, and the institutional context in a large urban hospital. *Pediatrics,* 77(3), 357-365.

World Health Organization (1981). International code of marketing of breast-milk substitutes. *WHO Chronicle,* 35, 112-117.

Wright, P. (1987). Hunger, satiety and feeding behavior in early infancy. In R. Boakes, D. Popplewell, and M. Burton (Eds.), *Eating habits, food, physiology and learned behavior* (pp. 75-106). New York: Wiley.

Breast-feeding

Adcock, A., Burleigh, A., and Scott-Heads (1988). Hind milk as an effective topical application in nipple care in the post-partum period. *Breastfeeding Review,* 13, Abstract 68.

American Academy of Pediatrics (1978). Breast-feeding. *Pediatrics,* 62, 591-601.

Baer, E. (1981). Promoting breastfeeding: A national responsibility. *Studies in Family Planning,* 12, 198-206.

Canadian Pediatric Society (1978). Breast-feeding: What is left besides the poetry? *Canadian Journal of Public Health,* 69, 13-20.

Casey, C., and Hambridge, K. (1983). Nutritional aspects of human lactation. In M. Neville and M. Neifert (Eds.), *Lactation physiology, nutrition and breast-feeding* (pp. 199-248). New York: Plenum.

Cunningham, A. (1988). Studies of breastfeeding and infections. How good is the evidence? *Journal of Human Lactation,* 4, 54-56.

Driscoll, J., and Sheehan, C. (1985). Breast-feeding and premature babies: Guidelines for nurses. *Neonatal Network,* 5(1), 18-24.

Food and Drug Administration. (1988, September 13). Lanolin contaminated with pesticides. Talk paper. (T-88-66).

Glasier, A., McNeilly, A., and Howie, P. (1984). The prolactin response to suckling. *Clinical Endocrinology,* 21(2), 109-116.

Hopkinson, J., Schanler, R., and Garza, C. (1988). Milk production by mothers of premature infants. *Pediatrics,* 81(6), 815-820.

Humenick, S. (1987). The clinical significance of breast milk maturation rates. *Birth,* 14, 174-181.

Jones, D., and West, R. (1985). Lactation nurse increases duration of breast-feeding. *Archives of Disease in Childhood,* 60(8), 772-774.

Keith, D., McInnes, S., and Keith, L. (1982). *Breastfeeding twins, triplets and quadruplets: 195 practical hints for success.* Chicago: Center for the Study of Multiple Birth.

Klaus, M. (1987). The frequency of suckling: A neglected but essential ingredient of breast-feeding. *Obstetrics and Gynecology Clinics of North America,* 14(3), 623-633.

Lauwers, J., and Woessner, C. (1989). *Counselling the nursing mother* (2nd ed.). Wayne, NJ: Avery.

Lawrence, R. (1989). *Breastfeeding – a guide for the medical profession* (3rd ed.). St. Louis: Mosby.

Leventhal, J., Shapiro, E., Aten, C., Berg, A., and Egerter, S. (1986). Does breast-feeding protect against infections in infants less than 3 months of age? *Pediatrics,* 78, 896-903.

Meier, P., and Pugh, E. (1985). Breastfeeding behavior of small preterm infants. *MCN,* 10(6), 396-401.

Myres, A., Watson, J., and Harrison, C. (1981). The national breast-feeding promotion program 1. professional phase – a note on its development, distribution and impact. *Canadian Journal of Public Health,* 72, 307-311.

Neifert, M., and Seacat, J. (1988). Practical aspects of breast-feeding the premature infant. *Perinatology-Neonatology,* 12(1), 24-31.

Neville, M. (1983). Regulation of mammary development and lactation. In M. Neville and M. Neifert (Eds.), *Lactation physiology, nutrition and breast-feeding* (pp. 103-140). New York: Plenum.

Newman, J. (1986). Breast-feeding: The problem of 'not enough milk'. *Canadian Family Physician,* 32, 571-574.

Royal College of Midwives. (1988). *Successful breastfeeding – a practical guide for midwives.* Oxford: Holywell Press.

Smith, W., Erenberg, A., and Nowak, A. (1988). Imaging evaluation of the human nipple during breast-feeding. *American Journal of Diseases in Children,* 142(1), 76-78.

Storr, G.B. (1989). Breastfeeding premature triplets — one woman's experience. *Journal of Human Lactation,* 5(2), 74-77.

U.S. Department of Health and Human Services. (1984). *Report on the surgeon general's workshop on breastfeeding and human lactation* (DDHS Publication No. HRS-D-MC 84-2). Washington, DC: U.S. Government Printing Office.

Weber, F., Woolridge, M., and Baum, J. (1986). An ultrasonographic study of the organization of sucking and swallowing by newborn infants. *Developmental Medicine & Child Neurology,* 28(1), 19-24.

Woolridge, M. (1986). The anatomy of infant sucking. *Midwifery,* 2(4), 164-171.

Woolridge, M. (1989, July 8). The physiology of suckling and milk transfer. Paper presented at ILCA Conference, Toronto.

Formula-feeding

Fomon, S. (1987). Reflections on infant feeding in the 1970s and 1980s. *American Journal of Clinical Nutrition,* 46, 171-82.

Jason, J., Nieburg, P., and Marks, J. (1984). Mortality and infectious disease associated with infant-feeding practices in developing countries. *Pediatrics,* 74 (4, Pt. 2), 702-727.

Kovar, M., Serdula, M., Marks, J., and Fraser, D. (1984). Review of epidemiologic evidence for an association between infant feeding and infant health. *Pediatrics,* 74 (4, Pt. 2), 615-638.

Kramer, M. (1988). Infant feeding, infection and public health. *Pediatrics,* 81(1), 164-166.

Cultural references

Armstrong, H. (1987). Breastfeeding and low birth weight babies: Advances in Kenya. *Journal of Human Lactation,* 3, 34-37.

Gabriel, A., Gabriel, K. R., and Lawrence, R. (1986). Cultural values and biomedical knowledge: Choices in infant feeding. *Social Science and Medicine,* 23(5), 501-509.

Nursing research

Hewat, R., and Ellis, D. (1986). Similarities and differences between women who breastfeed for short and long duration. *Midwifery,* 2(1), 37-43.

Hewat, R., and Ellis, D. (1987). A comparison of the effectiveness of two methods of nipple care. *Birth,* 14(1), 41-45.

Jones, D., West, R., and Newcombe, R. (1986). Maternal characteristics associated with duration of breast-feeding. *Midwifery,* 2(3), 141-146.

McCoy, R., Kadowski, C., Wilks, S., Engstrom, J., and Meier, P. (1988). Nursing management of breastfeeding for preterm infants. *Journal of Perinatal Neonatal Nursing,* 2(1), 42-55.

Meier, P. (1988). Bottle and breast feeding: Effects on transcutaneous oxygen pressure and temperature in small preterm infants. *Nursing Research,* 37(1), 36-41.

Storr, G.B. (1988). Prevention of nipple tenderness and breast engorgement in the postpartal period. *JOGNN,* 17(3), 203-209.

High-Risk Neonates

The high-risk neonate is one who has an increased chance of dying during or shortly after delivery or who has a congenital or perinatal problem necessitating prompt intervention. As medicine continues to develop more treatments for perinatal problems, many high-risk neonates who formerly would have died after mere hours or days now survive; many have few or no residual effects of the crisis that marked their first hours after birth.

NEONATAL INTENSIVE CARE

Many high-risk neonates require care in a neonatal intensive care unit (NICU). Besides a highly skilled, round-the-clock medical and nursing staff, the NICU offers full life-support, resuscitation, and monitoring equipment and extensive ancillary support staff and services.

REGIONALIZATION OF CARE

To ensure the highest quality of care for high-risk neonates, the American Academy of Pediatrics (1988) has established a system of "leveled" regionalized care in which a neonate is referred to the facility with the most appropriate staff and equipment to manage the neonate's specific problems. Ideally, regionalized care allows the most efficient use of resources by eliminating the need for all facilities to acquire the expensive equipment and staff for an NICU.

Every hospital in the United States is assigned to a region and classified according to the level of neonatal care provided. Level 1 care (as in the normal neonatal nursery) is most appropriate for uncomplicated deliveries; level 2 care, for neonates with mild to moderate problems; level 3 (NICU) care, for more serious problems.

Some neonatal care regions cross state lines; others include only a portion of a single state. Based on their needs and interdependence, facilities within each region are clustered to form referral networks. Within each region, one facility (or, in some cases, two) is designated as a regional referral center (a level 3 facility). Depending on the specific problems involved, a high-risk neonate who is delivered at a level 1 facility will be transported to a level 2 or level 3 facility.

Obstetric facilities also are classified according to the level of care provided; in some cases, this means that a mother may be cared for in a different facility than her neonate. For example, when no perinatal problems are anticipated, a woman may deliver in a level 1 obstetric facility with a level 1 nursery; if her neonate develops unexpected problems, he or she will require transport to a level 3 neonatal facility. (When a high-risk delivery is anticipated, however, the mother may be transported before delivery to a facility with level 3 neonatal care so that she and her neonate can be together.)

Sometimes a neonate is returned to the referring facility after treatment in a regional center; this is referred to as reverse transport. Candidates for reverse transport include neonates in whom the problem has resolved completely or neonates who have recovered sufficiently to be managed by the referring facility. Benefits of reverse transport include a decrease in the level 3 neonatal population and, in many cases, closer proximity to the family.

GOALS OF NEONATAL INTENSIVE CARE

The goals of neonatal intensive care include averting or minimizing complications, subjecting the neonate to as little stress as possible, and furthering parent-infant bonding. To achieve these goals, the NICU staff:
- anticipates, prevents, and detects potential or actual perinatal problems
- intervenes early for identified problems
- carries out care procedures in a way that minimizes disturbance to the neonate
- uses a family-centered approach.

ETHICAL AND LEGAL ISSUES

As treatment advances increase the survival odds for high-risk neonates, debate over various ethical and legal issues grows. Economic factors are intertwined with these issues; as the financial burden of providing medical care for high-risk neonates increases, economic considerations may influence the treatment measures used for a particular neonate.

Resuscitation and life-support decisions

A major ethical and legal dilemma centers on which neonates should be resuscitated — specifically, the gestational age limit below which delivery room resuscitation or other aggressive measures should not be attempted. For example, before 23 weeks' gestation, the respiratory system is too immature to sustain extrauterine survival; thus, some care providers may forgo aggressive measures for a neonate born before this time. Most clinicians use 24 weeks' gestation as the cut-off point because the distance between the fetus's alveoli and arterial capillaries makes gas exchange — and thus extrauterine survival — difficult before this time. However, in some cases, fetal stress (for instance, from intrauterine growth retardation and certain other conditions) stimulates respiratory development, making extrauterine survival possible and increasing the chance that resuscitation will succeed.

Other specific topics of debate are the number of rounds of resuscitative drugs to administer and the circumstances that warrant ventilatory support and experimental therapies. Some facilities have protocols to address these issues; others rely on physicians to make judgments in individual cases.

A closely related issue concerns the "Do not resuscitate" order, which specifies the circumstances under which life support can be withheld legally. In some states, technological support may be discontinued when well-documented evidence strongly suggests that the neonate's condition will not improve. Other states require evidence that supports the poor prognosis, including a flat electroencephalogram for 24 hours in the absence of drugs that depress the central nervous system (CNS).

Quality-of-life considerations

Quality of life becomes a consideration for some high-risk neonates. Many congenital anomalies, for instance, can be corrected by surgery; however, the child may be left with serious disabilities that necessitate costly, lifelong care. For example, neonates with meningomyelocele, a congenital neurologic anomaly, may suffer paralysis despite surgery. In some cases, the physician or parents may believe that the poor quality of life that awaits the child justifies withholding treatment; the expense of lifelong care is a complicating issue.

Decision-making power

Further clouding such dilemmas is the question of who should make care decisions for a neonate. For instance, the choice to allow a severely disabled neonate to die formerly was left mainly to the parents. Now, however, the child's rights sometimes are weighed against the parents'. If caregivers believe that the parents are acting in their own best interests rather than the child's, they may ask the courts to remove the parents as legal guardians. As technology advances, decision making becomes increasingly complex.

PERINATAL PROBLEMS

The most common problems seen in NICUs are prematurity and its sequelae, congenital heart defects, and congenital anomalies requiring emergency surgery (such as omphalocele and tracheoesophageal fistula).

GESTATIONAL-AGE AND BIRTH-WEIGHT VARIATIONS

Variations of gestational age (prematurity and postmaturity) and birth weight (small or large size for gestational age) predispose the neonate to various problems. (For information on the causes and consequences of these variations, see *Gestational-age variations,* pages 168 to 170, and *Birth-weight variations,* pages 171 to 174.)

RESPIRATORY PROBLEMS

In utero, the placenta supplies oxygen to body tissues; the respiratory arterioles remain partially closed so that blood is diverted through the ductus arteriosus and away from the lungs. At birth, the neonate's lungs must take over the task of providing oxygen for body tissues. For this to happen, lung fluid must be replaced by air and the arterioles must dilate to allow more blood into the lungs. The healthy neonate accomplishes this within seconds.

However, some neonates have trouble initiating respirations or develop respiratory distress after breathing is established. For instance, problems may arise if fluid remains in the lungs or if the

(Text continues on page 170.)

GESTATIONAL-AGE VARIATIONS

Birth before or after full-term gestation markedly increases the risk of perinatal problems. In the past 25 years, advances in research and technology have improved the survival rate dramatically for neonates with gestational-age variations—even extremely preterm neonates.

Preterm neonate

The preterm neonate—the classic high-risk neonate—is one born before completion of week 37 of gestation. The risks of preterm birth and the associated economic burden are tremendous. Neonatal mortality and morbidity are highest among preterm neonates; each day of prematurity can represent thousands of dollars in medical care and significantly reduces the chance for a positive outcome.

Delivery of a preterm neonate is more likely with any of the following maternal conditions:

- age extreme (under 19 or over 34)
- low socioeconomic status
- poor nutritional status
- poor prenatal care
- exposure to known teratogens (including drugs, alcohol, cigarette smoke, and hazardous chemicals)
- chronic disease (such as cardiovascular disease, renal disease, or diabetes mellitus)
- antepartal trauma, infection, or pregnancy-induced hypertension
- uterine anomalies or cervical incompetency
- a history of previous preterm delivery.

Other predisposing factors include more than one fetus, hydramnios (excessive amniotic fluid), fetal infection, premature rupture of the membranes, abruptio placentae, and placenta previa.

Perinatal problems. General immaturity can lead to dysfunction in any organ or body system. Thus, the preterm neonate risks a wide range of problems, including respiratory distress syndrome, apnea, bronchopulmonary dysplasia, patent ductus arteriosus, ineffective thermoregulation, hypoglycemia, intraventricular hemorrhage, gastrointestinal dysfunction, retinopathy, hyperbilirubinemia, and infection. The preterm neonate also may suffer ineffective development from the effects of intensive medical treatment (such as sensory overload and environmental stress); an immature central nervous system compounds this risk. Also, mother-infant bonding may be jeopardized. (The pathophysiology, assessment, and treatment of the problems listed above are discussed in detail throughout this chapter.)

Postterm neonate

The postterm neonate is one whose gestation exceed 294 days or 42 weeks. Typically, the neonate's weight falls above the ninetieth percentile on the Colorado intrauterine growth chart (discussed in Chapter 2, Neonatal Assessment).

GESTATIONAL-AGE VARIATIONS *(continued)*

Perinatal problems. Problems associated with postmaturity include fetal dysmaturity syndrome, asphyxia, meconium aspiration, polycythemia, hypothermia, and birth trauma (Fanaroff and Martin, 1987).

Fetal dysmaturity syndrome. Some 20% to 40% of post-term neonates experience placental insufficiency leading to fetal dysmaturity syndrome and a diagnosis of small for gestational age (SGA). After 280 days of gestation, the risk of placental insufficiency, fetal growth retardation, and chronic hypoxia increases. Fetal weight plateaus around the term date until week 42 (typically from placental lesion formation and decreased placental weight), then drops rapidly. Placental dysfunction after week 42 impairs fetal oxygenation and nutrition and exhausts placental reserves, retarding fetal growth (Resnick, 1989).

Fetal dysmaturity occurs in three forms: chronic, acute, and subacute placental insufficiency. Each form has distinctive manifestations. With *chronic placental insufficiency,* no meconium staining occurs but the neonate appears malnourished, with skin defects and an apprehensive look reflecting hypoxia. *Acute placental insufficiency* leads to a malnourished and apprehensive appearance and green meconium staining of the skin, umbilical cord, and placental membranes. With *subacute placental insufficiency,* the skin and nails are stained bright yellow (from breakdown of green-bile meconium stain), and the umbilical cord, placenta, and placental membranes may be stained greenish brown (Vorherr, 1975).

Asphyxia and meconium aspiration. The postterm neonate has a high risk of birth asphyxia and meconium aspiration. Usher, Boyd, McLean, and Kramer (1988) found that meconium release (defecation) occurs twice as frequently and meconium aspiration syndrome eight times as frequently in postterm neonates than in other neonates. Some researchers suggest that the postterm fetus reacts more dramatically than the term fetus to episodes of asphyxia, experiencing fetal heart abnormalities, gasping, and meconium release.

Oligohydramnios (presence of less than 300 ml of amniotic fluid at term) increases the risk of asphyxia and aspiration by making meconium less diluted and thus unusually thick (Eden, Seifert, Winegar, and Spellacy, 1987). Normally, amniotic fluid volume peaks at 1,000 to 1,200 ml at about 38 weeks' gestation, then decreases rapidly. By week 42, it drops to approximately 300 ml; further decreases occur at 43 and 44 weeks. In the neonate with no congenital anomalies, oligohydramnios confirms postmaturity and has been linked to fetal decelerations (as shown on fetal monitoring strips), bradycardia, or both (Phelan, Plah, Yeh, Broussard, and Paul, 1985).

Other perinatal problems. Intrauterine hypoxia in the postterm fetus may trigger increased red blood cell production, causing polycythemia, which in turn may lead to sluggish perfusion and complications associated with hyperviscosity. Subcutaneous fat deficiency caused by skin wasting predisposes the postterm neonate to hypothermia, despite a

(continued)

GESTATIONAL-AGE VARIATIONS *(continued)*

mature thermoregulatory system. Thus, a postterm neonate exposed to cold stress may develop respiratory compromise and hypoglycemia (Fanaroff and Martin, 1987).

Delivery complications. The risk of delivery complications increases after 280 days (40 weeks) of gestation. Excessive size may cause a dysfunctional labor and shoulder dystocia, possibly necessitating cesarean delivery. Because of maternal uterine inefficiency and cephalopelvic disproportion, postterm neonates have a higher-than-average rate of surgical deliveries (Boyd, Usher, McLean, and Kramer, 1988).

blood perfusion of the lungs does not increase; neonates with apnea at birth or a weak respiratory effort (from such conditions as prematurity, asphyxia, or maternal anesthesia) are predisposed to respiratory distress.

Asphyxia and apnea

Asphyxia may occur late in gestation or during delivery. Chemically, this condition is defined as insufficient oxygen in the blood (hypoxemia), excessive carbon dioxide in the blood, and a decreased blood pH. As carbon dioxide accumulates, respiratory acidosis occurs; poor tissue oxygenation leads to buildup of lactic acid, resulting in metabolic acidosis. If hypoxia is prolonged, the foramen ovale and ductus arteriosus — fetal shunts that normally close shortly after delivery — may reopen. This causes a return to fetal circulatory pathways to maintain circulation to the heart and brain.

Asphyxia causes rapid breathing at first. If asphyxia continues, apnea (absence of respirations) ensues, respiratory movements cease, and the heart rate starts to drop. Deep, gasping respirations then begin, the heart rate continues to fall, and blood pressure drops. Respirations weaken progressively until they stop altogether. Because hypoxemia and acidosis cause arteriolar constriction, lung perfusion is poor; consequently, the body cannot be oxygenated.

Without immediate resuscitation, the neonate will die. Complications of prolonged asphyxia include cerebral hypoxia, seizures, intraventricular hemorrhage (IVH), renal failure, necrotizing enterocolitis (NEC), and metabolic imbalances.

(Text continues on page 174.)

BIRTH-WEIGHT VARIATIONS

Like the neonate with a gestational-age variation, one whose weight is inappropriate for the estimated gestational age is at high risk for perinatal problems.

Small-for-gestational-age (SGA) neonate

The SGA neonate is one whose birth weight falls below the tenth percentile for gestational age. SGA status results from intrauterine growth retardation (IUGR), an abnormal process in which fetal development and maturation are delayed or impeded. After prematurity, IUGR is the leading cause of death during the perinatal period (Cassady and Strange, 1987).

Causes of IUGR. IUGR may result from maternal conditions, genetic factors (for example, trisomies), fetal and placental abnormalities, infection, fetal malnutrition caused by placental insufficiency, or exposure to such teratogens as drugs and alcohol.

Maternal conditions. The most common causes of IUGR are maternal conditions that reduce uteroplacental perfusion, such as toxemia, chronic hypertensive vascular disease, and renovascular and cardiac disorders. Maternal hypertension, smoking, renal disease, and diabetes mellitus that progresses to renovascular compromise also can result in IUGR. Ounsted, Moar, and Scott (1985) estimate that the SGA incidence could be reduced by 60% by eliminating such risk factors as smoking and hypertensive disorders.

During early pregnancy, smoking is the most important risk factor for IUGR. Typically, the neonate of a woman who smokes weighs 150 to 200 g less than other neonates. Fetal hypoxia, carbon monoxide poisoning of hemoglobin, and the vascular effects of nicotine have been suggested as smoking-related factors that contribute to IUGR.

The role of maternal nutrition in fetal growth remains unclear. Some researchers minimize its importance while others emphasize it. Those who minimize it point out that despite the high incidence of infertility and spontaneous abortion during famines and wars, only severe maternal starvation during the last trimester has reduced birth weight.

Fetal and placental abnormalities. IUGR can result from infarction, hemangiomas, aberrant cord insertion, single umbilical artery, and umbilical vascular thrombosis. Premature placental separation and other conditions that diminish placental surface area and thus decrease fetal-placental exchange capability also may cause IUGR.

Placental insufficiency. Placental insufficiency is the inadequate or improper functioning of the placenta, leading to a compromised intrauterine environment. Causes of placental insufficiency include systemic diseases (such as diabetes mellitus and infection) and placental abnormalities that impair fetal circulation and compromise fetal nutrition and oxygenation (such as abnormal placental implantation, abnormal cord attachment, and placental membrane abnormalities). Although placental insufficiency is most common in the postterm period, it may occur at

(continued)

BIRTH WEIGHT VARIATIONS *(continued)*

any time during gestation. The severity of IUGR arising from placental insufficiency depends on the duration of fetal distress.

Exposure to drugs and alcohol. Maternal use of heroin, cocaine, and methadone significantly reduces the neonate's weight, length, and head circumference at birth (Chasnoff, Bussey, Savich, and Stack, 1986). The neonate of a heroin-addicted mother, for instance, typically is SGA, preterm, and weighs less than 2,500 g. Maternal alcohol consumption may cause fetal alcohol syndrome (FAS). Some neonates show severe manifestations whereas others appear normal. Besides mental retardation — the most serious and common effect — FAS may reduce the neonate's weight and length at birth (Wright, 1986).

Perinatal problems. Although the SGA neonate may avoid the problems stemming from organ system immaturity seen in the preterm neonate, other perinatal problems may arise.

Asphyxia and meconium aspiration. The SGA neonate who suffered placental insufficiency risks asphyxiation during labor and delivery, as the flow of oxygen and nutrients slows and uterine contractions reduce placental perfusion. Also, the neonate may aspirate meconium that has entered the amniotic sac. Respiratory distress, cyanosis, pulmonary air trapping, pneumothorax, and pulmonary hypertension may result, along with severe asphyxia and cerebral hypoxia (Fanaroff and Martin, 1987).

Organ size variations. Relative to body weight, the SGA neonate has a larger brain and heart than the preterm neonate but smaller adrenal glands and a smaller liver, spleen, thymus, and placenta.

Hematologic and metabolic problems. The SGA neonate may experience hematologic changes from chronic fetal hypoxia, a condition that triggers compensation through increases in red blood cell (RBC) volume (polycythemia) and erythropoietin levels. Polycythemia, in turn, may cause hyperviscosity and sluggish microcirculation perfusion.

Disturbed carbohydrate metabolism and inefficient hepatic gluconeogenesis and glycogenolysis may lead to hypoglycemia. With increased energy requirements but inadequate glycogen and fat reserves, the SGA neonate is predisposed to hypoglycemia (Lubchenco and Koops, 1987). A stressful labor may further deplete already deficient energy reserves.

Long-term problems. An SGA neonate later may suffer developmental, immunologic, and neurologic problems.

Slowed growth and immunologic deficiencies. Growth rate depends on when IUGR occurred and how long it lasted. Commonly, the child who was SGA at birth remains slimmer and shorter than other children of the same gestational age or birth weight. The rate of catch-up growth depends on causative factors and postnatal events. Head growth may equal or exceed weight and height increases.

BIRTH WEIGHT VARIATIONS *(continued)*

Impaired fetal skeletal growth may contribute to delayed tooth eruption and enamel hypoplasia. Severely growth-retarded neonates also have an increased incidence of infection, possibly from immunologic deficiency.

Neurologic impairment. IUGR-induced brain damage and its potential effect on neurologic development remains a major medical concern. Most investigators believe IUGR has more serious neurologic consequences in the preterm than the term SGA neonate. Follow-up evaluations in children who experienced IUGR in utero have revealed defects in speech and language comprehension; outcome studies have described hyperactivity, short attention span, poor fine-motor coordination, hyperreflexia, and learning problems. Stunted growth and delayed intellectual or neurologic development were found in children who experienced both short and long periods of IUGR. Other factors that worsen the neurologic prognosis include male sex and low socioeconomic status, regardless of the severity of compromise (Teberg, Walther, and Pena, 1988).

Large-for-gestational-age (LGA) neonate

The LGA neonate is one whose birth weight exceeds the ninetieth percentile for gestational age. A neonate delivered at term is considered to be LGA if the birth weight exceeds 4,000 g (8 lb, 13 oz). The leading cause of LGA status is maternal diabetes mellitus.

Traditionally, the large neonate was considered a healthy one. However, clinicians now know that the accelerated intrauterine growth of the LGA fetus poses a threat to both mother and neonate during delivery and increases the risk of complications and death in the early neonatal period.

Intrapartal problems. When the membranes rupture, large fetal size and possible high station may result in umbilical cord prolapse. Uterine overdistention from an LGA fetus increases the risk of premature labor. Usually, the physician will initiate labor and delivery before term (once fetal lung maturity has been confirmed) because of the high incidence of unexplained death among term LGA fetuses. If the mother has an adequate pelvis, the physician typically administers oxytocin to induce labor; otherwise, cesarean delivery may be necessary. Shoulder dystocia stemming from cephalopelvic disproportion also may necessitate cesarean delivery, with all the inherent risks.

During vaginal delivery, the neonate's large size may cause birth injury, such as clavicular fracture resulting from shoulder dystocia, skull fracture from increased head size, or other traumatic head injuries (such as cephalhematomas, facial nerve damage, and intracranial bleeding). A difficult delivery also may lead to phrenic nerve damage or brachial plexus palsy.

(continued)

BIRTH WEIGHT VARIATIONS *(continued)*

Perinatal problems. If the mother is diabetic, the neonate may suffer hypocalcemia (possibly from depressed parathyroid function), hypoglycemia (from maternal hyperglycemia that stimulates fetal hyperinsulinism), and polycythemia (from RBC overproduction). Other problems associated with excessive size include congenital anomalies (such as transposition of the great vessels), erythroblastosis fetalis (hemolytic anemia), and Beckwith's syndrome (a hereditary disorder associated with neonatal hypoglycemia and hyperinsulinemia).

If the mother had postconceptional bleeding causing an error in the calculated delivery date, the LGA neonate may be delivered postterm and thus experience respiratory distress from meconium aspiration or intrauterine asphyxiation. The LGA neonate delivered before term to prevent fetal death or intrapartal complications of excessive size may suffer respiratory distress syndrome, hyperbilirubinemia, and other problems linked to prematurity.

Several days after delivery, apneic episodes (cessation of breathing for more than 15 seconds) are common among preterm neonates, many of whom have irregular respiratory patterns from neuronal immaturity. Such episodes may result from acidosis, anemia, hypoglycemia, hyperglycemia, hypothermia, hyperthermia, patent ductus arteriosus (PDA), abdominal distention, regurgitation, sepsis, or IVH. Central apnea (caused by insufficient neural impulses from the respiratory center) and obstructive apnea (resulting from upper airway obstruction) also occur in some preterm and low-birth-weight neonates.

Meconium aspiration syndrome

A lung inflammation, meconium aspiration syndrome (MAS) results from aspiration of meconium-stained amniotic fluid in utero or as the neonate takes the first few breaths after delivery. Meconium staining of amniotic fluid results from fetal asphyxia: In response to asphyxia, intestinal peristalsis increases, the anal sphincter relaxes, and meconium enters the amniotic fluid.

As meconium obstructs the bronchi and bronchioles, it creates a ball-valve effect: Air can enter but not exit the bronchi and bronchioles because meconium acts as a ball, plugging the alveolar sac. Alveoli then become overdistended; pneumothorax, bacterial pneumonia, or pulmonary hypertension may develop secondarily.

Respiratory distress syndrome

Respiratory distress syndrome (RDS; also called hyaline membrane disease) is characterized by respiratory distress and impaired gas exchange. RDS affects mainly preterm neonates, who have highly pliable and easily overinflated thoracic muscles, weak intercostal muscles, and insufficient surfactant. A lipoprotein synthesized by type II alveolar cells, surfactant is necessary to keep alveoli expanded. Although surfactant production begins at around weeks 22 to 24 of gestation, it is inadequate at this time to prevent alveolar collapse. Surfactant production probably becomes sufficient only after about week 35.

Insufficient surfactant causes alveolar collapse, leading to decreased lung volume and compliance. The resulting atelectasis causes hypoxia and acidosis, which in turn lead to anaerobic metabolism. As lactic acid accumulates in body tissues, myocardial contractility diminishes, impairing cardiac output and arterial blood pressure. Organ perfusion then diminishes; eventually respiratory failure occurs.

Transient tachypnea

This disorder, characterized by transient episodes of tachypnea (accelerated breathing), stems from incomplete removal of fetal lung fluid. Usually accompanied by cyanosis, it affects mainly full-term or nearly full-term neonates born by cesarean delivery (this delivery method eliminates fetal lung compression by the birth canal, which normally helps expel lung fluid).

Bronchopulmonary dysplasia

In this lung disease, the bronchiolar epithelial lining and alveolar walls become necrotic; in some cases, right-sided heart failure develops as a complication. Bronchopulmonary dysplasia (BPD) occurs mainly in preterm neonates as a complication of oxygen therapy or assisted mechanical ventilation — common treatments for RDS. The neonate with BPD typically becomes ventilator-dependent. Low birth weight and overhydration (in a neonate with PDA) may contribute to BPD.

RETINOPATHY OF PREMATURITY

Retinopathy of prematurity (ROP; formerly called retrolental fibroplasia) may lead to blindness. It begins with retinal vasoconstriction, which eventually causes vessels in some portions of the retina to become ischemic. To compensate for ischemia, new capillaries develop to provide oxygen and nutrients to the damaged tissue. However, lacking sufficient structural integrity, the new vessels rupture and hemorrhage. This leads to formation of scar tissue, which grows rigid and shortens, causing traction that results in retinal detachment and eventual blindness. In some cases, however, early retinal changes revert spontaneously, sparing the neonate's vision.

Immature retinal vessels are particularly vulnerable to ROP; the disorder is most common in the preterm neonate of less than 35 weeks' gestation who receives supplemental oxygen. Most experts attribute ROP to high concentrations of administered oxygen leading to an elevated partial pressure of arterial oxygen (PaO_2); even brief PaO_2 elevations have been linked with ROP. However, researchers suspect that coexisting factors must be present. These may include prematurity, blood transfusions, IVH, PDA, apnea, infection, vitamin E deficiency, lactic acidosis, administration of prostaglandin synthetase inhibitors, and prenatal and genetic factors. A study conducted by Subramanian, et al. (1985) shows a link between ROP and continuous exposure to bright lights in the nursery.

The precise PaO_2 level and the duration of the elevation that may cause ROP have not been determined. To minimize the risk, neonatologists now recommend that the PaO_2 level of a neonate receiving oxygen be kept at 60 to 80 mm Hg. (For more information on monitoring the neonate receiving supplemental oxygen, see the "Planning and implementation" section of this chapter.)

All preterm neonates who have received supplemental oxygen should have their eyes examined by the physician before discharge. Abnormal findings are graded I through IV, with I signifying minimal change and IV indicating severe retinal damage and blindness.

INTRAVENTRICULAR HEMORRHAGE

Fragile periventricular capillaries predispose the preterm neonate to IVH, or bleeding into the ventricles of the brain. IVH is associated with increased venous pressure and increased blood osmolarity. RDS also may lead to IVH because it typically causes hypoxia and hypercapnia. (Hypoxia can lead to vessel damage because it interrupts the brain's autonomic regulatory functions, hypercapnia because it causes cerebral vasodilation.)

NECROTIZING ENTEROCOLITIS

An acute inflammatory gastrointestinal (GI) mucosal disease, NEC may develop after hypoxic injury to the bowel at birth or during the early neonatal period. (Most commonly, it arises within the first 2 weeks after birth.) Hypoxia causes shunting of blood away from the GI tract to vital organs; the resulting intestinal ischemia predisposes the bowel to bacterial invasion, leading to necrotic lesions and possible perforation.

NEC has been linked to prematurity, which may predispose the neonate to anoxia and subsequent bowel ischemia. Intrauterine infection, maternal diabetes, multiple gestation (more than one fetus), and other conditions that cause fetal stress also may contribute to NEC.

NEONATE OF A DIABETIC MOTHER

Long-standing maternal diabetes mellitus or gestational diabetes mellitus (diabetes that arises during pregnancy) may cause various fetal and neonatal complications. Maternal serum insulin and glucose levels typically increase during pregnancy from increased tissue resistance to insulin in response to secretion of human placental lactogen and rising estrogen and progesterone levels. If the glucose level remains elevated, as in poorly controlled diabetes, the fetus responds by producing more insulin to combat hyperglycemia. Continued glucose elevations result in fetal hyperinsulinism, leading to changes in fetal glucose metabolism, growth, and development. Exposure to high glucose levels early in gestational development may have a teratogenic effect, causing various congenital anomalies, including heart defects, sacral agenesis, renal vein thrombosis, and small left colon (Fanaroff and Martin, 1987).

The neonate of a woman with diabetes (sometimes called an infant of a diabetic mother, or IDM) also has an increased risk of asphyxia, prematurity, infection, respiratory distress, severe hypoglycemia, hypocalcemia, hyperbilirubinemia, polycythemia, and neonatal death; unexplained fetal death also is higher than normal in IDMs. Typically, the IDM is large for gestational age (with a birth weight exceeding the ninetieth percentile for gestational age) and thus may suffer birth trauma, such as shoulder dystocia, cephalhematoma, subdural hemorrhage, ocular hemorrhage, or brachial plexus injury (Fanaroff and Martin, 1987).

Previously, large fetal size and the high incidence of fetal death late in gestation led many obstetricians to advise early delivery for pregnant diabetic clients. However, that approach has changed slightly, partly because the fetus affected by maternal diabetes has delayed alveolar maturation and thus cannot synthesize adequate surfactant to establish respirations after delivery. If early delivery is mandatory, however, it typically is scheduled for the thirty-seventh week of gestation.

METABOLIC DISORDERS

The most common metabolic disorders in high-risk neonates are hypoglycemia, hypocalcemia, and hyperbilirubinemia and jaundice.

Hypoglycemia

This condition is defined as two serum glucose levels below 35 mg/dl in the first 3 hours, less than 40 mg/dl from 4 to 24 hours, or less than 45 mg/dl from 24 hours to 7 days of age in a term neonate. In a preterm neonate, hypoglycemia is diagnosed when two serum glucose values are below 25 mg/dl during the first 72 hours. Hypoglycemia typically results from prematurity, low birth weight, severe fetal or neonatal stress, or maternal diabetes. Because fetal glycogen is deposited during the last few gestational months, the preterm neonate has deficient glycogen stores; if a stressful event, such as respiratory distress, develops at birth, these stores quickly become depleted. The low-birth-weight neonate has a high metabolic rate and inadequate enzyme supplies to activate glucogenesis — conditions that contribute to hypoglycemia.

Poorly controlled maternal diabetes, on the other hand, triggers increased insulin production by the fetal pancreas. After birth, the neonate continues to produce high levels of insulin; this facilitates the entry of glucose into muscle and fat cells, rapidly depleting serum glucose. Glucose expenditure during the transition to the extrauterine environment and sudden cessation of maternal glucose when the umbilical cord is clamped further tax the neonate's glucose stores.

Hypocalcemia

Defined as a serum calcium level below 7 mg/100 ml, hypocalcemia typically arises within the first 2 days or at 6 to 10 days after birth. It affects about half of neonates born to women with type I (insulin-dependent) diabetes mellitus. Other risk factors include small-for-gestational-age (SGA) status, prematurity, and birth asphyxia.

During pregnancy, the maternal parathyroid glands attempt to increase the maternal serum calcium level to compensate for loss of the calcium transferred to the fetus. The fetal parathyroid glands respond to this increase by a reduction in function; this in turn may cause hypoparathyroidism and subsequent hypocalcemia. After delivery, the neonatal serum calcium level drops further.

Hyperbilirubinemia and jaundice

Hyperbilirubinemia — an elevated serum level of unconjugated bilirubin — is common among both low-risk and high-risk neonates. It results from overproduction or underexcretion of bilirubin, as from liver immaturity or increased hemolysis. The disorder sometimes leads to jaundice, a yellow discoloration of the skin and sclerae. Types of jaundice include physiologic jaundice, which commonly arises 48 to 72 hours after birth and peaks by the third to fifth day; and pathologic jaundice, which arises secondary to another disorder, appears within the first 24 hours, and is characterized by a serum bilirubin level above 20 mg/dl. Pathologic jaundice, seen mainly in high-risk neonates, results from blood type or blood group incompatibility; infection; or biliary, hepatic, or metabolic abnormalities. (For more information on bilirubin production and excretion and physiologic jaundice, see Chapter 1, Neonatal Adaptation, and Chapter 3, Care of the Normal Neonate.)

The risk of hyperbilirubinemia is greatest in preterm neonates, those who are ill, those with isoimmune hemolytic anemia, and those who experienced a traumatic delivery leading to bruising and polycythemia. Such conditions as hypoxia and hypoglycemia (characterized by bilirubin displacement from binding sites) predispose the preterm neonate to hyperbilirubinemia (Fanaroff and Martin, 1987).

A serum bilirubin level of 15 to 20 mg/dl (or even lower in the preterm neonate) may lead to bilirubin encephalopathy (kernicterus), a condition in which unconjugated bilirubin crosses the blood-brain barrier and accumulates in the brain. This may result in damage to the brain and other organs, such as the kidneys, intestines, and pancreas (Fanaroff and Martin, 1987).

INEFFECTIVE THERMOREGULATION

All neonates are in danger of ineffective thermoregulation – particularly hypothermia (an abnormally low body temperature). However, the risk is greatest in the preterm neonate, who has an immature temperature-regulating center, reduced body mass-to-surface ratio, decreased subcutaneous fat, inability to shiver or sweat, and inadequate metabolic reserves.

Hypothermia or hyperthermia (an abnormally high body temperature) can cause dramatic changes in vital signs (including tachycardia or bradycardia, tachypnea, and apnea) and increase energy consumption – especially dangerous in a high-risk neonate. Hypothermia increases oxygen consumption, predisposing the neonate to hypoxia. When hypothermia begins, skin temperature decreases first; without intervention, the core temperature falls and irreversible hypothermia may ensue, leading to death.

The body attempts to compensate for hypothermia by increasing the basal metabolic rate (BMR). If the BMR increases above the normal baseline level, however, energy supplies may become depleted, leading to acidosis. This, in turn, causes changes in subcutaneous tissue; decreased peripheral perfusion may lead to tissue damage and necrosis in the cheeks and buttocks, cessation of GI motility, and internal hemorrhage. Hypoglycemia may occur as glucose is metabolized in an effort to meet cellular energy demands. Less commonly, hypothermia causes coagulation changes (Fanaroff and Martin, 1987).

Other changes that may result from hypothermia include pulmonary vasoconstriction, decreased surfactant production, exacerbation of RDS, and impaired weight gain (Fanaroff and Martin, 1987).

POLYCYTHEMIA

In this disorder, the number of red blood cells (RBCs) increases, as reflected by a hematocrit elevation. Polycythemia can result from maternal-fetal transfusion, delayed umbilical cord clamping, or placental insufficiency.

As RBCs increase, blood viscosity increases, leading to impaired blood pumping through vessels. Respiratory compromise, cardiac problems, and thrombosis may ensue; hyperbilirubinemia may develop as the excess RBCs are destroyed.

ISOIMMUNE HEMOLYTIC ANEMIAS

In these disorders (also called erythroblastosis fetalis), RBCs are destroyed prematurely. Two hemolytic anemias occurring in neonates are Rhesus (Rh) incompatibility and ABO blood group incompatibility.

Rh incompatibility

This blood incompatibility, which may cause critical illness in the neonate, occurs when an Rh-negative woman (one who lacks the Rh factor in the blood) carries an Rh-positive fetus. If maternal and fetal blood mix (as from a placental tear, prenatal bleeding, or a previous delivery), the mother may develop antibodies against fetal Rh antigens — a response called Rh sensitization. The antibodies cross the placenta, causing hemolysis of fetal RBCs. The resulting anemia may stimulate release of immature RBCs into the circulation; hemoglobin from hemolyzed RBCs breaks down to bilirubin.

In the fetus, the liver may enlarge to the point where it compresses the umbilical vein, compromising circulation and oxygen delivery. If hypoxia arises, the cardiovascular reserve is depleted rapidly and fluid accumulates, causing ascites. Also, as the liver becomes congested, hepatic protein synthesis may diminish, causing a life-threatening condition called hydrops fetalis, characterized by massive fetal edema (Nicholaides, 1989).

RBC destruction continues after delivery, causing severe anemia and jaundice in the neonate. Fortunately, Rh-negative women now receive $Rh_o(D)$ immune globulin (RhoGAM) within 3 days of a delivery or an abortion. Thus, Rh incompatibility now is rare.

ABO blood group incompatibility

This condition results from an antigen-antibody reaction by maternal RBCs, causing hemolysis of fetal RBCs. ABO incompatibility is most common when the mother has type O blood and the fetus has type A, B, or AB blood. Usually, it causes signs and symptoms similar to but far less severe than those seen in Rh incompatibility.

EFFECTS OF MATERNAL SUBSTANCE ABUSE

Maternal use of alcohol, narcotics, and other chemical substances during pregnancy can have devastating effects on the fetus and neonate.

Fetal alcohol syndrome

This syndrome involves alterations in intrauterine growth and development. A common finding in the NICU, fetal alcohol syndrome (FAS) may lead to growth deficiency, microcephaly, mental retardation, poor coordination, facial abnormalities, behavioral deviations (such as irritability), and cardiac and joint anomalies.

Alcohol crosses the placenta in the same concentration as is present in the maternal circulation. Damage to fetal cells may result from alcohol itself or from acetaldehyde, an alcohol oxidation product. Such damage is not limited to a particular gestational period. Also, researchers cannot pinpoint a safe level of alcohol consumption; even moderate drinking during the first trimester can cause physical characteristics of FAS. Consequently, pregnant women should be advised to avoid all alcohol (Jones, 1986). (Alcoholic beverages now carry labels warning that alcohol ingestion during pregnancy may affect the fetus.)

Drug exposure, addiction, and withdrawal

Maternal drug use during pregnancy is a serious and growing problem. Most drugs cross the placenta, with potentially devastating effects on the fetus. Depending on the stage of fetal development during exposure, maternal narcotic use may cause subtle or profound effects, including congenital anomalies, asphyxia, prematurity, respiratory and cardiac disorders, CNS abnormalities, and death. Intrauterine growth retardation leading to reduced neonatal weight also may occur, possibly from drug-induced slowing of blood flow to the placenta, which reduces nutrient delivery to the fetus. A fetus exposed to such drugs as heroin, methadone, or barbiturates also may become addicted and must go through withdrawal after birth.

A pregnant woman who uses drugs also puts her fetus in jeopardy by increasing her risk of poor nutrition, anemia, systemic or local infection, preeclampsia, and exposure to such diseases as human immunodeficiency virus (HIV), the virus that causes acquired immunodeficiency syndrome (AIDS). Intrapartal effects of maternal drug use include fetal distress and preterm delivery. After delivery, the neonate who is going through withdrawal may exhibit behavioral deviations that hinder parent-infant bonding, including irritability, continual crying, and poor feeding.

Ironically, the fetal stress caused by maternal heroin use has one positive consequence: It accelerates respiratory maturation. Consequently, the incidence of respiratory infections and RDS is relatively low among neonates of heroin users (Flandermeyer, 1987).

Maternal use of cocaine — a powerful CNS stimulant causing vasoconstriction, hypertension, and tachycardia — may result in various perinatal problems, depending on the gestational period and duration of exposure. These problems include profound congenital anomalies (such as urogenital anomalies in male neonates), abruptio placentae, altered brain-wave activity, cerebral infarcts (which may develop as late as 40 weeks' gestation), and prune-belly syndrome (characterized by a protruding, thin-walled abdomen; bladder and ureter dilation; small, dysplastic kidneys; undescended testes; and absence of a portion of the rectus abdominis muscle). Death also may occur (Kennard, 1990).

INFECTION

An infection can be acquired in utero, during labor and delivery, or after birth. The preterm neonate is especially vulnerable to postnatal infection because of reduced transmission of maternal immunoglobulins, including IgM and IgA. Unable to produce antibodies, the preterm neonate also cannot effectively phagocytose foreign proteins or mount a sufficient inflammatory response.

Agents that can infect the fetus or neonate, causing potentially morbid effects, are referred to as TORCH agents. This acronym stands for toxoplasmosis, others, rubella, cytomegalovirus, and herpes. Most TORCH infections are acquired in utero.

Cytomegalovirus (CMV) is the most common transplacentally acquired infection; it also can be acquired during delivery. CMV may result in CNS damage, although typically it causes no detectable signs at birth. Rubella, another transplacentally acquired infection, also causes serious sequelae. If acquired during the first trimester, it may result in CNS damage and cardiac defects; after the fourteenth week of gestation, the major sequela is deafness. Other transplacentally acquired infections include measles, chickenpox, smallpox, vaccinia, hepatitis B, HIV, toxoplasmosis, and syphilis.

Bacterial pneumonia, which can lead to intrauterine death, may be acquired by the fetus after prolonged rupture of the membranes (more than 24 hours), in which vaginal organisms may migrate upward. Bacterial organisms that can cause intrauterine bacteria pneumonia include nonhemolytic streptococci, *Escherichia coli* and other gram-negative organisms, *Listeria monocytogenes,* and *Candida.*

HIV can be acquired transplacentally at various times in gestation, intrapartally through contact with maternal blood and secretions, and postnatally through breast milk. The neonate with HIV typically has a distinctive facial dysmorphism (malformation) and suffers such problems as interstitial pneumonia, hepatosplenomegaly, recurrent infections, behavioral deviations, and neurologic abnormalities. In many cases, the neonate with HIV is small for gestational age and suffers failure to thrive. (For information on this problem, see *Child abuse and failure to thrive in the high-risk neonate,* pages 185 and 186.)

Infections that can be acquired as the fetus passes through the birth canal include:

• *Chlamydia trachomatis,* which may lead to conjunctivitis or pneumonia (if secretions pass into the eyes or oropharynx)

• *Neisseria gonorrhoeae,* which may cause ophthalmia neonatorum, an acute purulent conjunctivitis

• herpes simplex virus, which may result in skin vesicles, lethargy, respiratory problems, convulsions, disseminated vascular coagulation, hepatitis, keratoconjunctivitis, and death.

A pregnant client with known herpes simplex virus should be observed closely through frequent cervical cultures to determine whether the virus is active. Active virus at the time of delivery usually warrants cesarean delivery — an approach that has reduced the number of neonatal herpes cases (Hager, 1983).

CONGENITAL ANOMALIES

Many congenital anomalies are life-threatening and warrant immediate intervention and referral to a level 3 nursery. Such disorders include tracheoesophageal malformations, diaphragmatic hernia, choanal atresia, omphalocele, gastroschisis, meningomyelocele, encephalocele, and imperforate anus. Other anomalies do not require immediate treatment but may lead to chronic disability or deformity.

The exact cause of many congenital anomalies remains unknown. Some have been linked to genetic or chromosomal disorders, congenital rubella, exposure to radiation, maternal diabetes, and maternal drug use. Increased maternal age also has been associated with certain anomalies, including the trisomy disorders.

CHILD ABUSE AND FAILURE TO THRIVE IN THE HIGH-RISK NEONATE

Potential long-term effects of high-risk status at birth include child abuse and failure to thrive.

Child abuse

Although studies have failed to show a clear link between child abuse and preterm birth or chronic illness, both preterm status and congenital anomalies are associated with child abuse. However, the actual cause of abuse usually is secondary; for instance, frustration brought on by the combined pressures of the child's high-risk status and other family circumstances, such as poor financial resources (White, Benedict, Wulff, and Kelley, 1987). Therefore, identifying potential sources of stress and planning interventions to help parents deal with them is a crucial focus of nursing care.

If other factors with a high incidence in child-abuse cases also are present in a high-risk neonate's family, the potential for abuse—and thus the need for further assessment and intervention—may increase. These factors include:

• family or social isolation
• history of family abuse or neglect
• marital problems
• insufficient child-care arrangements
• siblings close in age
• decreased parent-neonate contact in the neonatal intensive care unit (Hunter, Kilstrom, Kraybill, and Loda, 1978).

If indications of a potential problem appear, the nurse should assess further and, as necessary, arrange for follow-up counseling with a nurse specialist in family therapy, a social worker, or other professional to help family members deal with pressures before they lead to child abuse. The nurse who suspects that abuse already has occurred should follow legal requirements and facility policy for reporting suspected child abuse.

Failure to thrive

In a full-term neonate or infant, failure to thrive is defined as a length and weight below the third percentile. For a preterm neonate or infant whose birth weight was significantly below normal, failure to thrive must be judged in terms of progress; the term should not be applied as long as the infant gains steadily over time, even if length and weight are below the third percentile.

Failure to thrive occurs because the neonate or infant cannot grow and develop normally—for organic reasons, inorganic reasons, or a combination of the two. In *organic* failure to thrive, physiologic problems (some of which may be associated with a high-risk birth) prevent the neonate or infant from digesting or ingesting sufficient nutrients to maintain normal growth. In *inorganic* failure to thrive, diagnosed when no organic cause can be found, the neonate or infant does not develop a

(continued)

CHILD ABUSE AND FAILURE TO THRIVE IN THE HIGH-RISK NEONATE *(continued)*

bond with the caregiver; even with sufficient intake, the child has poor weight gain and may fail to achieve developmental milestones.

Failure to thrive occurs in high-risk neonates for both organic and inorganic reasons. Not only may a physical defect or repeated illness interfere with growth, but lengthy hospitalization may prevent the formation of a trusting relationship with a permanent caregiver. Likewise, parents who fear that their seriously ill child will die may hold back from forming a normal parent-infant bond.

In the high-risk neonate or infant, lack of steady growth progress, poor eye contact, decreased interaction with the environment, and heightened irritability or lethargy may indicate failure to thrive. If such signs appear, the nurse should report them to the physician while working with the parents to strengthen their bond with the child.

CNS anomalies

More congenital anomalies involve the CNS than any other body system. Some CNS anomalies result in only minimal dysfunction; others have devastating consequences.

Meningomyelocele. In this anomaly (also called spina bifida), part of the meninges and spinal cord substance protrude through the vertebral column; the defect may be covered by a thin membrane. (When only the meninges protrude, the anomaly is called a meningocele.) Meningomyelocele results from defective neural tube formation during embryonic development. Hydrocephalus (discussed below) commonly accompanies the anomaly.

Consequences of meningomyelocele may be severe – for instance, paralysis below the defect. The child's appearance may be noticeably abnormal even after surgical correction.

Encephalocele. In this anomaly, the meninges and portions of brain tissue protrude through the cranium, usually in the occipital area. Typically, it occurs at the midline, through a suture line. Like meningomyelocele, encephalocele results from failure of the neural tube to close during embryonic development, may be accompanied by hydrocephalus, and may lead to paralysis.

Congenital hydrocephalus. In this disorder, excessive cerebro-spinal fluid (CSF) accumulates within the cranial vault, leading to suture expansion and ventricular dilation. This anomaly may result from obstruction of the foramen of Monro — a passage allowing communication between the lateral and third ventricles. Hydrocephalus sometimes is associated with meningomyelocele and other neural tube defects, intrauterine infection, meningitis, cerebral hemorrhage, head trauma, or Arnold-Chiari malformation (herniation of the brain stem and lower cerebellum through the foramen magnum into the cervical vertebral canal).

Anencephaly and microcephaly. In anencephaly, the cephalic end of the spinal cord fails to close, causing absence of the cerebral hemispheres. Anencephaly commonly causes stillbirth; if not, the neonate typically lives only a few days.

In microcephaly, the head is abnormally small and the brain underdeveloped, usually resulting in severe mental retardation and motor dysfunction. Microcephaly may result from an inborn error of metabolism (such as uncontrolled maternal phenylketonuria), intrauterine infection, or severe prolonged intrauterine hypoxia. (For a description of some inborn errors of metabolism, see *Inborn errors of metabolism,* pages 188 to 190.)

Teratoma. This neoplasm, which may be solid or fluid-filled, consists of various cell types, none of which normally occur together. The most common site is the sacrococcygeal area, although it may occur anywhere. Teratoma develops if the primitive streak (a dense area on the central posterior region of the embryonic disk) fails to disappear. This gives rise to a mass that may contain calcium and other tissue fragments (visible on X-ray).

Cardiac anomalies

Congenital cardiac anomalies — structural defects of the heart and great vessels — can occur during any stage of embryonic development. Cardiac structures are most susceptible to defects from the third to ninth weeks of gestation. In most cases, the cause remains unknown, although researchers believe that genetic and environmental factors play a role. Defects become noticeable after delivery when fetal circulation normally changes to neonatal circulation.

(Text continues on page 190.)

INBORN ERRORS OF METABOLISM

An inborn error of metabolism is a genetic condition in which a defect of a specific enzyme disrupts metabolism and nutrient use. The involved enzyme may not be produced or its action may be blocked by lack of a precursor necessary for a crucial chemical reaction.

The nursing goal for a neonate with an inborn error of metabolism is early detection and prevention of complications. The chart below describes these disorders and presents nursing implications for each.

CONDITION	DESCRIPTION	NURSING IMPLICATIONS
Congenital hypothyroidism	Deficiency of thyroid hormone secretion during fetal development or early infancy. The condition (also known as cretinism) typically stems from defective embryonic development causing absence or underdevelopment of the thyroid gland or severe maternal iodine deficiency; in some cases, it is inherited as an autosomal recessive disorder involving an enzymatic defect in the synthesis of the thyroid hormone thyroxine. Untreated, congenital hypothyroidism can lead to respiratory compromise and persistent physiologic jaundice.	• Signs of congenital hypothyroidism in the neonate include inactivity, jaundice, excessive sleep, hoarse cry, constipation, and feeding problems. • Many states require measurement of thyroid hormone levels at birth to detect congenital hypothyroidism early and thus help minimize mental and physical retardation. The disorder is confirmed by an elevated serum level of thyroid-stimulating hormone (TSH) and a low serum thyroxine (T_4) level. (However, test results may be misleading in the preterm neonate – especially one with respiratory distress syndrome, who typically has abnormal TSH and T_4 levels.) • Treatment involves lifelong administration of L-thyroxine, with periodic dosage adjustments to meet the demands of rapid growth periods. During the neonatal period, thyroxine can be given mixed with several milliliters of formula or crushed and mixed with rice cereal or applesauce when the infant begins eating solid foods.
Galactosemia	Hereditary autosomal recessive disorder in which deficiency of the enzyme galactose-1-phosphate uridyltransferase leads to inability to convert galactose to glucose and subsequent galactose accumulation in the blood. The disorder can be fatal if not detected and treated within the first few days after birth.	• Because the affected neonate cannot tolerate lactose, feeding problems may be the first sign of the disorder. Such problems may include anorexia, diarrhea, vomiting, jaundice, hepatomegaly, growth failure, lack of a red light reflex during eye examination, cataracts, and mental retardation (from elevated fetal galactose levels). Also, birth weight may be somewhat low. With early detection and treatment, these problems may subside. • Diagnosis is confirmed by the galactosemia tolerance test and examination of red blood cells revealing deficient galactose-1-phosphate uridyltransferase activity.

INBORN ERRORS OF METABOLISM   *(continued)*

CONDITION	DESCRIPTION	NURSING IMPLICATIONS
Galactosemia *(continued)*		• In some cases, galactosemia may be detected in utero by amniocentesis. In such cases, the mother should be placed on a galactose-restricted diet to prevent fetal complications and mental retardation. • Treatment involves lifelong avoidance of galactose-containing foods (milk and milk products).
Maple syrup urine disease	Autosomal recessive disorder characterized by an enzyme deficiency in the second step of branched-chain amino acid (BCAA) catabolism. BCAAs accumulate in the blood and urine, causing severe ketoacidosis soon after birth. Without intervention, the neonate progresses rapidly to death (usually from pneumonia and respiratory failure).	• The neonate typically appears normal at birth but deteriorates within 1 week as respirations become rapid and shallow and the level of consciousness declines. Other signs of the disorder include lethargy, alternating muscle hypotonicity and hypertonicity, brief tonic (rigid) seizures, hypoglycemic manifestations (from altered glucose metabolism), and a maple syrup odor to the urine. • Diagnosis is confirmed by a 2,4-dinitrophenylhydrazine test and serum elevation of the essential amino acids leucine, isoleucine, and valine. • Management involves lifelong dietary restriction of BCAAs and close monitoring of serum leucine, isoleucine, and valine levels. An acute episode warrants peritoneal dialysis.
Phenylketonuria (PKU)	Autosomal recessive disorder characterized by the abnormal presence of metabolites of phenylalanine (such as phenylketone) in the urine. It results from deficiency of phenylalanine hydroxylase, the enzyme responsible for converting the amino acid phenylalanine to tyrosine. Phenylalanine is transaminated to phenylpyruvic acid or decarboxylated to phenylthalanine, which then accumulates in the blood. Prolonged exposure to high serum levels of phenylalanine may cause severe brain damage and mental retardation.	• Most states require PKU screening at birth. The test usually is done within the first 24 to 48 hours after birth. If results are positive, retesting and referral should take place immediately to ensure early treatment. • Obtain blood for the screening test by heel stick. To prevent a false-negative test result, make sure the neonate has received adequate dietary protein and had no contraindications for oral feedings for 24 to 48 hours before the test. • Immediately after diagnosis, the neonate should be given Lafenalac (if the overall condition permits). This formula has a phenylalanine concentration of about 0.5% (in contrast to the 5% found in most infant formulas).

(continued)

INBORN ERRORS OF METABOLISM *(continued)*

CONDITION	DESCRIPTION	NURSING IMPLICATIONS
Phenylketonuria *(continued)*		• Usually, Lafenalac must be substituted for milk throughout the child's growing periods. Dietary restriction of phenylalanine must continue lifelong. Serum phenylalanine blood levels must be monitored closely throughout childhood. • Provide teaching, nutritional counseling, and emotional support to the neonate's family. Emphasize that the neonate cannot be given substitutions for prescribed food products, especially for Lafenalac. Refer the family to any available support groups for help in coping with the disease. • A woman with PKU who contemplates pregnancy should be warned about the possible effects of an elevated maternal phenylalanine level on the developing fetus (including congenital anomalies and mental retardation).

Congenital cardiac anomalies are classified as acyanotic or cyanotic. Acyanotic defects include atrial septal defect, ventricular septal defect, coarctation of the aorta, pulmonic stenosis, and PDA. These anomalies do not interfere with shunting of oxygenated blood from the left to the right side of the heart; the left side continues to eject oxygenated blood, preventing cyanosis. However, pulmonary blood flow to the right ventricle increases, placing the neonate at risk for pulmonary edema and congestive heart failure.

Cyanotic defects include tetralogy of Fallot, transposition of the great vessels, and tricuspid atresia. In such defects, abnormally high pressure in the right side of the heart permits left-to-right shunting of unoxygenated blood. As this blood mixes with oxygenated blood, arterial blood oxygen becomes desaturated. Peripheral perfusion then decreases and cyanosis develops. (For descriptions and illustrations of specific acyanotic and cyanotic defects, see *Congenital cardiac anomalies,* pages 191 to 193.)

CONGENITAL CARDIAC ANOMALIES

Abnormalities during fetal development may cause structural defects of the heart and great vessels. These defects probably stem from a combination of genetic or chromosomal disorders and environmental factors. Maternal alcoholism, malnutrition, rubella, or diabetes mellitus may contribute to cardiac anomalies. In the illustrations, blood flow is indicated by arrows—red arrows for adequately oxygenated blood and black arrows for poorly oxygenated blood.

Atrial septal defect
In this defect, an abnormal opening in the atrial septum allows blood to shunt from the left to right atrium. In many cases, it results from failure of the foramen ovale to close. Increased blood flow to the right heart and pulmonary arteries causes the right ventricle and atrium to enlarge.

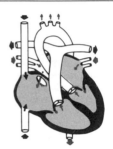

Ventricular septal defect
In this defect, an abnormal opening in the ventricular septum allows oxygenated blood to flow from the left to right ventricle; blood recirculates through the lungs and pulmonary artery. If the defect is large, pulmonary vascular resistance increases, causing elevated pulmonary and right ventricular pressures.

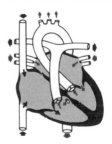

Coarctation of the aorta
This anomaly obstructs preductal or postductal blood flow, causing increased pressure in the left ventricle. To compensate, collateral circulation develops, enhancing blood flow from the proximal arteries and bypassing the obstructed area.

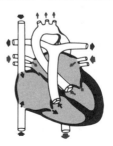

(continued)

CONGENITAL CARDIAC ANOMALIES *(continued)*

Pulmonic stenosis
This defect may be characterized by poststenotic dilation of the pulmonary trunk and concentric hypertrophy of the right ventricle, which cause a systolic pressure differential between the right ventricular cavity and pulmonary artery.

Patent ductus arteriosus
This anomaly occurs when the ductus arteriosus—a tubular connection that shunts blood away from the fetus's pulmonary circulation—fails to close after birth. Blood then shunts from the aorta to the pulmonary artery.

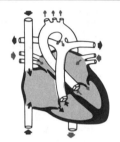

Tetralogy of Fallot
This anomaly consists of four defects—ventricular septal defect, overriding aorta, pulmonic stenosis, and right ventricular hypertrophy. Hemodynamic changes depend on the severity of these defects and may range from a left-to-right shunt to a right-to-left shunt, in which unoxygenated blood from the right ventricle enters the aorta directly.

Transposition of the great vessels
In this anomaly, the pulmonary artery arises from the left ventricle and the aorta from the right ventricle, preventing the pulmonary and systemic circulations from mixing. Without associated defects that allow these circulatory systems to mix—such as a patent ductus arteriosus or septal defect—the neonate will die.

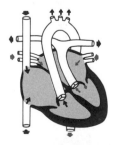

CONGENITAL CARDIAC ANOMALIES *(continued)*

Tricuspid atresia
In this defect, which usually is accompanied by an atrial or ventricular septal defect (both shown), the tricuspid valve is absent or incomplete, preventing the flow of blood from the right atrium to the right ventricle. Right atrial blood then shunts through an atrial septal defect into the left atrium.

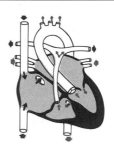

Respiratory tract anomalies

The most common respiratory tract anomaly is diaphragmatic hernia. In this defect, the various segments of the diaphragm fail to fuse during embryonic development, causing the abdominal contents to protrude from the abdominal cavity into the thoracic cavity at birth. Diaphragmatic hernia occurs in 1 of every 2,000 births. In the United States, it is twice as common in males as in females (Harjo, Kenner, and Brueggemeyer, 1988).

The defect may be unilateral or bilateral; most commonly, it occurs on the posterolateral aspect of the diaphragm on the left side. In a left-sided defect, the stomach and intestines typically protrude into the thoracic cavity; protrusion of the liver, spleen, and other abdominal organs is rare.

Most neonates with diaphragmatic hernia have impaired lung development — typically only a lung bud is present (a condition known as hypoplastic lung). This may lead to profound respiratory compromise and death if intervention does not begin immediately after delivery.

GI tract anomalies

These anomalies include tracheoesophageal malformations, abdominal wall defects (omphalocele and gastroschisis), meconium ileus, imperforate anus, and cleft palate and lip.

Tracheoesophageal malformations. Tracheoesophageal malformations, which occur in 1 of every 1,500 live births (Harjo, Kenner, and Brueggemeyer, 1988), result from altered embryonic development of the trachea and esophagus. These anomalies sometimes occur as part of the VACTERL syndrome — vertebral, anal, cardiac, tracheal, esophageal, renal, and limb anomalies. Types of tracheo-esophageal anomalies include tracheoesophageal fistula (an abnormal connection between the trachea and esophagus), esophageal atresia (closure of the esophagus at some point), and absence of the esophagus. Usually, tracheoesophageal fistula occurs in tandem with esophageal atresia. In the most common tracheoesophageal malformation, esophageal atresia accompanies distal tracheoesophageal fistula; the upper esophageal section ends in a blind pouch (atresia) that does not connect with the stomach. (For an illustration of this and other types of tracheoesophageal malformations, see *Tracheoesophageal malformations,* pages 195 and 196.)

Abdominal wall defects. Omphalocele and gastroschisis occur in approximately 1 of every 7,000 births (Harjo, Kenner, and Brueggemeyer, 1988). In omphalocele, a portion of the intestine protrudes through a defect in the abdominal wall at the umbilicus, in the midline. A thin, transparent membrane composed of amnion and peritoneum typically covers the protruding part. (The membrane sometimes ruptures during delivery and thus may not be visible by the time the neonate is admitted to the NICU.) The defect may be quite large — or small enough to elude detection on brief inspection.

Omphalocele arises during embryonic development when the abdominal contents migrate into the umbilical cord. Normally, at 9 weeks' gestation, the abdominal contents recede from the umbilical cord, regressing into the abdominal cavity; if the contents fail to recede, omphalocele occurs.

Gastroschisis refers to incomplete abdominal wall closure not involving the site of the umbilical cord insertion. Usually, the small intestine and part of the large intestine protrude. No membranous sac covers the protrusion.

Meconium ileus. This intestinal obstruction results from obstruction of the terminal ileum by viscous meconium. Beyond the ileal obstruction, the colon atrophies and narrows in diameter. In at least 95% of cases, it is a sign of cystic fibrosis, a genetic disease resulting from a pancreatic enzyme deficiency.

TRACHEOESOPHAGEAL MALFORMATIONS

Tracheoesophageal malformations result from incomplete separation of the trachea and esophagus during the first trimester of pregnancy. Among the most serious surgical emergencies in neonates, they require immediate correction. In many cases, they are accompanied by other congenital anomalies. Common variations of tracheoesophageal malformations are illustrated here.

Esophageal atresia with distal tracheoesophageal fistula is the most common variation.

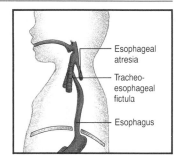

Esophageal atresia

Tracheo-esophageal fistula

Esophagus

In **esophageal atresia without tracheoesophageal fistula,** the upper esophageal portion ends in a blind pouch, the upper and lower esophageal portions do not connect, and the trachea and esophagus are not linked by a fistula.

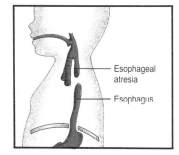

Esophageal atresia

Esophagus

Tracheoesophageal fistula without esophageal atresia (sometimes called an H-type tracheoesophageal fistula) is characterized by an intact esophagus and a connection between the trachea and esophagus.

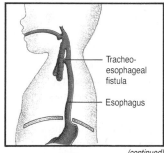

Tracheo-esophageal fistula

Esophagus

(continued)

TRACHEOESOPHAGEAL MALFORMATIONS (continued)

In some cases, **esophageal atresia** occurs with a **proximal fistula.**

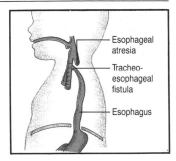

Esophageal atresia

Tracheo-esophageal fistula

Esophagus

Esophageal atresia sometimes occurs with a **double** (proximal and distal) **fistula.**

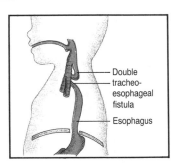

Double tracheo-esophageal fistula

Esophagus

Imperforate anus. In this malformation, the anus is closed abnormally. Occurring in 1 of every 20,000 live births, the disorder is more common in males than females (Harjo, Kenner, and Brueggemeyer, 1988). It results from persistence of the membrane that separates the lower rectum from the lower aspect of the large intestine. (Normally, this membrane disappears by the ninth week of gestation, leading to formation of a patent tube from the intestine to the rectum.) In many cases, imperforate anus is associated with other defects, such as rectourethral and rectovaginal fistula (both of which permit abnormal evacuation of fecal matter from the rectum).

Imperforate anus occurs as several variants. In anal agenesis, the most common variant, the rectal pouch ends blindly above the surface of the perineum; an anal fistula commonly is present. In anal stenosis, the anal aperture is abnormally small. In anal membrane atresia, the anal membrane covers the aperture, creating an obstruction.

Imperforate anus also may be classified as high or low. In the high form, a fistula links the upper rectal pouch to the bladder, urethra, or vagina. If a fistula is absent, bowel obstruction occurs and the neonate has a large, distended abdomen. In low imperforate anus, intestinal patency may be compromised by a membrane at the anal sphincter level.

Cleft palate and cleft lip. These congenital defects, which occur in 1 of every 1,000 live births (Harjo, Kenner, and Brueggemeyer, 1988), sometimes result from chromosomal abnormalities. Cleft palate occurs when the sides of the palate fail to fuse during embryonic development, leading to a fissure in the palatal midline. The fissure may be complete, extending through both the hard and soft palates into the nasal cavities, or incomplete.

In cleft lip (harelip), one or more clefts appear in the upper lip resulting from failure of the maxillary and median nasal processes to close during embryonic development. The defect, which is more common in males than females, may be unilateral or bilateral and sometimes occurs in conjunction with other anomalies. It commonly accompanies cleft palate.

Genitourinary tract anomalies
Genitourinary tract anomalies include renal agenesis, polycystic kidney disease, posterior urethral valves, and external genital ambiguity.

Renal agenesis. One of the most common congenital anomalies in males, renal agenesis may be unilateral (absence of one kidney) or bilateral (absence of both kidneys). The bilateral form (also called Potter's association) is incompatible with life and typically causes stillbirth or death during the neonatal period; autopsies of neonates with bilateral renal agenesis show hypoplastic lung and multiple pneumothoraces. With unilateral agenesis, the single kidney enlarges to maintain normal renal function.

Polycystic kidney disease. In this disorder, which occurs as an autosomal recessive disease in the neonate and as an acquired disease in the adult, multiple cysts form within the kidney. As the cysts enlarge, adjacent tissue is destroyed. At birth, the neonate with polycystic kidney disease typically suffers renal failure, respiratory distress, congestive heart failure, and hypertension.

Posterior urethral valves. This anomaly, which occurs only in males, causes urinary tract obstruction, hydronephrosis, impaired urine flow, and (when untreated) profound renal damage. Typically, the obstructing valves are exaggerations of two mucosal folds that normally are continuous with the lower end of the urethera where the ejaculatory ducts open.

External genital ambiguity. This problem may reflect a developmental defect, genetic abnormality, or hormonal influences. In some cases, it complicates determination of the neonate's sex. In males, genital ambiguity typically stems from a developmental abnormality. In females, a common cause is congenital adrenal hyperplasia, a condition stemming from blockage of cortisol precursors (enzymes that convert cholesterol to cortisol). The resulting corticotropin deficiency leads to increased secretion of cortisol precursors and androgens and subsequent masculinization of the female external genitalia.

Musculoskeletal anomalies
The most common congenital musculoskeletal anomaly is clubfoot (talipes). This deformity involves unilateral or bilateral deviation of the metatarsal bones; talus deformation and a shortened Achilles tendon give the foot a clublike appearance. Clubfoot sometimes is associated with other anomalies, such as meningomyelocele.

The second most common musculoskeletal disorder is congenital hip dysplasia. This disorder occurs more commonly in females.

ASSESSMENT

In many — perhaps most — cases, delivery of a high-risk neonate can be predicted from the maternal health history or from antepartal or intrapartal data. For instance, fetal distress (signaled by an abnormal fetal heart rate, meconium-stained amniotic fluid, or a fetal scalp blood pH below 7.25) warns strongly of a high-risk delivery. Thus, anticipation and preparation can help prevent or minimize perinatal problems. When a client is due to deliver, check the calculated date of delivery and review the history for factors that help predict neonatal outcome. (For more information, see *Risk factors for perinatal problems,* pages 200 and 201.)

If a high-risk neonate is expected, a brief assessment immediately after delivery verifies the endangered status, as when the neonate fails to breathe spontaneously or has central cyanosis or an inadequate heart rate. Poor 1-minute and 5-minute Apgar scores also may confirm or suggest high-risk status. In some cases, however, a perinatal problem is not discovered until a complete examination is conducted several hours or days later. (For a detailed discussion of neonatal assessment, see Chapter 2, Neonatal Assessment.)

GESTATIONAL-AGE AND BIRTH-WEIGHT VARIATIONS
In many cases, maternal, antepartal, and intrapartal factors give advance warning of these problems — particularly preterm or postterm status.

Maternal, antepartal, and intrapartal history
The preterm neonate is the classic high-risk neonate, making prematurity the leading predictor of high-risk status. Prematurity and postmaturity usually can be anticipated from maternal, antepartal, and intrapartal data; the calculated delivery date; and ultrasound evaluation. For example, maternal weight loss, decreased abdominal circumference, and reduced uterine size during pregnancy may indicate an altered fetal growth pattern reflecting postterm gestation; ultrasound can be used to estimate gestational weeks.

The diagnosis of large for gestational age (LGA) typically comes during the antepartal period, when fundal height appears disproportionate to gestational weeks (and ultrasound determines exact fetal size). Also, because maternal diabetes mellitus is a leading cause of accelerated intrauterine growth, this condition suggests an LGA fetus.

About two-thirds of SGA neonates are born to women with SGA-associated risk factors (Cassady and Strange, 1987). Consequently, check the maternal history for such factors as low socioeconomic status, age extreme, increased parity, short stature, low prepregnancy weight, and previous delivery of an SGA neonate.

RISK FACTORS FOR PERINATAL PROBLEMS

The health care team can anticipate a neonate's high-risk status from the maternal, antepartal, or intrapartal history or from certain neonatal conditions present at birth.

MATERNAL RISK FACTORS

- Age over 34 or under 19
- Alcohol or drug use during pregnancy
- Chronic illness (including diabetes mellitus, anemia, hypertension, kidney disease, or heart disease)
- Cigarette smoking
- Death of a previous fetus
- Death or illness of a previous neonate
- Exposure to toxic chemicals, radiation, or other hazardous substances or conditions
- Exposure to infection during pregnancy
- Family history of a genetic disease (such as Down's syndrome)
- Hereditary disease
- Isoimmunization
- Low socioeconomic status
- More than seven previous pregnancies
- Poor prenatal care
- Previous multiple fetuses
- Short interval between pregnancies (less than 18 months)

ANTEPARTAL RISK FACTORS

- Abruptio placentae
- Accelerated fetal growth
- Fetal surgery
- First-trimester bleeding
- Hydramnios
- Intrauterine growth retardation
- Multiple fetuses
- Placenta previa
- Pregnancy-induced hypertension
- Premature rupture of the membranes

INTRAPARTAL RISK FACTORS

- Abnormal fetal presentation
- Cesarean delivery
- Fetal distress (as indicated by late decelerations and decreased beat-to-beat variability)
- Maternal anesthetics or analgesics

RISK FACTORS FOR PERINATAL PROBLEMS *(continued)*

INTRAPARTAL RISK FACTORS *(continued)*

- Prolonged labor
- Umbilical cord prolapse
- Use of forceps during delivery

NEONATAL RISK FACTORS

- Abnormal placental weight or appearance
- Cardiorespiratory depression
- Congenital anomaly
- Low Apgar score
- Lack of spontaneous respirations
- Meconium-stained amniotic fluid
- Prematurity
- Postmaturity
- Small or large size for gestational age
- Unusual number of umbilical vessels

Neonatal findings

After delivery, assess the neonate for physical signs of gestational-age and birth-weight variations as well as perinatal problems associated with these variations. For example, the preterm neonate may appear inactive, with extended positioning at rest, splayed legs, and arms held away from the body. The respiratory pattern typically is irregular, possibly with apneic episodes. Other signs of prematurity include translucent, ruddy skin; visible blood vessels; absent skin folds (from decreased subcutaneous fat); thick vernix caseosa, especially around the neck and thighs; prominent lanugo across the back and face; long, thin fingers with soft, pliable nails; sparse or absent breast tissue; and immature external genitalia.

Physical examination of the postterm neonate typically reveals macrosomic (excessively large) features. Some postterm neonates also have green, brown, or yellow meconium staining of the skin, nails, umbilical cord, or placental membranes. A postterm LGA neonate may show signs of birth trauma and hypoglycemia. With a postterm SGA neonate, expect dry, cracked, wrinkled skin with decreased subcutaneous fat; no visible vernix caseosa or lanugo;

skin maceration; long, thin arms and legs; long nails; and full hair growth.

Although birth weight must be correlated with gestational age to verify SGA or LGA status, assess for associated physical signs and perinatal problems if either problem is suspected. The typical SGA neonate has loose, dry skin with diminished skinfold thickness; reduced breast tissue (from soft-tissue wasting); skin wasting in the buttocks and thighs; widened skull sutures with large fontanels; and shortened crown-to-heel, femoral, and foot lengths (from bone growth failure). In a neonate with these findings, also check for congenital anomalies, which are 10 to 20 times more common in SGA neonates than normal neonates.

With the LGA neonate, assess for signs of birth injury, congenital anomalies, hypoglycemia, and polycythemia. If the LGA neonate is preterm, check for signs of respiratory distress and hyperbilirubinemia. With a postterm LGA neonate, expect respiratory distress from meconium aspiration syndrome or asphyxiation. With the LGA neonate of a diabetic mother, check for signs of hypoglycemia and hypocalcemia.

RESPIRATORY PROBLEMS
Signs of a respiratory problem may be obvious, immediate, and life-threatening, such as with birth asphyxia or apnea, or may arise hours, days, or even weeks later.

Asphyxia and apnea
The cardinal sign of asphyxia is deep gasping or failure to breathe spontaneously at delivery. Associated signs include a slow heart rate, abnormally low blood pressure, poor muscle tone, and poor reflexes. To help anticipate birth asphyxia, check for such risk factors as maternal diabetes, infection, pregnancy-induced hypertension, or anesthesia; more than one fetus; prolonged labor; prolapsed umbilical cord; abruptio placentae; placenta previa; prolonged rupture of the membranes; meconium-stained amniotic fluid; oligohydramnios; hydramnios; umbilical cord compression; placental insufficiency; abnormal fetal heart rate patterns; isoimmunization; delivery complications; excessive fetal size; abnormal presentation; or neonatal prematurity, postmaturity, or congenital anomalies.

Apneic episodes commonly manifest as rapid respirations punctuated by brief pauses. Hypoxemia, cyanosis, and bradycardia may ensue. With central apnea, expect absence of respiratory efforts and muscle flaccidity. With obstructive apnea, expect respiratory motions accompanied by hypoxemia and bradycardia (from inability to draw air into the lungs).

Meconium aspiration syndrome

In MAS, signs of respiratory distress may be mild, moderate, or severe. The neonate typically appears barrel chested because of an increased anteroposterior chest diameter (from bronchial obstruction by meconium or tension pneumothorax). Skin and nails may be meconium stained.

Respiratory distress syndrome

Signs of RDS may appear at delivery or within a few hours. They include tachypnea (a respiratory rate over 60 breaths/minute), labored respirations, grunting, nasal flaring, cyanosis, and chest retractions. The neonate may become restless and agitated (probably from the increasing $PaCO_2$ level) and show fatigue even after simple care procedures. Complex procedures, such as endotracheal suctioning, may thoroughly exhaust the neonate's limited energy reserves, leading to bradycardia and hypoxia.

The likelihood of RDS may be determined antenatally from analysis of amniotic fluid lipids; a lecithin-sphingomyelin ratio below 2 and a phosphatidylglycerol level below 3% suggest fetal lung immaturity and a high risk for RDS.

RDS affects mainly preterm neonates. Other risk factors include maternal diabetes mellitus, infection, or hemorrhage; maternal steroid or analgesic use; more than one fetus; abruptio placentae; umbilical cord prolapse; meconium-stained amniotic fluid; fetal distress; and breech presentation.

Transient tachypnea

Tachypnea — alone or accompanied by hypoxemia, cyanosis, grunting, and chest retractions — is the hallmark of this disorder. Cesarean delivery and term or near-term gestation are common history findings.

Bronchopulmonary dysplasia

Because BPD typically occurs as a complication of treatment for RDS, signs usually arise after supplemental oxygen administration or mechanical ventilation. The severity of these signs reflects the degree of disease progression and pulmonary dysfunction. Expect nasal flaring, retractions, tachypnea, and grunting. However, the first clue to BPD may be difficulty weaning the neonate from a ventilator. As the disease progresses, carbon dioxide retention and pulmonary secretions increase and crackles can be auscultated. Bronchospasm may result from bronchial smooth muscle hypertrophy. Typically, the neonate's condition worsens and oxygen dependency occurs. (Conversely, decreased oxygen dependency may be the earliest sign of recovery.)

RETINOPATHY OF PREMATURITY
Ophthalmoscopic examination of the neonate with ROP reveals a proliferation of dilated, tortuous retinal vessels; edema; and retinal detachment.

INTRAVENTRICULAR HEMORRHAGE
Typically, IVH causes bulging fontanels, increasing head size, hypotonia, forceful vomiting, downward eye deviation, seizures, lethargy, and extreme irritability. Also assess for generalized signs of hemorrhage, including temperature instability, bradycardia, increasing respiratory distress, apnea, and hypotension.

NECROTIZING ENTEROCOLITIS
Signs of NEC may be generalized—for instance, apnea, hypothermia, lethargy, and irritability—or restricted to the GI tract. GI signs include abdominal distention and tenderness; absent bowel sounds; visible distended, ropelike bowel loops; vomiting; increased gastric residual matter; bloody stools; and feeding problems. Also, stools may contain positive reducing substances—various forms of glucose in abnormal amounts—which indicate impaired intestinal carbohydrate absorption caused by NEC-induced tissue damage.

Determine the neonate's glucose level from a copper reduction tablet test and perform a guaiac test to check for occult blood in the stool. X-ray evidence of pneumatosis (air within the intestinal walls), adynamic ileus (intestinal obstruction caused by reduced intestinal motility), thickened bowel walls, and free air in the peritoneum or portal system confirm the diagnosis.

NEONATE OF A DIABETIC MOTHER

Typically, this neonate is macrosomic, with a birth weight in the upper percentile range for gestational age. The face is round with chubby cheeks and the skin is ruddy to bright red. Signs of hypoglycemia and hypocalcemia (discussed below) may be present; however, over half of neonates of diabetic mothers have asymptomatic hypoglycemia. Assess for signs of birth trauma, such as bruising, ecchymosis, and shoulder dystocia (sometimes manifested as a flaccid or unusually positioned arm).

For the neonate whose mother had questionably or poorly controlled diabetes during pregnancy, assess for signs of hypoglycemia and check blood-glucose levels using a glucose oxidase dipstick at delivery and 30 minutes afterward.

METABOLIC DISORDERS

Signs of metabolic disorders range from extremely mild to severe.

Hypoglycemia

Signs of hypoglycemia include apnea or bradycardia, seizures, irregular respirations, cyanosis, irritability, listlessness, lethargy, tremors, feeding problems, vomiting, hypotonia, and a high-pitched cry. Also, neurologic immaturity may prevent homeostasis in the hypoglycemic neonate, leading to unstable vital signs. However, some hypoglycemic neonates are asymptomatic.

Besides maternal diabetes, risk factors for hypoglycemia include prematurity, SGA status, severe isoimmune hemolytic anemia, and birth asphyxia.

A glucose oxidase dipstick value below 25 mg/100 ml indicates hypoglycemia and warrants a venous blood sample to confirm the diagnosis. Hypoglycemia is confirmed by a blood-glucose level below 40 mg/dl before the first day after birth or below 45 mg/dl on or after the third day.

Hypocalcemia

The hypocalcemic neonate may have seizures, irritability, hypotonia, poor feeding, a high-pitched cry, and signs associated with hypoglycemia. Suspect hypocalcemia in the neonate of a diabetic mother. Other at-risk neonates include those who are preterm or SGA and those who experienced birth asphyxia.

To assess for hypocalcemia, attempt to elicit Chvostek's sign by tapping the skin over the sixth cranial nerve (in front of the ear); unilateral contraction of the muscles surrounding the eye, nose, and mouth indicates tetany, a sign of hypocalcemia. A serum calcium level below 7 mg/100 ml confirms the diagnosis.

Hyperbilirubinemia and jaundice

The neonate with hyperbilirubinemia has yellow skin and sclerae. For the most accurate assessment, apply pressure over the tip of the neonate's nose; a yellow tinge appearing as circulation returns indicates jaundice.

With pathologic jaundice (the more dangerous jaundice form), the serum bilirubin level rises above 13 mg/dl within the first 24 hours after delivery. Transcutaneous bilirubinometry (reflective photometry) sometimes is used as a screening tool for hyperbilirubinemia. This method detects bilirubin levels through the skin and is considered superior to observation of the skin or sclera color alone. However, its accuracy may be reduced in neonates with dark skin.

With severe hyperbilirubinemia (bilirubin encephalopathy), signs vary with the disease phase. Phase 1 signs include hypotonia, vomiting, lethargy, a high-pitched cry, a poor sucking reflex, a decreased or absent Moro reflex, and diminished flexion. During phase 2, spasticity develops; this may take the form of opisthotonus, a prolonged, severe muscle spasm in which the back arches acutely, the head bends back on the neck, the heels bend back on the leg, and the arms and hands flex rigidly at the joints.

In phase 3, spasticity diminishes, the sclera shows above the iris (a condition called sunset eyes), and seizures may occur. During phase 4, gastric, pulmonary, and CNS hemorrhages may develop (these problems also may occur during phase 2). A neonate who survives phase 4 usually has residual effects, such as mental retardation, cerebral palsy, and such sensory alterations as deafness and poor visual acuity or blindness.

INEFFECTIVE THERMOREGULATION

Hypothermia (a body temperature below 99.5° F [37.5° C]) causes an accelerated respiratory rate, labored respirations, an increased metabolic rate, and signs of hypoglycemia (indicating greater use of glucose stores).

Hyperthermia (a core temperature above 99.5° F) may cause skin reddening, dehydration, irritability, and an initial rise, then gradual drop, in the heart and respiratory rates.

POLYCYTHEMIA

The neonate with polycythemia may have such signs as tachypnea, cyanosis, seizures, jaundice, and pleural and scrotal effusions. However, most polycythemic neonates are asymptomatic (Cassady and Strange, 1987).

ISOIMMUNE HEMOLYTIC ANEMIA

When isoimmunization has occurred in utero, antepartal ultrasound evaluation may reveal fetal hepatomegaly and hydramnios; fetal monitoring may detect an abnormal heart rate pattern caused by tissue hypoxia at the level of the medulla oblongata (which controls cardiac function via the autonomic nervous system).

The neonate with Rh incompatibility typically is anemic at birth, as indicated by pale mucous membranes, and has massive generalized edema; with severe disease, expect pathologic jaundice, congestive heart failure, an enlarged liver and spleen, and generalized ascites. The neonate with ABO incompatibility may have anemia at birth and develop hyperbilirubinemia after delivery.

EFFECTS OF MATERNAL SUBSTANCE ABUSE

The neonate with FAS may have cardiac anomalies, decreased joint mobility, behavioral deviations, kidney defects, labial hypoplasia, and distinctive facial features. The latter include short palpebral fissures (eye openings); ptosis (drooping eyelids); strabismus (eye muscle deviation); a thin, smooth upper lip with a long philtrum (vertical groove) above it; a short, upturned nose; and a receding jaw. Behavioral deviations include irritability, excessive crying, and poor feeding.

The neonate affected by maternal drug abuse may have muscle tremors, twitching, or rigidity, with inability to extend the muscles; seizures; temperature instability; GI disturbances, including vomiting and diarrhea; tachycardia; tachypnea; diaphoresis with mottling over the extremities; and excessive sneezing and yawning. If the mother used heroin or methadone during pregnancy, the neonate may be SGA or have a low birth weight with cardiorespiratory depression at delivery.

Typically, the behavior pattern of the drug-addicted neonate is disorganized, with marked fussiness and irritability (which may be exacerbated by eye contact), prolonged periods of high-pitched crying, and poor consolability. Normal neonatal reflexes, especially the Moro reflex, are highly exaggerated. The sucking reflex is strong and the neonate may suck on the hands and fists frequently. However, sucking may be poorly coordinated with swallowing, impairing feeding. Sleep periods may be abnormally short; unlike the normal neonate, who spends more time asleep than awake, the addicted neonate may have a sleep-awake ratio of 1 to 3.

Signs of drug withdrawal typically begin about 12 to 48 hours after birth. (For a list of these signs, see *Assessing for drug withdrawal.*) As withdrawal progresses, these signs worsen. Try to verify that the mother used drugs during pregnancy if neonatal drug addiction or withdrawal is suspected. However, keep in mind that some women may deny or misrepresent drug use.

If the neonate's mother used I.V. drugs, an HIV test should be done. Maternally conferred IgG may interfere with the accuracy of an HIV antibody test for the first few months after birth; therefore, an HIV antigen test is preferred. Assess for signs of HIV infection, including facial dysmorphism, hepatosplenomegaly, interstitial pneumonia, subtle neurologic abnormalities, behavioral changes, and recurrent infection.

INFECTION

The neonate with an infection may be SGA at birth, with a nonspecific rash, pallor, hypotonia, jaundice, lethargy, hyperthermia, or hypothermia. Other common signs accompanying infection include apnea or tachypnea, tachycardia or bradycardia, abdominal distention, hepatomegaly, splenomegaly, seizures, diarrhea, occult blood in the stool, and bleeding disorders. The behavior pattern may be abnormal and the reflexes diminished; poor feeding may cause failure to thrive.

With an intrapartally acquired infection, the neonate may not appear ill at birth but will show gradual deterioration in vital signs over the next 6 to 12 hours. However, with group B streptococcal infection — a commonly acquired intrapartal infection — the neonate may have dyspnea and cyanosis and appear quite ill. However, RDS and congenital cardiac anomalies can cause similar signs and must

ASSESSING FOR DRUG WITHDRAWAL

The neonate whose mother used such drugs as narcotics, barbiturates, or cocaine during pregnancy may be addicted at birth and go through withdrawal. Classic signs of neonatal drug withdrawal are listed below.

VITAL SIGN DEVIATIONS

- Profound diaphoresis
- Skin mottling
- Tachycardia or bradycardia (depending on the drug involved)
- Tachypnea
- Temperature instability (fever followed by hypothermia)

NEUROMUSCULAR SIGNS

- Absent or strong sucking reflex (may be poorly coordinated with swallowing reflex)
- Exaggeration of other neonatal reflexes
- Difficulty extending muscles
- Jerky movements
- Muscle rigidity with flexion
- Muscle twitching
- Seizures
- Tremors

BEHAVIORAL SIGNS

- Decreased sleep periods and lengthened awake periods
- Dislike for cuddling and close body contact
- Frequent or prolonged sneezing or yawning
- High-pitched or weak cry, inconsolability
- Irritability

GASTROINTESTINAL SIGNS

- Frequent vomiting
- Increased gastrointestinal motility, with diarrhea and rapid (possibly visible) peristalsis

be ruled out. The following laboratory results suggest perinatal infection:

- an increased number of immature cells, as shown by the white blood cell (WBC) differential
- a WBC count above 20,000/mm^3, reflecting leukocytosis (an abnormal increase in the number of WBCs)

- an absolute neutrophil count exceeding 60%
- a thrombocyte count below 100,000/mm³ with an abnormally high reticulocyte count.

A neonate who acquired HIV intrapartally may be preterm or SGA, with an abnormally small head and distinctive facial features. Disorders seen in neonates with HIV infection include oral candidiasis (thrush) and lymphoid interstitial pneumonitis. Later, such problems as lymphadenopathy, chronic diarrhea, viral and bacterial infections, *Pneumocystis carinii* pneumonia, and parotid gland enlargement may occur.

Because maternal HIV antibodies are transferred to the fetus, a neonate whose mother has the virus may test positive for HIV antibodies even when not infected. Consequently, an HIV culture or antigen test must be used to confirm infection.

CONGENITAL ANOMALIES
Antepartal factors suggesting congenital abnormalities include increased or decreased amniotic fluid volume. For example, hydramnios (excess amniotic fluid) may accompany tracheoesophageal anomalies; oligohydramnios (insufficient amniotic fluid) may signify a genitourinary tract anomaly. If a congenital anomaly is discovered in one body system, other systems should be investigated thoroughly because congenital anomalies commonly occur in tandem.

CNS anomalies
Most CNS anomalies are apparent even on rapid inspection.

Meningomyelocele. Most commonly, this anomaly appears in the lumbosacral region of the vertebral column. CSF may leak through the defect. Sometimes it is covered only by a thin, membranous sac; otherwise, nerve tissue is exposed. In less obvious cases, the defect manifests as a slight indentation or dimple over the lumbosacral region, detected on palpation; sometimes the indentation is covered by a mole with hair follicles. Such a dimple or mole should be reported for further evaluation. If meningomyelocele is detected, also check for associated anomalies, such as hip dislocation, knee and foot deformities, and hydrocephalus.

If the defect appears above the lumbosacral region, the lower extremities may lack sensation and movement and the bladder and bowel may lack innervation, causing impaired bladder and bowel function. To assess bowel innervation, test for an anal wink by lightly stroking the anus with a cotton-tipped applicator; absence of anal sphincter constriction indicates lack of bowel innervation.

Encephalocele. Suspect this defect when the meninges protrude through the cranium. The defect may be covered with skin or membrane and may be accompanied by hydrocephalus, paralysis, and seizures.

Hydrocephalus. The neonate with this abnormality has an enlarged head with an excessive diameter (the occipitofrontal circumference typically exceeds the ninetieth percentile by 2 cm). Wide or bulging fontanels, a shiny scalp with prominent veins, and possible separation of the suture lines are common. Also check for downward eye slanting caused by increased intracranial pressure, and for sunset eyes (appearance of the sclera above the iris), reflecting upper lid retraction.

Associated findings include an abnormal heart rate (usually bradycardia), apneic episodes, vomiting, irritability, excessive crying, and reduced alertness.

Anencephaly and microcephaly. Suspect anencephaly if the neonate lacks a forehead and has a minimal posterior cranium. Suspect microcephaly if head circumference is more than three standard deviations below the average for age, sex, race, and gestational age (Brann and Schwartz, 1987); the forehead is narrow and receding; the occiput (back of the head) is flattened; and the vertex (top of the head) is pointed.

Teratoma. This tumor may be visible on inspection of the sacral area; it may be completely or partly external.

Cardiac anomalies

A heart murmur, which can be assessed on auscultation, is common to most cardiac anomalies. Other general signs of cardiac anomalies include diminished capillary refill time, tachypnea, dyspnea, and tachycardia.

With acyanotic defects, cyanosis usually is absent. Atrial and ventricular septal defects may cause no signs at birth (although a systolic murmur is possible with the atrial defect). PDA causes a continuous or systolic heart murmur, increased heart pulsation (a heartbeat palpable over the precordium), tachycardia, tachypnea, hepatomegaly, bounding pulses, a palpable thrill over the suprasternal notch, bounding peripheral pulses, widened pulse pressure, and signs of respiratory distress or congestive heart failure (CHF), such as increasing respiratory effort, crackles or other moist breath sounds, feeding intolerance, fatigue, and decreasing urine output.

Coarctation of the aorta also may cause CHF as well as systolic hypertension in the arms, systolic hypotension in the legs, weak or absent femoral pulses, and a systolic ejection murmur at the left sternal border.

With cyanotic cardiac defects, expect cyanosis, especially during hypoxic spells. With tetralogy of Fallot, also expect dyspnea and a continuous murmur heard across the back. Transposition of the great vessels may cause tachypnea, poor feeding, dyspnea, and a soft murmur at the midsternal border. With tricuspid atresia, a systolic murmur at the second intercostal space along the left border may be auscultated. Expect signs of CHF with transposition and tricuspid atresia.

Respiratory tract anomalies

Cyanosis and respiratory compromise are the first signs of diaphragmatic hernia; the more severe the defect, the greater the respiratory compromise. The chest typically appears asymmetrical and the abdomen concave (from lack of abdominal contents). Substernal, intercostal, and suprascapular retractions usually occur over the unaffected side. The neonate usually is tachypneic, with a respiratory rate of at least 80 breaths/minute.

Record the neonate's temperature and assess pulse and respirations. Also, auscultate breath sounds over the entire chest wall; expect diminished or absent breath sounds on the affected side. A decrease or other change in breath sounds usually signifies gastric distention, which can lead to further respiratory compromise. Depending on the extent of the defect, heart sounds may be displaced.

GI tract anomalies

Except for meconium ileus, signs of these anomalies are obvious.

Tracheoesophageal malformations. In almost half of affected neonates, the maternal history includes hydramnios. After delivery, suspect a tracheoesopagheal malformation if the neonate has labored breathing, chest retractions, nasal flaring, cyanosis, or frothy secretions. Difficulty inserting a nasogastric tube and choking or aspiration during oral feedings are other suggestive signs.

Abdominal wall defects. Omphalocele and gastroschisis are apparent from the protruding intestine. Evaluate the defect for signs that the exposed viscera are becoming dry or infected. Also observe for fluid loss through the defect, which may be considerable, and for signs of gastric distention (such as a distended abdomen). If the neonate has omphalocele, examine carefully for associated anomalies.

Meconium ileus. This disorder manifests as abdominal distention, bilious vomiting, and distended bowel loops in the right lower quadrant (found on palpation).

Imperforate anus. This anomaly usually is obvious at delivery, although in some cases it is detected only during an attempt to take a rectal temperature. With a complete defect, the anus appears as a dimple in the perineal skin; an incomplete defect may manifest as a narrow opening where the anus should appear. If this anomaly is accompanied by bowel obstruction, the abdomen will be distended. The neonate typically does not pass meconium; however, sometimes meconium passes through a fistula or misplaced anus.

The level of the defect commonly is diagnosed by abdominal X-rays. A lateral abdominal X-ray with the neonate inverted distinguishes high from low imperforate anus. If air appears below a line drawn from the pubis to the sacrococcygeal junction (with a marker placed over the rectum), the defect is low. Air appearing above the line indicates a high defect.

Cleft palate and cleft lip. Except when the cleft affects the soft palate only, these anomalies are obvious. (For a description, see "Cleft palate and cleft lip" in the "Perinatal problems" section earlier in this chapter.) The neonate may have difficulty sucking, with expulsion of milk or formula through the nose. With cleft lip, the neonate may have signs of localized infection in the oral cavity, causing a fever, crying, and irritability.

Genitourinary tract anomalies

An anomaly involving the kidneys commonly causes acute renal failure, as reflected by oliguria or anuria. In many cases, the neonate has associated signs, such as hypoplastic lungs or GI defects.

Renal agenesis. Maternal oligohydramnios during pregnancy is a predictor of this anomaly; fetal ultrasound examination can confirm it before delivery. With bilateral renal agenesis, stillbirth occurs or the neonate dies within a few days after birth. Check for Potter facies: low-set ears; prominent skin folds beneath the eyes; a small, flattened nose; and a small chin and mandible with excessive skin folds. Oliguria or anuria within the first 48 hours after birth is diagnostic of this disorder. Skeletal anomalies that sometimes accompany renal agenesis include bowed legs and flat or broad hands and feet.

Polycystic kidneys. A protruding abdomen and greatly enlarged kidneys suggest this disorder; the liver also is enlarged. Fluid buildup may cause signs of acute renal failure, such as oliguria or anuria, edema, and blood pressure fluctuations.

Posterior urethral valves. A dribbling urine stream in a male neonate suggests this defect.

Genital ambiguity. In the affected female, androgen hypersecretion may cause such genital abnormalities as a small penis and the beginning of a scrotal sac. In the male, genital abnormalities may include abnormally small or undescended testes, hypospadias, and incomplete scrotal fusion.

The nurse who detects ambiguous genitalia should notify the physician immediately so that genetic evaluation can begin. Sex determination not only permits prompt treatment of the underlying adrenal disorder but may help reduce parental anxiety. Definitive sex determination may take up to 2 weeks. Meanwhile, review the prenatal history, especially noting any maternal exposure to hazardous environmental substances, and check the family history for associated problems.

Musculoskeletal anomalies

Clubfoot may be mild to severe and occurs in several varations. In equinovarus, the most common form, the heel turns inward from the midline of the leg, the foot is plantarflexed, the inner border of the foot is raised, and the anterior part of the foot is displaced so that it lies medial to the vertical axis of the leg. Other forms of clubfoot include calcaneovalgus, metatarsus adductus, and metatarsus varus.

If the neonate has an obvious foot deformity, first rule out "apparent clubfoot" (caused by fetal positioning) by taking the foot through the full range of motion. If the foot does not revert to a natural position with manipulation, suspect true clubfoot.

NURSING DIAGNOSIS

After gathering all assessment data, the nurse must review it carefully to identify pertinent nursing diagnoses for the neonate. (For a partial list of applicable diagnoses, see *Nursing diagnoses: High-risk neonate,* page 216.)

PLANNING AND IMPLEMENTATION

Once a fetus or neonate is identified as high risk (such as when fetal distress has been detected late in pregnancy), initial intervention should focus on preventing complications and death. Some high-risk neonates require emergency interventions; others, such as those with relatively minor congenital anomalies, are fairly stable at birth but require prompt treatment to prevent complications.

EMERGENCY INTERVENTION

In most cases, the need for resuscitation at delivery can be anticipated from maternal, antepartal, or intrapartal factors (as discussed in the "Assessment" section of this chapter). Immediately after delivery, the neonate must be evaluated to determine the need for resuscitation. Depending on the neonate's condition and response to each resuscitative measure, neonatal resuscitation typically involves some combination of the following:

• free-flow oxygen

HIGH-RISK NEONATE

The following are potential nursing diagnoses for problems and etiologies that a nurse may encounter when caring for a high-risk neonate. Specific nursing interventions for many of these diagnoses are provided in the "Planning and implementation" section of this chapter.

- Altered family processes related to the birth of a high-risk neonate and the adjustments necessitated by the neonate's condition and hospitalization
- Altered growth and development related to functional immaturity, prolonged environmental stress, a congenital anomaly, or lack of stimulation appropriate for gestational age and physical status
- Altered nutrition: less than body requirements, related to increased caloric requirements, respiratory distress, gastrointestinal immaturity, a weak sucking reflex, or metabolic dysfunction
- Fluid volume deficit related to renal immaturity or increased fluid loss
- Hypothermia related to an immature temperature-regulating center, decreased body mass-to-surface ratio, reduced subcutaneous fat, inability to shiver or sweat, and inadequate metabolic reserves
- Impaired gas exchange related to surfactant deficiency and altered alveolar function
- Ineffective airway clearance related to inability to expel excess secretions
- Ineffective breathing pattern related to respiratory and neurologic immaturity
- Potential altered parenting related to the neonate's condition, difficulty coping with a less-than-perfect neonate, and enforced separation of neonate and parents
- Potential aspiration related to meconium in amniotic fluid
- Potential impaired skin integrity related to frequent invasive procedures
- Potential for infection related to immunologic immaturity, altered ventilation, ineffective airway clearance, or frequent invasive procedures
- Potential for injury related to lack of cushioning from inadequate subcutaneous fat

- positive-pressure ventilation (PPV)
- closed-chest cardiac massage
- gastric decompression
- emergency drugs

● endotracheal intubation.

Preparation for resuscitation

Before every delivery, verify that emergency equipment and supplies are present, in working order, and ready to use; ideally, all items should be double-checked. This helps avert problems during resuscitation, when replacement of a missing supply or malfunctioning part could cause a dangerous treatment delay. (For a list of equipment and supplies, see *Resuscitation equipment and supplies,* pages 218 and 219.)

Resuscitation personnel

Every delivery should be attended by at least one person skilled in all resuscitation techniques and another person who is an experienced resuscitation assistant. When asphyxia is likely, a third person also should be present in the delivery room to manage the mother so that the resuscitators can attend solely to the neonate.

Before performing resuscitation on a neonate, an inexperienced nurse should observe a skilled nurse performing the procedures, then practice on a mannequin to the point of proficiency. The first few times the nurse resuscitates a neonate, close supervision is mandatory.

Resuscitation procedure

Initial neonatal evaluation and subsequent resuscitative measures are based on respirations, heart rate, and skin color – not on the 1-minute Apgar score (American Heart Association and American Academy of Pediatrics, 1987). Waiting until the end of the first minute to start resuscitation makes the procedure more difficult and increases the chance for brain damage and death. With a severely asphyxiated neonate, a delay is especially dangerous. (However, Apgar scores *should* be used to help determine whether resuscitative measures are effective.)

Like any resuscitation, the goal of neonatal resuscitation is to ensure the ABCs – airway, breathing, and circulation. Resuscitation follows an orderly sequence; after each intervention, the team quickly evaluates the neonate's condition and response to the intervention, then decides which further measures, if any, are necessary.

(For a detailed description of the steps used in resuscitation, see *Psychomotor skills: Resuscitating a neonate,* pages 220 to 224.)

RESUSCITATION EQUIPMENT AND SUPPLIES

To help ensure the most effective resuscitation, the nurse should be familiar with the delivery room equipment and supplies listed below.

BAG-AND-MASK EQUIPMENT

- Face masks (sizes 0.1 and 2)
- Infant resuscitation bag (anesthesia bag or self-inflating bag) capable of delivering 90% to 100% oxygen
- Oxygen delivery unit with adjustable fraction of inspired oxygen, humidification source, flowmeter, tubing, pressure gauge or pressure-release (pop-off) valve (40 to 60 cm H_2O)
- Oropharyngeal airway (sizes 000, 00, and 0)

EMERGENCY DRUGS AND SOLUTIONS

- Dextrose 10% in water
- Epinephrine 1:10,000
- Naloxone 0.02 mg/ml
- Normal saline solution
- Sodium bicarbonate 4.2% (5 mEq/10 ml)
- Volume expander (albumin, normal saline solution, or lactated Ringer's solution)

INTUBATION EQUIPMENT

- Endotracheal tubes with adapters (sizes 2.5, 3, 3.5, and 4 mm)
- Extra bulbs and batteries
- Gloves
- Laryngoscope with straight blades (sizes 0 and 1)
- Magill forceps
- Wire stylet for tubes
- Scissors

SUCTION EQUIPMENT (80 TO 100 MM HG)

- Bulb syringe
- DeLee mucus trap
- Mechanical suction machine
- Suction catheters (#5, #6, #8, and #10 Fr.)

OTHER ITEMS

- Adhesive tape
- Blood pressure cuff and gauge
- Cardiorespiratory monitor
- Clock or timer

RESUSCITATION EQUIPMENT AND SUPPLIES *(continued)*

OTHER ITEMS *(continued)*

- Electrocardiograph electrodes
- I.V. solution and tubing
- Water-soluble lubricating jelly (such as K-Y jelly)
- Nasogastric tube
- Radiant warmer resuscitation bed (preheated)
- Sterile gloves
- Sterile water
- Stethoscope
- Syringes (tuberculin 3, 5, and 10 ml)
- Umbilical artery catheter tray (including #3.5 and #5 Fr.)

Respirations. If the neonate lacks spontaneous respirations, PPV with a bag and mask must begin immediately. If the neonate is breathing (as indicated by chest movements), the resuscitation team moves on, evaluating heart rate.

Heart rate. If the heart rate is below 100 beats/minute, closed-chest cardiac massage (chest compression) typically begins as PPV continues. (PPV should be initiated whenever the heart rate is below 100, even if the neonate has spontaneous respirations.) If the heart rate is above 100 beats/minute, the team evaluates skin color.

Skin color. If the neonate has central cyanosis, reflecting lack of oxygen in the blood, the team administers free-flow oxygen by holding the end of an oxygen tube close to the neonate's nose or by holding an oxygen mask over the neonate's mouth and nose.

Special considerations
Although most neonates respond to PPV and chest compressions, some require other measures.

Gastric decompression. Bag-and-mask ventilation forces air to enter the stomach, which can prevent full lung expansion, cause aspiration of gastric contents, and lead to abdominal distention (which impedes breathing). Consequently, when bag-and-mask ven-

(Text continues on page 225.)

RESUSCITATING A NEONATE

The neonate with birth asphyxia or another form of cardiopulmonary compromise needs immediate resuscitation after delivery. The guidelines below, which describe the essential steps in neonatal resuscitation, reflect the recommendations of the American Heart Association and American Academy of Pediatrics (1987).

Suctioning the airway

1 Dry the neonate and place on a firm surface under a preheated radiant warmer. Extend the neck slightly to the "sniff" position. To maintain this position, place a rolled towel or blanket under the shoulders to raise them ¾" to 1" off the surface.

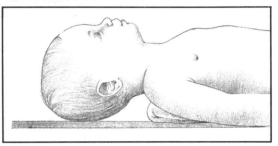

2 Using a soft catheter, mechanical suction, or a bulb syringe, suction the mouth, then the nose, to remove blood, meconium, or other matter. If the neonate has copious oral secretions, turn the head to the side to facilitate suctioning. To avoid stimulating the vagal reflex, which could cause bradycardia or apnea, avoid suctioning too vigorously or for more than 10 seconds.

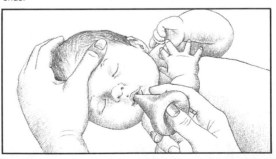

RESUSCITATING A NEONATE *(continued)*

Administering positive-pressure ventilation

1 If drying, suctioning, or other tactile stimulation (such as tapping the soles or rubbing the back) does not induce respirations immediately, begin positive-pressure ventilation with a bag and mask at once. Attach the resuscitation bag to an oxygen source and select a mask of the correct size (size 0 for the preterm neonate, size 1 for the term neonate). Connect the mask to the resuscitation bag.

2 Standing at the neonate's side or head, apply the mask so that it covers the neonate's nose and mouth, with the edge of the neonate's chin resting within the rim of the mask. To obtain an airtight seal, use light downward pressure on the rim to apply the mask.

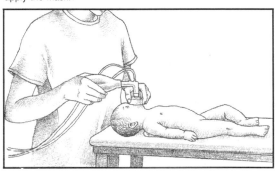

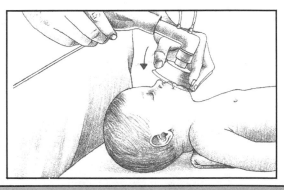

(continued)

RESUSCITATING A NEONATE *(continued)*

3 Check the seal and the ventilation technique by ventilating two or three times and watching for chest movement. (Make sure to squeeze the bag with the fingertips only, not the entire palm.) The neonate's chest should rise slightly, as in a shallow breath. A deep breath indicates that the lungs are being overinflated from excessive pressure on the bag.

If the neonate's chest does not rise, suspect an inadequate seal, a blocked airway, or insufficient pressure delivered by the bag. Correct these problems by reapplying the mask; repositioning the neonate's head; checking for secretions and suctioning, if necessary; or increasing the pressure to 20 to 40 cm H_2O or until the pop-off valve activates.

4 If the chest rises slightly, give an initial ventilation of 15 to 30 seconds with 100% oxygen at a rate of 40 ventilations/minute. Initial breaths may require a pressure of up to 40 cm H_2O; for subsequent ventilations, use only the minimum pressure necessary to move the chest.

5 Subsequent actions depend on the heart rate. Check the heart rate with a cardiac monitor (if a monitor is not available, listen to the apical beat with a stethoscope or feel the umbilical pulse at the base of the cord). To estimate the 1-minute heart rate, count the heartbeat for 6 seconds and multiply by 10.
• If the heart rate is above 100 beats/minute and the neonate is breathing spontaneously, discontinue bag-and-mask ventilation and provide gentle stimulation (for instance, by rubbing the skin). Monitor the neonate to assess for stabilization.
• If the heart rate is above 100 beats/minute but the neonate is not breathing spontaneously, continue to ventilate at a rate of 40 breaths/minute.
• If the heart rate is 60 to 100 beats/minute and increasing, continue to ventilate. If the heart rate is between 60 and 100 but *not* increasing, continue to ventilate and verify that the chest is moving properly and that 100% oxygen is being delivered.
• If the heart rate is less than 60 beats/minute or between 60 and 80 beats/minute and *not* increasing, another member of the team must start closed-chest cardiac massage (chest compressions) at once while the first resuscitator continues to ventilate.

RESUSCITATING A NEONATE (continued)

Performing chest compressions

1 To ensure the best outcome, resuscitation team members should position themselves so that each can work effectively without hindering the other.

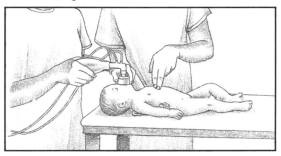

2 The resuscitator who administers chest compressions may use either the thumb method or the two-finger method.

For the **thumb method,** place both thumbs side-by-side over the midsternum, with the hands encircling the chest and the fingers supporting the neonate's back (illustration at left). If the neonate is very small, one thumb can be placed over the other (illustration at right).

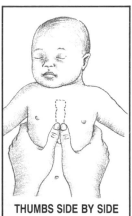

THUMBS SIDE BY SIDE

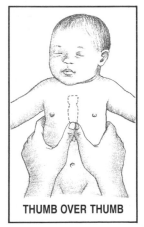

THUMB OVER THUMB

(continued)

RESUSCITATING A NEONATE (continued)

For the **two-finger method,** place the tips of the middle finger and the ring or index finger over the midsternum in the midline while supporting the neonate's back with the other hand.

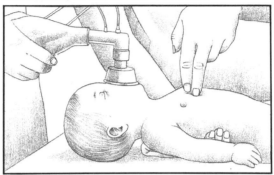

3 With either method, depress the sternum ½" to ¾", then release the pressure to allow the heart to refill; keep the thumbs or fingertips in contact with the sternum at all times, even during the release. Deliver 120 compressions/minute (one compression equals the downward stroke plus the release). When delivering compressions, take care not to squeeze the chest with the whole hand or apply pressure to the xiphoid process.

4 To determine if chest compressions are effective, one resuscitator should check the pulse after 30 seconds of compressions, then periodically (by counting for 6 seconds). Once the neonate's heart rate reaches 80 beats/minute, chest compressions should be discontinued. However, ventilations should continue until the heart rate exceeds 100 beats/minute and the neonate is breathing spontaneously.

If the heart rate is below 80 beats/minute, chest compressions and ventilation must continue; in some cases, emergency drugs are administered at this point. If the neonate still shows no response, resuscitation continues until the physician decides to stop it.

RESUSCITATION DRUGS

For the neonate with no detectable heartbeat at delivery, the physician typically orders emergency drugs immediately (along with bag-and-mask ventilation and chest compressions). Drugs also are indicated for a neonate whose heart rate remains below 80 beats/minute despite adequate bag-and-mask ventilation and chest compressions. The chart below summarizes indications and nursing considerations for drugs recommended for neonatal resuscitation by the American Heart Association and American Academy of Pediatrics (1987).

DRUG	INDICATIONS	NURSING CONSIDERATIONS
dopamine	Poor peripheral perfusion, thready pulses, and continuing signs of shock after administration of epinephrine, a volume expander, and sodium bicarbonate	• Administer as a continuous I.V. infusion in a prepared solution. • Use an infusion pump to control the infusion rate.
epinephrine	Heart rate of 0 or heart rate below 80 beats/minute after 30 seconds of ventilation with 100% oxygen and chest compressions	• Prepare 1 ml 1:10,000 dilution in a syringe for I.V. or endotracheal administration. • Administer rapidly.
sodium bicarbonate	Metabolic acidosis	• Prepare two prefilled syringes (10 ml) or draw 20 ml into a syringe for I.V. administration. • Give over at least 2 minutes.
naloxone hydrochloride (neonatal narcan)	Severe respiratory depression in a neonate whose mother received a narcotic no more than 4 hours earlier	• Draw 2 ml 0.02 mg/ml dilution into a syringe for I.V., I.M., subcutaneous, or endotracheal administration. • Inject rapidly.

tilation is required for more than 2 minutes, an orogastric tube must be inserted to suction gastric contents; the tube is left in place throughout resuscitation to vent air.

Emergency drugs. Drugs may be administered if the neonate fails to respond to bag-and-mask ventilation and chest compressions. Such drugs typically are administered via the umbilical vein or, in some cases, through a peripheral vein (such as a scalp or extremity vein) or an endotracheal tube. (For information on drugs recommended for use in neonatal resuscitation, see *Resuscitation drugs*.)

Endotracheal intubation. This intervention, which should be performed only by an experienced intubator, is indicated when diaphragmatic hernia is suspected, when the neonate requires prolonged ventilation, or when prolonged bag-and-mask ventilation proves ineffective.

Endotracheal intubation also is necessary when MAS is suspected. If the amniotic fluid contains thick meconium — a sign of asphyxia experienced in utero — the neonate has a nursing diagnosis of *potential for aspiration related to meconium in the respiratory tract*. As soon as the neonate's head is delivered, the mouth, oropharynx, and hypopharynx must be suctioned with a flexible suction catheter. Immediately after delivery, an experienced intubator visualizes the larynx with a laryngoscope, then intubates the trachea and suctions any meconium from the lower airway — preferably by applying suction to an endotracheal tube. After the tube has been inserted, continuous suction is applied as the tube is withdrawn. This procedure is repeated until no more meconium is suctioned.

Post-resuscitation care

After resuscitation, observe the neonate closely for signs of respiratory distress, including cyanosis, apnea, tachypnea, and inspiratory retractions. Blood pressure and perfusion are other key indicators; if either is inadequate, expect to administer volume expanders to reverse shock.

If an endotracheal tube is in place, observe for tube dislodgement, signs of tube obstruction, and associated complications, such as pneumothorax. To monitor tube placement, check tube length (from the point where it leaves the mouth to the connection point) and assess for equal bilateral breath sounds and symmetrical chest expansion.

If the neonate was severely asphyxiated at delivery, the physician may want to maintain serum glucose at 100 to 150 mg/dl; expect to administer dextrose 10% in water and monitor the serum glucose level. Also monitor the hematocrit and assess renal status by measuring fluid intake and checking for abrupt weight changes, which may signal renal complications of asphyxia. Ensure thermoregulation by keeping the neonate under a radiant warmer and monitoring skin temperature.

If the neonate requires transport to a level 3 nursery, make preparations according to institutional protocol and notify the nursery of the impending admission as soon as possible so that staff and necessary equipment can be mobilized.

GENERAL NURSING GUIDELINES

Although the neonate's condition will dictate the specifics of nursing care, the same nursing goals apply to all high-risk neonates: Ensure oxygenation, ventilation, thermoregulation, nutrition, and fluid and electrolyte balance, prevent and control infection, and provide developmental care.

Supporting oxygenation and ventilation

Most neonates who have been successfully resuscitated — as well as many other high-risk neonates — need supplemental oxygen to prevent or correct hypoxia. Supplemental oxygen can be administered by hood, nasal cannula, or continuous positive-airway pressure (CPAP); it always should be warmed and humidified. To avoid a nursing diagnosis of *impaired gas exchange related to surfactant deficiency and altered alveolar function* or *ineffective breathing pattern related to respiratory and neurologic immaturity,* be alert to neonates who require additional ventilatory support in the form of mechanical ventilation.

The goal of supplemental oxygen therapy is to maintain a PaO_2 of 60 to 80 mm Hg. A higher level may lead to ROP; a lower level, to profound hypoxia and CNS problems (including cerebral hemorrhage and brain damage). Record the fraction of inspired oxygen (FIO_2) as a percentage (however, for the older neonate who is receiving oxygen by nasal cannula, FIO_2 may be recorded in liters/ minute). FIO_2 ranges from 21% (the oxygen concentration in room air) to 100%.

Because oxygen is a drug, the nurse must be familiar with its potential adverse effects and ways to avoid them. For instance, to prevent or minimize the risk of ROP, always administer oxygen at the lowest concentration that will correct hypoxia, using an oxygen analyzer to determine the actual concentration of delivered oxygen.

To ensure therapeutic efficacy and avoid oxygen toxicity, monitor the neonate's oxygenation status continuously with a noninvasive technique, such as transcutaneous oxygen pressure ($tcPO_2$) monitoring or pulse oximetry. With a $tcPO_2$ monitor, the probe measures oxygen diffusion and carbon dioxide perfusion across the skin; with pulse oximetry, the probe measures beat-to-beat arterial oxygen saturation. Be sure to place the probe in a well-perfused area. $TcPO_2$ readings should range from 50 to 80 mm Hg; oximetry readings should be no less than 90% (Chatburn and Carlo, 1988).

However, tcPO$_2$ or oximetry values alone are not adequate; they must be correlated with simultaneously obtained arterial blood gas (ABG) samples drawn every 3 to 4 hours. To obtain ABG samples, use a heparinized syringe; place the samples on ice to prevent oxygen and carbon dioxide diffusion.

Oxygen hood and nasal cannula. An oxygen hood, which fits over the neonate's head, can deliver up to 100% oxygen and allows easy access to the rest of the neonate's body for care procedures. A nasal cannula delivers oxygen concentrations above room air (21%); typically, it is used for a neonate with BPD or a congenital cardiac defect (the minimal equipment involved allows frequent cuddling and other stimulation).

CPAP. CPAP usually is implemented if the PaO$_2$ level of a neonate receiving an FIO$_2$ of 60% or higher drops below 60 mm Hg. CPAP delivers air at a constant pressure throughout the respiratory cycle, keeping the lungs expanded at all times to reduce shunting and improve oxygenation. CPAP may be delivered via a nasopharyngeal tube or an endotracheal tube inserted through the mouth or nose. Some neonatologists believe a nasal tube is more secure than an oral tube. However, prolonged nasal intubation may cause anterior naris (nostril) damage and deviation or nasal septal erosion. An excessively long oral tube, on the other hand, may become kinked. With either tube, take steps to avoid accidental extubation.

During CPAP therapy, monitor the neonate's vital signs, blood pressure, and respiratory effort; stay especially alert for tachycardia, tachypnea, and arrhythmias.

Mechanical ventilation. Mechanical ventilation usually is used instead of CPAP if any of the following criteria are present:
- PaO$_2$ level below 50 mm Hg with administration of 100% oxygen (Goldsmith and Karotkin, 1988)
- PaCO$_2$ level above 80 mm Hg
- arterial pH below 7.2.

During mechanical ventilation, assess the neonate's vital signs, breath sounds, chest movement, respiratory effort, and oxygenation status every hour. When assessing breath sounds, keep in mind that in a mechanically ventilated neonate, breath sounds normally are loud and high-pitched. However, extremely high-pitched sounds may signal excessive secretions. A pitch decrease, in contrast, may reflect atelectasis or pulmonary air leakage.

As necessary, suction the endotracheal tube to maintain a patent airway, making sure to apply suction only while removing the catheter. If possible, use a suctioning remethod that does not necessitate interruption of mechanical ventilation. Report any change in the amount or consistency of secretions.

Be sure to assess endotracheal tube positioning and patency regularly; a tube resting along the tracheal wall may impair ventilation. Also check ventilator function periodically, making sure all alarms are working. Assess the system for leaks.

Maintaining thermoregulation

An essential part of care for all neonates, thermoregulation is particularly crucial to the high-risk neonate, whose oxygen and energy reserves may be depleted rapidly by illness. The preterm neonate especially is at risk for cold stress because of limited subcutaneous fat, an extremely high surface-to-mass ratio, inability to shiver, and minimal brown fat (a type of fat that provides body heat).

Heat loss may result from radiation, conduction, evaporation, or convection (as discussed in Chapter 1, Neonatal Adaptation). A neonate who suffers heat loss and subsequent cold stress may experience peripheral vasoconstriction, hypoglycemia, reduced cerebral perfusion, metabolic acidosis, exacerbation of RDS, decreased surfactant production, impaired kidney function, GI disturbances, hypoglycemia, and, ultimately, death.

A first step in preventing hypothermia is to minimize cooling at delivery; such cooling may delay adequate thermoregulation for hours. During the initial examination and resuscitation, the neonate should be placed under a radiant heat warmer. Wrap the neonate in a plastic bag or thermal foil blanket as soon as possible after resuscitation, and then transfer the neonate to an incubator or radiant warmer bed. The practice of drying the neonate thoroughly after birth has been found to cause cold stress (Perlstein, 1988).

Because heat loss from the neonate's head is considerable, keep the neonate's head covered at all times. Also, warm the hands before touching the neonate to prevent conductive heat loss through handling.

Neutral thermal environment. Throughout care, aim for a neutral thermal environment (NTE), a narrow range of environmental temperature (89.6° to 93.2° F [32° to 34° C]) that maintains a stable core (rectal) temperature with minimal caloric and oxygen expenditure. Although NTE may prove hard to achieve, certain measures may help prevent a nursing diagnosis of *hypothermia related to an immature temperature-regulating center, decreased body mass-to-surface ratio, reduced subcutaneous fat, inability to shiver or sweat, and inadequate metabolic reserves.* For instance, use of a warmed, humidified incubator with an air temperature of 96.8° F (36° C) helps maintain proper skin temperature (Perlstein, 1988).

Thermoregulation during transport. Special measures must be taken if the neonate requires transport to another facility. Causes of heat loss during transport include poor heat retention in the transport bed, radiant heat loss within the transport vehicle, and drafts as the transport bed passes through unheated corridors or as the door or hood to the transport bed is opened to place the neonate inside. To help minimize the risk of cold stress from these causes, provide an NTE before transport (for instance, by protecting the neonate from heat loss during examinations or care procedures). Also, wrap the neonate before transport or place a warming mattress in the transport bed to enhance its heating capacity.

Providing adequate nutrition

The accelerated metabolic rate and energy expenditure of the high-risk neonate may lead to a nursing diagnosis of *altered nutrition: less than body requirements, related to increased caloric requirements, respiratory distress, GI immaturity, a weak sucking reflex, or metabolic dysfunction.* Respiratory distress, for instance, increases caloric requirements 50% to 75%; the metabolic response to surgery, by 30% (Kaempf, Bonnabel, and Hoy, 1989).

The preterm neonate may need 104 to 130 calories/kg/day, compared to the normal healthy neonate, who requires 100 to 120 calories/kg/day. However, caloric requirements change over time and should be adjusted depending on the neonate's tolerance.

For the high-risk neonate who can take nourishment by mouth, breast milk is the preferred nutritional form. If the neonate cannot receive breast milk, the physician may order a special high-calorie infant formula to provide 24 or 27 calories/oz (in contrast to the

20 calories/oz in standard formulas). In some cases, a neonate may begin feedings with half-strength formula and gradually increase to three-quarters-strength, then full-strength.

Enteral nutrition (gavage feedings). To avoid aspiration resulting from a weak sucking reflex, uncoordinated sucking and swallowing, or respiratory distress, many high-risk neonates must be fed enterally, typically through a tube passed through the nose or mouth into the stomach. (However, some neonates must be fed through a surgically placed gastrostomy tube.)

Although a nasogastric tube typically is used to provide enteral feedings, some neonatologists prefer a nasojejunal or orojejunal tube. A nasojejunal tube is passed from the nose through the stomach to the jejunum; an orojejunal tube is passed from the mouth to the jejunum. Because of a possible link between jejunal tubes and NEC, some authorities do not recommend them for neonates weighing less than 2,000 g (Moyer-Mileur, 1986). Nonetheless, jejunal tubes are used with increasing frequency in neonates with gastric reflux and a high risk for aspiration pneumonia. With either tube, placement usually is confirmed by X-ray and aspirate pH values.

If intermittent bolus feedings are prescribed, a tube is passed with each feeding; continuous feedings are administered through an indwelling tube. Typically, the delivery rate for enteral feedings is increased at 12-hour intervals; the increase must be gradual to avoid complications associated with poor feeding tolerance, such as dehydration, diarrhea, vomiting, and abdominal distention. Monitor the neonate closely for these signs.

Check tube placement every 4 hours; remove the tube immediately if the neonate begins to choke or cough or becomes cyanotic — signs that the tube has entered the trachea. To prevent aspiration, keep the mattress elevated 30 degrees for 30 minutes after intermittent bolus feedings and at all times for continuous feedings.

To check gastric residual matter, aspirate gastric contents every 4 hours by attaching a syringe containing 0.5 to 1 ml of air to the tubing. Inject the air while listening through a stethoscope over the epigastric area for a rush of air. Note the color, amount, and consistency of gastric contents; more than 15 ml of matter aspirated before a feeding may signal poor tolerance of feedings.

Parenteral nutrition. This method, in which nutrients are administered by the I.V. route, may be required by the preterm or postsurgical neonate who cannot tolerate oral or enteral feedings. Parenteral nutrition requirements depend on birth weight and diagnosis. For many high-risk neonates, a solution of dextrose 5% or 10% in water (80 to 100 ml/kg/day) is initiated in the delivery room or soon after transfer to the NICU. Electrolytes typically are added to the solution 24 hours after delivery; the most commonly administered electrolytes are sodium and potassium chloride.

Monitor urine and serum glucose levels carefully during parenteral nutrition to prevent glycosuria and hyperglycemia; if these conditions develop, expect to reduce the dextrose concentration. For the preterm neonate, hyperglycemia is confirmed by a glucose oxidase dipstick or heelstick glucose value above 150 mg/100 ml.

If the neonate will not be fed orally for more than 3 days, expect the physician to order total parenteral nutrition (TPN), which provides adequate carbohydrates, amino acids, lipids, glucose, vitamins, and electrolytes for growth and development. When caring for the neonate who is receiving TPN, monitor the serum glucose level with a glucose oxidase dipstick and the urine glucose level with a copper reduction tablet or glucose oxidase dipstick. Obtain hematocrit and serum electrolyte and urea levels to assess how well the neonate is tolerating TPN. (Required laboratory values vary from one facility to another; however, expect to obtain calcium, phosphate, magnesium, alkaline phosphate, protein, and transaminase levels at least weekly.)

Any substance with a dextrose concentration above 12.5% must be administered via a central line (such as an umbilical vessel catheter); peripheral administration of fluids with a higher dextrose concentration can cause tissue swelling, necrosis, and cellular death at the infusion site. When administering parenteral nutrition via a central line, maintain meticulous aseptic technique and clean the infusion site according to facility protocol to minimize the risk of contamination. Also make sure the line remains intact to prevent the introduction of organisms that may cause systemic infection. Keep the dressing over the insertion site occlusive; if it appears loose, change it immediately.

In some facilities, blood cultures and cultures from the infusion site are obtained routinely; in others, cultures are required only if infection is suspected. With the extremely preterm neonate, who has limited vascular volume, avoid obtaining blood cultures unless an infection is suspected.

Maintaining fluid and electrolyte balance

Renal immaturity, small fluid reserves, a high metabolic rate, and pronounced insensible fluid losses make even the normal, healthy neonate susceptible to fluid and electrolyte imbalance. Perinatal problems—especially those causing diarrhea, vomiting, or high fever—and surgery can further upset fluid balance in the high-risk neonate, leading to a nursing diagnosis of *fluid volume deficit related to renal immaturity or increased fluid loss.*

Both clinical and environmental conditions influence fluid requirements. For example, CHF, certain renal disorders, and use of a thermal blanket or mist tent reduce the fluid requirement. On the other hand, the neonate who is receiving phototherapy has a greater need for fluid, as does one with respiratory distress or blood loss. Likewise, use of a radiant warmer increases fluid needs by enhancing insensible fluid losses. After surgery, a neonate is particularly vulnerable to fluid volume deficit—not only is hypovolemia a natural response to surgery, but the neonate loses blood during surgery and loses insensible fluids in the cool, dry operating room. To counter environmental conditions that promote insensible fluid loss, provide an NTE whenever possible.

I.V. fluid requirements for the high-risk neonate range from 60 to 200 ml/kg/day. To maintain fluid balance, give sufficient fluids to maintain a urine output of about 1 ml/kg/hour and a specific gravity of 1.005 to 1.012. However, if gastric compression is used, give additional fluids, as prescribed, to counter gastric fluid losses.

Measure fluid intake and urine output hourly for each shift, and at 24-hour intervals by using a urine collection bag or by weighing diapers. Weigh the neonate daily, using the same scale if possible, and compare fluid intake to output for each shift and at 24-hour intervals. Also monitor laboratory data (hematocrit, blood pH, and serum electrolyte, blood urea nitrogen, creatinine, and uric acid levels) to evaluate acid-base status. Assess urine specific gravity with each voiding or at least every 4 hours.

Stay alert for signs of fluid deficit and fluid excess; the latter is most likely with a cardiac or renal problem. (For signs of fluid deficit and excess, see *Assessing fluid status,* page 234.)

ASSESSING FLUID STATUS

Various factors place the high-risk neonate in danger of fluid imbalance – particularly fluid volume deficit. To assess for fluid volume deficit or excess, check for the signs listed below.

SIGNS OF FLUID VOLUME DEFICIT (DEHYDRATION)

- Dry mucous membranes
- Elevated hematocrit, hemoglobin level, and blood urea nitrogen value
- Increasing heart and respiratory rates
- Low-grade fever
- Poor skin turgor
- Slightly decreased blood pressure
- Sunken eyeballs or fontanels
- Urine output less than 1 ml/kg/hour
- Urine specific gravity above 1.013
- Weight loss

SIGNS OF FLUID VOLUME EXCESS (OVERHYDRATION)

- Chronic cough
- Crackles
- Dyspnea
- Edema
- Increasing central venous pressure
- Rhonchi
- Tachypnea
- Urine output exceeding 5 ml/kg/hour

Assess the neonate's electrolyte status by monitoring serum electrolyte levels. As a general rule, serum sodium should approximate 133 to 146 mmol/liter; serum calcium, 6.1 to 11.6 mg/dl; serum potassium, 4.6 to 6.7 mmol/liter; and serum chloride, 100 to 117 mmol/liter.

Preventing and controlling infection

Nearly all high-risk neonates have a nursing diagnosis of *potential for infection related to immunologic immaturity, altered ventilation, ineffective airway clearance, or frequent invasive procedures.* Consequently, take the following precautions to help minimize the risk of infection.

• Practice meticulous hand washing. Scrub for 3 minutes before entering the nursery and wash hands frequently throughout caregiving activities. After providing care, perform a 1-minute scrub.

• Pay meticulous attention to asepsis during all care procedures. Maintain sterile technique during invasive procedures, such as suctioning and drawing blood from arterial lines. As permitted by facility protocol, use triple-dye alcohol or an antimicrobial agent when caring for the umbilical cord and any puncture sites.

• Make sure all equipment used for neonatal care is sterile or has been cleaned thoroughly. A stethoscope should be assigned to each neonate to prevent cross-contamination, and health care providers should refrain from using their own equipment when providing neonatal care.

• Avoid wearing rings and other jewelry. Many facilities also prohibit nursery staff from using hand lotions, which serve as a breeding ground for pathogenic organisms.

• Wear gloves and follow other universal precautions when changing diapers and performing other activities involving contact with body secretions.

• If an I.V. line is in place, document the appearance of the I.V. site every 30 minutes to 1 hour, depending on the solution being given. If redness or swelling appears, indicating infiltration, the infusion site may have to be changed. However, never stop a glucose or calcium infusion abruptly without immediately restarting it because this may cause serum glucose or calcium levels to fluctuate widely.

• When bathing the neonate, use mild soap and wash only creases and soiled areas. Avoid harsh chemicals, such as alcohol and povidone-iodine, and carefully rinse the neonate's skin after using any irritating substance.

• Maintain an intact skin barrier — especially if the neonate has a nursing diagnosis of *potential impaired skin integrity related to frequent invasive procedures* — by using as little tape as possible to secure I.V. catheters, urine collection containers, feeding tubes, and other equipment (tape removal may peel off the epidermis). Also, first apply an adhesive removal pad when removing ECG leads.

• To help prevent pressure-point breakdown, change the neonate's position, provide range-of-motion exercises, and place the neonate on sheepskin or a waterbed. Assess the skin for redness (especially over bony prominences), which indicates poor circulation to the reddened area. To guard against skin tears and scrapes when turning or moving the neonate, apply a protective transparent covering over elbows, knees, and other vulnerable joints.

• Evaluate all visitors for signs of infection.

• Any staff member with active herpes simplex lesions (those that have not reached the crusting stage) should refrain from working in the nursery. Even after lesions have crusted, the person should wear gloves and wash hands before and after contact.

To detect infection early, assess the neonate regularly for such systemic signs as hypothermia or hyperthermia, lethargy, jaundice, petechiae, respiratory distress, purulent drainage from the eyes or umbilical site, and subtle behavioral changes. Also check for signs of localized infection from the umbilical and I.V. sites.

If the neonate has potential signs of infection, place in an incubator and, if possible, an isolation room to protect other neonates. Expect the physician to prescribe prophylactic antibiotics (typically ampicillin and gentamicin) and a septic workup, which routinely includes cultures of blood, CSF, and urine; a chest X-ray; serum electrolyte analysis; and a complete blood count (CBC) with differential.

Once culture and sensitivity test results determine the infectious organism, the physician may change the antibiotic prescribed; in most cases, a combination of antibiotics is used. If the physician prescribes gentamicin, obtain peak and trough serum blood levels after the third dose to detect or prevent adverse drug reactions; obtain a trough level 30 minutes before administering the next dose and a peak level 30 to 45 minutes afterward. Antibiotic therapy typically continues for 10 days, with reevaluation at the end of the course.

During antibiotic therapy, assess the neonate for signs of drug-induced nerve damage, including palsy, decreased arm or leg mobility, and tremors; also check for behavioral changes, which could signal decreased tolerance of antibiotic therapy. Monitor fluid intake and output every 4 to 8 hours, and notify the physician if output falls below normal.

For a group B streptococcal infection, monitor blood pressure, including mean arterial pressure. Decreasing blood pressure may warrant administration of plasmanate to expand blood volume and correct the shock response resulting from this infection. Unless immediate aggressive interventions begin, this infection carries a mortality rate as high as 90% (Nelson, Merenstein, and Pierce, 1986).

Providing developmental care and environmental support

Research from the past 20 years shows that the neonate is aware of surroundings and responds to sensory stimulation. Within the past decade, health care providers increasingly have aimed to establish a developmentally appropriate environment for the high-risk neonate by reducing detrimental stimulation, providing appropriate stimulation during caregiving activities, and teaching parents how to provide appropriate stimulation.

To reduce environmental noise, for example, eliminate loud music and loud talking near the neonate and make sure doors, trash-can bottoms, and incubator portholes are padded. Also, dim the lights and minimize handling of the neonate. When trying to arouse the neonate, use a soft voice and call the neonate by name.

For the neonate with a nursing diagnosis of *altered growth and development related to functional immaturity, prolonged environmental stress, and lack of stimulation appropriate for gestational age and physical status,* nursing interventions include:
• initiating direct-care procedures only when the neonate is alert
• providing rest periods between activities
• encouraging parents to interact with the neonate in ways that promote optimal development
• providing tactile, auditory, visual, and vestibular stimulation (handling) according to the neonate's tolerance. Activities that provide such stimulation include gentle stroking, caressing (especially during feeding), talking, singing, calling the neonate by name, playing a tape of the parents' voices, promoting eye contact with visitors, displaying pictures and designs near the neonate, holding the neonate in a ventral (face-down) position during burping, and stroking the back until the neonate burps. Also, continually assess the neonate's response to stimulation.

Ensuring preoperative and postoperative care

For the neonate who requires surgery, preoperative nursing care includes monitoring vital signs, maintaining a patent airway, assessing respiratory status, ensuring fluid balance, and maintaining adequate nutrition (as with enteral or parenteral feedings). Depending on the neonate's specific problems, other measures may be warranted—for example, providing gastric decompression via a nasogastric tube; preventing trauma, heat loss, and infection at a defect site (such as with encephalocele or gastroschisis); and administering broad-spectrum antibiotics.

After surgery, check vital signs for the first 24 hours—every 15 minutes for the first hour, every 30 minutes for the next 2 hours, every hour for the next 4 hours, then every 2 hours. Maintain patency of the airway and any airway tubes by suctioning frequently and checking for signs of respiratory distress. Support oxygenation and ventilation by giving supplemental oxygen or maintaining mechanical ventilation, as appropriate, and by turning the neonate from side to side every few hours.

Ensure fluid and electrolyte balance by monitoring fluid intake and output and checking serum electrolyte levels. If the neonate must be fed through a gastrostomy tube, give feedings by slow gravity drip. If possible, have the neonate suck on a pacifier to stimulate the sucking and swallowing reflexes.

Maintain skin integrity at the surgical site by cleaning frequently (as specified by facility protocol) and observing for signs of infection, such as skin breakdown, erythema, edema, or bloody or purulent drainage. To prevent disruption of the suture line, use restraints if necessary.

If a nasogastric tube is present for postoperative gastric decompression (to prevent stress on the surgical site), tape the tube to the neonate's face. Irrigate the tube frequently to ensure patency and drainage, and connect it to low-intermittent suction.

If a chest tube is present, check for patency of the system by observing for a consistent flow of bubbles in the underwater seal container. Auscultate breath sounds frequently; diminishing breath sounds may signal a developing pneumothorax.

If a colostomy was performed (as with certain GI defects), check the amount, color, and consistency of stools. When changing dressings, avoid applying undue friction when cleaning around the stoma. Check for skin breakdown and bleeding near the stoma.

For the neonate recovering from surgery for a neurologic anomaly, check neurologic status frequently by assessing pupil size and response, level of consciousness, behavior and activity levels, motor function, and firmness of fontanels. Also evaluate for signs of increased intracranial pressure (such as lethargy, a high-pitched cry, and sunset eyes) and measure head circumference daily. Monitor fluid intake and output and observe extremities for mottling and poor capillary refill.

After surgery for a cardiac anomaly, frequently assess vital signs, breath sounds, and results of ABG analysis and blood tests (especialy hematocrit and hemoglobin values). Maintain electronic cardiorespiratory monitoring and assess urine output hourly.

Carrying out special procedures

Many high-risk neonates require phototherapy or exchange transfusion to treat hyperbilirubinemia; a few require extracorporeal membrane oxygenation (ECMO). General nursing measures during phototherapy and exchange transfusions focus on maintaining body temperature, proper timing of care to avoid unnecessary stress, and assessing oral intake, urine output, and stools. With any of the procedures described in this section, observe the neonate closely for respiratory compromise. The neonate with hyperbilirubinemia is at risk for asphyxia and respiratory distress; the neonate who requires ECMO commonly has preexisting respiratory distress.

Phototherapy. In this procedure, used to treat hyperbilirubinemia, the neonate is placed unclothed approximately 18″ under a bank of lights for several hours or days until the serum bilirubin level drops to within acceptable limits. Phototherapy lights decompose bilirubin in the skin through oxidation, facilitating biliary excretion of unconjugated bilirubin.

Nursing responsibilities. To prevent retinal damage, an opaque mask must be placed over the neonate's eyes. Make sure that the mask is tight enough to stay in place but not so tight that it impedes circulation or puts pressure on the eyeballs (direct pressure may cause reflex bradycardia). Also keep the genitals covered with a mask or small diaper to catch urine and stool while leaving the skin surface open to the light. Observe for signs of pressure caused by eye and genital coverings. Turn the neonate every 2 hours to relieve pressure on the knees, hips, and other joints and to allow exposure of all skin surfaces.

Turn off the phototherapy lights for 2 to 5 minutes at least every 8 hours to assess the eyes for irritation or redness and help the neonate establish a normal sleep-awake pattern (phototherapy may lengthen sleep). Monitor the number and consistency of stools;

bilirubin breakdown increases gastric motility, resulting in loose stools that can cause skin excoriation and breakdown. Be sure to clean the neonate's buttocks after each stool to help maintain skin integrity.

Check the serum bilirubin level every 4 to 8 hours to determine if phototherapy is effective, and frequently assess skin and sclera color to check the degree of jaundice. Also estimate fluid losses and check for dehydration, which occurs as GI hypermotility pulls fluids into the intestines; if dehydration occurs, notify the physician. To minimize insensible fluid losses, place the neonate in an incubator if possible, and provide I.V. fluids, as prescribed.

Complete exchange transfusion. Hyperbilirubinemia that does not respond to phototherapy may necessitate a complete exchange transfusion. In this procedure, the neonate's blood is removed via an umbilical catheter and replaced with fresh whole donor blood to remove the unconjugated bilirubin in the serum. The procedure carries a risk of transfusion reaction and subsequent death.

To minimize the risk of cardiovascular complications, isovolumetric exchange transfusion may be used. In this method, both the umbilical vein and umbilical artery are catheterized: One catheter is inserted into the umbilical artery and another into the umbilical vein. A three-way stopcock is placed at the end of each catheter and a syringe is connected to the arterial catheter at the junction of the stopcock; the arterial catheter serves as the site for blood withdrawal. After the neonate's blood is withdrawn, warmed whole blood is administered via the venous catheter.

In the most common isovolumetric technique, 5 to 10 ml of the neonate's blood are removed and the same amount of warmed donor blood administered via the venous catheter over at least 2 minutes. Withdrawing or administering blood at a faster rate may lead to life-threatening arrhythmias. Half-way through the exchange transfusion, calcium gluconate is administered to prevent hypocalcemia and consequent cardiac irritability.

The procedure takes 1 to 2 hours, depending on the volume of blood exchanged and the neonate's condition. (The volume of blood to be exchanged typically is calculated by multiplying kilograms of body weight by 180 ml.) An exchange transfusion may be repeated if the serum bilirubin level continues to rise.

In some facilities, fetal exchange transfusion is used to treat isoimmune hemolytic anemia in utero. In this technique, introduced by Liley (1963), fetal blood is withdrawn and donor blood administered through an umbilical artery catheter. Although fetal exchange transfusion can predispose the fetus to infection and hemorrhage, it has proven successful. Fetal transfusions usually are carried out at regional centers with little risk to the mother and a success rate of 65% to 70% (Pringle, 1989).

Nursing responsibilities. For several hours before an exchange transfusion, withhold oral intake to decrease the risk of aspirating saliva or feeding matter (the neonate must be strapped into a supine position during the procedure, increasing the aspiration risk). Also obtain a blood sample for laboratory analysis of the total and conjugated serum bilirubin levels.

Donor blood should be checked by two staff members to verify that it is the correct blood. During the transfusion, vital signs are assessed every 5 to 15 minutes; a running total of the amount of blood administered and withdrawn is kept. The best way to accomplish this is for an assistant to call out the amounts — for example, by stating "5 ml of blood out" and "5 ml of blood in." The exact time of blood administration and withdrawal should be documented. The heart and respiratory rates displayed on the monitor should be noted and the cardiac monitor observed for arrhythmias, which may signal poor tolerance of the transfusion.

When the procedure is completed and the catheter is withdrawn, assess the infusion site for bleeding; expect to transfer the neonate to the phototherapy unit. For the next several hours, monitor the neonate closely for signs of complications, such as metabolic acidosis, hypothermia, circulatory overload, electrolyte disturbances, air embolism, arrhythmias, infection, and hypoglycemia.

Check serum bilirubin levels every 4 to 8 hours to determine if the exchange transfusion was effective. (Always draw blood with the phototherapy lights off to prevent misleading laboratory results.) Approximately 4 hours after the transfusion, check serum electrolyte and glucose levels; if these levels are below normal, a corrective I.V. solution may be ordered.

ECMO. In major neonatal centers, ECMO may be used to maintain gas exchange and perfusion during preoperative management of diaphragmatic hernia or for selected neonates with refractory respiratory failure or MAS. In this technique, the neonate's blood is oxygenated outside the body through an arterial shunt to maintain ventilation and oxygenation; this permits cardiopulmonary recovery at low FIO_2 levels and ventilator settings.

In the neonate, ECMO usually involves venoarterial bypass, in which a cannula is inserted into the right atrium via the right internal jugular vein and the aortic arch is cannulated via the right common carotid artery. Blood circulates through tubing via a pumping device, then through a membrane oxygenator. After blood is oxygenated, it flows through a heating device and into the carotid cannula. The neonate continues on mechanical ventilation during ECMO, with ventilator settings reduced to the minimum level required.

Nursing responsibilities. A specially trained nurse perfusionist typically manages the neonate during ECMO, drawing blood samples for ABG analysis hourly from the neonate and at specified intervals from the ECMO circuit. This nurse also monitors laboratory values (including CBC, platelet count, hemoglobin, hematocrit, and serum electrolytes) and adjusts the heparin drip, as needed, to maintain optimal clotting times.

The nurse assigned to the neonate should change the neonate's position and check vital signs frequently. Weigh dressings under the neonate's neck and assess for blood leakage at the cannulation site. Be sure to monitor fluid intake and output and $tcPO_2$ or pulse oximetry readings frequently. Also, check neurologic status hourly; suction the endotracheal tube and collect tracheal aspirate, as prescribed.

Supporting the family and promoting parent-infant bonding

The birth of a critically ill neonate creates a crisis for family members. Provide emotional support to the family throughout the neonate's stay but especially during each parent's first visit to the NICU — a potentially overwhelming experience. Explain the use of monitors and other supportive equipment to lessen the intimidating effect these machines can have. To help the parents adjust to their child's appearance, emphasize the neonate's normal features.

The parents may be especially anxious if their child is being cared for in a regional center located far from their home. For the family with a nursing diagnosis of *potential altered parenting related to the neonate's condition, difficulty coping with a less-than-perfect neonate, and enforced separation,* make sure to keep communications open and pay special attention to the family's needs. Encourage the parents to visit frequently; if this is not possible, ask them to keep in touch with the NICU staff by telephone. Give them the names and telephone numbers of the physician, primary nurse, social worker, and other contact persons.

To promote parent-infant bonding, encourage the parents to contribute to their child's environment by attaching a small family item, such as a family photograph, to the neonate's bed. Allow the parents to touch and hold their child whenever possible and provide them with simple caregiving tasks, such as diaper changes. Point out how their child responds to their presence, voice, and touch, and show them how to offer appropriate sensory stimulation so that they can take an active role in their child's development — a measure that enhances their self-esteem.

If the neonate's problem has an underlying genetic cause, refer the parents for genetic testing, as appropriate. Throughout nursing care, consider the neonate's discharge planning needs to ease the transition to the home.

MANAGEMENT OF SELECTED PERINATAL PROBLEMS

This section presents an overview of the management of selected problems seen in high-risk neonates. (For a summary of treatments used for all of the perinatal problems discussed in this chapter, see *Medical management of perinatal problems,* pages 244 to 247.)

Respiratory problems

Serious respiratory depression at birth calls for immediate resuscitation (as discussed earlier). After resuscitation, monitor the neonate's cardiopulmonary status and skin temperature. Obtain blood samples for ABG analysis at least every 4 hours (or as needed); obtain samples for serum electrolyte analysis on admission and 24 hours after delivery. Monitor arterial blood pressure at least every 2 hours; stay alert for subtle changes, which may signal an impending change in respiratory status.

For RDS, standard interventions include administration of supplemental oxygen and positive-pressure ventilation. If the severity

(Text continues on page 247.)

MEDICAL MANAGEMENT OF PERINATAL PROBLEMS

Management of a perinatal problem may involve any or all of the measures specified in the chart below. (For details on nursing care for a neonate with some of these problems, see the "Planning and implementation" section of this chapter.)

Birth asphyxia

• Immediate resuscitation followed by supplemental oxygen, continuous positive-airway pressure (CPAP), or mechanical ventilation

Meconium aspiration syndrome

• Immediate resuscitation, with endotracheal intubation and suctioning of the lower airway

Episodic apnea

• Treatment of the underlying disorder (such as intracranial hemorrhage or hypoglycemia)
• Aminophylline or theophylline to stimulate respirations
• CPAP

Respiratory distress syndrome

• Supplemental oxygen, CPAP, or mechanical ventilation, with close monitoring of oxygenation status
• Preventive therapies, such as maternal betamethasone administration to stimulate fetal surfactant production or administration of exogenous surfactant to the neonate

Transient tachypnea

• Oxygen administration (or, rarely, CPAP or mechanical ventilation) with close monitoring of oxygenation status

Bronchopulmonary dysplasia

• Close monitoring of oxygenation status during supplemental oxygen therapy
• Gradual weaning from mechanical ventilation
• Nutritional support (typically enteral or parenteral feedings)
• Fluid restriction and diuretics to prevent pulmonary edema

Retinopathy of prematurity

• Close monitoring of oxygenation status during supplemental oxygen therapy
• Frequent ophthalmologic evaluations
• Reduced intensity of nursery lighting
• Cryosurgery

Intraventricular hemorrhage

• Supportive treatment, typically including vitamin K, platelets, and anticonvulsant medication

MEDICAL MANAGEMENT OF PERINATAL PROBLEMS *(continued)*

Intraventricular hemorrhage *(continued)*

- Reduced environmental stimulation and handling
- Close monitoring of neurologic status

Necrotizing enterocolitis

- Colostomy
- Parenteral nutrition
- Antibiotics

Neonate of a diabetic mother

- Treatment of associated birth trauma
- Correction of associated metabolic and electrolyte imbalances

Hypoglycemia

- Early oral feedings or I.V. glucose (typically as dextrose 10% in water)
- Close monitoring of serum glucose level

Hypocalcemia

- Supplemental calcium (typically as I.V. or oral calcium gluconate)

Hyperbilirubinemia and jaundice

- Early, frequent feedings
- Phototherapy
- Exchange transfusion

Polycythemia

- Partial exchange transfusion

Ineffective thermoregulation

- Maintenance of neutral thermal environment
- Gradual rewarming (1°/hour)

Rh incompatibility

- Complete exchange transfusion with Rh-negative red blood cells, sometimes followed by phototherapy
- Close monitoring of hematocrit and serum bilirubin level

ABO blood group incompatibility

- Correction of hyperbilirubinemia (as with phototherapy)
- Close monitoring of hematocrit and serum bilirubin level

Fetal alcohol syndrome

- Developmental care
- Reduced environmental stimulation
- Enteral feedings if the neonate has incoordinated sucking and swallowing

Drug exposure, addiction, or withdrawal

- Developmental care
- Reduced environmental stimulation

(continued)

MEDICAL MANAGEMENT OF PERINATAL PROBLEMS *(continued)*

Drug exposure, addiction, or withdrawal *(continued)*

- Enteral feedings, if the neonate has incoordinated sucking and swallowing
- Swaddling and frequent feedings to decrease irritability and tremors
- Phenobarbitol to control seizures (for a neonate going through drug withdrawal)

Infection

- Antibiotics
- Infection control measures (including universal precautions)

Meningomyelocele

- Surgery
- Proper positioning

Encephalocele

- Surgery
- Proper positioning

Congenital hydrocephalus

- Surgical placement of a ventriculoperitoneal or ventriculoatrial shunt
- Proper positioning

Microcephaly

- Supportive treatment
- Anticonvulsant medications

Teratoma

- Surgical tumor excision
- Proper positioning

Cardiac anomalies

- Palliative or corrective surgery
- Diuretics or digoxin to control congestive heart failure
- Supportive therapy (such as I.V. fluids and iron supplements to correct anemia)

Diaphragmatic hernia

- Respiratory support
- Gastric decompression
- Extracorporeal membrane oxygenation
- Surgical restoration of abdominal contents to their proper anatomic position
- Postsurgical endotracheal intubation and chest tube placement
- Antibiotics

Tracheoesophageal malformations

- Surgical separation of the trachea and esophagus (with gastrostomy tube placement to prevent aspiration and provide access for feedings)
- Continuous low-pressure suction of blind pouch
- Oxygen therapy

Omphalocele or gastroschisis

- Oxygen therapy
- Immediate positive-pressure ventilation followed by I.V. fluid administration
- Coverage of defect with sterile dressings (to keep tissues moist and reduce heat loss)

MEDICAL MANAGEMENT OF PERINATAL PROBLEMS *(continued)*

Omphalocele or gastroschisis *(continued)*

- Gastric decompression
- Surgical reduction of defect or creation of pouch around herniated abdominal contents to reduce tissue swelling (with placement of gastrostomy tube to provide access for feedings)

Meconium ileus

- Enemas and fluid administration
- Ileostomy

Imperforate anus

- Gastric decompression
- Colostomy

Cleft palate and cleft lip

- Later surgical repair
- Use of special nipple for feeding
- Close monitoring for ear infection

Unilateral renal agenesis

- Surgical removal of affected kidney (If other kidney is functional, surgery may not be necessary.)

Polycystic kidney disease

- Surgical removal of the affected kidney
- Gastric decompression
- Dialysis
- Antibiotics for urinary tract infection

Posterior urethral valves

- Surgical correction of the obstruction
- Placement of nephrostomy tube or stent for drainage
- Open fetal surgery for temporary relief of obstruction (if diagnosed antepartally)

Genital ambiguity

- Hydrocortisone (if caused by congenital adrenal hyperplasia)
- Later surgical reconstruction of external genitalia

Clubfoot

- Corrective shoes, casts, or braces
- Later corrective surgery, if necessary

---

of RDS has not been determined, the neonate typically is given supplemental oxygen or positive-pressure ventilation (CPAP or positive end-expiratory pressure). Assess the neonate every 30 minutes during this therapy.

To help prevent RDS, exogenous surfactants may be administered to preterm neonates via an endotracheal tube to stimulate surfactant production (Jobe, 1988). However, this experimental treatment is available only in selected regional centers. Antenatally, several approaches are available. For instance, ritodrine may be administered to prevent premature labor and delivery before the fetal lungs have matured; subsequent lecithin-sphingomyelin ratios are determined to assess fetal lung maturity. If the pregnancy is threatened at 28 to 32 weeks, betamethasone or another glucocorticoid may be given 24 hours before delivery to stimulate fetal surfactant production.

Necrotizing enterocolitis

For NEC, parenteral nutrition is necessary to allow the bowel to rest. A temporary colostomy may be performed. A portion of localized necrotic bowel may be excised; widespread bowel necrosis may necessitate massive bowel resection, with resulting short-gut syndrome, a condition characterized by impaired nutrient digestion. Expect to administer antibiotics to control secondary infection.

Neonate of a diabetic mother

Assess for signs of birth trauma (for example, by evaluating mobility, especially in the upper extremities), correct any fluid or electrolyte imbalances, and assess for complications stemming from widely fluctuating serum glucose, calcium, and bilirubin levels. Also monitor the neonate's vital signs, $tcPO_2$ or pulse oximetry values, and ABG values. (For specific interventions associated with hypoglycemia, hypocalcemia, and hyperbilirubinemia, see the "Metabolic disorders" section below.)

Metabolic disorders

For hypoglycemia, if the neonate has no other problems, early feedings may be initiated to counteract the glucose imbalance. In other cases, expect to give glucose I.V., as 3 ml/kg of dextrose 10% in water. (The use of dextrose 25% to 50% in solution is contraindicated because it can cause vascular damage leading to ischemic necrosis.)

For hypocalcemia, expect to administer I.V. or oral supplemental calcium. The typical I.V. dosage is 24 mg/kg/day; the typical oral dosage, 75 mg/kg/day (Kliegman and Wald, 1986). When administering calcium by slow infusion, check the pulse frequently to detect bradycardia. Assess the infusion site every 30 minutes for signs of infiltration, which may cause tissue necrosis and sloughing. Monitor the serum calcium level every few hours, or according to facility policy. Once the serum calcium level stabilizes, draw daily blood samples.

For hyperbilirubinemia, the treatment depends on the serum bilirubin level. If the level is elevated only moderately or begins to fall by the fourth or fifth day after birth, the physician may order only early, frequent feedings, which increase intestinal motility and thus speed bilirubin excretion. However, persistent or severe hyperbilirubinemia commonly warrants phototherapy or complete exchange transfusion to prevent bilirubin encephalopathy.

The serum bilirubin level at which these treatments are ordered depends on the physician, facility policy, and the neonate's gestational age and condition. Some physicians initiate treatment when the bilirubin level measures 15 to 20 mg/100 ml; others wait until it reaches 20 mg/100 ml. (However, the preterm neonate may receive prophylactic phototherapy.) The nurse caring for a neonate undergoing phototherapy or exchange transfusion should perform the measures described earlier under "Carrying out special procedures."

Polycythemia

For an asymptomatic neonate, the physician may order only close observation and monitoring of the serum bilirubin level and fluid status. For a symptomatic neonate, a partial exchange transfusion may be ordered.

Isoimmune hemolytic anemia

Care for the neonate with Rh or ABO incompatibility centers on correcting anemia, managing hyperbilirubinemia, and preventing complications. Typically, these disorders warrant exchange transfusion followed by phototherapy.

To prevent Rh isoimmunization, expect the physician to administer prophylactic anti-D immunoglobulin (RhoGAM) to a woman with Rh-negative blood during the twenty-eighth week of pregnancy (Fanaroff and Martin, 1987) and within 48 to 72 hours of delivery of an Rh-positive neonate.

Effects of maternal substance abuse

For FAS, no treatment exists because the structural damage occurs in utero. Supportive management focuses on developmental care and environmental support. If the neonate has poorly coordinated sucking and swallowing reflexes, expect to give enteral feedings to prevent aspiration; physical therapy also may be implemented to help alleviate this problem.

For the neonate who is addicted to maternal drugs or going through drug withdrawal, nursing goals include:

- ensuring adequate nutritional intake
- improving coordination of the sucking and swallowing reflexes
- reducing irritability by minimizing environmental stimulation
- avoiding abrupt movements near the neonate
- promoting a normal sleep-awake cycle to prolong sleep
- stabilizing body temperature.

To reduce tremors and extraneous movement, swaddle the neonate and touch the tremulous area firmly and calmly. To minimize muscle rigidity or hypertonicity, bathe the neonate in warm water, massage gently, and swaddle in a flexed position. Do not leave the neonate in a supine position that maintains muscle extension or stiffness.

For the neonate going through withdrawal, treatment varies with the health care facility and the substance involved. Seizures may be controlled with phenobarbital (5 to 8 mg/kg/day).

Congenital anomalies

For a potentially life-threatening congenital anomaly, immediate interventions must begin; the neonate may require corrective surgery within hours. Specific management varies with the anomaly and the neonate's condition.

Meningomyelocele. This condition calls for surgery — perhaps within a few hours after birth. The surgeon removes the herniated tissue and covers the defect with surrounding skin.

Before surgery, if the defect is open, cover it immediately with warm saline-solution compresses and plastic wrap. To reduce pressure on the defect and minimize tissue damage, position the neonate to avoid pressure on the defect; be sure to support the defect when moving the neonate.

After surgery, place a rolled towel under the neonate's hips to maintain the legs in a relaxed position. Observe the suture line for signs of CSF leakage and infection, indicated by redness or swelling. Closely monitor neurologic status and assess movement; lack of movement suggests neurologic damage (from the anomaly or surgery). Also monitor for skin mottling, coolness of the legs and arms, decreased capillary refill, and reduced muscle tone.

Prevent contamination of and trauma to the wound and stay alert for signs of infection (particularly meningitis). To prevent fecal contamination of the suture line, tape a cup or a plastic diaper lining to the lower part of the surgical dressing to cover the anus. Because surgery for this disorder may cause hydrocephalus, check head circumference daily.

If the neonate's bladder function is disturbed, monitor fluid intake and output and observe for bladder distention. With lack of innervation (neurogenic bladder), an indwelling catheter may be necessary both before and after surgery. However, in some facilities, the Credé method is used to remove urine from the urethra. In this method, gently roll the fingers from the umbilicus toward the symphysis pubis; pushing on the bladder forces urine into the urethra for elimination. (However, be aware that this method may cause infection from reflux of urine from the lower urinary tract to the bladder.)

Encephalocele. This defect must be closed surgically, necessitating removal of external brain tissue. Surgery may cause such problems as paralysis, mental retardation, or even death.

Preoperatively, position the neonate to avoid pressure on the defect. To prevent infection at the defect, administer antibiotics, as prescribed; cover the defect if CSF leakage occurs. Postoperatively, monitor neurologic status and vital signs frequently; assess motor function in all extremities. If the neonate cannot breathe independently, support respirations by maintaining mechanical ventilation. Inspect the dressing for drainage or CSF leakage; to avoid serious neurologic complications, maintain its sterility. Avoid placing the neonate on the suture site.

Congenital hydrocephalus. This disorder typically warrants surgical placement of a ventriculoperitoneal shunt (or, rarely, a ventriculoatrial shunt). The shunt drains CSF from the dilated ventricle into the peritoneal cavity or atrium for absorption and removal; it must be revised periodically as the child grows.

Preoperatively, keep the neonate comfortable. To prevent apnea caused by backward head movement, position the neonate on one side and keep the head of the bed flat or slightly elevated. Postoperatively, maintain suture line integrity and observe for signs of CSF leakage and infection.

To monitor for increasing intracranial pressure, measure and record head circumference once during each shift. As head circumference decreases, discomfort should subside and oral feedings may begin slowly. Also assess for suture line integrity, check the alertness level, and note how well the neonate tolerates enteral or oral feedings.

Teratoma. In most cases, this tumor is excised within the first 28 days after birth. The surgical procedure depends on the tissue involved and the amount of associated tissue. If the tumor is in the sacrococcygeal area, the coccyx may be removed along with the tumor to avoid tumor recurrence. (The nursing measures described below apply mainly to a neonate with a sacrococcygeal tumor.)

Before surgery, position the neonate to minimize pressure on the affected area. After surgery, assess neurologic function by observing movement and color of the legs. Also assess the appearance and amount of drainage from the incision site. Keep the neonate prone, and place sheepskin under the knees to prevent skin irritation and breakdown. To assess for urine retention, measure urine by weighing diapers; if urine output diminishes, notify the physician. Take measures to help prevent infection and minimize stress on the incision line; if necessary, use loose leg restraints to prevent suture line trauma.

Cardiac anomalies. Treatment may be medical or surgical, depending on the specific defect. For an acyanotic defect, corrective surgery may be delayed in favor of symptomatic treatment. For instance, indomethacin, a synthetic prostaglandin inhibitor, may be administered I.V. to close a PDA. However, if this defect is accompanied by severe CHF, the duct is ligated surgically.

For temporary or palliative surgical treatment of an atrial or ventricular septal defect, a band may be placed around the pulmonary artery to decrease blood flow into the pulmonary circulation and alleviate CHF. Other treatments are aimed at managing CHF and include diuretic therapy and digoxin to support cardiac output. When the child is older, a patch graft may be placed to correct the defect.

Surgical correction of coarctation of the aorta, attempted during the toddler or preschool years, involves resection of obstructed blood flow through placement of a graft over the stenotic area; the two segments then are anastomosed on either side of the stenosis.

With a cyanotic defect, palliative surgery typically is performed during the neonatal period. For example, balloon septostomy may be used to open atrial shunts or an artificial graft may be placed. Palliative medical treatments aim to prevent complications of hypoxemia — for instance, iron supplements may be given to correct anemia and fluids and nutritional therapy to prevent fluid overload or dehydration. (Oxygen administration will not improve the neonate's color because cyanosis does not result from pulmonary compromise.) A temporary shunt may be placed to increase pulmonary blood flow.

Nursing goals for the neonate with a congenital cardiac anomaly include maintaining adequate cardiopulmonary function and preventing complications. The neonate will require intensive, expert care and close monitoring. Assess for cyanosis, heart murmurs, arrythmias, absent or unequal pulses, and respiratory distress, and monitor daily weight and fluid intake and output.

Diaphragmatic hernia. Although recent changes in surgical technique have decreased mortality from this anomaly, the neonate with a diaphragmatic hernia poses a challenge for the health care team. Gastric decompression is necessary to relieve gastric distention caused by pressure over the stomach and decreased intestinal motility. The sooner the defect is corrected, the better the prognosis. Surgery for diaphragmatic hernia involves a transthoracic or transabdominal incision to restore the abdominal contents to their proper anatomic position. The surgeon pulls the outer skin layers to cover the abdominal wall defect.

Unfortunately, surgical repair does not guarantee survival. If the neonate has respiratory complications or if the unaffected lung is compromised and the affected lung is hypoplastic, the prognosis is guarded at best.

Preoperatively, the main nursing goal is to stabilize and support respiration. Expect to administer prophylactic antibiotics and I.V. fluids; as prescribed, give dextrose 10% in water for the first 24 hours after birth. As appropriate, obtain samples for CBC, WBC differential, serum electrolyte levels, and ABG analysis.

Postoperatively, stay alert for signs of complications, such as a right-to-left shunt, pneumothorax, and pulmonary arterial hypertension. Maintain airway patency, respiratory support, and fluid and electrolyte balance. Auscultate breath sounds every 1 to 2 hours to detect a developing pneumothorax, indicated by diminished breath sounds. Check the incision site every 1 to 2 hours for signs of leakage or infection. As prescribed, institute feedings gradually once the neonate no longer requires ventilatory assistance.

The neonate probably will require endotracheal intubation; perform endotracheal suctioning and maintain ventilatory support, as needed. To help reinflate the lung on the affected side, a chest tube also is placed. Maintain chest tube patency by monitoring tube drainage every hour and moving the contents away from the chest wall toward the collection system. Be sure to monitor the amount and color of drainage. If chest tube patency appears questionable or drainage suddenly increases or decreases markedly, notify the physician.

Tracheoesophageal malformations. Surgical intervention is necessary to separate the trachea and esophagus and to maintain the patency of each structure. The surgical procedure used depends on the specific malformation. A gastrostomy tube commonly is inserted during surgery to prevent gastric reflux and aspiration pneumonia. Some neonates also require cervical esophagostomy to drain saliva and mucus from an atretic area (this procedure is performed only when no tracheoesophageal fistula is present).

Nursing goals include maintaining a patent airway and ensuring fluid and electrolyte balance before and after surgery. Preoperatively, if a blind pouch has been diagnosed, observe secretions for color and amount. As requested, insert a nasogastric tube and connect it to the blind pouch to provide continuous low-pressure suction and prevent aspiration. Check tube patency hourly, and assess vital signs every 1 to 2 hours.

Oxygen therapy may be required if the neonate's breathing effort increases or if cyanosis develops. A warmed mist, delivered by an oxygen hood or through a closed incubator, may be used to thin secretions. Monitor vital signs, respiratory effort, skin color, appearance of the I.V. infusion site, and the amount of secretions suctioned.

Postoperative nursing interventions resemble those used for the neonate with diaphragmatic hernia, except that no chest tube is present. Turn the neonate every 2 hours to prevent atelectasis. If the neonate can tolerate it, perform nasopharyngeal suctioning with a marked catheter, as ordered, to a depth just short of the suture line to help prevent suture perforation during suctioning.

If the nasogastric tube remains in place for gastric decompression, maintain its patency by inserting 2 ml of air every 2 hours. If cervical esophagostomy was performed, maintain skin integrity by cleaning the skin, applying petroleum jelly to create a waterproof barrier, and applying a secretion-absorbing dressing every 4 hours. Diminished secretions suggest that the stoma is closing, necessitating surgical dilatation with a soft rubber catheter.

Keep the neonate in an upright position before and after surgery — for instance, by using a cholasia chair, which allows the neonate to remain upright after feeding to prevent reflux of secretions. Maintain patency of the gastrostomy tube by inserting 2 ml of air every 2 to 4 hours (gravity drainage typically is used). Also, note how well the neonate tolerated medical and nursing procedures, and assess the appearance of secretions, the neonate's breathing effort, and skin color.

Once enteral feedings begin, assess the neonate's tolerance for them. Any aspirate found before the next feeding may indicate impaired intestinal activity; make sure to document and report this finding.

Bottle feedings typically can begin once an intact suture line is verified. Expect to begin bottle feedings gradually with a clear electrolyte solution, such as Pedialyte. Give feedings slowly to prevent aspiration and gastric distention. Methylene blue, a dye, commonly is added to feedings to reveal suture line leakage. If a fistula is present, this dye appears in the chest tube; dye appearing only in the gastrostomy tube means that the suture line is intact.

If the esophagus has been pulled taut and stretched to make the ends meet, gastrostomy feedings may be needed and the surgeon may perform dilatation with increasing catheter sizes several weeks after surgery. When these feedings begin, evaluate how well the neonate tolerates them. A dusky skin color or choking during feedings may indicate fistula leakage; increased mucus may indicate stenosis around the surgical site.

Abdominal wall defects. The neonate with gastroschisis or omphalocele requires immediate intervention in the delivery room — ventilatory support followed by peripheral line placement for I.V. fluid administration. As soon as possible, cover the defect with sterile gauze dressings moistened with warm normal saline solution; place plastic wrap on top of the dressings to help keep tissues moist and reduce heat loss. Maintain gastric decompression with a nasogastric tube.

Corrective treatment of a small defect involves complete or primary surgical reduction. In the operating room, the bowel and protruding tissues are inspected for trauma that could cause loss of GI contents and bacterial wound contamination. If the protruding contents are too large to return to the abdominal cavity, a silastic pouch is placed around them. Later, keep this pouch (now referred to as a silo) suspended from the top of the incubator to help reduce tissue swelling and facilitate eventual return of the abdominal contents to the abdominal cavity. Position the neonate supine and moisten the silo with povidone-iodine every 8 hours (or as specified by facility protocol).

If the defect is large, the reduction must be performed in stages to prevent excessive pressure on the diaphragm and resulting complications, such as respiratory compromise and tissue hypoxia. In some cases, reduction may be performed in the NICU; in others, the neonate must return to the operating room.

The nursing goal is to minimize the risk of infection and maintain the herniated tissue and organs in optimal condition. Be sure to maintain sterile technique throughout caregiving procedures. Before surgery, keep the dressings sterile and moist and evaluate for skin breakdown from supine positioning. If appropriate, place an air mattress or sheepskin under the neonate to minimize skin breakdown.

After the neonate's final surgical closure, expect to administer feedings through a gastrostomy tube. Begin feedings gradually and increase the volume based on the neonate's tolerance. Usually, a central line also must be inserted for administration of parenteral nutrition, which will continue for several days or weeks.

Monitor for changes in respiratory status and vital signs (especially during the immediate postoperative period), and assess tolerance of feedings once these begin. Also evaluate the appearance of the defect, checking closely for signs of infection. To assess for circulatory compromise caused by pressure from the defect, check capillary refill in the legs.

Imperforate anus. The neonate with this anomaly requires surgical restoration of the anal canal to achieve urinary and bowel continence. For a low defect, a peripheral anoplasty typically is performed during the neonatal period. For an intermediate defect, a colostomy is performed in most cases, with further surgery performed several months later. A high defect always necessitates a colostomy.

Nursing goals include preventing gastric distention and dehydration. Preoperatively, nursing measures depend on the severity of the defect. Expect to maintain gastric decompression and initiate I.V. therapy.

Postoperatively, position the neonate on the stomach or side. Maintain gastric decompression until 24 hours before feedings are to begin. If anoplasty was performed, assess the site for skin breakdown, redness, and drainage. Clean it regularly and after every stool; avoid taking rectal temperatures or examining the rectum. To minimize stool formation until the incision heals, delay feedings at least 24 hours after surgery.

If the neonate has a colostomy, assess the suture line and skin around the stoma for color, swelling, and drainage; check for separation of the suture line. As needed, change the dressing to prevent infection, and change the colostomy bag to prevent leakage.

Cleft palate and cleft lip. Surgical repair of these anomalies usually is delayed to prevent disruption of facial growth and tooth-bud formation. However, it must occur early enough so that the defect does not interfere with speech development. Repair of cleft lip (cheilorrhaphy, or Z-plasty) commonly takes place when the child is 3 months old; repair of cleft palate (by joining of the palatal segments) typically is performed when the child is 9 to 15 months old.

Ensure adequate nutrition before and after surgery because air leaks around the cleft and nasal regurgitation typically cause feeding problems. Many neonates with cleft lip can be breast-fed (except after surgery); the mother may provide breast milk she has pumped. With cleft palate, a feeding neonate requires a syringe or cleft palate feed or a special elongated nipple (such as a Martin's nipple). When using an elongated nipple, be sure to place it far into the mouth — but not far enough to induce gagging. Burp the neonate frequently while feeding because cleft lip or palate causes swallowing of much air during feeding. To prevent aspiration of feeding matter through the palatal opening and the nares, elevate the head of the bed or place the neonate in an infant seat or on the stomach after feedings.

The neonate's abnormally short eustachian tubes provide easy access for nasal and oral bacteria, increasing the risk of ear infection. To help reduce this risk, clean the nose and oral cavities after feedings, and assess frequently for fever, irritability, and other signs of ear infection. To remove excess formula, rinse the neonate's mouth with water after feedings.

Be sure to teach the parents how to provide the special care their child requires. Cleft palate and lip can cause long-term speech, dental, hearing, and other problems, so the nurse should refer parents to appropriate professionals for follow-up care.

Polycystic kidney disease and posterior urethral valves. A polycystic kidney is removed surgically. Before surgery, monitor the neonate for infection (especially of the urinary tract). Afterward, maintain gastric decompression and monitor urine output, urine specific gravity, and dipstick for blood every 2 hours. Report any decrease in urine output.

With posterior urethral valves, the obstruction is corrected surgically and a nephrostomy tube or stent is placed to drain the ureter that has been anastomosed around the stenotic area. Sometimes, temporary relief of the obstruction is achieved antenatally with open fetal surgery. This procedure has the highest reported success rate of any fetal surgery attempted (Pringle, 1989).

Nursing goals include maintaining fluid and electrolyte balance and supporting respiration (hypoplastic lungs accompany some renal problems). If surgery is scheduled, preoperative nursing care centers on maintaining fluid and electrolyte balance. Assess intake and output every 4 to 8 hours, and check urine specific gravity every 4 hours. Support respiratory efforts, as needed, by maintaining oxygen therapy or assisted ventilation.

Assess the neonate before and after surgery for signs of acute renal failure, such as oliguria or anuria, edema, blood pressure fluctuations, and cardiopulmonary compromise secondary to fluid accumulation. Take postoperative measures to prevent infection. Also, assess for signs of respiratory compromise, decreased urine output, and drainage from the nephrostomy tube or stent. Evaluate renal status by comparing vital sign measurements with baseline values. Also compare fluid intake and output from the previous 24 hours to detect any difference.

Observe and evaluate output from any nephrostomy tube or stent. To help prevent infection, protect the dressing at the suture line and observe this site closely. Keep all dressings dry; as needed, replace dressings at the suture line and around tubes.

Genital ambiguity. If genital ambiguity stems from congenital adrenal hyperplasia, hydrocortisone is given to arrest the disorder; with severe adrenal hyperplasia, hydrocortisone must be administered immediately to prevent acute adrenocorticol failure — a fatal condition. Later, surgical reconstruction of the external genitalia may be attempted.

Expect to assist in genetic testing and determination of the neonate's underlying problem if this has not been established. Providing support to the family is a nursing priority. Refer them to a psychiatrist or other professional for help in coping with this problem. Also, advise them to select a unisex name for their child. Some professionals encourage parents to delay the announcement of their child's birth until the sex can be determined; others believe that a delay exacerbates parental anxiety.

Clubfoot. Typically, corrective shoes, casts, or braces are used as soon as possible to correct the deformity. If these measures fail, surgery may be performed when the child is several years old. Inform the parents of the need for early and continual medical evaluation to avoid problems when the child begins to walk.

Congenital hip dysplasia. Treatment involves pressing the femoral head against and into the acetabulum. This pressure allows formation of an adequate socket before ossification is complete. To abduct and externally rotate the leg and flex the hip, a triangular pillow is applied over the diaper. At a later date, the neonate typically is placed in a spica cast.

EVALUATION

During this step of the nursing process, the nurse evaluates the effectiveness of the care plan by ongoing evaluation of subjective and objective criteria. Evaluation findings should be stated in terms of actions performed or outcomes achieved for each goal. The following examples illustrate appropriate evaluation statements for the high-risk neonate.

• The neonate's vital signs improved.

• The neonate maintained an adequate core temperature.

• The neonate's cardiopulmonary status improved or remained within acceptable limits.

• The neonate maintained fluid and electrolyte balance, as evidenced by adequate urine output, no signs of dehydration or fluid overload, and acceptable serum electrolyte levels.

• The neonate tolerated feedings.

• The I.V. infusion site remained free of signs of infiltration.

• Skin integrity remained intact.

• The neonate's parents showed positive coping mechanisms in response to their child's problem.

• The neonate's parents know how to obtain appropriate counseling and support.

For the neonate with respiratory problems, these additional evaluation statements may be appropriate.

• Signs of increased breathing effort diminished.

• The neonate's ABG and $tcPO_2$ or pulse oximetry values approached normal limits.

• The neonate had no episodes of apnea.

For the neonate with infection, this additional evaluation statement may be appropriate.

• The neonate showed a positive response to antibiotic therapy, as evidenced by improved vital signs and reductions in behavioral deviations, high-pitched crying, and temperature instability.

For the neonate with hyperbilirubinemia or isoimmune hemolytic anemia, these additional evaluation statements may be appropriate.

• The serum bilirubin level decreased to normal or near-normal limits.

• Jaundice diminished, as evidenced by improved skin and sclera color.

• The neonate was free of complications, such as transfusion reaction or infection, after exchange transfusion.

For the neonate who underwent surgery, these additional evaluation statements may be appropriate.

• The neonate's vital signs remained normal.

- No signs of postoperative complications appeared.
- The suture line remained intact.
- The incision site remained clean and free of redness or swelling.

DOCUMENTATION

All steps of the nursing process should be documented as thoroughly and objectively as possible. Thorough documentation not only allows the nurse to evaluate the effectiveness of the care plan, but it also makes this information available to other members of the health care team, helping to ensure consistency of care.

Documentation for the high-risk neonate should include the following points:
- vital signs and alertness level
- changes in status
- serum bilirubin, calcium, and glucose levels
- fluid intake and output
- stool characteristics
- tolerance for feedings
- location and appearance of any I.V. infusion site
- presence of any gastric distention
- presence of an indwelling nasogastric tube
- amount and appearance of secretions obtained by suctioning
- tolerance for medical and nursing procedures
- parents' level of acceptance of their child's problem.

For the neonate with respiratory problems, documentation also should include the following points:
- breathing effort
- any apneic episodes
- administration route and FIO_2 of supplemental oxygen (if given)
- ABG and $tcPO_2$ or pulse oximetry values
- ventilator pressure, rate, and positive end-expiratory pressure settings (if the neonate is on a mechanical ventilator).

For the neonate with a diagnosed infection, documentation also should include the following points:
- behavioral and physical changes indicative of infection
- the time when antibiotic therapy began and ended
- response to and tolerance of antibiotic therapy
- any cultures or blood samples taken.

For the neonate receiving phototherapy, documentation also should include the following points:

- number of stools
- skin turgor
- skin and sclera color
- amount and color of urine.

For the neonate who underwent exchange transfusion, documentation also should include the following points:

- tolerance for the procedure
- neurologic status.

For the neonate who underwent surgery, documentation also should include the following points:

- preoperative and postoperative vital signs
- the time when feedings were instituted
- tolerance for feedings
- respiratory effort
- appearance and amount of drainage from the incision site
- appearance of the suture line
- presence of bladder distention
- need for Credé's maneuver.

BIBLIOGRAPHY

American Academy of Pediatrics. (1988). *Guidelines for Perinatal Care* (2nd ed.). Chicago: Author.

American Heart Association and American Academy of Pediatrics. (1987). *Textbook of Neonatal Resuscitation.* Dallas.

Chatburn, R.L., and Carlo, W.A. (1988). Assessment of neonatal gas exchange. In W.A. Carlo and M. Lough (Eds.), *Neonatal Respiratory Care* (2nd ed.). Chicago: Year Book Medical Publishers.

Fanaroff, A.A., and Martin, R.J. (1987). *Behrman's neonatal-perinatal medicine: Diseases of the fetus or infant.* St. Louis: Mosby.

Hager, J.J. (1983). Characteristics and management of pregnancy in women with genital herpes simplex virus infection. *American Journal of Obstetrics and Gynecology,* 145, 784.

Harjo, J., Kenner, C., and Brueggermeyer, A. (1988). Alterations in effective breathing patterns. In C. Kenner, J. Harjo, and A. Brueggermeyer (Eds.), *Neonatal Surgery: A nursing perspective.* (pp. 79-120). Orlando, FL.: Grune & Stratton.

Harjo, J., Kenner, C., and Brueggermeyer, A. (1988). Alterations in the gastrointestinal system. In In C. Kenner, J. Harjo, and A. Brueggermeyer

(Eds.), *Neonatal Surgery: A nursing perspective.* (pp. 121-189). Orlando, FL.: Grune & Stratton.

Jobe, A. (1988). *Surfactant replacement therapy.* Workshop presented at the National Perinatal Association Conference, Perinatal Health: Facing the 21st Century, San Diego, CA.

Kaempf, J.W., Bonnabel, C., and Hoy, W.W. (1989). Neonatal nutrition. In G.B. Merenstein and S.L. Gardner (Eds.), *Handbook of Neonatal Care* (p. 185). St. Louis: Mosby.

Kliegman, R.M., and Wald, M.K. (1986). Problems in metabolic adaptation: Glucose, calcium, and magnesium. In M.H. Klaus and A.A. Fanaroff (Eds.), *Care of the High Risk Neonate* (3rd ed.). Philadelphia: Saunders.

Moyer-Mileur, L.J. (1986). Nutrition. In N.S. Streeter (Ed.), *High-risk neonatal care* (p. 276). Rockville, MD: Aspen.

Nelson, S.N., Merenstein, G.B., and Pierce, J.R. (1986). Early onset group B streptococcal disease. *Journal of Perinatology, 6*, 234.

Nicolaides, K.H. (1989). Studies on fetal physiology and pathophysiology in Rhesus disease. *Seminars in Perinatology, 13*(4), 328-337.

Perlstein, P.H. (1988). The thermal environment. In A.A. Fanaroff and R.J. Martin (Eds.), *Behrman's neonatal-perinatal medicine: Diseases of the fetus or infant.* St. Louis: Mosby.

Pringle, K.C. (1989). Fetal diagnosis and fetal surgery. *Clinics in Perinatology, 16*(1), 13-22.

Subramanian, K.N.S., Glass, P., Avery, G.B., Kolinjavadi, N., Keys, M.P., Sostek, A.M., and Friendly, D.S. (1985). Effect of bright light in the hospital nursery on the incidence of retinopathy of prematurity. *New England Journal of Medicine, 313*(7), 401-404.

Birth-weight and gestational-age variations

Boyd, M.E., Usher, R.H., McLean, F.H., and Kramer, M.S. (1988). Obstetric consequences of postmaturity. *American Journal of Obstetrics and Gynecology, 158*(2), 334-338.

Cassady, G., and Strange, M. (1987). The small-for-gestational-age (SGA) infant. In G.B. Avery (Ed.), *Neonatology: Pathophysiology and management of the newborn* (pp. 299-378). Philadelphia: Lippincott.

Resnick, R. (1989). Post-term pregnancy. In R.K. Creasy and R. Resnick (Eds.), *Maternal-fetal medicine: Principles and practice* (2nd ed.; pp. 505-509). Philadelphia: Saunders.

Teberg, A.J., Walther, F.J., and Pena, I.C. (1988). Mortality, morbidity, and outcome of the small-for-gestational age infant. *Seminars in Perinatology, 12*, 84-94.

Failure to thrive and child abuse

Hunter, R.S., Kilstrum, N., Kraybill, E.N., and Loda, F. (1978). Antecedents of child abuse and neglect in premature infants: A prospective study in a newborn intensive care unit. *Pediatrics, 61*(4), 629-635.

White, R., Benedict, M.I., Wulff, L., and Kelley, M. (1987). Physical disabilities as risk factors for child maltreatment: A selected review. *American Journal of Orthopsychiatry, 57*(1), 93-101.

Maternal substance abuse

Flandermeyer, A.A. (1987). A comparison of the effects of heroin and cocaine abuse upon the neonate. *Neonatal Network, 6*(3), 42-48.

Jones, K.L. (1986). Fetal alcohol syndrome. *Pediatrics in review, 8*(4), 122-126.

Kennard, M. J. (1990). Cocaine use during pregnancy: Fetal and neonatal effects. *Journal of Perinatal and Neonatal Nursing, 3*(9), 53-63.

Neonatal mortality

National Center for Health Statistics. (1989a, March 28). *Monthly vital statistics report—Births, marriages, divorces, and deaths for 1988.* U.S. Dept. of Health and Human Services Publication No. (PHS) 89-1120. Hyattsville, MD: U.S. Public Health Service.

National Center for Health Statistics. (1989b, June 29). *Monthly vital statistics report—Advance report of final natality statistics, 1987.* U.S. Dept. of Health and Human Services, 38, (3). Hyattsville, MD: U.S. Public Health Service.

Nursing research

Meier, P. (1988, January-February). Bottle- and Breast-feeding: Effects on transcutaneous oxygen pressure and temperature in preterm infants. *Nursing Research, 37*(1), 36-41.

Care of the Families of High-Risk Neonates

With the birth of a high-risk neonate (one who is preterm or very ill), family members experience a sense of loss. Even the family of a preterm neonate who becomes healthy enough to leave the neonatal intensive care unit (NICU) within a few weeks must work through some grief at the loss of the expected "perfect" child before they can bond strongly to the imperfect one. The family of a neonate with a chronic illness or congenital anomaly must find ways to cope with long-term grief and develop strategies to provide the special care the condition will require (and perhaps to balance these care needs with those of other children). If the neonate is stillborn or dies within a few hours or days after birth, family members must complete their bonding with the neonate, then detach themselves gradually so they can focus again on the family's life and needs.

To provide care in the first weeks after the birth of a high-risk neonate, the nurse must:
• understand the function of grief
• recognize the stages of grief in individual family members
• assess how family members are responding to and coping with the crisis of the high-risk neonate
• identify and implement strategies to help family members cope
• help family members identify support systems that can provide further help
• teach family members about the condition and care of the high-risk neonate
• maintain empathetic contact with family members as they work to integrate care of the high-risk neonate into family life.

FAMILY REACTIONS

To the family, the birth of a high-risk neonate may seem like a tragedy. Over the course of the pregnancy, they built expectations of a child whose features would reflect their own, whose abilities they could nurture, and whose interests they would share. With the neonate's birth, the family experiences the loss of the "perfect" child of their dreams. They must deal with that loss and the grief it causes and find ways of adjusting their expectations and plans to match the reality of the child born to them.

GRIEF

Because of the enormity of a perinatal loss, parents and other family members must adapt slowly to the situation – or experience overwhelming anxiety and pain. The degree of parental feelings of grief do not correlate with the severity of the neonate's condition (Benefield, Leib, and Reuter, 1976).

Before the family can accept their loss, they must progress through several stages of grief. Various researchers and theorists have developed concepts of grieving. Among the most influential is that of Kübler-Ross (1969), who proposed that a person encountering death or another type of loss progresses through five stages: denial, anger, bargaining, depression, and acceptance. Sahu (1981) and other authorities apply these stages specifically to perinatal loss. Based on studies by Bowlby (1961) and Parkes (1970) as well as on original research, thanatologist Glen Davidson (1984) describes four phases, or dimensions, of grief that survivors of loss may move among: shock and numbness, yearning and searching, disorientation, and reorganization.

Regardless of the grief model used, the nurse should regard the stages of grief as descriptive rather than clearly defined. Rather than progressing through the stages in an orderly manner, the parents and other family members may experience aspects of several stages at once or may regress to a stage previously experienced.

Denial

In this first stage, the parents attempt to deny the reality or seriousness of their child's condition; this allows them to hope that the child may improve. They cannot let go abruptly of the hopes and dreams they developed during the pregnancy. By postponing recognition of their child's condition, they protect themselves until they are ready to face and cope with the situation.

Anger

As awareness of the situation develops, the parents progress to this stage. Anger may take the form of resentment, bitterness, rage, blaming, or envy of others with healthy neonates. Needing to hold something or someone accountable for their child's condition, parents may direct their anger outward. For instance, they may accuse members of the health care team of not caring properly for their child; or they may accuse each other of some past action that caused the situation — for example, the mother's smoking during pregnancy. Some parents, especially those who cannot express their anger, may direct their feelings inward, becoming depressed and guilt-ridden as they blame themselves for their child's condition.

Bargaining

During this stage, a parent may be willing to do anything that might help the neonate or delay the perinatal loss. Bargaining may involve religious beliefs ("I'll go to church every Sunday if God will let my baby get better") or the desire to try new forms of medical therapy.

Depression

In this stage, feelings of hopelessness, powerlessness, or despair predominate. Some depressed parents put their feelings into words; others become noncommunicative and wish to be left alone. Still others, such as the previously well-groomed parent who begins neglecting his or her appearance, signal depression through behavior. As long as it does not continue for an excessive time, this stage represents real progress toward acceptance because it signals recognition of the neonate's situation and its potential impact on the present and future.

Acceptance

This final stage, which takes most people at least several months and can take as long as 2 years to achieve, is marked by resumption of normal daily activity and diminishing preoccupation with the loss (Lindemann, 1944). Parents whose child has died continue to experience sadness when they remember their loss; at certain times, such as the anniversary of the child's birth or death, they again may pass through denial, anger, and depression (all usually less acute) before returning to acceptance. However, they manage to incorporate the memory of their loss into their lives and move on.

For the family of a child who survives with a chronic disability, however, complete acceptance may be difficult or even impossible to achieve. The chronic condition necessitates continual adaptation and coping; the disability and the limitations it places on the child's life remain a constant cause of sorrow (Lemons, 1986). Olshansky (1962) termed this persistent effect *chronic sorrow*.

COPING MECHANISMS

Parents may use various coping mechanisms to deal with the sadness and worry they feel for a high-risk neonate. Denial and anger, the first and second stages of grief, are coping mechanisms; so are withdrawal (one manifestation of depression, the fourth stage) and guilt (the form anger takes if it turns inward). A fifth method of coping is intellectualizing.

Denial

Shock and disbelief are the most common first reactions to the birth of a high-risk neonate (Tarbert, 1985). Although denial serves a protective purpose for a brief time, as long as parents cling to denial they cannot participate in care decisions or make realistic plans. Should the neonate die, they may be unable to grieve successfully.

Anger

Anger and hostility may succeed denial as parents attempt to deal with their shock (Brooten, et al., 1988). Needing a way to feel power over their situation, parents may direct their anger against the health care team, blaming them for their child's condition.

Guilt

Many parents of a high-risk neonate try to cope with their power-lessness through guilt, telling themselves that they did something to cause their child's abnormality or failed to do something to prevent it (Cordell and Apolito, 1981). Like denial and anger, guilt is a mechanism parents must move beyond to function effectively.

Withdrawal

Parents who have progressed to the stage of depression in the grief process may withdraw emotionally to protect themselves from the anticipated pain of losing their child. Even though they may visit regularly, they invest little energy into building a parent-child relationship.

Intellectualizing

Some parents attempt to retreat from the painful emotions they feel by searching for meaning in the situation; knowing about such matters as blood values and oxygen levels can give them something to focus on. These parents need the assurance of receiving accurate information and having their questions answered carefully, but they also may need help to refocus on the neonate.

ASSESSMENT

During the assessment, the nurse should keep in mind the various stages of grief; this helps identify the family's need for practical and emotional support. Because parents usually are the family members most closely involved with the neonate, this chapter focuses mainly on them. However, the nurse should not overlook the neonate's siblings, grandparents, and other close family members.

Parents

Already upset by the arrival of a high-risk neonate, parents may feel further stress within the NICU, with its sophisticated equipment, flashing monitors, buzzing alarms, and hurrying staff members. For this reason, the nurse should try to conduct the assessment in a quiet, unhurried, and straightforward manner.

Assessment of the parents should include the following:
• age, experience as parents, and history of previous childbirths
• understanding of and feelings about the neonate's condition
• concerns about the neonate's care
• family and home care arrangements
• response to the NICU
• grieving behavior and coping mechanisms.

Age, experience, and history

Find out the parents' age and their experience as parents. Young or first-time parents may have little experience dealing with illness. Especially if they are young enough to require parenting themselves, they may feel particularly inadequate about coping with a high-risk neonate.

Ask about any family history of problem pregnancies or deliveries. Parents who have experienced a previous perinatal illness or death may fear or believe that the past problem and this one are related. Even if their anxiety is inappropriate, it may impair their ability to cope with their neonate. On the other hand, parents whose earlier pregnancies and deliveries were problem-free may have trouble accepting that this delivery has produced a high-risk neonate.

To determine whether genetic counseling might be advisable eventually, look for indications of a genetic cause for the neonate's condition. Ask about the presence, in this or previous generations, of such conditions as inherited disorders, metabolic disorders, or chromosomal disorders. Even if parents are not aware of any history of these problems, such a condition in the neonate suggests a genetic link.

Understanding and feelings

Ask the parents what they understand about their child's condition and how it makes them feel. Although grief and anxiety are natural reactions to the delivery of a neonate who is preterm or born with a severe illness or an obvious physical anomaly, parents may feel perinatal loss for other reasons as well. Because of the value society places on physical beauty, any physical irregularity may cause great anxiety. (Even the birth of a neonate who is healthy but not of the desired sex or whose physical features differ from the expected ones can result in a sense of loss.) Knowing the cause of the parents' grief is essential in planning interventions to help them deal with it; even if their grief seems out of proportion, it is real and must be addressed. Here and throughout the assessment, stay alert for signs of stress developing between the parents.

Concerns about care of the neonate and its effects

To determine where counseling and teaching can decrease anxiety, explore the parents' feelings about their ability to care for their child. They may express doubt about being able to care for their child at home and may worry about financial consequences of giving up work days to spend time with their child and about long-term medical expenses.

Also look and listen for signs of emotional discomfort. A parent who feels anxious and powerless may have trouble absorbing and putting into practice information about caregiving. A parent who hesitates to participate in simple neonatal care may be establishing emotional distance from the neonate.

Family and home care arrangements

Ask the parents about arrangements they have made for care of other children at home and other family concerns. Even parents who have made adequate care arrangements may worry that they are short-changing their other children. Assess whether they need help allocating their time or arranging care for the children.

Also ask them how their other children are responding to the birth of a high-risk neonate. Under these circumstances, an older child's relationship with the parents may change (Trahd, 1986). However, parents may not be aware of this in the first days and weeks, when the neonate holds so much of their attention. Most parents probably realize that siblings are likely to feel neglected or jealous because of the disruptions in routine and the time parents spend at the NICU. However, parents may not be aware of other feelings the high-risk neonate may evoke, including fear and guilt that they somehow are responsible for the neonate's illness. Asking what responses parents have noticed may help them relate better with their other children and also will help focus teaching plans for preparing the neonate's siblings to visit the NICU.

Response to the NICU

Find out what previous experience the parents have had with health care facilities. The less experience they have, or the less recent their experience, the more unsettling they may find the NICU and the more help they may need in understanding that many of the procedures and equipment that seem extraordinary actually are routine.

The apparent ease with which the NICU staff functions may increase parents' doubts about their own ability to provide care, especially if no one explains what is happening and why. To plan ways to make parents more comfortable in the NICU, ask how much they understand about the equipment being used to help their child and invite questions about the care being given.

Also assess the effect of the NICU location on the developing parent-infant bond and on the relationship between the parents. For most parents, the ideal situation is an NICU located within the mother's obstetric unit. Here, both parents can visit the neonate in the first few days after delivery with little or no trouble. However, if the neonate must be transferred to a distant tertiary care center, only the father may be able to visit for the first several days. Ask whether the mother was able to spend time with the neonate before the transfer and what effect the transfer has had on each parent. Particularly if the mother did not see the neonate before the transfer, she may feel isolated and resentful of the father's greater contact (Consolvo, 1984); the father, meanwhile, may feel uncomfortable in the primary parent role in which circumstances have placed him.

If the NICU is relatively far from the home, neither parent may be able to visit frequently. Assess for signs that the parents' lack of physical contact is delaying parent-infant bonding. Without such bonding, their interest and motivation may not be strong enough to meet their child's long-term needs.

Grieving behavior and coping mechanisms

Throughout the neonate's hospitalization, parents typically exhibit signs of grief. Determine each parent's grief stage (as described earlier in the "Family reactions" section). However, keep in mind that grief expression may depend somewhat on cultural background, but avoid drawing conclusions based on culture alone.

Also determine which coping mechanism each parent is using — denial, anger, guilt, intellectualizing, or withdrawal. (Remember, though, that coping mechanisms may vary from day to day or even moment to moment.) Accurately identifying the coping mechanisms that parents use is crucial to planning nursing interventions that respond to their needs.

To assess for denial, look for signs that parents are denying the reality of the neonate's condition. Normally, parents move beyond denial on their own, so assess for signs that this transition is occurring; if it is not, they may require help.

If parents exhibit anger or hostility (such as toward the health care team), assess for any misunderstanding of the neonate's condition. Keep in mind that angry parents usually are reacting to the situation and rarely feel real hostility toward health care personnel.

Clues that a parent is using guilt to cope include such obvious statements as, "It's all my fault" as well as more subtle indications, such as utterances beginning with "If only I..." In guilt statements, listen for misunderstandings of the causes of the neonate's condition.

Parents who focus on the cause of their child's condition more than on the neonate as a person are using intellectualizing as a coping mechanism. These parents may ask many questions about their child's treatment and seem hesitant to focus on the child.

Assess for withdrawal by observing how the parents relate to their child. Withdrawn parents may not touch or hold their child or may look away while doing so.

SUPPORT SYSTEMS

Coping with the birth of a high-risk neonate is not something that one parent — or even both — can handle alone. Parents need help from various sources.

Family and friends

For most parents, the first line of support comes from within the family. In a two-parent family, the partners typically form each other's base of support. If one parent is unavailable — for example, as in the case of a single mother — another family member or a close friend may assume the support role. Assess parents to determine which family members or close friends make up their support base and how nursing care can assist the supporters.

Ask about the relationship between the neonate's parents and grandparents. In many cases, grandparents can provide both emotional and practical support.

Other support sources

Beyond the circle of family and friends, additional support may be available to parents through religious practices, cultural customs, and support groups consisting of other parents.

Religious practices. The birth of a high-risk neonate may pull the parents back to their religious roots. They may find comfort in speaking with a member of the clergy, reading scripture, or participating in religious services. Assess parents for their interest in seeing a chaplain or their own priest, minister, or rabbi. Ask whether they would like any religious practices to be observed for their neonate; members of some Christian churches, for example, may wish to have their child baptized. Even parents who might not think of asking for such support may use it if they know it is available.

Cultural customs. If cultural identity is important to the family, they may derive additional support from observing traditional care customs with their child. In assessing cultural customs, however, bear in mind that although cultural norms exist, variations do occur. Also, the beliefs one generation holds to strongly may be less important to a second or third generation. Athough an overall awareness of such beliefs is helpful, assess the parents for their own beliefs as individuals.

Begin the cultural assessment by asking about the main elements of values and beliefs the parents hold and the customs these values dictate regarding childbirth in general and the birth of a high-risk neonate in particular. Then focus on specific care concerns parents may want addressed.

Support groups. Assess parents for their awareness of parent-to-parent support groups — including national organizations, local groups, and groups associated with the health care facility.

NURSING DIAGNOSIS

After gathering assessment data, the nurse must review it carefully to identify pertinent nursing diagnoses for the family. (For a partial list of applicable diagnoses, see *Nursing diagnoses: Family of a high-risk neonate.*)

PLANNING AND IMPLEMENTATION

The goal of nursing care is to help the family develop the understanding, skills, and confidence to give competent care after the neonate's discharge. Thus, the nurse should plan interventions to help them deal with the crisis of a high-risk neonate and to meet the neonate's needs. Such interventions should focus on the neonate's

NURSING DIAGNOSES

FAMILY OF A HIGH-RISK NEONATE

The following are potential nursing diagnoses for problems and etiologies that a nurse may encounter when caring for the family of a high-risk neonate. Specific nursing interventions for many of these diagnoses are provided in the "Planning and implementation" section of this chapter.

- Anticipatory grieving related to the prospect of the neonate's death
- Anxiety related to the neonate's condition and unknown outcome
- Defensive coping related to the seriousness of the neonate's condition and long-term implications
- Denial related to immediate and long-term implications of the neonate's condition
- Ineffective family coping: compromised, related to family disorganization secondary to the neonate's condition
- Ineffective individual coping related to family disorganization secondary to the neonate's condition
- Ineffective individual coping related to the stress of a preterm birth
- Knowledge deficit related to the hospital course and care of the high-risk neonate
- Parental role conflict related to limited opportunities to care for the neonate
- Potential altered parenting related to poor parent-infant bonding
- Powerlessness related to the health care environment and limited interaction with the neonate

physical and developmental needs and the family's practical and emotional needs.

Whenever possible, involve family members in planning. This not only helps ensure that they can carry out the planned interventions, but it also makes them active participants in their child's care. Such involvement particularly helps the family with a nursing diagnosis of *powerlessness related to the health care environment and limited interaction with the neonate.*

Interventions for the family of a high-risk neonate fall into four main categories:
- providing information
- strengthening support systems
- teaching caregiving skills
- enhancing parent-infant bonding.

Depending on the neonate's status, the nurse also may need to help the family plan for their child's discharge or help them cope with their child's death.

PROVIDE INFORMATION

Two nursing diagnoses that apply to almost every family of a high-risk neonate are *knowledge deficit related to the hospital course and care of a high-risk neonate* and *anxiety related to the neonate's condition and unknown outcome.* Nursing care is essential in helping the family with either diagnosis. In many cases, the family relies mainly on the nurse — not just for information but for help in understanding that information. Although the physician initially may identify the neonate's medical condition to the parents and may speak with them regularly, the nurse typically provides daily reports and thus may be the person to whom parents turn with questions.

The more thorough the parents' understanding, the better equipped they will be to cope with the crisis and achieve the eventual goal of adequate caregiving at home. To give them the most complete picture possible, cover the following topics:
- the neonate's medical condition, its cause (if known), and its long-term implications
- potential length of stay and probable course of treatment in the NICU
- ways parents can enhance their contact with their child
- ways parents can participate in their child's care.

Present, reinforce, and reinterpret

Such factors as familiarity with health care facilities, previous experience with health problems, and emotional state affect parents' ability to comprehend information the health care team gives them. Thus, adapt teaching strategies to parents' needs and assess the parents' comprehension frequently.

Recognize emotional blocks to understanding. Especially during denial, the first stage of grief, parents may not absorb all the information they receive about their child's condition. Although parents with a nursing diagnosis of *denial related to the immediate and long-term implications of the neonate's condition* can be frustrating to work with, the problem arises from grief. Acknowledge the parents' feelings, but persist, presenting the information in small chunks and reinforcing it patiently. Eventually, parents will move beyond denial and begin to take in the facts.

Review and clarify. Even after progressing past denial, parents may need help to grasp their child's condition fully. Try to be present whenever the physician talks with them, and review any new information with them afterward to clarify uncertainties and correct misunderstandings. Invite their questions, and encourage them to talk over what they have learned.

Once parents become hungry for information, they may seek it constantly – for example, in conversation with other parents with children in the NICU. Listen for such conversations, and intervene if necessary to clarify differences so that parents do not expect their child to have the same course of illness as another with a different diagnosis or maturity level.

Recognize parents' concerns. In seeking information, parents' main concerns may differ from those of the health care team. For example, they may focus on their child's long-term problems before short-term problems have been overcome.

Augment spoken information. To give parents a clearer idea of neonatal care procedures, use any available illustrations or photographs. Also provide information booklets, written in lay terms, that address the neonate's condition. (Several national support groups, such as the March of Dimes, publish such booklets.) As they read this material at home, they may develop a better understanding of what they have been told.

Reassure parents about their responses. Parents may need help in understanding what is happening to them emotionally. Explain that anxiety, fear, anger, and guilt are common among parents of high-risk neonates. To provide further reassurance and help them deal with their feelings, discuss the stages of grief.

Familiarize parents with the NICU
To most parents, the NICU is an alien and frightening environment. To make them feel more comfortable, describe the neonate's care routine, identifying each piece of equipment used and explaining its purpose. Be aware that anything attached to the neonate – even

a temperature probe taped to the abdomen — may look threatening. If a new piece of equipment is introduced after the parents' first visit, explain its purpose and operation. Also encourage parents to enliven their child's surroundings with photographs or toys. If they have other children, suggest that they have the children draw pictures to tape near the neonate's incubator or crib.

Outline the course of treatment
As far as possible, explain the probable course the neonate's treatment will take and the time that may be involved. Prepare parents for the chance that their child may need oxygen therapy or assisted ventilation at some point.

Be realistic
An insistent question among parents of high-risk neonates is whether their child will survive. A problem that the health care team regards as minor may seem to parents like a sign of impending death. While not playing down the likelihood of death if the neonate's condition is life-threatening, do not minimize the chance for survival, either. Advise parents that although the usual hospital course of a high-risk neonate is unstable at best, the health care team may be surprised by the amount of fight in even the smallest and sickest neonate.

Maintain communication
For the parents with a nursing diagnosis of *potential altered parenting related to poor parent-infant bonding,* foster attachment and reduce anxiety by letting them know by frequent communication that they are welcome partners in their child's care. Even if the parents visit frequently, encourage them to phone daily. Initiate calls to them from time to time simply to give progress reports or to check with them about points brought up in their last visit. Include news of milestones achieved by their child, such as a weight gain, as well as a condition update.

If parents live so far away that daily phone calls are too costly, write them a note every few days to give them a sense of their child's course between one visit and the next. If possible, occasionally include a photograph of their child.

STRENGTHEN SUPPORT SYSTEMS
The family of a high-risk neonate needs a tremendous amount of support. The nurse should plan interventions that help parents make good use of the support sources they know of and identify other potential sources.

Enhance parents' support systems
Ensure that parents make the best possible use of familiar support systems by encouraging them to communicate with each other and by providing opportunities for them to discuss their feelings.

Promote communication between parents. Even if the parents normally serve as each other's greatest source of emotional support, their ability to meet each other's needs may fall short in a crisis. Also, they may move through grief at vastly different rates. However, one parent may assume that the other is at the same stage; when that assumption proves wrong, anger and resentment on both sides may result. To counter this potential, urge them to keep communication open.

Provide openings to discuss feelings. When parents visit their child, invite them to express their feelings. Such a comment as, "You must feel overwhelmed by all this" may release a flood of feelings. If one parent speaks but not the other, ask the silent parent what his or her reactions are.

Given an opening for honest discussion, parents may find common ground in their concerns and a sense of relief at not being alone. Even if they are not at the same stage of grief, one may be able to affirm the other's feelings as something he or she went through. If parents cannot reach common ground in their perceptions, urge them to find another family member – a grandparent, for example – who is understanding and supportive. Likewise, encourage a single parent to look to another family member or close friend for support.

Especially in the first few days after the neonate's birth, the parents' needs may differ. The mother, physically weakened and perhaps feeling isolated from other family members and from her child while in the maternity unit, may not have her usual control of her feelings. She may depend heavily on the father's visits for emotional support; between these visits, she may feel particularly alone. Even after her discharge, such feelings may persist because of her separation from her hospitalized child.

The father, too, needs support. The comfort he provides to the mother may drain his reserves. Should he believe he must be strong in crisis, he may be reluctant to reach out to other family members. His sense of isolation may increase further if friends and coworkers lack sympathy for any life-style changes he makes in response to family needs (Battles, 1988).

Each parent may feel so overwhelmed by the situation as to be unaware of the emotional drain made on the other. Help them open up to each other and discuss their feelings, which can strengthen understanding between them.

Also encourage parents to find time alone together — perhaps something as simple as a regular stop at a coffee shop on the way home from a visit to the NICU. Such an occasion, away from the pressures of home and hospital, may help them replenish their mental and emotional reserves.

Encourage family support

Among the most important interventions by the nurse caring for the family of a high-risk neonate are those that promote interaction among all family members. The family can be the strongest source of support for individual family members in a crisis. Conversely, physical or emotional isolation of any one member from the rest may put tremendous stress on all members and on the family as a whole.

Help siblings cope. Unless their needs receive attention, siblings of a high-risk neonate may face lifelong problems in dealing with the changes such a birth creates. Communication problems may develop (Scheiber, 1989), and siblings may experience conflicting feelings about the neonate.

Besides helping parents balance the needs of the neonate and siblings for attention, make sure they are aware of the feelings siblings may be experiencing. For example, siblings may become fearful as they sense their parents' fear. If they are not old enough to understand the neonate's health problem or if no one explains it to them, they may fear "catching" the same ailment. In many cases, siblings fear that the neonate will take their mother away from them.

Siblings also may feel guilt over the neonate's condition. Not wanting to share the parents' attention with another child, for example, a sibling earlier may have wished that the birth would not occur and now may fear that the neonate's condition is a punishment for that wish. Preschool-age children, who believe that their thoughts have the power of actions (Gardner and Merenstein, 1989), are particularly likely to feel guilty.

Jealousy and anger may occur as siblings see how much of the parents' time and energy the neonate has captured. To regain some attention for themselves, they may display signs and symptoms similar to those of the ill neonate. If the siblings are staying with friends or relatives while the mother is hospitalized, they may be angry with the neonate for disrupting their home life.

Using terms the siblings can understand, explain to them the neonate's condition. Also, urge the parents to let siblings visit and care for the neonate and reassure them that their lives will not change drastically.

Encourage closeness between parents and other family members. Let parents know that they are not expected to spend every possible moment with the neonate. Discuss with them their own needs and those of children at home, and help them set priorities for meeting these needs along with the neonate's.

For a family with a nursing diagnosis of *ineffective family coping: compromised, related to family disorganization secondary to the neonate's condition,* help parents explore ways of scheduling regular family time together at home and of making sure that birthdays and other special occasions are not neglected. Suggest, for example, that parents ask grandparents or other relatives to help with housekeeping chores so that when parents are home they can devote attention and energy to family interaction, not just to home care.

Encourage family members to interact with the neonate. Help parents plan ways to include grandparents, siblings, and other family members in visits to the NICU. If the neonate is stable and the facility's physical layout and policies permit, suggest bringing the whole family together in a private area near the NICU. If no such area is available but sibling visits are permitted, family members can take turns visiting the neonate; the time they spend together in the waiting area may provide the chance for them to interact with and support one another. Grandparents and older, responsible siblings also may take part in the neonate's care.

Make parents aware of support groups

Inform parents of support groups available within the facility, locally, and nationally. Many facilities with NICUs have parent or family support groups, organized by parents or the nursing or social services staff. Parent-to-parent support groups in particular can provide emotional support and practical advice. Parents who take part in these groups can discuss their concerns, learn how parents of neonates with similar problems have coped, and find out about available community resources. If an in-house support group is available, let parents know its meeting time and place.

National support groups include those tied to a specific problem, such as spina bifida, and those with a more general scope, such as the March of Dimes. Provide parents with names, addresses, and phone numbers for local chapters (or, if no local group exists, national headquarters). Many national groups provide practical help. For instance, the United Way and the March of Dimes may provide funding for medical care, equipment, and transportation for follow-up care. Encourage parents to talk with the facility's social worker about applying for such assistance.

TEACH CAREGIVING SKILLS

To promote parenting skills and parent-infant bonding, the nurse should involve parents in their child's care. With few exceptions, parents can provide some care for even the sickest neonate (Kelting, 1986). Although some parents welcome the chance to do this, others express doubts. These doubts may reflect insecurity about their own abilities or reluctance to establish a relationship with the neonate. If parents are uncomfortable with the idea of becoming caregivers, recognize their fears and work toward overcoming them. To do this, begin with the simplest procedures and increase the parents' participation only as they indicate readiness.

Increase the family's comfort level

To help the parents feel comfortable around their child, arrange for the neonate and parents to be together as much as possible. Take the mother to the NICU as soon as she has recovered sufficiently from delivery; if the neonate's health status permits, let the mother hold as well as see her child for a few minutes. Encourage her to touch her child if she seems hesitant.

Whenever parents come to the NICU, help them feel physically close to their child—for instance, by arranging chairs to let them comfortably see and touch their child. When their child is in a quiet but alert state, in which interaction is least stressful, encourage the parents to use gentle touch to get acquainted. Try to provide privacy and minimize interruptions at this time.

Involve parents in basic care

As the neonate's condition permits, encourage the parents to perform basic care. For instance, if the neonate is stable, invite the parents to participate in feeding. Show them how to hold their child during and after feeding, and explain how to perform simple mouth care. If the mother is considering breast-feeding, explain that giving breast milk may be beneficial physically and psychologically to her child and to her (Steele, 1987). Even if the neonate cannot suckle, the mother can provide breast milk she has pumped.

If the neonate must be gavage-fed, show the parents how to assist by holding the feeding tube or cylinder or by pouring the milk into the container. Invite them to supply a pacifier for their child to use between feedings.

Bathing the neonate can be a special time for parents. For the first bath with parents present, explain any special precautions they must take and encourage parents to watch their child respond to gentle touch; on future occasions, parents may give the bath with minimal supervision.

Diapering provides another opportunity for parents to strengthen their caregiving skills and perhaps also a chance to make some care decisions. Even if the neonate's fecal output must be monitored carefully, parents can change the diaper, weighing it themselves or saving it for a staff member to weigh. Offer parents their choice of several diaper ointments and creams, and encourage them to apply whatever they choose with a gentle touch.

As parents become more familiar with neonatal care needs, encourage them to rely less on staff supervision during caregiving—for example, suggest that they perform routine bottle- or breast-feeding on their own. The more successfully they function on their own as caregivers, the more confident they will feel when caring for their child at home.

An ideal way to enhance and evaluate parents' caregiving ability is to observe them as they care for their child. Such supervision also may decrease anxiety in parents before discharge and may prove particularly helpful if the neonate has complex care needs. Many facilities provide this experience by means of a care-by-parent unit. In this arrangement, one or both parents live with the neonate for 18 to 36 hours in a private room within or near the NICU.

Involve parents in developmental care

To help parents participate in developmental care, which can reduce some physical and mental limitations resulting from high-risk birth, suggest that they bring in items that stimulate vision and hearing, such as brightly colored toys or mobiles, tape recordings of family members' voices, or toys that make soothingly rhythmic sounds. Devices that mimic the sound of the maternal heartbeat are especially effective in calming a fussy neonate.

Invite participation in decision making

Ask parents how they would like their child's daily care routine to be adjusted to give them maximum participation. For example, they may ask that bath time be set for when they can be present and routine medical procedures scheduled to avoid interfering with visiting time. Accommodate the parents' desires as much as possible; if something will not fit in, explain the problem to them.

Involve parents in decision making on as many levels as possible, both simple and complex. Even when the physician must make the final decision, help them to understand the options and the reason for the physician's choice so that they become partners in the decision.

ENHANCE PARENT-INFANT BONDING

Parents whose neonate is critically ill or separated from them for long periods may show poor bonding with the neonate for several years (Plunkett, Meisels, Stiefel, Pasick, and Roloff, 1986). However, to withstand the rigors of caregiving for a high-risk neonate, they must develop a strong bond. The nurse can promote bonding by continuing to encourage frequent visiting, caregiving, phone calls, and other interaction. Also, give the parents the fullest possible picture of their child's characteristic behavior, including patterns of fussiness and wakefulness, so that they know what to expect once their child is discharged. Such advance knowledge minimizes strains on parent-infant bonding.

PLAN FOR THE NEONATE'S DISCHARGE

As technological advances have increased survival rates, many high-risk neonates who only a few years ago would have lived hours or days now survive and eventually go home with their parents. However, some require complex, demanding, and expensive care for years—perhaps the rest of their lives. Nursing care for the family of a high-risk neonate should aim to ensure that the family will know how to provide this level of care. (For details on discharge planning, see Chapter 7, Discharge Planning and Care at Home.)

Preparation of the family for the neonate's discharge requires an evaluation of their concerns and any weaknesses in their caregiving ability. The nurse must look not only for the skills they demonstrate but for any persisting fears—understandable as they face the prospect of taking over care of a neonate whose life so far has been supported by advanced equipment. For example, they may fear that they will not recognize signs of a sudden downturn until too late.

Evaluate readiness to assume care

To determine whether the family needs further nursing intervention before the neonate's discharge, evaluate the parents for their emotional and practical readiness to assume primary care. Discharge to a poorly prepared family could result in such problems as failure to thrive or abuse of the neonate by a family member.

Although careful teaching can prepare most parents to be effective caregivers, some parents need more than this. Carefully evaluate the parents' ability and motivation to care for their child, and inform the physician if they display any of the following behaviors as the neonate's discharge date nears:

• delay in arranging for medical-support equipment in the home
• infrequent calls or visits to the NICU
• apparent lack of interest in giving simple care to their child in the NICU.

Explain further care needs and options

Make sure parents understand which kinds of continuing care their child will require after discharge. For parents whose child is likely to remain technologically dependent for life, the availability of health services is a major concern — not just whether they exist but whether they are affordable and available nearby. Help parents identify facilities in their area that offer continuing support, and encourage them to enlist the social worker's help in applying for funds from institutional, governmental, and support-group sources.

HELP THE FAMILY DEAL WITH DEATH

If the neonate has a poor prognosis or if death appears imminent, the nurse can help the family deal with the prospect of death as well as the event itself. Fetal loss and stillbirth also warrant special nursing interventions.

Perinatal death

The kinds of interventions family members need before and after a neonate's death depend somewhat on the relationship they have formed with the neonate and on the stage of grief they are in. To facilitate a healthy resolution of grief, carry out measures that help family members complete their bond with the neonate. Some family members experience a brief denial phase after the death of a high-risk neonate; others skip denial and show signs of anger, guilt, or despair.

Prepare the family for the neonate's death. Even if the parents have spent little time with their child, their emotional bond probably has been developing since pregnancy. To resolve their grief, they must complete their bonding with the neonate as their child and a member of their family, building memories to sustain them in the future.

To promote bonding, encourage the parents to name their child (if they have not done so already). As they look at the child, point out physical features that resemble those of family members; this may help them put their thoughts about their child into words (Krone and Harris, 1988). Find out whether they want the child to be baptized or to receive some other blessing, and make appropriate arrangements. If possible, let them hold their child; otherwise, encourage gentle touching and stroking.

Also plan interventions to help family members deal with their grief. For family members in denial, do not attempt to force them past denial, but provide and reinforce clear, accurate information about the child's condition.

For family members feeling anger, provide the opportunity to vent feelings. However, if one family member blames another for the child's condition, point out that in most cases, preterm birth, neo-natal illness, and birth defects result from a combination of factors. Even if the action of one or both parents seems to have been the immediate cause, laying blame serves no purpose.

Use similar reasoning to help family members put aside guilt, a form of self-targeting anger. Although the mother is more likely to express feelings of guilt — remembering a week of unauthorized di-eting or a single glass of wine — the father may feel guilt for not being committed enough to the mother's care while she was preg-nant.

Anticipatory grieving can occur during the fourth stage of grief — depression and withdrawal. If the neonate is in critical condition and not expected to live, the parents may begin grieving by with-drawing from the neonate (Lindemann, 1944). Even if the parents say nothing, reduced attention to their child may signal that they have begun to withdraw.

Anticipatory grieving and emotional withdrawal may occur briefly or continue throughout the neonate's hospitalization. Although these behaviors can ease pain when an anticipated perinatal death occurs, they also can create problems in bonding if the neonate survives. For the family with a nursing diagnosis of ***anticipatory grieving related to the prospect of the neonate's death,*** make sure the parents' understanding of their child's condition is not bleaker than the sit-uation warrants, and inform them that even critically ill neonates may recover.

Make arrangements for the death. Keep parents informed of changes in their child's condition. Assure them that the staff will do its best to let them know when death appears near so that they can be with their child.

Before the family arrives, dress the neonate in regular baby cloth-ing (some units keep a supply of baby clothes to use if the parents have not provided any). If family members will be permitted to hold their child, have a receiving blanket ready for wrapping the neonate; later, parents may wish to have the blanket as a keepsake.

When the family arrives, provide as much privacy as possible. Move the neonate to a private area (or at least to the quietest corner of the NICU). Post a sign near the entrance to this area, alerting staff to the family's need for quiet. When no additional medical intervention is planned, let the family spend the last few moments alone with the neonate.

Provide support after the death. Family members need support to cope with the immediate reality of their child's death and to deal with their grief. After the neonate has died, the nurse should give family members all the time they need to say goodbye to and hold the child.

If the family was absent at the time of death, check with the physician about notification procedure. Some physicians prefer to inform the family personally rather than by telephone. Offer to be present to give support when the family is notified. (For information about organizations that help bereaved parents cope with perinatal loss, see *Resources for dealing with perinatal loss*.)

Prepare the body. If the family arrives after the neonate has died, prepare the body for them to see. Wash, dress, and wrap the neonate in a way that displays positive features and covers disfigurements. With the physician's permission, remove all tubes and lines (except where removal might affect the outcome of an autopsy); disconnect, tie off, and secure those lines under the clothing while the family visits. Remove drainage stains and tape marks; cover surgical wounds or puncture sites with small dressings.

Place the wrapped body in a cool area until just before the family arrives. Then, before presenting the body to them, wrap it in warmed linens, which will transfer some of the warmth to the neonate's skin.

Preserve mementos. To provide the family with tangible memories of the neonate, assemble a memory packet, including such items as photographs, a lock of hair, the identification bracelet, a footprint, caps, and blankets. If the family does not wish to take these items home, let them know that the packet will be kept in case they want it later; when they are past the initial shock, these mementos may help them through grief.

Help with funeral arrangements. For some parents, making funeral arrangements for their child is calming; focusing on the task at hand helps them accept their loss and deal with their grief. Recognize, however, that parents who have never before experienced the death

RESOURCES FOR DEALING WITH PERINATAL LOSS

The grief and loss experienced by the family of a neonate who dies last far longer than the brief time most neonatal nurses are in contact with the family. Consequently, the nurse should be aware of support groups that can help family members deal with their loss in the months and years to come.

Pregnancy and Infant Loss Center (PILC)
1421 E. Wayzata Boulevard, Suite 40
Wayzata, MN 55391
612-473-9372

Resolve Through Sharing
La Crosse Lutheran Hospital
1910 South Avenue
La Crosse, WI 54601
608-791-4747

Source of Help in Airing and Resolving Experiences (SHARE)
St. Elizabeth's Hospital
211 South 3rd Street
Belleville, IL 62222
618-234-2415

of a close relative may need help to identify what needs to be done; particularly distraught parents may be unable to face the task at all. Discuss with them — or have the chaplain or social worker discuss — possible funeral and burial choices (including having the hospital take care of the body, if that option is available).

If the parents' reactions to the death are so intense that they cannot make arrangements, call on a family support source, such as a grandparent, to help out. (However, do not seek help if parents can do their own planning; a well-meaning relative or friend who takes over may deprive parents of tasks that would help them resolve grief.)

Even if the parents can make their own arrangements, talk with other family members about ways to help them out at home. Relatives may think they should remove all signs of preparation for the child's birth — crib, toys, clothing — and keep the mother so busy once she comes home that she has no chance to think about her loss. Explain that such tasks as packing up these items may help parents come to terms with their loss. Suggest that offering an afternoon's child care or other practical help might be more appropriate.

Help with resolving grief. Between experiencing and accepting their child's death, parents go through a lengthy internal struggle. The aim of nursing interventions during this period is twofold: help maintain basic family functioning and help family members work through grief to a healthy resolution.

Identify and intervene in dysfunctional grief. Be familar with signs of dysfunctional grief. After their child's death, parents may experience disorganization and physical ailments. For instance, various studies show that the risk of disease increases during bereavement. Parkes (1970) described psychosomatic pain, especially chest pain, among bereaved adults. Mourners also have a higher risk of serious illness than nonmourners (Rees and Lutkins, 1967). Lynch (1979) found a twofold risk of myocardial infarction in mourners compared to nonmourners and, depending on the region in which they lived, a threefold risk of gastrointestinal cancer.

Some bereaved parents may be unable to eat, sleep, or make decisions; they may seem caught up in anger at the health care team or in depression about their inability to produce a healthy child. In some cases, they may fail to cope with everyday experiences or to meet their own and their children's basic needs.

To assess for these problems, monitor the parents' physical appearance, if possible. Also talk with them frequently about how they are managing home affairs, and be ready to call in a friend or relative who can help keep the family functioning until the parents can resume their normal roles. Suggest that they undergo a physical examination approximately 4 months after the loss to ensure early detection of any physical problems associated with bereavement. (For more information about dysfunctional grief, see *Pathologic mourning.*)

Counter misunderstandings. Because family members may pass through the stages of grief at different rates, misunderstandings may arise. Most commonly, the mother's grief takes longer to resolve. Her attachment may be greater because of the special bond she developed with the fetus during pregnancy. Thus she may find grief resolution more difficult. The father, meanwhile, may seem to have

PATHOLOGIC MOURNING

Ultimately, grief results in healing. When the process is completed, family members can resume normal functioning, remembering the dead neonate with sorrow but able to move on. In a few cases, however, mourning (the outward expression of grief) becomes pathologic—most commonly when a parent tries to suppress grief (Gardner and Merenstein, 1989) instead of letting the process work through. The family member may never reach resolution without intervention by a professional skilled in grief counseling.

The nurse who cares for the family of a neonate who has died should stay alert for indications that a family member is fighting recognition of grief. If any of the following signs or symptoms appear, alert other members of the health care team and refer the family member to an expert:
- agitated depression
- changes in relationships with family or friends
- hostility toward specific individuals
- illness that may be psychosomatic (for example, chronic fatigue and headache)
- inability to function productively
- loss of social-interaction patterns
- overactivity with no sense of loss
- schizophrenia-like formality of manner
- symptoms resembling those of the neonate.

distanced himself from the dead child. His grief may not be evident, even though his sense of loss may be great.

To help reduce misunderstandings, teach the parents about the grief stages and encourage them to communicate with each other about their feelings — not only about the loss of their child, but about the pressures they feel in its aftermath. The father, for example, may explain that although the loss is painful for him, he feels he must be stoic, fearing that the same people who sympathize with the mother's expression of grief would disapprove of his. If the parents have trouble understanding each other, suggest that they talk together with the social worker, chaplain, or another counselor.

Also talk with other family members. As they reach their own points of grief resolution, they may become impatient with the mother (or both parents) for being "preoccupied" with the child's death. When the mother attempts to discuss her feelings, for example, other family members may urge her to stop dwelling in the past. They even may encourage her to start a "replacement" child before she is ready to consider another pregnancy.

To avert such well-meaning intrusion, discuss with other family members the individuality of grieving. Assure them that 6 weeks of acute mourning are by no means unusual, that full resolution of grief may take 2 years, and that accepting the mother's feelings will help her resolve her grief.

Fetal death

Because parents can begin bonding with a child as soon as they are aware of a pregnancy, the death of a fetus can be as traumatic as the death of a neonate. Nursing interventions similar to those provided after a neonate's death can help parents who suffer a fetal loss; however, depending on when in the pregnancy the fetal loss occurs, opportunity to provide such interventions may be limited. Thus the timing and circumstances of the fetal loss guide nursing interventions.

First-trimester fetal death. With a first-trimester loss (usually a spontaneous abortion), the mother may have been unaware of the pregnancy — and she may not be hospitalized for treatment. If she simply is treated in the physician's office, little opportunity exists for nursing intervention; yet she may need such intervention.

On the other hand, if the mother was aware of the pregnancy, she and her partner may have begun their emotional investment; if so, they will need to grieve. Unfortunately, family and friends may minimize a first-trimester fetal loss, believing that the pregnancy cannot have meant that much yet and thus fail to give parents support. Nursing interventions in this situation include affirming the parents' right and need to grieve, explaining the stages of grief to them, and encouraging them to communicate with and support each other.

Second-trimester fetal death. Fetal death at this stage typically results in spontaneous abortion. In most cases, the parents were aware of the pregnancy and had invested themselves emotionally in the forthcoming birth. Nursing interventions include helping the parents express their grief, explaining the stages of grief, and encouraging them to communicate with each other and other family members.

Third-trimester fetal death. As pregnancy progresses and parents invest more time and energy in the fetus, bonding with the expected child increases. Thus third-trimester fetal loss may be quite traumatic. The mother may have to go through labor to expel the fetus, adding to the trauma. Parents in this situation need much support from each other, other family members, and friends. Nursing interventions may include suggesting that they pack up whatever clothes, toys, and other items they had begun accumulating to help them complete their bonding with the expected child. Although this may be a difficult task, it can help parents face their loss and express their feelings (Limbo and Wheeler, 1986).

Stillbirth

Stillbirth — the death shortly before or during delivery of a fetus that had been expected to live — is a wrenching experience as happy anticipation suddenly vanishes. If fetal death occurs before labor begins, the parents also must deal with feelings of helplessness as they wait for delivery to occur. Because grieving will be easier if they complete their bonding with the child, encourage the parents to look at, touch, and hold the stillborn neonate. Also, provide solitude as they say goodbye to their child.

EVALUATION

During this step of the nursing process, the nurse evaluates the effectiveness of the care plan by ongoing evaluation of subjective and objective criteria. Evaluation findings should be stated in terms of actions performed or outcomes achieved for each goal. Keep in mind that while the neonate is hospitalized, the nurse may have difficulty evaluating the effect of care for the family because full results of some interventions may not be apparent until after the neonate is discharged.

The following examples illustrate appropriate evaluation statements for the family of a high-risk neonate.

• The parents demonstrated specific caregiving skills required by their neonate during and after hospitalization.

• The parents identified and used available support sources during and after the neonate's hospitalization.

• The parents' verbal and nonverbal behaviors reflected at least a moderate level of comfort in meeting the neonate's physical and emotional needs.
• The parents demonstrated an understanding of and used appropriate coping mechanisms.
• The parents expressed grief in a constructive manner.
• The parents demonstrated an accurate perception of the neonate's condition and have realistic expectations.

DOCUMENTATION

Documentation for the parents of a high-risk neonate should include:
• signs of individual expressions of grief
• length and frequency of visits to the neonate
• nature of the interaction with the neonate
• ability to express feelings about the neonate
• ability to identify and provide for the neonate's care needs
• ability to accept help and advice from the health care team
• verbal expression of coping ability
• expression of comfort with caring for the neonate at home
• willingness to make necessary arrangements for home care
• ability to identify appropriate follow-up medical care for the neonate
• contact with the deceased neonate if perinatal death has occurred.

Documentation for the neonate with regard to family interaction should include the following points:
• physiologic response to parents' care, including response to feeding and simple caregiving activities
• eye contact and other signs of interaction with parents
• response to interaction by the parents (for example, "Takes feeding easily from mother; no vomiting after eating; quiet after feeding").

BIBLIOGRAPHY

Plunkett, J.W., Meisels, S.J., Stiefel, G.S., Pasick, P.L., and Roloff, D.W. (1986). Patterns of attachment among preterm infants of varying biological risk. *Journal of the American Academy of Child Psychiatry,* 25(6), 794-800.

Wranesh, B.L. (1982). The effect of sibling visitation on bacterial colonization rate in neonates. *JOGNN,* 11(4), 211-213.

Cultural references

Leininger, M.M. (1985). Transcultural care diversity and universality: A theory of nursing. *Nursing and Health Care,* 6(4), 208-212.

Manio, E.B., and Hall, R.R. (1987). Asian family traditions and their influence in transcultural health care delivery. *Children's Health Care,* 15(3), 172-177.

Tripp-Reimer, T., Brink, P. J., and Saunders, J. M. (1984). Cultural assessment: Content and process. *Nursing Outlook,* 32(2), 78-82.

York, C.R., and Stichler, J.F. (1985). Cultural grief expressions following infant death. *Dimensions of Critical Care Nursing,* 4(2), 120-127.

Families in crisis

Battles, R.S. (1988). Factors influencing men's transition into parenthood. *Neonatal Network,* 6(5), 63-66.

Kelting, S. (1986). Supporting parents in the NICU. *Neonatal Network,* 4(6), 14-18.

Lemons, P.M. (1986). Beyond the birth of a defective child. *Neonatal Network,* 5(3), 13-20.

Scheiber, K.K. (1989). Developmentally delayed children: Effects on the normal sibling. *Pediatric Nursing,* 15(1), 42-44.

Steele, K.H. (1987). Caring for parents of critically ill neonates during hospitalization: Strategies for health-care professionals. *MCN,* 16(1), 13-27.

Tarbert, K.C. (1985). The impact of a high-risk infant upon the family. *Neonatal Network,* 3(4), 20-23.

Trahd, G.E. (1986). Siblings of chronically ill children: Helping them cope. *Pediatric Nursing,* 12(3), 191-193.

Grief

Benefield, D.G., Leib, S.A., and Reuter, J. (1976). Grief response of parents after referral of the critically ill newborn to a regional center. *New England Journal of Medicine,* 294(18), 975-978.

Bowlby, J. (1961). Process of mourning. *International Journal of Psychoanalysis,* 42, 317-340.

Cordell, A.S., and Apolito, R. (1981). Family support in infant death. *JOGNN,* 10(4), 281-285.

Davidson, G.W. (1984). *Understanding mourning: A guide for those who grieve.* Minneapolis: Augsburg Publishing House.

Gardner, S.L., and Merenstein, G.B. (1989). *Handbook of neonatal intensive care.* St. Louis: Mosby.

Krone, C., and Harris, C.C. (1988). The importance of infant gender and family resemblance within parents' perinatal bereavement process: Establishing personhood. *Journal of Perinatal and Neonatal Nursing,* 2(2), 1-11.

Kübler-Ross, E. (1969). *On Death and Dying.* New York: Macmillan.

Limbo, R.K., and Wheeler, S.R. (1986). *When a baby dies: A handbook for healing and helping.* Holmen, WI: Harsand Press.

Lindemann, E. (1944). Symptomatology and management of acute grief. *American Journal of Psychiatry,* 101: 141-148.

Lynch, J.J. (1979). *The broken heart: The medical consequences of loneliness.* New York: Basic Books.

Olshansky, S. (1962, April). Chronic sorrow: A response to having a mentally defective child. *Social Casework,* 43, 190-193.

Parkes, C.M. (1970). "Seeking" and "finding" a lost object: Evidence from recent studies of the reaction to bereavement. *Social Science and Medicine,* 4(2), 187-201.

Rees, W.D., and Lutkins, S.G. (1967). The mortality of bereavement. *British Medical Journal,* 4(570), 13-16.

Sahu, S. (1981). Coping with perinatal death. *Journal of Reproductive Medicine,* 26(3), 129-132.

Nursing research

Blackburn, S., and Lowen, L. (1986). Impact of an infant's premature birth on the grandparents and parents. *JOGNN,* 15(2), 173-178.

Brooten, D., Gennaro, S., Brown, L.P., Butts, P., Gibbons, A.L., Bakewell Sachs, S., and Kumar, S.P. (1988). Anxiety, depression, and hostility in mothers of preterm infants. *Nursing Research,* 37(4), 213-216.

Choi, E.C. (1986). Unique aspects of Korean-American mothers. *JOGNN,* 15(5), 394-400.

Discharge Planning and Care at Home

In the past decade, dramatic changes in health care — economic pressures, advances in the treatment of high-risk neonates, and the desire by families for more active participation in health care — have led to a growing demand for home health care and other community-based services.

Philosophical changes within the neonatal health care community also have played a role. For example, early discharge is now standard for normal, healthy neonates. For the nurse working within the setting of a health care facility, early discharge means less time to plan for the neonate's discharge — yet a greater need for thorough discharge planning. For the nurse who makes postdischarge visits to the home, early discharge may mean a longer period of follow-up with a greater need for family support and individualized attention.

Also, high-risk neonates who survive their initial problems and become medically stable commonly require further treatment at home. Many have multiple chronic problems that call for specialized, complex home care; some depend on monitors and other technological devices. In 1988, for example, an estimated 10,000 American families experienced the birth of a catastrophically ill child (National Association of Children's Hospitals and Related Industries, Inc., 1989). Thus, home health care for neonates has become increasingly complex as well as common. The long-term success of the sophisticated technology now available for home use may hinge on how effectively the nurse and other health care professionals can extend their specialized knowledge and skills to the home.

To meet the challenges of home health care, the nurse must have expert assessment skills — sophisticated and holistic in scope, yet specific. Discharge planning must be the focus of care from the time of the neonate's admission to the nursery. As the main liaison between the family and other health care professionals, the nurse must possess a wealth of knowledge about neonatal and pediatric home health care and act as family advocate in determining the appropriateness of this care.

DISCHARGE PLANNING

Discharge planning involves the formulation of a program by the health care team, client, family, and appropriate outside agencies to meet the client's physical and psychosocial needs after discharge. Discharge planning for a neonate prepares the neonate and family (or other primary caregivers) for care at home or in another health care facility.

The American Nurses' Association (1975) defines discharge planning as "that part of the continuity of care...designed to prepare the client for the next phase of care, whether it be self care, care by family members, or care by an organized health care provider."

All clients have the right to planned continuity of care after discharge. When effective, discharge planning improves both the continuity and cost-effectiveness of care. In response to fiscal restraints and pressure from third-party payers, most health care facilities now emphasize discharge planning.

NURSE'S ROLE

The nurse's role in discharge planning is delineated in the standards of neonatal nursing established in 1986 by NAACOG, the organization for obstetric, gynecologic, and neonatal nurses.

• The nurse develops the discharge plan, making referrals as necessary to help the family cope with the neonate's condition.

• The nurse helps integrate the neonate into the family.

• The nurse provides the family with health education to promote neonatal and infant care.

• The nurse initiates and participates in neonatal care conferences with the family and other members of the health care team.

DISCHARGE PLANNING SYSTEMS

Although nurses are responsible for the health care aspects of discharge planning, some health care facilities have centralized discharge planning conducted by social workers or by a combination of social workers and nurses. With this system, the discharge planning department receives a list of new admissions every morning and identifies those neonates who will need extensive discharge planning.

Other facilities have a decentralized system, in which the nurse who works most closely with the client is responsible for discharge planning; as necessary, this nurse consults with other professionals for help with special aspects of planning, such as obtaining financial assistance.

The high-risk screen, a popular tool used by admitting offices, categorizes clients according to the intensity of their discharge planning needs. Most commonly, it is used in centralized discharge planning systems to "red-flag" and prioritize clients. In primary or secondary perinatal care facilities, the high-risk screen is used at nursery admission to identify:
- preterm neonates
- neonates of adolescent mothers
- neonates of mothers who used drugs or other substances during pregnancy
- neonates with no insurance coverage.

The use of high-risk screens is less helpful in a tertiary (intensive care) center, where almost every neonate fits the high-risk category.

DISCHARGE PLANNING RESOURCES

Discharge planning requires close collaboration among health care team members. In most cases, the nurse can refer the family to any professional for discharge planning assistance (although in some cases a physician's order is required for a referral to a specialist from another discipline). Typically, in-facility resource personnel involved in discharge planning include:
- clinical nurse specialist
- physician
- social worker
- financial counselor
- speech, hearing, occupational, and physical therapists
- utilization review nurse

- dietitian
- respiratory therapist
- child life therapist.

For example, the nurse would collaborate with a social worker when planning the discharge of a preterm neonate of an unwed mother who rarely visits and is undecided about keeping her child. In this case, the nurse documents lack of visits by the mother and any conversations with other family members; the social worker determines whether the child should be discharged to another family member or to foster care if the mother chooses not to keep the child.

Complex discharge

For help with a complex discharge, particularly on weekends or holidays when other resource personnel may be unavailable, the nurse may refer to unit discharge planning manuals. Also, some facilities have parent libraries that offer information at the layperson's level on diseases, medical procedures, child development, and community resources; toy libraries may be available to lend toys adapted for children with special needs. For help in identifying appropriate home care resources within the community, a community nurse may prove invaluable.

Nurses and other professionals who are experts in discharge planning may belong to the American Association for Continuity of Care. This organization holds annual conferences and state-level meetings where members share information. The legislative arm lobbies for continuity-of-care issues at the national level.

Family involvement

To enhance their commitment to and confidence in the discharge plan, the neonate's parents should be allowed to participate actively in discharge planning and set realistic goals mutually with the health care team. The Joint Commission on Accreditation of Healthcare Organizations (JCAHO; 1989) stipulates that the medical record document the parents' involvement in discharge planning. To help ensure parental involvement, the nurse may use a questionnaire, such as the one shown in *Discharge planning questionnaire,* pages 301 and 302.

DISCHARGE PLANNING QUESTIONNAIRE

To help assess the neonate's and family's discharge planning needs, the nurse may ask the parents (or other primary caregiver) to complete a questionnaire, such as the one shown here.

1. What is your name and your relationship to the infant?

_____

2. During which times of day will you be able to visit your infant here at the health care facility?

_____ Mornings   _____ Nights

_____ Afternoons   _____ Not sure

_____ Evenings

3. How will you get here to visit your infant?

_____ Own car   _____ Relative or friend
                                    will bring

_____ Public   _____ Other
          transportation

4. Who will be caring for your infant after discharge?

_____ Mother   _____ Friend

_____ Father   _____ Day care

_____ Babysitter   _____ Other

_____ Relative

5. Who will be able to help you with your infant's care at home?

_____ Spouse   _____ Other

_____ Relative   _____ No one available

_____ Friend

6. What kinds of help do you think your family will need to care for your infant at home?

_____

7. Would you like to see a social worker who can help your family work out problems you might be having while your infant is in the health care facility?

_____ Yes   _____ No

(continued)

DISCHARGE PLANNING QUESTIONNAIRE *(continued)*

8. Do you have any questions about your insurance coverage for your infant's home care?

_____ Yes _____ No

9. Would you like to see a financial counselor to discuss your insurance coverage or to obtain information on applying for financial assistance?

_____ Yes _____ No

10. Please indicate if you would like to see any of these professionals.

_____ Chaplain _____ Dietitian

_____ Child life therapist _____ Other

Adapted with permission from Children's Hospital Medical Center, Cincinnati.

IDENTIFYING DISCHARGE PLANNING NEEDS

To help avoid a delay in discharge once the neonate is medically ready, the nurse or other discharge planner should begin family preparation and arrangements for needed services at the time of delivery or, at the latest, by the time the neonate is admitted to the nursery. The nurse assesses the discharge planning needs of both the neonate and parents, using information from the nursing admission assessment and from ongoing assessment. (For details on gathering relevant data from admission information, see *Assessing discharge planning needs*.)

Neonatal needs

Assess the scope and complexity of the neonate's physical care needs, which may vary from routine care and arrangements for follow-up medical visits for the normal neonate to complex, high-technology care for the special-needs neonate. Identify the neonate's primary caregiver and at least one secondary caregiver who will be responsible for care in the primary caregiver's absence. Also determine which community agencies may need to be involved in home health care, which equipment and supplies will be required at home, and whether the home is adequate and safe for health care. To determine

ASSESSING DISCHARGE PLANNING NEEDS

To obtain sufficient information to formulate a discharge plan, the nurse may want to use information obtained from the neonate's parents by an admission assessment tool, such as the one shown here. Each question is accompanied by a rationale that explains how the answer might affect the neonate's discharge planning needs.

Is this your first child?
Rationale: For parents of a first child, teaching of routine neonatal care is essential. However, all parents can benefit from a review of routine neonatal care.

Where does your family live?
Rationale: A family living in a rural area may have trouble obtaining follow-up care at a tertiary perinatal center for a special-needs neonate. Also, certain high-technology home care services may not be available in isolated areas.

Who will be the caregiver at different times of the day?
Rationale: Secondary caregivers and babysitters may need to learn special care techniques.

How do you plan on paying for home health care?
Rationale: For the neonate with a chronic illness or an anticipated long-term need for home health care, public and private insurers may cover only some costs, if any. Thus, the family will need financial counseling about alternative financial sources.

Is your family experiencing much stress right now? How extensive is your family's support system?
Rationale: To provide a safe environment for home care, the family may need help to minimize stress or enhance their support systems before the neonate's discharge. For the family with significant stress or little support, a referral to a social service agency may be necessary.

How much do you know about your child's medical condition?
Rationale: General teaching usually can begin soon after the neonate's admission to the nursery. (However, predicting what the neonate's condition will be at discharge or exactly which equipment and services will be needed at home may be impossible.)

the latter, consider arranging for a predischarge home visit by a community health nurse.

Parental needs
To determine the parents' discharge planning needs, assess their:
- ability and willingness to care for their child at home
- ability to bond with their child
- understanding of growth and development
- knowledge of neonatal and infant care techniques
- physical and psychosocial support systems
- need for additional caregivers
- stress level
- medical insurance and financial resources
- psychosocial adaptation to the changing family structure.

Assessing the feasibility of home care
Although caring for the neonate at home may sound ideal, this is not always best for the neonate or family. The parents and health care team must consider many factors when determining the most appropriate postdischarge care setting, especially if the neonate has special needs.

Neonate's health status. Usually, the neonate must be in stable condition to be cared for at home. If the neonate will need high-technology equipment or extensive professional services, a final decision on the suitability of home care should be delayed until the neonate is medically stable. Continuing instability or the need for frequent laboratory tests usually necessitates institutional care.

Parental willingness and ability. For home care to succeed, the parents must be willing and able to take on primary responsibility for the neonate's health care. Some parents — those who are ill themselves, for instance — are unable physically to care for a child. Others cannot afford to quit a job to stay home with the child, particularly if the employer pays for medical insurance. Home care also may be out of the question if the neonate needs complex or frequent care — a situation requiring two or more caregivers so that one can relieve the other.

The nurse should not assume that all parents want to care for a special-needs child at home. Some parents feel intimidated by medical equipment and overwhelmed by the demands of providing complex care. Some are unwilling to add the burden of health care to their other responsibilities or to make the necessary life-style changes to accommodate complex home care. A few parents, unable to cope with an uncertain future, are unsuited psychologically to caring for a special-needs child.

In some cases, parents express the desire to care for their child at home but repeatedly fail to attend learning sessions; this may indicate that they have unexpressed concerns about their ability to provide home care. Other parents are willing but lack the ability to learn caregiving skills.

Practical and psychosocial support. The parents of a special-needs child must have sufficient physical and psychosocial support to cope with home health care. Yet these parents may not get the support they need. The General Accounting Office (GAO; 1989) identified lack of information about available services or a resource person to contact when parents need help with home care as among the most common reasons why families with special-needs children have trouble obtaining support services.

Ideally, friends and other family members should be available to help care for other children and perform household chores. Respite for the parents also is crucial; a secondary caregiver who is trained in the required skills should be available to relieve the parents periodically from caregiving.

Psychosocial support is particularly important; parents of chronically ill children perceive less social support than parents of well children (Ferrari, 1986). Knowing that someone understands what the parents are going through, cares about them, and is available to offer emotional support can help the parents withstand the emotional rigors of caring for a special-needs child.

Cost considerations. In the United States, cost is a major issue when planning for discharge. Most major insurers provide only minimal coverage, if any, for home care even though home care usually costs significantly less than institutional care of comparable duration. Also, few insurers will pay for home care if it costs more than institutional care — a situation that may occur with a special-needs child who requires one-to-one nursing care.

When home care is covered by insurance, the family may have to pay a yearly deductible of $100 to $500 before the insurer will begin to reimburse 80% of the charges. Also, some insurers cover only certain types of equipment; for instance, they may pay for durable medical equipment, such as enteral feeding pumps, but not for disposables, such as the feeding bags and tubes used with such pumps. Moreover, most third-party payers limit the amount they will reimburse yearly for home nursing services; the average $5,000 limit would cover just 1 week of around-the-clock nursing care at $30/hour (this amount includes indirect costs as well as the nurse's wage). Many special-needs children nearly exhaust their lifetime maximum insurance benefits before discharge; further medical costs may devastate the family financially. This is a major concern for U.S. citizens, legislators, and health care providers and has sparked the introduction of catastrophic health care legislation.

Hidden costs usually are not reported in comparisons of institutional and home health care expenses; however, such costs can be substantial. Hidden costs include lost income when a family member must take time off from work to care for the child, higher home electricity bills (such as when the neonate requires mechanical ventilation), modifications of the home or family vehicle to accommodate special equipment, and transportation to and from physician appointments.

Other factors. The family considering home care must have transportation for follow-up medical visits. Also, the home environment must be suitable for caregiving, with adequate space to store supplies and set up equipment. Preferably, it also should have indoor plumbing, refrigeration, electricity, and a telephone (or easy access to one). Availability of services also must be considered. For instance, private-duty nurses may not be available in rural areas.

Supporting the family's decision. The nurse and other members of the health care team must be willing to support the family's informed decision regarding their child's placement. This is particularly important if the parents are considering an alternative care setting and have unresolved doubts about their moral, ethical, and legal obligations to their child; reinforcement of these doubts by the nurse could cause overwhelming parental guilt.

Likewise, the nurse should avoid imposing personal values on the parents. A parent's unkempt appearance or unhealthful life-style, for instance, may offend the nurse; lack of toilets and running water in the home may not conform to the nurse's view of a safe, healthful home environment. However, make an effort to maintain objectivity when considering whether such deficiencies represent real threats to the child's health and safety. After all, many children thrive even in the harshest environments. Also, the nurse who tries to "make the picture perfect" stands a good chance of encountering repeated disappointments and may have trouble establishing a positive relationship with the family. In any event, making referrals to the appropriate social service agencies and other resources fulfills the nurse's responsibility.

On the other hand, if the parents seem incapable of responsible parenting and their behavior or attitude suggests that the neonate will be neglected or abused after discharge, the nurse should consider notifying a social worker, who may attempt to have the court place the neonate in protective custody.

Ongoing assessment of discharge planning needs

Obviously, the nurse cannot assess all discharge planning needs at the time of nursery admission but must continue to assess these needs throughout the neonate's stay in the health care facility. As new needs arise, they must be incorporated into the discharge plan.

Many health care facilities conduct ongoing assessment of discharge planning needs during weekly discharge planning rounds and regularly scheduled client care conferences in addition to daily nurse-physician rounds. Topics discussed in these forums typically include the parents' understanding of and attitude toward the neonate's condition, the parents' coping ability and capacity to provide adequate care at home, the home environment, the family's need for support services and community resources, and the neonate's readiness for discharge.

Discharge planning rounds. During discharge planning rounds, each client on the unit is discussed briefly by a multidisciplinary team consisting of nurse, physician, social worker, occupational or physical therapist, dietitian, child life therapist, and perhaps a utilization review nurse and financial counselor. The team discusses assessment findings and ways to meet the neonate's and family's discharge planning needs.

Each team member is assigned specific tasks. The physician, for instance, typically will record which pediatrician or other primary care physician the parents have chosen for postdischarge care. The nurse will provide parent teaching (such as how to perform cardiopulmonary resuscitation [CPR], if appropriate), and make referrals to home health care companies. The social worker will determine if friends or other family members will be available to help with household tasks. The financial counselor will determine if the family's medical insurance covers private-duty home nursing care and, if so, to what dollar limit.

This discussion is documented in the client progress notes. In subsequent days or weeks, members of the health care team report on their assignments and work to finalize the discharge plan.

Client care conference. This forum, usually used to discuss a single client in depth, aids in the development and implementation of the discharge plan for the neonate who requires special planning. For some special-needs neonates, several such conferences may be required. The nurse may call the conference to conduct prospective planning or to discuss a new development or health crisis. To minimize the miscommunication and differences of opinion that can arise when several professionals are involved in a client's care, all major health care team members should take part in the conference; to help ensure continuity of care, the neonate's private physician also should attend. Usually, the parents are invited to attend, at least for the summary.

The physician or primary nurse usually chairs the conference, describing the neonate's current situation and requesting clarification and consensus on the plan of care. The nurse should ensure that the parents are supported rather than intimidated at the conference and that any questions or concerns they bring up are addressed adequately. As with discharge planning rounds, the client care conference is summarized by the primary nurse and recorded in the neonate's medical record.

IMPLEMENTING THE DISCHARGE PLAN

To implement the discharge plan, the nurse prepares the parents by teaching them about the care their child will require, helps them select a home health agency and order medical equipment and supplies, arranges for follow-up medical visits, makes appropriate referrals to community health services and other resources, and verifies that a family support system is in place by the time the neonate is discharged.

For the neonate with special needs, the American Academy of Pediatrics (1984) recommends that the discharge plan include a primary care physician, a case coordinator, a defined backup system for medical emergency care, verification of family access to a telephone, and a means of monitoring and adjusting the care plan as necessary. If the neonate requires special equipment, some health care facilities require that the equipment be brought there and used to check its operation and familiarize the parents with it.

Preparing the parents for the neonate's discharge

The nurse must ensure that the parents learn caregiving skills before the neonate's discharge. Besides routine neonatal and infant caregiving techniques, teaching topics may include emergency interventions, signs and symptoms of medical problems, use of special equipment, the purpose and adverse effects of medications, and names of people to contact when the parents have questions.

Use of written, standardized teaching plans ensures that teaching content is congruent over time and among professionals; however, when using such plans, make sure to individualize them so that they are relevant to the family's unique situation. Also, provide adequate learning time, making allowances for such problems as tardiness or missed appointments because of work responsibilities, lack of transportation, or difficulty finding a babysitter.

During parent preparation, keep in mind the various factors that can affect a parent's readiness and ability to learn: anxiety, previous experiences with illness, physical and mental capacities, cultural and ethnic background, language, family relationships, and motivation. As necessary, adjust the teaching plan around these factors. Because many parents are under stress when learning new information or skills and may not absorb information completely, be sure to reinforce verbal teaching with printed materials written at a fourth-grade reading level; preferably, these materials should have pictures or diagrams. Topics covered in such handouts should include illnesses, medications, special procedures, and well-baby care. (Use of written teaching materials also makes documentation of teaching more efficient and consistent.)

Besides verbal and written instruction, another useful teaching strategy is demonstration. Asking for a return demonstration of skills demonstrated by the nurse gives parents the chance to practice these skills and allows the nurse to check for evidence of their caregiving competence and confidence.

Videotapes are increasingly used as a teaching tool because they allow demonstration of skills with maximum consistency of content. Many nurses find that one-to-one teaching time is reduced when parents have seen a videotape. Many videotaped teaching resources are available for parents.

Selecting home health care services

Over the past 10 years, the home health care industry has seen phenomenal growth. However, not every agency or company that describes itself as a home health care service specializes in neonatal or pediatric care. The discharge planning staff should steer the parents toward agencies and companies with neonatal and pediatric expertise.

To avoid problems with reimbursement that could delay the neonate's discharge, the nurse should aim for early identification of the home health care services the child will need. (For specific information on home health care services, see the "Home health care" section of this chapter.)

Planning for payment of home health care

If third-party payment is unavailable, refer the family to a financial counselor for information on alternative funding sources, such as private, religious, local, and national associations and foundations, as well as specialized support groups, such as the March of Dimes Foundation.

Arranging for follow-up care

Verify that the parents know the dates and times of scheduled follow-up medical visits; this information should be supplied to them in writing. Also make sure they will have transportation for these visits. If they do not have transportation, refer them to a social worker, who can inform them of transportation services. Also make sure the parents know whom to call with questions and concerns about their child's health care. To evaluate the effectiveness of the discharge plan and to provide emotional support, arrange to call the parents a few days after discharge.

Preparing discharge instructions

Discharge instructions may take the form of written materials, such as booklets and printed instruction sheets for specific diseases, medication, or equipment; however, be sure to individualize such materials. Give discharge information to the parents early enough to allow them to read it, absorb it, and come up with questions that can be answered before the neonate's discharge, while the health care team is most accessible. Make sure to give parents emergency numbers to keep by the telephone at home. However, tell them that they are welcome to place nonemergency calls to ask any questions that may arise.

Send a copy of the discharge instructions and information about the neonate's status at discharge to the private physician's office and to the health care agency that will follow the child at home. If the parents received teaching handouts, also send a copy of these to the home health care agency to ensure continuity of care.

DOCUMENTING THE DISCHARGE PLAN

The JCAHO (1989) stipulates that the discharge plan be recorded in the client's medical record; this promotes continuity of care, provides a communication link for other team members, and serves as a reference for legal and other purposes. Make sure the medical record includes:
• assessment of the neonate's needs, problems, capabilities, and limitations
• evidence of parental participation in discharge planning
• evidence of parental learning of information provided
• availability of recommended services for the family
• the neonate's medical status at discharge
• the actual discharge plan, including prescribed medications, follow-up medical appointments, and any referrals to community agencies.

HOME HEALTH CARE

The services, supplies, and equipment provided to a client at home help to maintain or promote the client's physical, mental, or emotional health. Home health care also can reduce the cost of neonatal — actually, infant — care while providing support to the family.

Studies show that home health care can be safe and cost-effective even for high-risk children. Brooten, et al. (1986) randomly assigned low-birth-weight neonates to two groups. One group was discharged according to routine nursery criteria. The second group was discharged an average of 11 days earlier and weighed 200 g (7 oz) less; a perinatal nurse specialist provided evaluation and parent teaching and support for this group before discharge, during home visits 1 week after discharge, and periodically afterward. The researchers found no difference between the groups in number of rehospitalizations or in physical and mental growth and development, but health care costs per child in the group discharged earlier were $18,560 lower than for the other group.

Home health care also may improve mother-infant interaction. Norr, Nacion, and Abramson (1989) studied interaction between low-income, inner-city mothers and their neonates in three groups:
• simultaneous early discharge of mother and neonate (24 to 47 hours after delivery)
• early discharge of the mother, with discharge of the neonate after 48 hours
• simultaneous conventional discharge of mother and neonate (48 to 72 hours after delivery).

The selection criteria ensured that only low-risk mothers and neonates were discharged early. A nurse and community aide visited the simultaneous early-discharge group 1 to 2 days after discharge to conduct physical examinations and phenylketonuria and bilirubin testing; provide standard teaching on health, safety, and infant growth and development; and discuss the mothers' concerns. The researchers found stronger mother-infant bonding, fewer maternal concerns, and greater maternal satisfaction with postpartal care in this group, with no increase in maternal or neonatal morbidity in the first 2 weeks after discharge. However, all of the subjects in this study required careful health monitoring, and the mothers needed considerable teaching during the first month at home.

As these studies suggest, including a perinatal nurse specialist in a home health care program helps ensure that the parents receive expert advice and that any problems with their child are prevented or detected early through comprehensive assessment. In regions where perinatal nurse specialists are not available, home nurse generalists must maintain conscientious communication with nurse specialists and physicians to provide continuity of care.

HOME HEALTH CARE SERVICES, EQUIPMENT, AND SUPPLIES

Home health care services may be provided by public agencies or private companies. Equipment, supplies, and other products used for home care typically are obtained from private companies. The tremendous expansion in home health care has led to increased competition among providers of services and products. However, many services are geared to geriatric clients; therefore, careful selection is crucial.

Services

Formerly, home health care was the nearly exclusive province of the public health nurse, who provided not only illness care but health promotion and comprehensive family care. However, the passage of Medicare and Medicaid legislation led to dramatic changes in payment and provision systems and in client eligibility for home care. As physicians' roles in home care enlarged, such care became less comprehensive and more narrowly focused on illness care. Currently, professionals who may provide home health care include nurses, physicians, social workers, dietitians, and speech, hearing, occupational, and physical therapists. Many clients also require home health aides and homemaker services.

Nurses involved in home health care include public or community health nurses, private-duty nurses, and nurses from home care departments of local hospitals or for-profit (proprietary) home health care companies. These nurses and other professionals can be hired through a public, proprietary, or hospital-based agency.

A certified home care nursing agency (which may be run privately or publicly) is one that is subject to certain standards of care and has been certified for Medicare reimbursement. Such an agency can provide nurses for intermittent visits and also may provide speech, hearing, occupational, and physical therapists; homemakers; and home health aides. Many certified agencies also can supply private-duty or hourly nurses for families who have private insurance or can pay directly for nursing care.

Equipment and supplies

Home health care equipment and supplies can be obtained from durable medical equipment companies, surgical pharmacies, and home infusion therapy services. Selection of a vendor should take into account the company's pediatric experience and the range of equipment and supplies provided. Optimally, the vendor should offer preventive maintenance, free loaner equipment during repairs, 24-hour availability for emergency service, and prompt response to service calls.

Durable medical equipment companies provide respiratory equipment, such as oxygen tanks, mechanical ventilators, and apnea monitors; most also can supply hospital beds (but usually not cribs), wheelchairs, phototherapy equipment, enteral feeding pumps, and other supplies for home use. These companies usually employ a nurse or respiratory therapist to manage the home use of their equipment. Home infusion therapy services can provide home chemotherapy, pain control therapy, antibiotic therapy, and enteral feedings. For neonates and infants, home infusion therapy is used mainly to deliver total parenteral nutrition.

CASE MANAGEMENT

Case management is a system whereby a single person manages a client's care, helping to prevent duplication of services, to decrease costs (by assuring timely services and preventing complications), and to promote continuity of care. In the home care setting, the case manager may be responsible for advising the family on the services they need, arranging for nurses and equipment, arranging for payment of services, solving problems, and visiting the family regularly. For home care, the community health nurse is especially well-suited to serve as case manager.

Ironically, case management has become so popular that several case managers may be assigned to a family — perhaps one from the insurance company, another from the home health care agency, and yet another from developmental services. However, not every family requires case management; many need information only and can act as their own case managers. Case management is most helpful for

CRITERIA FOR HOME MECHANICAL VENTILATION

The decision to care for a mechanically ventilated infant at home is a difficult one. The parents must undergo extensive predischarge teaching, and the child's prolonged need for complex care creates an enormous emotional and financial drain on the family. Also, home assessment of the mechanically ventilated infant can be challenging. In the health care facility, blood gas analysis, transcutaneous monitoring, and pulse oximetry help the health care team assess the neonate's ventilatory requirements. At home, where these evaluative mechanisms usually are not available, management is based on skin color, absence or presence of signs of respiratory compromise, and, in some cases, apnea monitoring.

On the other hand, the ventilator-dependent infant who is cared for at home usually has a decreased infection risk, greater socialization, and better stimulation for growth and development (Donar, 1988).

Ahmann (1986) identifies the following criteria for mechanical ventilation at home.

- The infant must have a stable underlying disease and continued inability to be weaned from mechanical ventilation.
- The infant must be able to maintain an adequate nutritional intake, as measured by consistent growth and development.
- The parents must have a positive attitude, motivation, and willingness to make a 24-hour commitment to their child's care.
- The family must have access to a community source for equipment and supplies, emergency care, and home nursing personnel and must have the financial resources to support the cost of prolonged, complex care.
- The home must support the mechanical and electrical needs of the ventilator and have adequate space for caregiving activities and storage of equipment and supplies.

parents who lack the ability or means to coordinate their child's care and for those whose child has multiple needs necessitating the involvement of several agencies and support services (GAO, 1989).

HOME HEALTH CARE NEEDS

The trend toward early discharge has increased the need for home health care for both normal, healthy neonates and special-needs neonates. (For information on when mechanical ventilation may be appropriate, see *Criteria for home mechanical ventilation*. For indications for nutritional therapy and applicable nursing considerations, see *Home nutrition therapy,* pages 317 to 319.)

Routine and basic care

For the normal, healthy infant, home health care typically involves assessment of the infant and teaching, counseling, and support for the family. Areas of particular interest to the nurse include the infant's nutritional status, healing of the umbilicus and circumcision site, feeding patterns, urinary and bowel elimination patterns, and sleep-awake patterns. As necessary, the nurse may draw blood samples for various laboratory tests (such as serum bilirubin analysis).

The nurse also assesses the parents' ability to provide routine care (such as bathing, feeding, diapering, stimulation, and cord and circumcision care) and perform basic health care procedures (such as taking rectal temperature, administering vitamins and medications, and suctioning with a bulb syringe).

Some otherwise healthy infants require phototherapy at home for the treatment of jaundice or an elevated serum unconjugated bilirubin level. Phototherapy, which involves exposure of the infant's skin to various lights, previously necessitated continued hospitalization. The significant cost of the treatment in this setting and the enforced separation from parents led practitioners to attempt home phototherapy (Heiser, 1987). Home phototherapy with supportive teaching for parents is a safe, satisfactory intervention that produces substantial savings for families, health care facilities, and insurance providers (Heiser, 1987).

Candidates for home phototherapy typically include term neonates who tolerate oral feedings well and lack underlying hemolytic disease. Also, the parents must be willing and able to manage this treatment at home and to arrange for serial laboratory bilirubin testing.

Specialized care

Besides routine and basic care, the high-risk or special-needs child requires sophisticated, complex care at home. Such care may involve apnea monitoring, suctioning, chest physiotherapy, oxygen therapy, tracheostomy care, mechanical ventilation, enteral or parenteral nutrition, medication administration, and developmental stimulation programs.

HOME NUTRITION THERAPY

The infant who cannot ingest sufficient nutrients orally or whose gastro-intestinal (GI) tract cannot be used for nutritional replenishment may require enteral or parenteral (I.V.) nutrition therapy at home to ensure adequate nutrition.

Enteral nutrition

The preferred method for nutritional support, enteral nutrition is the administration of nutrients through a feeding tube to the GI tract. Besides helping to maintain GI function, enteral therapy has fewer risks and costs less than parenteral nutrition. Enteral therapy may be required to supplement oral feedings or to supply the total caloric intake for the infant with a vomiting disorder (such as gastroesophageal reflux), an inadequate sucking reflex (for instance, from prolonged mechanical ventilation), or a respiratory or cardiac disorder that reduces the energy available for oral feeding.

Administration routes. High-risk infants usually receive enteral nutrition through a nasogastric (NG) tube or an orogastric tube — methods known as gavage feeding. In some cases, however, a gastrostomy tube is used. Gavage feeding commonly is used for intermittent or short-term home use but also may be appropriate for long-term home use. The tube may be made of polyurethane, polyvinyl chloride, or silicone (Silastic) material. Although Silastic tubes are more expensive than ones made of harder plastic, they are preferred for home use because they are easier to insert and cause less irritation to the GI mucosa. For home use, they can be reused after washing with soap and water.

Gastrostomy feedings necessitate surgical placement of a tube in the abdomen to deposit feedings directly into the stomach. Gastrostomy feedings are the preferred method for long-term home enteral nutrition.

Administration methods. The method used to administer gavage or gastrostomy feedings depends on the infant's GI tolerance. Bolus feedings can be given by gravity through a syringe attached to the tube; larger volumes are introduced into the stomach at a rate similar to that of normal sucking on a breast or bottle. Some high-risk infants given bolus feedings experience feeding intolerance, manifested as diarrhea or vomiting. Bolus feedings are contraindicated in neonates or infants with a history of gastroesophageal reflux (unless the cardiac sphincter has been repaired) because they may precipitate regurgitation or aspiration.

With continuous feedings, a pump and administration set are used to deliver small volumes of formula continuously. Although continuous feedings usually are tolerated better than bolus feedings, they restrict the infant's mobility because the pump and tubing must remain attached. However, scheduling most feedings at night minimizes the need to restrict daytime activities (if appropriate, oral feedings can be given during the day). Because the family must rent the pump and buy the tubing, continuous feedings are relatively expensive.

(continued)

HOME NUTRITION THERAPY *(continued)*

Enteral nutrition formulas. The high-risk infant may need a high-calorie enteral nutrition formula (27 to 30 calories/oz) to meet energy and growth demands. Some of these formulas are hyperosmolar, however, and may cause diarrhea and subsequent weight loss.

Parenteral nutrition

Parenteral nutrition refers to the I.V. administration of fluids containing glucose, amino acids, electrolytes, vitamins, and minerals in specific proportions necessary for growth. In most cases, parenteral nutrition is administered as total parenteral nutrition (TPN), a nutritionally complete form usually delivered through a central venous catheter inserted into a large neck or chest vessel. Many neonates and infants receive a combination of TPN and enteral nutrition.

Candidates for parenteral therapy include infants who cannot receive adequate food through the GI tract. For instance, those with congenital GI anomalies, such as omphalocele (protrusion of an intestinal portion through an abdominal wall defect at the umbilicus) or gastroschisis (protrusion of an intestinal portion through a defect elsewhere in the abdominal wall), may have suffered significant small intestine loss during surgery or may have developed multiple obstructions secondary to adhesions. Thus, they may be unable to tolerate any enteral formula.

Nursing considerations

• For enteral feedings, teach the parents to position the infant prone, with the shoulders at least 30 degrees higher than the feet, and to maintain this position for at least 20 minutes after the feeding.

• If the infant has gastroesophageal reflux, inform the parents that the head must remain higher than the stomach to reduce the risk of aspiration. If appropriate, teach them how to use a special harness to maintain proper positioning, with the head of the crib elevated 30 to 45 degrees.

• To help prevent aspiration of enteral feedings, show the parents how to aspirate stomach contents to check for residual matter before feedings. Also teach them how to use a stethoscope to auscultate air insertion through the tube when checking tube placement before feedings.

• Make sure the parents know how to prepare and administer feedings. For example, teach them to warm the formula to room temperature. Explain how to attach the filled drip set to the tube and regulate the flow using the clamp or pump. Advise them to burp the infant periodically and at the end of the feeding and to position the infant on the right side afterward.

• Instruct the parents to call the physician if the feeding tube becomes blocked or dislodged; insertion of a new tube may be necessary.

• Teach the parents how to provide skin care around the tube insertion site or stoma. Advise them to tape the NG tube without applying upward pressure against the nostril. Instruct them to clean the infant's nose or stoma with soap and water (or the prescribed solution) and to keep the area dry.

> ## HOME NUTRITION THERAPY (continued)
>
> • Instruct the parents how to prepare a high-calorie enteral formula, if ordered; proper preparation helps minimize diarrhea. Make sure they know how to assess for diarrhea and other complications of tube feedings, such as vomiting, aspiration of feeding matter (from improper tube position), abdominal cramps (from rapid feeding administration), and skin breakdown around the stoma of the gastrostomy tube.
> • Mouth care is especially important for infants who are fed enterally or parenterally. Instruct the parents to swab the infant's mouth with moistened sponge-tipped swabs or gauze to keep it clean and moist and to apply white petrolatum to the lips to help prevent drying and cracking.
> • Instruct the parents to weigh the infant regularly to monitor nutritional status.

The typical infant who requires specialized home care is preterm or low birth weight and has one or some combination of the following disorders: respiratory distress, bronchopulmonary dysplasia, apnea of prematurity, patent ductus arteriosus, hearing or visual impairment, hydrocephalus, intraventricular hemorrhage, seizures, or necrotizing enterocolitis. Congenital anomalies and the effects of maternal substance abuse also may necessitate specialized home care. (For information on the pathophysiology and management of these and other perinatal disorders, see Chapter 5, High-Risk Neonates.)

Psychosocial support is a key aspect of home care for the family of the special-needs child. The transition from the intensive care unit to the home can be stressful for parents; although they are relieved that their child is well enough to be discharged, they also may have doubts and fears about their ability to provide care at home.

ASSESSMENT

Before the first home visit, the nurse should review the discharge plan to become acquainted with the neonate's hospital course, discharge medications, and care instructions and to determine the parents' caregiving skills, confidence level, and teaching and support needs.

First home visit

Make every effort to establish a rapport so that the parents will feel free to discuss their concerns openly. Avoid medical jargon and be attentive and nonjudgmental as the parents discuss their concerns. Keep in mind that the home, unlike the health care facility, is the family's territory; an intrusive, domineering approach here could make the family resent the nurse's presence.

Obtain baseline information about the infant's physical status, growth, and development, and make a preliminary assessment of the parents' caregiving knowledge and skills and the family's support system. Also assess the home environment and the family's emergency plans, and confirm that any required equipment is functioning properly and that all needed supplies are present. Obtain information for insurance and other financial matters, and have the parents sign any necessary forms. At this visit and all subsequent visits, ask the parents what their main concerns are and then address these concerns.

Also obtain a health history and perform a physical assessment; however, if this will take more time than the family can spare, the history may be obtained gradually over subsequent visits. For the high-risk child, gear the physical assessment toward the specific condition, as described below under "Assessment of the special-needs child."

If the neonate is taking medications, review the dosages and schedules with the parents. If the schedules are inconvenient, with nighttime doses and many separate dosage times, consider asking the physician to modify them.

Parental caregiving knowledge and skills. Assess the parents' ability to perform routine and basic neonatal health care. Also evaluate their ability to provide any specific interventions, such as phototherapy, that the neonate requires. If the neonate needs specialized care, such as enteral or parenteral feeding, apnea monitoring, or oxygen therapy, assess the parents' understanding of the purpose of this care and the proper operation of equipment and medical supplies; make sure they know how to examine their child for problems related to the use of such equipment. (For detailed assessment information, see *Assessment guidelines for the infant who requires special equipment,* pages 321 to 323.) If premixed solutions are required, such as for nutritional therapy, verify that the family

ASSESSMENT GUIDELINES FOR THE INFANT WHO REQUIRES SPECIAL EQUIPMENT

The chart below shows key assessment guidelines if the infant requires special medical equipment. Before the first home visit, the nurse should obtain the health history to review the reason for the equipment and the neonate's hospital course. On each home visit, verify that all equipment is functioning properly; conduct a rapid review of functional patterns and body systems, then focus the assessment on the infant's specific problem.

EQUIPMENT AND INDICATIONS	HEALTH HISTORY AND PHYSICAL ASSESSMENT DATA	PARENTAL KNOWLEDGE AND SKILLS	EQUIPMENT-RELATED DATA
Apnea monitor Apnea of prematurity, respiratory compromise, tracheostomy use, acute drug withdrawal, family history of apnea or sudden infant death	• Vital signs • Respiratory status • Frequency and duration of predischarge apneic episodes, need for resuscitation after an episode, and any associated signs or precipitating factors • Postdischarge history of pallor, cyanosis, or hypotonia • Postdischarge history of apnea or bradycardia alarms, their frequency and duration, and type of stimulation required to arouse the infant	• Understanding of apnea and purpose of monitor • Knowledge of correct monitor settings • Operation of monitor • Safety precautions; proper response to monitor alarms • Ability to keep an accurate apnea log • Knowledge of infant cardiopulmonary resuscitation (CPR) procedure	• Presence of all needed supplies in the home, including lead wires, patches, and an instruction manual • Use of grounded outlet for monitor • Appropriateness and accuracy of monitor settings • Proper monitor placement (on a hard surface at the bedside with sufficient ventilation behind and above monitor) • Correct placement of electrodes (they must contact sides of chest wall)
Oxygen therapy Respiratory or cardiac disorder	• Vital signs • Respiratory status • Skin color changes, such as peripheral cyanosis and signs of respiratory distress	• Understanding of purpose and use of oxygen therapy • Competence and confidence in using equipment • Knowledge of safety precautions	• Accuracy of concentration and liter flow • Use of recommended equipment • Correct number of hours of daily oxygen therapy • Proper equipment function • Adequate supply level of oxygen source • Use of a humidity source (if prescribed) and proper humidifier function and settings • Proper use of prescribed delivery method (such as cannula or mask)

(continued)

ASSESSMENT GUIDELINES FOR THE INFANT WHO REQUIRES SPECIAL EQUIPMENT *(continued)*

EQUIPMENT AND INDICATIONS	HEALTH HISTORY AND PHYSICAL ASSESSMENT DATA	PARENTAL KNOWLEDGE AND SKILLS	EQUIPMENT-RELATED DATA
Tracheostomy Upper airway obstruction, respiratory failure from mechanical or neurologic problems, chronic aspiration, long-term mechanical ventilation	• Vital signs • Respiratory status • Quality, color, viscosity, and odor of tracheal secretions • Condition of skin at tracheostomy site	• Purpose of tracheostomy • Indications for suctioning (such as wheezing breath sounds, sounds of bubbling of secretions in the airway, and signs of respiratory distress) • Competence and confidence in performing tracheostomy care (such as routine daily cleaning of the tracheostomy site, daily changing of tracheostomy ties, suctioning, and tube insertion and removal) • Knowledge of modified CPR procedure	• Proper use of humidification source (such as compressor with a nebulizer or cascade, room humidifier, or tracheostomy humidifying filter) • Correct size of tracheostomy tubes and suction catheter
Mechanical ventilator Respiratory disorder	• Vital signs (compare observed respiratory rate against ventilator rate) • Skin color, respiratory pattern, and rise and fall of chest with each breath	• Understanding purpose, function, and operation of ventilator • Ability to assess for signs of respiratory distress, fatigue, and periorbital edema • Ability to prevent atelectasis through frequent positioning changes, hyperinflation, chest physiotherapy, and suctioning • Ability to check for proper ventilator function and settings • Knowledge of proper response to ventilator alarms • Ability to use other required equipment (such as oxygen therapy or apnea monitor)	• Proper ventilator settings • Correct bellows functioning • Alarm lights on • Connections secure • Tubing unkinked • Humidifier filled • Availability of backup power supply (such as batteries or a generator)

ASSESSMENT GUIDELINES FOR THE INFANT WHO REQUIRES SPECIAL EQUIPMENT *(continued)*

EQUIPMENT AND INDICATIONS	HEALTH HISTORY AND PHYSICAL ASSESSMENT DATA	PARENTAL KNOWLEDGE AND SKILLS	EQUIPMENT-RELATED DATA
Enteral or parenteral nutrition therapy Inability to ingest adequate calories by mouth	• Nutritional status (such as growth parameters and daily tube or I.V. intake) • Skin condition around tube or I.V. insertion site	• Knowledge and ability to prepare and administer feedings correctly • Ability to assess for proper tube placement before each tube feeding (using a stethoscope to auscultate air insertion through tube) • Ability to identify such problems as tube dislodgement and nasal irritation • Knowledge of proper interventions for tube dislodgement • Ability to identify and troubleshoot equipment problems • Ability to provide mouth care and assess and intervene for complications of tube feedings (such as vomiting, diarrhea, aspiration of feeding matter, and abdominal cramps) or parenteral nutrition (such as air embolism, infection, metabolic problems, and fluid extravasation) • Understanding of special positioning requirements during feedings	• Correct function of feeding pump • Appropriateness of feeding technique; enteral or I.V. formula; placement, size, and type of tube; administration method; feeding frequency and duration; and infant positioning • Availability of refrigeration for storage of feeding solutions • Adequate home sanitation to allow sterile procedures required for nutritional therapy

has a refrigerator for solution storage; if not, find out if the home infusion therapy service can supply refrigeration, and if so, whether they will charge for this.

Support system. Although the hospital discharge planning staff makes a preliminary assessment of the support system that may be available to the family after discharge, the home health care nurse has the advantage of assessing the support system in action, determining its extent and reliability. The major support needs of the family caring for a special-needs child at home are physical support for caregiving and household tasks, respite care, and psychosocial support.

Physical support. Assess how much physical support the parents need and how much they are receiving. Many parents of special-needs children must rely on help from friends and relatives because few community support agencies are geared toward the special-needs child. Meals On Wheels, for example, provides hot meals for people physically unable to cook for themselves but not for parents struggling with an ill child. Also, many insurance companies reimburse homemaker services for adults who cannot physically maintain their homes but not for parents of ill children, on the grounds that the parents are physically able to perform household tasks.

Also assess whether the parents have a realistic attitude toward their need for physical support. Many parents are reluctant to ask for help, feeling that they should be able to care for their special-needs child round the clock while keeping house, attending to other children, and meeting their personal needs.

Respite care. Determine whether a secondary caregiver is available. The parents of a child who requires high-technology or other complex care need occasional respite, or relief, from caregiving but may have trouble finding it. Some regional perinatal centers provide respite care. Also, respite care is available through various community programs; however, the caregivers provided by these programs rarely are trained to care for special-needs neonates or infants. On the other hand, friends and relatives may be intimidated by the idea of caring for a child who depends on medical equipment; although wishing they could help, they may worry that they will not know what to do if something happens and that the child will die while in their care.

Thus, many parents of special-needs children discover that only a nurse is comfortable with, or capable of, caring for their child. But hiring a nurse to provide a few hours of respite care costs at least five times as much as a regular babysitter. Consequently, parents may forego respite care and never take a break from caregiving. Eventually, this can take a toll on the parents' health as well as the couple's relationship and other family relationships.

Psychosocial support. Determine if the parents are aware of support groups and other resources that can provide psychosocial support, especially if their child has special needs. Members of parent support groups have had first-hand experience in caring for special-needs children and can offer advice on which problems to anticipate, how to cope with problems, and where to find special supplies or services. For instance, Sick Kids Need Involved People (SKIP) is a support group for families of technology-dependent children, particularly those requiring tracheostomies and ventilatory support. Founded in 1980, it promotes specialized pediatric home care for medically fragile children.

Home environment. Assess whether the home has adequate facilities and space for caregiving. For the special-needs child, check for sufficient electrical outlets and adequate shelving or other storage arrangements for supplies (however, make sure supplies are not stored directly over the child's bed). Determine whether the family might benefit by installing ramps to allow easier movement of the child and equipment into and out of the house. Also observe for evidence that home health care may be disrupting family functioning; if so, assess whether the parents should consider converting a downstairs room into the child's bedroom to give them privacy from home health personnel.

Emergency plan. Determine if the family has a good emergency plan. A telephone is essential; if the home lacks one, find out if the parents have made other arrangements for obtaining help in an emergency. To help ensure prompt emergency intervention, verify that they have notified the police and fire departments in writing about their child's condition, medications, and treatments as well as the names of the child's health care providers and the health care facility to transport the child to in an emergency. Likewise, the parents should notify the telephone and electric companies requesting placement on a priority service list, advance notification of anticipated interruptions, and priority reinstatement of service after unexpected interruptions.

Also make sure parents and all other caregivers know how to administer infant CPR correctly and when to seek immediate medical attention for a problem. Check whether CPR instructions are posted near the child's bed and a list of emergency telephone numbers is located near all telephones.

Subsequent home visits

Once the nurse has established a rapport with the family and made baseline assessments, assessment during later visits should focus on detecting changes in the infant's physical status, observing the parents' caregiving skills for improvement, and assessing parent-infant interaction. For the high-risk or special-needs child, also assess specific aspects of the infant's condition (as described below under "Assessment of the special-needs child") and observe how the infant's care is affecting other family members.

Physical status. Take vital signs and assess for changes in the infant's condition. For the infant receiving phototherapy, assess for signs of treatment efficacy, such as improved color of the skin and mucous membranes. Also check for dehydration, an adverse effect of phototherapy, which may manifest as lethargy, poor feeding, and excessive, watery stools.

Parental caregiving skills. As the parents become more familiar and comfortable with infant care, expect their caregiving skills to improve. A deficiency in skills warrants additional teaching sessions.

Parent-infant interaction. The home is a good environment in which to observe parent-infant interaction, which is crucial to child growth and development. In some cases, the nurse may use a specific assessment tool to assess the mother-infant relationship. Also note the degree of eye contact between parent and infant and observe how frequently the mother fondles, kisses, and vocalizes with the infant. Keep in mind that problems in parent-infant bonding sometimes manifest in neonatal or infant behavioral problems, such as sleep disturbances, feeding disorders, failure to gain weight, and refusal to cuddle or feed.

Assessment of the special-needs child

For the special-needs child, augment routine assessment with an investigation tailored to the specific problem.

Respiratory disorder. Measure the pulse, respiratory rate, and temperature. A change from baseline values when unrelated to crying, position changes, feeding, or activity may signal cardiac or respiratory compromise. Auscultate the lungs, noting the general quality of breath sounds and checking for adventitious sounds.

Assess the skin color and respiratory pattern, and note any signs of respiratory distress, such as pallor, cyanosis, nasal flaring, chest retractions, edema, or diaphoresis. Ask the parents if they have noted irritability, appetite loss, or other signs of respiratory distress, such as color changes. Assess respiratory secretions for amount, consistency, color, and odor; suspect infection if secretions are foul-smelling, yellowish green, or more copious or viscous than normal. Also assess for medication efficacy and adverse effects; be sure to ask the parents whether they have noticed the latter.

Determine whether the parents understand respiratory anatomy and physiology as well as the pathophysiology, signs and symptoms, and course of the underlying respiratory disease and the purpose of each intervention. Also find out if they know how to assess the infant's respiratory status.

The infant with respiratory compromise is predisposed to respiratory infections; simple colds can rapidly progress to fulminant viral pneumonia, bronchopneumonia, respiratory syncytial virus, reactive airway disease, or bronchospasm. Assess whether the parents can identify signs of respiratory infection, such as irritability, fever, cyanosis, increased respiratory distress, pallor, tachypnea, increased oxygen requirements, increased secretions, cough, and poor feeding.

A respiratory disorder can compromise the infant's nutritional status; therefore, be sure to assess nutritional intake and growth.

If the infant is receiving nebulized medications, assess the parents' administration skills. Also, if appropriate, observe them as they perform chest physiotherapy, assessing whether they position their child correctly and use proper percussion techniques. Also observe the parents as they suction their child (performed after chest physiotherapy). Suctioning may be done with a bulb syringe or a catheter. In some cases, a suction machine is used at home; assess whether the parents know how to use this equipment properly.

Neurologic problem. In hydrocephalus, excessive cerebrospinal fluid (CSF) accumulates within the cranial vault, leading to suture expansion and ventricular dilation. The infant discharged with hydrocephalus may have a surgically placed ventricular shunt to drain excess CSF from the ventricles to a distal compartment, such as the peritoneum.

Before the first home visit, review the infant's health history for shunt location, serial head circumference measurements, neurologic status, and prognosis. On each visit, measure head circumference, noting any abnormally rapid increase. Assess the infant's mental status (orientation level, alertness, and behavior). Check range of motion of the neck, and assess eye movements for nystagmus, convergence, and ability to follow. Also evaluate the fontanels, which should be flat and soft, and palpate the sutures, which should not be split or overlapped.

Assess for shunt obstruction and infection, which may manifest in fontanel tenseness or bulging, increased head circumference, irritability, vomiting, appetite changes, sleepiness, and sunset eyes (upper lid retraction causing the sclera to show above the iris). Infection may cause fever, erythema, and tenderness along the shunt tract.

Determine if the parents understand the purpose of the shunt and know how to check the fontanel to assess for shunt obstruction and infection. Also make sure they know when to call the physician (such as for rapidly increasing head circumference, irritability, vomiting, or hypoglycemia, hypocalcemia, and decreased alertness).

The preterm and low-birth-weight infant are predisposed to seizures. A symptom rather than a disease in itself, a seizure may stem from such conditions as intraventricular hemorrhage, head trauma, or drug withdrawal. An infant with seizures usually is discharged on anticonvulsant therapy, which typically continues until the child is at least 6 months old.

Before the first home visit, review the health history for the type of seizure the infant has experienced, seizure signs observed, postseizure behavior, and medications. During each visit, assess vital signs, alertness level, and motor and ocular responses to stimulation. Ask the parents whether they have observed signs of a seizure. (Preferably, they should keep a seizure log.) A subtle seizure may manifest as eyelid fluttering, nystagmus, drooling, tongue thrusting, lip smacking, tonic limb positioning, bicycling movements of the legs, or apnea. Also assess whether the parents can differentiate a seizure from jitteriness (unlike seizures, jittery movements commonly subside when the limbs are restrained).

Determine whether the parents know how to assess the infant's neurologic status and behavior, care for their child during a seizure, observe activity during and after the seizure, and provide emergency interventions (including CPR) for apnea. Also assess whether they know when to seek medical attention (such as when a seizure is prolonged), and evaluate their understanding of anticonvulsant medication – its regimen, potential adverse effects, and the need to avoid abrupt discontinuation (which could cause seizures). Make sure they know how often blood samples will be required for blood drug level monitoring and understand that stressful events (such as immunizations, infections, fever, and emotional stress) may trigger a seizure. Determine their knowledge of safety precautions, such as secure positioning, and make sure they understand that the child's neurologic outcome may remain undetermined for some time.

Visual or hearing impairment. Conditions leading to visual impairment include retinopathy of prematurity (ROP) and rarely, congenital cataracts. A retinal disorder seen mainly in preterm and low-birth-weight neonates treated with oxygen therapy for respiratory distress, ROP can be detected as early as 6 weeks after birth. A congenital cataract is an opacification of the lens associated with such disorders as trisomy 13 and 18, galactosemia, and rubella syndrome. Many visually impaired neonates have multiple physiologic problems, including respiratory and neurologic compromise.

A neonate who receives oxygen therapy typically undergoes ophthalmologic examination before discharge. However, ROP usually is not detectable until after the neonatal period. Therefore, before the first home visit, be sure to review the medical records to determine if the neonate received oxygen therapy and is at risk for ROP.

During the first visit, perform a vision screening, examining the lids, pupils, sclera, and conjunctivae. Note any lesions, discharge, and unequal or absent pupillary reaction to light. Also assess for nystagmus, strabismus, and red reflex. Evaluate the infant's ability to focus on an object placed 8″ to 10″ directly ahead and to follow objects moving horizontally. If the results of this screening suggest a problem, refer the child to an ophthalmologist.

For the infant with a previously diagnosed visual impairment, assess the parents' understanding of the condition and their awareness of home stimulation programs. Such programs may involve placement of mobiles and colorful toys in the crib, shaking a colorful noise-maker, or slowly moving an object from side to side in front of the infant.

A hearing impairment is associated with such factors as low birth weight, congenital or perinatal infection, severe birth asphyxia, hyperbilirubinemia, exposure to high levels of environmental noise, chronic maternal illness, and malnutrition. The impairment may be unilateral or bilateral, may vary from mild to profound, and may involve low-frequency sound, high-frequency sound, or both. Depending on the auditory structures involved, a hearing impairment also may be classified as conductive (involving structures of the outer and middle ear), sensorineural (involving malformation of or damage to inner ear structures), or mixed (a combination of conductive and sensorineural).

A hearing impairment may not be detected before discharge. If a hearing problem is suspected, conduct an informal auditory behavioral screening, which determines responses to noisemakers with known intensity and frequency. If the results of this examination suggest a problem, refer the child for a complete audiologic and medical evaluation.

If a hearing impairment already has been diagnosed, find out if the child is wearing a hearing aid and whether the parents are aware of the benefits of a home stimulation program, which can teach them how to provide an optimal auditory environment and use alternative communication methods

Acquired immunodeficiency syndrome (AIDS). Every neonate born to a woman infected with human immunodeficiency virus (HIV) carries the mother's HIV antibodies. This complicates neonatal diagnosis because a neonate who tests positive for HIV at birth may not actually be infected. To make a definitive diagnosis, the physician must determine if the child is producing HIV antibodies, indicating true HIV infection; this may take up to 15 months (Cruz, 1988).

Keep in mind that signs and symptoms of HIV infection may not appear until age 6 months to 2 years. A distinctive facial dysmorphism can help with early detection, as can persistent oral candida infections and diaper rash from diarrhea. Other suggestive findings include failure to thrive, severe bacterial infections, chronic parotid swelling, and pulmonary lymphoid interstitial pneumonitis. Sometimes central nervous system abnormalities are the only signs of HIV infection. For instance, the infant may be microencephalic with delayed cognitive and motor functioning. In some cases, the brain is affected directly; at least 50% of affected infants have encephalopathy (Cruz, 1988).

If AIDS is suspected, perform a complete physical assessment of the infant. If AIDS already has been diagnosed, assess the parents' ability and willingness to care for their child at home, especially if a parent also has AIDS or abuses drugs. Determine how much the parents know about the disease and the care required for the infant (such as management of life-threatening opportunistic infections). Also find out if they know which precautions are necessary to prevent disease spread to other family members; a misinformed caregiver may be afraid of catching the disease through casual contact and thus avoid the infant, placing the infant at risk for inadequate care and sensory deprivation. (For home care guidelines, see *Parent teaching: When your infant has AIDS,* page 332.)

Effects of maternal substance abuse. The neonate affected by maternal substance abuse during pregnancy may remain in the health care facility until drug withdrawal is achieved. However, if this problem somehow eludes detection before discharge, the home health nurse who suspects it should check for such suggestive signs as abnormal reflex responses, marked irritability, continual high-pitched crying, poor feeding, muscle tremors, twitching, or rigidity with inability to extend the muscles.

Assessment of the family of the special-needs child

For the family of the special-needs child, discharge may herald a new crisis. Already grieving over the loss of the anticipated "perfect" child, they must now confront the challenge of providing complex care on their own. To ensure family-centered nursing care during this stressful transition, assess family members for the following factors, found by Wegener and Aday (1989) to increase the risk of stress in family members of special-needs children:
- discontinuous medical care of the infant
- financial problems

WHEN YOUR INFANT HAS A.I.D.S.

To care for your infant with AIDS, you will need to follow certain safeguards. Because of a weakened immune system, the child is more vulnerable to infection by germs that most children can fight off. Also, although AIDS cannot be transmitted through casual contact, you and other family members should avoid coming into direct contact with the infant's blood and body fluids. The precautions below can help ensure the safety of your infant as well as the rest of the family.

- Instruct all family members to wash their hands before eating and after using the toilet.
- To prevent the infant from developing an intestinal infection, use premixed commercial formulas, or prepare formula with pasteurized milk and milk products. Do not put the infant to bed with a bottle of milk or juice because bacteria grow rapidly in these fluids.
- Do not feed the infant directly from a jar; bacteria from the mouth may spoil the food that remains in the jar. Refrigerate opened jars and use the food within 24 hours.
- Cook or peel fruits and vegetables and cook meats thoroughly before giving them to the infant.
- Use a dishwasher or wash dishes in hot, sudsy water and air dry them.
- If possible, use disposable diapers. When changing diapers, wear disposable gloves; place used diapers in a sealed plastic bag.
- Keep diaper-changing areas separate from food preparation and serving areas. After each diaper change, clean the changing surface with a 1:10 solution of household bleach and water. (Be sure to wear disposable gloves when doing this.)
- Reserve separate towels and washcloths for the infant.
- Launder items soiled with the infant's blood or body fluids separately from the family laundry, and use hot sudsy water. The rest of the infant's laundry can be washed with other household laundry.
- Flush the infant's body wastes down the toilet and keep the infant's trash in a closed plastic container. Place needles and other sharp objects in an impenetrable container and arrange for their disposal.
- If you have a pet in the house, keep the animal's waste products away from the infant; do not allow animals that may bite or scratch to come near your child.

• many extended family members living in the household
• lack of a designated nurse-case manager at the time of the infant's discharge.

Also evaluate the parents for signs of grief and determine the coping mechanism each parent is using. Expect the parents to show signs of exhaustion and possibly marital strain. Assess siblings for overt or covert signs of jealousy and resentment of the infant. Also explore family dynamics, strengths, and weaknesses.

Parental grief and coping mechanisms. The parents of an infant with a chronic or disabling condition must pass through the stages of grief to deal with the loss of the "perfect" child and accept the real one. These stages typically include denial, anger, bargaining, depression, and acceptance. Like anyone faced with a stressful situation, parents of high-risk children also use certain coping mechanisms — denial, anger, withdrawal, guilt, and intellectualizing — to deal with their feelings. If possible, determine which stage of grief each parent is in and which coping mechanism each parent is using.

If the infant has a chronic condition, assessment of the parents in subsequent months or years may uncover chronic sorrow, a phenomenon first described by Olshansky (1962). The intensity of chronic sorrow varies from person to person and over time; it may disappear temporarily, only to recur. To assess for chronic sorrow, observe for sadness, fear, anxiety, anger, guilt, ambivalence, helplessness, or hopelessness. Keep in mind, however, that some parents conceal their sorrow; a few even try to suppress it to cope with the grim reality they face, seeming unduly optimistic about their child's condition.

Effect on the couple's relationship. Many parents of special-needs children report a strengthening of the marital relationship over time (Thomas, 1987). Also, studies show that parents of a special-needs child do not necessarily experience reduced marital satisfaction or have a shorter marriage duration. Nonetheless, the child's condition undoubtedly causes tremendous stress within the relationship, especially at first. Some couples may choose to stay together even though they do not derive support or enjoyment from the relationship.

Assess for both overt signs of marital stress, such as arguments, and more subtle indications, such as terse conversation and reluctance to acknowledge the partner's presence. If stress is apparent or suspected, consider tactfully suggesting that the couple see a marriage counselor.

Effect on siblings. Siblings of chronically ill children may be ill-informed about the nature of the infant's illness. Also, they may be unsure of what others expect of them and feel that their own identify is threatened. Anger, guilt, and resentment are common (Seligman, 1987). To help prevent or detect these problems, assess siblings for signs of behavioral changes and maladaptation — jealousy and resentment of the infant, aggressive behavior, fear, guilt, and anger.

NURSING DIAGNOSIS

After gathering assessment data, the nurse must review it carefully to identify pertinent nursing diagnoses for the infant. (For a partial list of applicable diagnoses, see *Nursing diagnoses: Infant receiving nursing care at home*.)

PLANNING AND IMPLEMENTATION

For the nurse who provides intermittent home visits, nursing goals include managing or correcting any problems detected during assessment and ensuring that the parents (or other primary caregivers) are providing safe, appropriate care. (For parent-teaching information on some specific equipment, see *Parent teaching: Using a home apnea monitor,* page 336, and *Parent teaching: When your infant is receiving oxygen by nasal cannula,* pages 337 and 338.)

Nursing care in the home calls for flexibility and innovation. Be patient and understanding about interruptions in teaching sessions and unanticipated household events. If the family has a diagnosis of ***altered family processes related to the arrival of a new family member or household disruption caused by the infant's care,*** help them devise individualized solutions to such problems as cramped quarters, inadequate storage space for equipment and supplies, and too few electrical outlets.

A key nursing intervention is to ensure that the infant has a source of primary pediatric care, that all of the infant's care is coordinated, and that the family's resources are adequate to provide appropriate, ongoing care. If necessary, help the family obtain a pediatrician; also facilitate communication and coordination among care providers. If the home lacks indoor plumbing, running water, hot water,

NURSING DIAGNOSES

INFANT RECEIVING NURSING CARE AT HOME

When caring for an infant at home, the nurse may find these examples of nursing diagnoses appropriate. Specific nursing interventions for many of these diagnoses are provided in the "Planning and implementation" section of this chapter.

FOR THE INFANT

- Altered growth and development related to impaired oral feeding and inadequate caloric intake
- Altered nutrition: less than body requirements, related to immature gastrointestinal function or inefficient feeding patterns
- Impaired physical mobility related to restrictions imposed by feeding tubes or I.V. lines
- Impaired skin integrity: potential, related to the presence of feeding tubes or I.V. lines
- Ineffective airway clearance related to pooling of secretions
- Potential for infection related to respiratory compromise
- Sensory-perceptual alteration: auditory, related to perinatal infection
- Sensory-perceptual alteration: visual, related to retinopathy of prematurity

FOR THE FAMILY

- Altered family processes related to the arrival of a new family member or household disruption caused by the infant's care
- Anxiety related to the infant's constant care needs or the demands of delivering complex, specialized care
- Grieving related to loss of the anticipated healthy neonate
- Ineffective family or individual coping related to the stress of caregiving procedures or fear that the infant will die
- Knowledge deficit related to the infant's medical condition or infant caregiving skills

or electricity, make sure a social service agency has been contacted. Besides city and county social services departments, resources for financial assistance include:
- state child services programs
- federal Special Supplemental Food Program for Women, Infants, and Children, Aid to Dependent Children program, and Aid to Dependent Families and Children program
- Salvation Army

USING A HOME APNEA MONITOR

Because your infant has had problems breathing, the doctor has determined that a home apnea monitor is necessary. The monitor will alert you to changes in your infant's heart rate or absence of breathing. By following the steps below, you can help ensure your infant's well-being when the monitor is in use.

General guidelines

• Prepare the home environment for monitoring – for instance, by providing a sturdy surface for the monitor and by displaying emergency telephone numbers (such as for the doctor and monitor dealer or vendor) in a prominent place.

• Make sure other family members know how to use the monitor.

• If your monitor has electrodes, make sure the respirator indicator goes on each time your infant breathes. If it does not, move the electrodes slightly until it does.

• If the apnea or bradycardia alarm goes off, check the color on the inside of the infant's mouth. If it is bluish and the infant is not breathing, try to stimulate breathing by calling loudly, then touching the infant. Use gentle touch at first, then stronger stimulation as necessary; do not shake the infant. If the infant does not respond, begin cardiopulmonary resuscitation (CPR).

• A loose-lead alarm may indicate a dirty electrode, a loose electrode patch, a loose belt, a disconnected or malfunctioning wire, or monitor malfunction. If this alarm sounds, see the equipment manual for instructions.

• Periodically review CPR and other lifesaving techniques you have been taught. Make sure that everyone who cares for your infant knows these techniques.

• Notify the local police, ambulance company, telephone company, and electric company that your infant is on an apnea monitor. Also make sure the pediatrician and visiting nurse know about the monitor.

• For two useful booklets – *A Manual for Home Monitoring* and *At Home with a Monitor* – write to the Sudden Infant Death Syndrome Alliance, 10500 Little Patuxent Parkway, Suite 420, Columbia, MD 21044 or call 1-800-221-SIDS.

• religious organizations and charities.

Be prepared to help the family through sudden financial crises triggered by the infant's care requirements. For example, mechanical ventilation may increase monthly electric bills substantially; if necessary, refer the family to a social service agency to arrange for

WHEN YOUR INFANT IS RECEIVING OXYGEN BY NASAL CANNULA

The doctor has prescribed oxygen therapy by nasal cannula for your infant. To improve the safety and effectiveness of this treatment, refer to the guidelines below.

Setting up the system

1 Make sure you have a nasal cannula, tubing, skin tape, oxygen tank, and humidifier (if prescribed). Also, keep a spare cannula available to use when the original one is being cleaned.

2 Fill the humidifier with sterile distilled water and attach it to the flowmeter.

3 Attach the flowmeter to the oxygen source and connect the cannula to the system.

4 To apply the cannula, slip it over the infant's head so that the nasal prongs curve inward toward the face. Tape the cannula to each cheek to secure it.

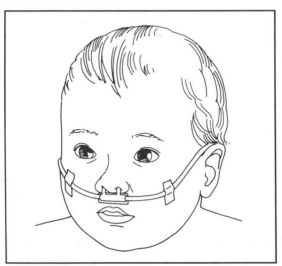

5 Adjust the flowmeter to the prescribed rate.

(continued)

WHEN YOUR INFANT IS RECEIVING OXYGEN BY NASAL CANNULA *(continued)*

Maintaining hygiene

• Once a week, or whenever the cannula appears dirty, wash it with soap and water; let it dry for 24 hours. Make sure no water remains in the cannula after cleaning, because this could block the flow of oxygen.
• Every day, remove the humidifier from the oxygen source, empty the remaining water from the tank, and clean it with equal parts water and hydrogen peroxide.

Ensuring safety

• Store the oxygen container upright and secure it to prevent it from falling (which may cause a leakage in the system).
• Keep the tank away from direct sunlight and do not store grease, oil, or other flammable materials nearby. Keep a fire extinguisher nearby.
• Keep the oxygen tank at least 5 feet from heat sources and electrical devices and ban smoking near the oxygen tank.
• Make sure the electrical equipment is properly grounded.
• Turn off both the volume regulator and flow regulator when oxygen is not in use to prevent oxygen leakage.
• Do not use alcohol-based or oil-based substances (such as petroleum jelly or baby oil) on your infant, because these substances are highly flammable.
• Dress the infant in flame-retardant clothing.
• Weaning from supplemental oxygen must be done gradually, as instructed by the doctor. Never discontinue oxygen therapy abruptly; this may cause serious harm to your infant.
• Notify the police and fire departments that oxygen tanks are in your home.

emergency financial assistance to pay these bills, or help them contact the electric company to make special payment arrangements.

Ensuring parental caregiving knowledge and skills

For parents with a nursing diagnosis of ***knowledge deficit related to the infant's medical condition or infant caregiving skills,*** reinforce discharge teaching about the underlying disease and the care

required. An effective way to do this is to observe the parents as they care for the infant, then demonstrate any aspect of their care that is incorrect and ask for a return demonstration.

A parent may feel overwhelmed by the responsibility of providing care, even when the infant's care needs seem fairly simple to the nurse. The parent's reaction may lead to a nursing diagnosis of *ineffective family or individual coping related to the stress of caregiving procedures or fear that the infant will die.* Even when the parents' caregiving skills are deficient, convey a sense of trust and confidence in their eventual ability to care for their child adequately at home.

Keep in mind that the addition of a dependent new family member can be enormously stressful, possibly resulting in a nursing diagnosis of *anxiety related to the infant's constant care needs or the demands of delivering complex, specialized care.* Reassure the parents that negative as well as positive feelings are bound to arise during the immediate postdischarge period; if necessary, refer them for counseling or other support resources to ease their child's transition to the home. Also, to reduce the burden presented by the infant's care demands, encourage the parents to seek and accept any offers of help.

Promoting positive parent-infant interaction

If parent-infant interaction suggests poor bonding, reinforce teaching about neonatal behavioral states, communication cues, growth and developmental patterns, and sleep-awake patterns. If poor interaction seems to stem from parental disappointment or grief over the infant's medical condition or physical appearance, encourage the parents to express their feelings freely, without fear of being judged as bad people or bad parents.

In some cases, poor parent-infant interaction or parental failure to provide proper care may reflect child neglect or abuse. The nurse who suspects this should contact the local child protective services agency.

Helping siblings adjust

The addition of a new family member may cause siblings to feel neglected and unloved, especially if the infant's care is demanding and time-consuming. If family assessment reveals sibling behavioral changes or maladaptation, urge the parents to help siblings under-

stand the infant's condition and express their fears and concerns, and to reassure siblings that they are not the cause of the infant's illness. Also encourage the parents to let siblings participate in the infant's care at a level appropriate for each sibling's developmental stage; this can help the sibling feel more involved in and important to the family. (However, if a sibling is assuming too much caregiving responsibility, point out to the parents that the sibling may need more time to be a child.) Also urge the parents to spend some time alone with each sibling regularly to convey the feeling that the sibling has a special place in the family.

EVALUATION

Evaluation findings should be stated in terms of actions performed or outcomes achieved for each goal. The following examples illustrate appropriate evaluation statements for the infant receiving care at home:

• The infant's physiologic status remained stable, with no changes in vital signs since the last visit.

• The infant maintained a satisfactory nutritional status based on a defined weight gain.

• The home environment is safe and adequate for the infant care required.

• The family has sufficient resources to care for the infant at home.

• All appropriate items required for the infant's care are present in the home.

• Medical equipment is functioning properly.

• The parents provide the required care in a competent and confident manner.

• The family shows a positive adjustment to the responsibility of providing complex care for their special-needs child.

DOCUMENTATION

Thorough documentation not only allows the nurse to evaluate the effectiveness of the care plan, but it also makes this information available to other members of the health care team, helping to ensure consistency of care.

Documentation of a home nursing visit should include:

• the infant's physiologic status, including vital signs

• the infant's nutritional status based on a defined weight gain

• the parents' ability to provide the required care

• the parents' ability to cope with infant care responsibilities and the infant's condition

• the parents' understanding of the infant care required.

BIBLIOGRAPHY

Discharge planning and home health care

Ahmann, E. (1986). *Home care for the high risk infant: A holistic guide to using technology.* Rockville, MD: Aspen.

American Nurses' Association (1975). *Continuity of care and discharge planning programs* (p. 3). New York: Author

General Accounting Office. (1989, June). *Health care – Home care experiences of families with chronically ill children* (GAO-HRD-89-73) (p. 3). Washington, DC: Author

Joint Commission for Accreditation of Healthcare Organizations (1989). *The joint commission 1990 AMH accreditation manual for hospitals* (p. 131). Chicago: Author.

NAACOG. (1986). *Standards for obstetric, gynecologic, and neonatal nursing* (3rd ed.; p. 32). Washington, DC: Author.

National Association of Children's Hospitals and Related Institutions, Inc. (1989). Fact sheet on catastrophically ill children. In *Pediatric nursing, forum on the future: Looking toward the 21st century.* Proceedings and report from an invitational conference, May 16-17, 1988 (p. 9). Pitman, NJ: Anthony J. Jannetti.

Norr, K., Nacion, K., and Abramson, R. (1989). Early discharge with home follow-up: Impacts on low-income mothers and infants. *JOGGN,* 18(2), 133-141.

Wegener, D.J., and Aday, L.A. (1989). Home care for ventilator-assisted children: Predicting family stress. *Pediatric Nursing,* 15, 371-376.

Special-needs children

American Academy of Pediatrics Ad Hoc Task Forces on Home Care of Chronically Ill Infants and Children. (1984). Guidelines for home care of infants, children, and adolescents with chronic disease. *Pediatrics,* 74, 434-436.

Cruz, L.D. (1988, November). Children with AIDS: Diagnosis, symptoms, care. *AORN Journal,* 48, 893-910

Donar, M.E. (1988). Community care: Pediatric home mechanical ventilation. *Holistic Nursing Practice,* 2(2), 68-80.

Hartsell, M.B. (1986). Home phototherapy. *Journal of Pediatric Nursing,* 1(4), 282-283.

Heiser, C.A. (1987). Home phototherapy. *Pediatric Nursing,* 13(6), 425-427.

Olshansky, S. (1962, April). Chronic sorrow: A response to having a mentally defective child. *Social Casework,* 43, 190-193.

Seligman, M. (1987). Adaptation of children to a chronically ill or mentally handicapped sibling. *Canadian Medical Association Journal*, 136(12), 1249-1252.

Thomas, R.B. (1987). Family adaptation to a child with a chronic condition. In M.H. Rose and R.B. Thomas (Eds.), *Children with chronic conditions* (p.39). Orlando: Grune & Stratton.

Family needs

Ferrari, M. (1986). Perceptions of social support by parents of chronically ill versus healthy children. *Children's Health Care*, 14, 26-31.

U.S. General Accounting Office. (1989, June). *Health care – Home care experiences of families with chronically ill children* (GAO-HRD-89-73) (p. 3). Washington, DC: Author

Nursing research

Brooten, D., Kumar, S., Brown, L., Butts, P., Finkler, S., Bakewell-Sachs, S., Gibbons, A., and Delivoria-Papadopoulos, M. (1986). A randomized clinical trial of early hospital discharge and home follow-up of very-low-birth-weight infants. *New England Journal of Medicine*, 315(15), 934-939.

Rawlins, P., and Horner, M. (1988). Does membership in a support group alter needs of parents of chronically ill children? *Pediatric Nursing*, 14(1), 70-72.

Appendices
and Index

NANDA TAXONOMY OF NURSING DIAGNOSES

A taxonomy for classifying nursing diagnoses has evolved over several years. The following list is grouped around nine human response patterns endorsed by the North American Nursing Diagnosis Association, as of summer 1990.

PATTERN 1. Exchanging: A human response pattern involving mutual giving and receiving

1.1.2.1. Altered nutrition: more than body requirements

1.1.2.2. Altered nutrition: less than body requirements

1.1.2.3. Altered nutrition: potential for more than body requirements

1.2.1.1. Potential for infection

1.2.2.1. Potential for altered body temperature

1.2.2.2. Hypothermia

1.2.2.3. Hyperthermia

1.2.2.4. Ineffective thermoregulation

1.2.3.1. Dysreflexia

1.3.1.1. Constipation

1.3.1.1.1. Perceived constipation

1.3.1.1.2. Colonic constipation

1.3.1.2. Diarrhea

1.3.1.3. Bowel incontinence

1.3.2. Altered urinary elimination

1.3.2.1.1. Stress incontinence

1.3.2.1.2. Reflex incontinence

1.3.2.1.3. Urge incontinence

1.3.2.1.4. Functional incontinence

1.3.2.1.5. Total incontinence

1.3.2.2. Urinary retention

(continued)

NANDA TAXONOMY OF NURSING DIAGNOSES *(continued)*

1.4.1.1. Altered (specify type) tissue perfusion (renal, cerebral, cardiopulmonary, gastrointestinal, peripheral)

1.4.1.2.1. Fluid volume excess

1.4.1.2.2.1. Fluid volume deficit

1.4.1.2.2.2. Potential fluid volume deficit

1.4.2.1. Decreased cardiac output

1.5.1.1. Impaired gas exchange

1.5.1.2. Ineffective airway clearance

1.5.1.3. Ineffective breathing pattern

1.6.1. Potential for injury

1.6.1.1. Potential for suffocation

1.6.1.2. Potential for poisoning

1.6.1.3. Potential for trauma

1.6.1.4. Potential for aspiration

1.6.1.5. Potential for disuse syndrome

1.6.2. Altered protection

1.6.2.1. Impaired tissue integrity

1.6.2.1.1. Altered oral mucous membrane

1.6.2.1.2.1. Impaired skin integrity

1.6.2.1.2.2. Potential impaired skin integrity

PATTERN 2. Communicating: A human response pattern involving sending messages

2.1.1.1. Impaired verbal communication

PATTERN 3. Relating: A human response pattern involving establishing bonds

3.1.1. Impaired social interaction

3.1.2. Social isolation

3.2.1. Altered role performance

3.2.1.1.1. Altered parenting

3.2.1.1.2. Potential altered parenting

NANDA TAXONOMY OF NURSING DIAGNOSES *(continued)*

3.2.1.2.1. Sexual dysfunction

3.2.2. Altered family processes

3.2.3.1. Parental role conflict

3.3. Altered sexuality patterns

PATTERN 4. Valuing: A human response pattern involving the assigning of relative worth

4.1.1. Spiritual distress (distress of the human spirit)

PATTERN 5. Choosing: A human response pattern involving the selection of alternatives

5.1.1.1. Ineffective individual coping

5.1.1.1.1. Impaired adjustment

5.1.1.1.2. Defensive coping

5.1.1.1.3. Ineffective denial

5.1.2.1.1. Ineffective family coping: disabling

5.1.2.1.2. Ineffective family coping: compromised

5.1.2.2. Family coping: potential for growth

5.2.1.1. Noncompliance (specify)

5.3.1.1. Decisional conflict (specify)

5.4. Health-seeking behaviors (specify)

PATTERN 6. Moving: A human response pattern involving activity

6.1.1.1. Impaired physical mobility

6.1.1.2. Activity intolerance

6.1.1.2.1. Fatigue

6.1.1.3. Potential activity intolerance

6.2.1. Sleep pattern disturbance

6.3.1.1. Diversional activity deficit

6.4.1.1. Impaired home maintenance management

6.4.2. Altered health maintenance

(continued)

NANDA TAXONOMY OF NURSING DIAGNOSES *(continued)*

6.5.1. Feeding self-care deficit

6.5.1.1. Impaired swallowing

6.5.1.2. Ineffective breast-feeding

6.5.1.3. Effective breast-feeding

6.5.2. Bathing or hygiene self-care deficit

6.5.3. Dressing or grooming self-care deficit

6.5.4. Toileting self-care deficit

6.6. Altered growth and development

PATTERN 7. Perceiving: A human response pattern involving the reception of information

7.1.1. Body image disturbance

7.1.2. Self-esteem disturbance

7.1.2.1. Chronic low self-esteem

7.1.2.2. Situational low self-esteem

7.1.3. Personal identify disturbance

7.2. Sensory or perceptual alterations (specify — visual, auditory, kinesthetic, gustatory, tactile, olfactory)

7.2.1.1. Unilateral neglect

7.3.1. Hopelessness

7.3.2. Powerlessness

PATTERN 8. Knowing: A human response pattern involving the meaning associated with information

8.1.1. Knowledge deficit (specify)

8.3. Altered thought processes

NANDA TAXONOMY OF NURSING DIAGNOSES *(continued)*

PATTERN 9. Feeling: A human response pattern involving the subjective awareness of information

9.1.1. Pain

9.1.1.1. Chronic pain

9.2.1.1. Dysfunctional grieving

9.2.1.2. Anticipatory grieving

9.2.2. Potential for violence: self-directed or directed at others

9.2.3. Post-trauma response

9.2.3.1. Rape-trauma syndrome

9.2.3.1.1. Rape-trauma syndrome: compound reaction

9.2.3.1.2. Rape-trauma syndrome: silent reaction

9.3.1. Anxiety

9.3.2. Fear

NEONATAL WEIGHT CONVERSION TABLE

The nurse can use the table below to convert a neonate's weight from customary units (pounds and ounces) to metric units (grams), or from metric to customary. The left column shows pounds; the top row shows ounces. The remaining numbers indicate grams.

Converting from customary to metric units

For a neonate weighing 4 pounds, 8 ounces, determine the weight in grams by finding *4 pounds* in the left column. Next, find *8 ounces* in the

	Ounces						
	0	1	2	3	4	5	6
Pounds	**Grams**						
0	—	28	57	85	113	142	170
1	454	482	510	539	567	595	624
2	907	936	964	992	1021	1049	1077
3	1361	1389	1417	1446	1474	1502	1531
4	1814	1843	1871	1899	1928	1956	1984
5	2268	2296	2325	2353	2381	2410	2438
6	2722	2750	2778	2807	2835	2863	2892
7	3175	3203	3232	3260	3289	3317	3345
8	3629	3657	3685	3714	3742	3770	3799
9	4082	4111	4139	4167	4196	4224	4252
10	4536	4564	4593	4621	4649	4678	4706
11	4990	5018	5046	5075	5103	5131	5160
12	5443	5471	5500	5528	5557	5585	5613
13	5897	5925	5953	5982	6010	6038	6067
14	6350	6379	6407	6435	6464	6492	6520
15	6804	6832	6860	6889	6917	6945	6973

top row. The intersecting number (2041) is the neonate's weight in grams.

Converting from metric to customary units

For a neonate weighing 4224 grams, find *4224* in the gram section. Read across to the left column (*9 pounds*), then read upward to the top row (*5 ounces*) to determine the neonate's weight in customary units (9 pounds, 5 ounces).

7	8	9	10	11	12	13	14	15
198	227	255	283	312	340	369	397	425
652	680	709	737	765	794	822	850	879
1106	1134	1162	1191	1219	1247	1276	1304	1332
1559	1588	1616	1644	1673	1701	1729	1758	1786
2013	2041	2070	2098	2126	2155	2183	2211	2240
2466	2495	2523	2551	2580	2608	2637	2665	2693
2920	2948	2977	3005	3033	3062	3090	3118	3147
3374	3402	3430	3459	3487	3515	3544	3572	3600
3827	3856	3884	3912	3941	3969	3997	4026	4054
4281	4309	4337	4366	4394	4423	4451	4479	4508
4734	4763	4791	4819	4848	4876	4904	4933	4961
5188	5216	5245	5273	5301	5330	5358	5386	5415
5642	5670	5698	5727	5755	5783	5812	5840	5868
6095	6123	6152	6180	6209	6237	6265	6294	6322
6549	6577	6605	6634	6662	6690	6719	6747	6776
7002	7030	7059	7087	7115	7144	7172	7201	7228

TEMPERATURE CONVERSION TABLE

The nurse can use this table to determine Fahrenheit (°F) and Celsius (°C) temperature equivalents. Alternatively, temperatures can be converted with the following formulas.

To convert from °F to °C:
$°F = (°C \times 1.8) + 32$

To convert from °C to °F:
$°C = (°F - 32) \div 1.8$

DEGREES FAHRENHEIT	DEGREES CELSIUS
93.2	34.0
93.6	34.2
93.9	34.4
94.3	34.6
94.6	34.8
95.0	35.0
95.4	35.2
95.7	35.4
96.1	35.6
96.4	35.8
96.8	36.0
97.2	36.2
97.5	36.4
97.9	36.6
98.2	36.8
98.6	37.0
99.0	37.2
99.3	37.4
99.7	37.6

TEMPERATURE CONVERSION TABLE *(continued)*

DEGREES FAHRENHEIT	DEGREES CELSIUS
100.0	37.8
100.4	38.0
100.8	38.2
101.1	38.4
101.5	38.6
101.8	38.8
102.2	39.0
102.6	39.2
102.9	39.4
103.3	39.6
103.6	39.8
104.0	40.0
104.4	40.2
104.7	40.4
105.2	40.6
105.4	40.8
105.9	41.0
106.1	41.2
106.5	41.4
106.8	41.6
107.2	41.8
107.6	42.0
108.0	42.2
108.3	42.4
108.7	42.6
109.0	42.8
109.4	43.0

SUPPORT RESOURCES FOR FAMILIES WITH SPECIAL-NEEDS NEONATES

The nurse may wish to refer families with special-needs neonates to some of the following organizations for specific advice and coping techniques.

BIRTH DEFECTS

Association of Birth Defect Children, Inc.
Orlando Executive Park
5400 Diplomat Circle
Suite 270
Orlando, FL 32810
407-629-1466

March of Dimes Birth Defects Foundation
1275 Mamaroneck Avenue
White Plains, NY 10605
914-428-7100

CEREBRAL PALSY

United Cerebral Palsy Associations, Inc.
1522 K Street, Suite 1112
Washington, DC 20005
800-USA-5UCP

Canadian Cerebral Palsy Association
880 Wellington Street, Suite 612
City Centre
Ottawa, Ontario
Canada K1R 6K7
613-235-2144

CRANIOFACIAL ABNORMALITIES

American Cleft Palate-Craniofacial Association
1218 Grandview Avenue
Pittsburgh, PA 15211
412-481-1376

Cleft Lip and Palate Program
Hospital for Sick Children
555 University Avenue
Toronto, Ontario
Canada M5G 1X8
416-598-6019

CYSTIC FIBROSIS

Cystic Fibrosis Foundation
6931 Arlington Road, #200
Bethesda, MD 20814
301-951-4422

Canadian Cystic Fibrosis Foundation
2221 Yonge Street, Suite 601
Toronto, Ontario
Canada M4S 2B4
416-485-9149

SUPPORT RESOURCES FOR FAMILIES WITH SPECIAL-NEEDS NEONATES *(continued)*

DOWN'S SYNDROME

National Down Syndrome Society
666 Broadway
New York, NY 10012
212-460-9330

Down Syndrome Association of Metropolitan Toronto
P.O. Box 490
Don Mills, Ontario
Canada M3C 2T2
416-690-2503

HYDROCEPHALUS

National Hydrocephalus Foundation
22427 South River Road
Joliet, IL 60436
815-467-6548

(For a Canadian organization, see the Spina Bifida and Hydrocephalus Association of Ontario, below.)

INTRAVENTRICULAR HEMORRHAGE (IVH)

IVH Parents
P.O. Box 56-1111
Miami, FL 33256-1111
305-232-0381

MENTAL RETARDATION AND DELAYED DEVELOPMENT

Association for Retarded Citizens of the United States
2501 Avenue J
Arlington, TX 76006
817-640-0204

Canadian Association for Community Living
York University Kinsmen Building
4700 Keele Street
Downsview, Ontario
Canada M3J 1P3
416-661-9611

PHYSICAL DISABILITIES

National Easter Seal Society, Inc.
70 East Lake Street
Chicago, IL 60601
312-726-6200

Easter Seals Canada
45 Sheppard Avenue, East
Suite 801
Toronto, Ontario
Canada M2N 5W9
416-250-7490

(continued)

SUPPORT RESOURCES FOR FAMILIES WITH SPECIAL-NEEDS NEONATES *(continued)*

RARE DISORDERS

National Organization for Rare Disorders
P.O. Box 8923
New Fairfield, CT 06812
800-999-NORD
203-746-6518

Lethbridge Society for Rare Disorders
100-542-7 Street, South
Lethbridge, Alberta
Canada T1J 2H1
403-329-0665

PARENTS OF PREMATURE AND HIGH-RISK INFANTS

Parent Care, Inc.
101½ South Union Street
Alexandria, VA 22314
703-836-4678

PHENYLKETONURIA (PKU)

PKU Parents
c/o Dale Hilliard
8 Myrtle Lane
San Anselmo, CA 94960
415-457-4632

SEVERE HANDICAPS

(TASH) The Association for Persons with Severe Handicaps
7010 Roosevelt Way NE
Seattle, WA 98115
206-523-8446

SIBLING SUPPORT

A.J. Pappanikou Center on Special Education and Rehabilitation
991 Main Street, Suite 3A
East Hartford, CT 06108
203-282-7050

SUPPORT RESOURCES FOR FAMILIES WITH SPECIAL-NEEDS NEONATES *(continued)*

SICKLE CELL DISEASE

National Association for Sickle Cell Disease
4221 Wilshire Boulevard
Suite 360
Los Angeles, CA 90010
800-421-8453
213-936-7205

Canadian Sickle Cell Society
1076 Bathurst
Toronto, Ontario
Canada M5R 3G8
416-537-3475

SPINA BIFIDA (MENINGOMYELOCELE)

Spina Bifida Association of America
1700 Rockville Pike
Suite 250
Rockville, MD 20852
301-770-SBAA

Spina Bifida and Hydrocephalus Association of Ontario
55 Queen Street East
Suite 300
Toronto, Ontario
Canada M5C 1R6
416-364-1871

TECHNOLOGY-DEPENDENT CHILDREN

SKIP: Sick Kids Need Involved People
990 Second Avenue
New York, NY 10022
212-421-9160

TURNER'S SYNDROME

Turner's Syndrome Society
York University
Administrative Studies Building
Room 006
Downsview, Ontario
Canada M3J 1P3
416-736-5023

VISUAL AND AUDITORY DEFICITS

American Society for Deaf Children
814 Thayer Avenue
Silver Spring, MD 20910
301-585-5400 (international office)

Helen Keller National Center for Deaf-Blind Youths and Adults
111 Middle Neck Road
Sands Point, NY 11050-1299
516-944-8900

GLOSSARY

ABO blood group incompatibility: isoimmune hemolytic anemia in which a maternal antigen-antibody reaction causes premature destruction of fetal red blood cells (RBCs).

Acrocyanosis: bluish discoloration of the hands and feet caused by vasomotor instability, capillary stasis, and high hemoglobin levels.

Anencephaly: congenital absence of the cerebral hemispheres in which the cephalic end of the spinal cord fails to close during gestation.

Anticipatory grief: sadness in anticipation of loss.

Apnea monitor: device that sounds an alarm when breathing or heartbeat stops or when the respiratory or heart rate drops below a preset level.

Appropriate for gestational age: term used to describe a neonate whose birth weight falls between the tenth and ninetieth percentile for gestational age on the Colorado intrauterine growth chart.

Asphyxia: condition caused by sustained oxygen deprivation and characterized by hypoxemia, hypercapnia, and acidosis.

Ballard gestational-age assessment tool: tool that examines seven physical (external) and six neuromuscular characteristics to determine a neonate's gestational age.

Bilirubin: yellow bile pigment; a product of red blood cell hemolysis.

Bonding: process through which an emotional attachment forms, which binds one person to another in an enduring relationship.

Brazelton neonatal behavioral assessment scale (BNBAS): tool that determines a neonate's interactive and behavioral capacities.

Bronchopulmonary dysplasia (BPD): lung disease characterized by bronchiolar metaplasia and interstitial fibrosis; associated with oxygen therapy and mechanical ventilation in preterm neonates.

Cephalocaudal: pertaining to the long axis of the body in a head-to-tail direction.

Child life therapist: professional who uses play activities to help ill children cope with their illness and medical environment.

Circumcision: surgical removal of the prepuce (foreskin) covering the glans penis.

Cleft lip: congenital defect caused by failure of the maxillary and median nasal processes to close during embryonic development.

Cleft palate: congenital defect in which a fissure appears in the palatal midline; caused by failure of the sides of the palate to close during embryonic development.

Clubfoot: congenital foot deformity characterized by unilateral or bilateral deviation of the metatarsal bones, causing the foot to appear clublike.

GLOSSARY *(continued)*

Colostrum: thin, yellow, serous fluid secreted by the breasts during pregnancy and the first postpartal days before lactation begins; consists of water, protein, fat, carbohydrates, white blood cells, and immunoglobulins.

Conduction: transfer of heat to a substance in contact with the body; a mechanism of heat loss or gain.

Congenital hydrocephalus: condition characterized by accumulation of excessive cerebrospinal fluid within the cranial vault.

Congenital hypothyroidism: deficiency of thyroid hormone secretion during fetal development or early infancy; also called cretinism.

Convection: transfer of heat away from a surface by movement of air currents; a mechanism of heat loss or gain.

Coping mechanism: conscious response to stress that allows an individual to confront a problem directly and solve it.

Cyanosis: bluish skin discoloration caused by an excess of deoxygenated hemoglobin in the blood.

Discharge planning: formulation of a program by the health care team, client, family, and appropriate outside agencies to ensure that the client's physical and psychosocial needs are met after discharge.

Dubowitz gestational-age assessment tool: tool that examines 11 physical (external) and 10 neuromuscular characteristics to determine a neonate's gestational age.

Ductus arteriosus: tubular connection that shunts blood away from the pulmonary circulation during fetal development.

Ductus venosus: circulatory pathway that allows blood to bypass the liver during fetal development.

Dysmaturity: undernourished fetus or neonate that is abnormally small for gestational age.

Encephalocele: congenital neural tube defect in which the meninges and portions of brain tissue protrude through the cranium.

En face position: position in which the neonate is held 8″ (20 cm) in front of the parent or other observer; allows direct eye contact.

Erythroblastosis fetalis: hemolytic disease of the neonate (Rh or ABO incompatibility) characterized by severe anemia, jaundice, edema, and enlargement of the heart, liver, and spleen.

Erythropoietin: hormone produced in the kidneys that regulates red blood cell production.

Evaporation: conversion of fluid to vapor; a mechanism of heat loss.

Everted nipple: nipple that is turned outward and becomes more graspable with stimulation.

Exchange transfusion: procedure in which the neonate's blood is removed and replaced with fresh whole donor blood to remove unconjugated bilirubin in serum; used to treat hyperbilirubinemia and hemolytic anemia.

Extracorporeal membrane oxygenation (ECMO): technique that maintains gas exchange and perfusion by oxygenating blood outside the body through an arterial shunt; used mainly to treat refractory respiratory failure or meconium aspiration syndrome.

(continued)

GLOSSARY *(continued)*

Fetal alcohol syndrome (FAS): syndrome caused by maternal alcohol consumption and characterized by altered intrauterine growth and development, resulting in mental and growth retardation, facial abnormalities, and behavioral deviations.

Fetal position: relationship of the landmark on the fetal presenting part to the front, back, and sides of the maternal pelvis.

Flat nipple: nipple that is hard to distinguish from the areola; changes shape only slightly with stimulation.

Fontanel: nonossified area of connective tissue between the skull bones where the sutures intersect; allows molding of the skull for passage through the pelvis during delivery.

Foramen ovale: opening in the interatrial septum that directs blood from the right to left atrium during fetal development.

Foremilk: thin, watery breast milk secreted at the of a feeding.

Functional residual capacity (FRC): volume of air remaining in the lungs after a normal expiration.

Galactosemia: hereditary autosomal recessive disorder in which deficiency of the enzyme galactose-1-phosphate uridyltransferase leads to galactose accumulation in the blood.

Gastroschisis: congenital condition characterized by incomplete abdominal wall closure not involving the site of umbilical cord insertion; typically, the small intestine and part of the large intestine protrude.

Gestational age: estimated age in weeks following conception.

Gestational-age assessment: evaluation of a neonate's physical and neurologic characteristics to determine approximate weeks of fetal development.

Glomerular filtration rate (GFR): volume of glomerular filtrate (a protein-free plasmalike substance) formed over a specific period

Glucuronyl transferase: liver enzyme necessary for bilirubin conjugation.

Grief process: cycle that follows a loss; the Kübler-Ross model progresses from denial through anger, bargaining, and depression to acceptance; stages may overlap or regress and may be repeated many times before acceptance is complete.

Habituation: gradual adaptation to a stimulus through repeated exposure.

Head lag: head position relative to the trunk when the neonate is in a sitting position.

Hemoglobin F: hemoglobin produced by fetal erythrocytes; has a higher affinity for oxygen than does adult hemoglobin (hemoglobin A), helping to ensure adequate fetal tissue oxygenation.

Hindmilk: high-fat breast milk secreted at the end of a feeding.

Hydramnios: excess amniotic fluid (also called polyhydramnios).

Hyperbilirubinemia: elevated serum level of unconjugated bilirubin.

Imperforate anus: congenital defect characterized by abnormal closure of the anus.

Incubator: fully enclosed, single-walled or double-walled bed containing a heating source and a humidification chamber.

GLOSSARY *(continued)*

Intrauterine growth retardation: abnormal process in which fetal development and maturation are impeded or delayed by maternal disease, genetic factors, or fetal malnutrition caused by placental insufficiency; seen in the small-for-gestational-age neonate.

Intraventricular hemorrhage (IVH): bleeding into the ventricles.

Inverted nipple: nipple that turns inward; occurs in three types: pseudoinverted (becomes erect with stimulation), semi-inverted (retracts with stimulation), and truly inverted (inverted both at rest and when stimulated).

Isoimmune hemolytic anemia: disorder in which an antigen-antibody reaction leads to the premature destruction of RBCs.

Jaundice: yellow skin discoloration caused by bilirubin accumulation in the blood and tissues.

Lanugo: fine hair covering the face, shoulders, and back of the fetus or neonate before 28 weeks' gestation.

Large for gestational age (LGA): term used to describe a neonate whose birth weight exceeds the ninetieth percentile for gestational age on the Colorado intrauterine growth chart.

Let-down reflex: milk ejection from the breast triggered by nipple stimulation or an emotional response to the neonate.

Lipolysis: decomposition of fat.

Low birth weight: birth weight of 1,500 to 2,500 g.

Macrosomia: large body size with a high birth weight (4,000 g or more at term).

Maple syrup urine disease: autosomal recessive disorder characterized by an enzyme deficiency in the second step of branched-chain amino acid catabolism.

Mature neonate: neonate of 38 to 42 weeks' gestation.

Meconium: thick, sticky, green-to-black material that collects in the fetal intestines and forms the first neonatal stool.

Meconium aspiration syndrome (MAS): lung inflammation resulting from aspiration of meconium-stained amniotic fluid in utero or as the neonate takes the first few breaths.

Meningomyelocele: congenital neural tube defect in which part of the meninges and spinal cord protrude through the vertebral column.

Microcephaly: congenital anomaly characterized by abnormal smallness of the head relative to the rest of the body and by underdevelopment of the brain, with resulting mental retardation.

Micrognathia: underdevelopment of the jaw, especially the mandible.

Moro reflex: normal neonatal reflex elicited by dropping the neonate's head backward in a sudden motion, resulting in extension and abduction of all extremities, formation of a "C" with the fingers, and adduction, then flexion, of all extremities (as in an embrace).

Motor maturity: full development of muscle tone and posture, including muscle coordination, muscle movements, and reflexes.

(continued)

GLOSSARY *(continued)*

Myoepithelial cells: smooth-muscle cells surrounding breast alveoli and ducts; with the let-down reflex, these cells contract and eject milk into breast ductules and sinuses.

Necrotizing enterocolitis (NEC): acute inflammatory bowel disorder occurring mainly in preterm neonates.

Neonatal adaptation: physiologic and behavioral changes during the first 24 hours after delivery through which the neonate makes the transition from the intrauterine to the extrauterine environment.

Neonatal intensive care unit (NICU): nursery that provides the highest level of life-support management, including ventilatory support; heart rate, blood pressure, cardiorespiratory, and blood gas monitoring; I.V. fluid therapy; and round-the-clock medical and nursing care.

Neonatal mortality: number of deaths per 1,000 live births within the first 28 days after birth.

Neutral thermal environment (NTE): range of environmental temperatures (89.6° to 93.2°F [32° to 34°C]) that maintains a stable core temperature with minimal caloric and oxygen expenditure.

Nipple confusion: condition in which the infant does not know how to suck properly from a nipple; caused by frequent nipple changes (such as from use of supplemental bottles during breast-feeding).

Nonshivering thermogenesis: heat production by lipolysis of brown fat; primary method through which the neonate produces heat.

Oligohydramnios: presence of less than 300 ml of amniotic fluid at term.

Omphalocele: congenital anomaly in which a portion of the intestine protrudes through a defect in the abdominal wall at the umbilicus.

Orientation: neonate's ability to respond to visual and auditory stimuli.

Oxytocin: hormone responsible for contraction of smooth muscles surrounding breast alveoli, causing release of milk; secreted by the posterior pituitary gland in response to infant sucking on the breast.

Patent ductus arteriosus (PDA): abnormal opening between the pulmonary artery and the aorta; results from failure of the fetal ductus arteriosus to close after birth (seen mainly in the preterm neonate).

Pathologic jaundice: condition marked by yellow skin discoloration and an increase in the serum bilirubin level (above 13 mg/dl); arising within 24 hours after birth, it results from blood type or group incompatibility, infection, or biliary, hepatic, or metabolic abnormalities.

Pathologic mourning: mourning that does not lead to resolution of grief.

Perinatal period: period extending from the twenty-eighth week of gestation to the end of the fourth week after birth.

Periods of neonatal reactivity: predictable, identifiable series of behavioral and physiologic characteristics occurring during the first hours after birth.

Phenylketonuria: autosomal recessive disorder characterized by the abnormal presence of metabolites of phenylalanine in the urine.

GLOSSARY   (continued)

Physiologic jaundice: common condition of the full-term neonate marked by yellow skin discoloration and an increase in the serum bilirubin level (4 to 12 mg/dl); arising 48 to 72 hours after birth and peaking by the third to fifth day, it results from hepatic immaturity.

Placental insufficiency: inadequate or improper functioning of the placenta, leading to a compromised intrauterine environment that jeopardizes the fetus.

Poikilotherm: neonate who takes on the temperature of the environment.

Polycystic kidney disease: condition characterized by formation of multiple cysts within the kidney, leading to kidney enlargement and destruction of adjacent tissue.

Polycythemia: abnormal increase in the number of RBCs; in the neonate, it results from maternal-fetal transfusion, delayed umbilical cord clamping, or placental insufficiency.

Posterior urethral valves: congenital anomaly characterized by urinary tract obstruction, hydronephrosis, and an impaired urinary flow.

Postterm neonate: neonate born after completion of week 42 of gestation; also called postmature neonate.

Preterm neonate: neonate born before completion of week 37 of gestation; also called premature neonate.

Prolactin: hormone causing breast milk production; secreted by the anterior pituitary gland in response to tactile stimulation of the breast.

Radiant heat warmer bed: open bed with an overhead radiant heat source.

Radiation: transfer of heat from one surface to another without contact between the surfaces; a mechanism of heat loss.

Reflex: involuntary function or movement of any organ or body part in response to a stimulus.

Renal agenesis: congenital absence of one kidney (unilateral renal agenesis) or both kidneys (bilateral renal agenesis).

Respiratory distress syndrome: acute, potentially fatal neonatal lung disorder (most common in preterm neonates), resulting from surfactant deficiency; characterized by a respiratory rate greater than 60 breaths/minute, lung inelasticity, nasal flaring, expiratory grunts, chest retractions, and peripheral edema.

Respite care: care provided by a secondary caregiver to relieve the primary caregiver; may be required for several hours to several weeks.

Retinopathy of prematurity (ROP): disease of the retinal vasculature associated with oxygen therapy in the preterm neonate; formerly called retrolental fibroplasia.

Rh incompatibility: isoimmune hemolytic anemia in which maternal antibodies cause destruction of fetal RBCs, leading to severe anemia and jaundice in the neonate.

Rooting reflex: normal neonatal reflex elicited by stroking the cheek or corner of the mouth with a finger or nipple, resulting in turning of the head toward the stimulus.

(continued)

GLOSSARY *(continued)*

Scarf sign: term describing the distance that the neonate's elbow can be extended across the chest toward the opposite side; an index of gestational age.

Self-quieting behaviors: actions the neonate uses to become quiet when crying, including hand-to-mouth movements, fist sucking, and attending to external stimuli.

Small for gestational age (SGA): term used to describe the neonate who experienced intrauterine growth retardation and whose birth weight falls below the tenth percentile for gestational age on the Colorado intrauterine growth chart.

Smegma: sebaceous secretion that accumulates under the foreskin of the penis and at the base of the labia minora.

Smith's minor anomalies: neonatal physiologic variations (such as abnormal dermal ridges) that may indicate major anomalies (for example, Down's syndrome).

Social behaviors: neonatal responses to others' actions (especially those of caregivers), including smiling, gazing, and cuddling.

Square window sign: term describing the degree to which the neonate's wrist can be flexed against the forearm; an index of gestational age.

Sucking reflex: normal neonatal reflex elicited by inserting a finger or nipple in the neonate's mouth, resulting in forceful, rhythmic sucking.

Surfactant: phospholipid produced by Type II alveolar cells in the alveolar lining of the lungs; decreases alveolar inflation pressures, improves lung compliance, and provides alveolar stability, thereby decreasing labor of breathing.

Synactive theory of development: Als's theory proposing that the neonate continuously interacts with the environment and that the neonate's physiologic status depends on the environmental stimuli received and processed.

Teratoma: congenital neoplasm consisting of various cell types, none of which normally occur together.

Term neonate: neonate of 38 to 42 weeks' gestation.

Tertiary care center: facility capable of providing care for the most critically ill neonates; offers the most advanced technological equipment and specialty care.

Thermoregulation: maintenance of body temperature by complex interaction between environmental temperature and body heat loss and production.

TORCH: acronym for a group of infections that include toxoplasmosis, other infections (chlamydia, group B beta-hemolytic streptococcus, syphilis, and varicella zoster), rubella, cytomegalovirus, and herpesvirus type 2.

Transient tachypnea: neonatal disorder characterized by rapid, shallow breathing (possibly accompanied by cyanosis) that lasts a few hours or days; caused by the retention of fetal lung fluid that follows cesarean delivery.

GLOSSARY *(continued)*

Transitional period: time during which the neonate experiences biological and behavioral adaptations to extrauterine life; normally lasts for about 24 hours.

Ventral suspension: term describing the degree to which the neonate extends the back, flexes the arms and legs, and holds the head upright when an examiner positions the neonate prone and places a hand under the chest; an index of gestational age.

Vernix caseosa: grayish white, cheeselike substance composed of sebaceous gland secretions and desquamated epithelial cells that covers the near-term fetus and neonate.

Very low birth weight: birth weight of 500 to 1,500 g.

---

i refers to an illustration; t refers to a table.